RESTORATION OF SPLIT MILK

RESTORATION OF SPLIT MILK

S.N. ROY CHAUDHURY

GYAN

Restoration of Split Milk

Rs. 630

ISBN: 978-81-212-1046-1

Published in 2011 in India by
Gyan Publishing House
23, Main Ansari Road, Daryaganj,
New Delhi - 110002
Phone : 23282060, 23261060
Fax : (011) 23285914
e-mail : books@gyanbooks.com
gyanbook@vsnl.com
website : gyanbooks.com

Laser Type Setting by: Rudra Computer Graphics, Delhi
Printed at : Gian Ridhi Offset Press, Delhi

DEDICATED TO MY MOTHER

THE MOTIVATION

India is perhaps the most complex region in the world to analyze for it's absence of unity as one Nation in the past now partitioned; economic development and poverty; knowledge and illiteracy; religions and perversions; poor initiation of scientific mind and desire for experimental and mathematical confirmation; poor exploitation of natural resources to develop mainly the rural poor and also the urban richer societies; endless platitudes on noble acts and nil desire towards their implementations. The ailments are too many, but curable through improved agronomy, literacy, education, skilled efforts on value added agronomy, and innovative industrial activities in rural areas where 800 million people (2008) currently live.

A fact needs recognition is that our country's poverty and illiteracy are attributable more to our own deficiencies than foreign invasions and submissions. They became rulers with active support of country's rich and traitorous acts against their own people, with hypocritical noble faces. This despicable strain is as old as 1500 B.C., when a non-ethnic race germinated with Aryan victory over Dravidian, and their acceptance of the existing culture of the land, initially with a conflicting mind. An Indo-Aryan race came in being, with inter marriages, but the superior Dravidian culture overwhelmed the Aryan religious practices. The country became a land of Indians retaining some of the Aryan strains. The harmful ones are creations of Princely States owning demarcated lands, and practicing lavish 'homa' on special occasions to seek blessings of God, simultaneously accepting knowledge based hymns to understand God's creations to sustain universe. The caste system was a well thought out managerial apparatus, totally different to the currently practiced graded hereditary system, although claimed as a derivative of the original ones.

The motivation to write the book on a 10,000 years old world's first civilized but mostly exploited subcontinent, is to bring home three facts;

(a) with innovative S &T, specifically on energy, if worked on with dedication, a ***prosperous NEW INDIA*** *will emerge. Such a creation is an unavoidable necessity now;*

(b) our literacy and education promotion programmes should not be limited to learning what current text books impart. Methods should be evolved, to sharpen our genetically intelligent minds at all levels of teachings, narrating about the existence of our basic innovative thinking and also about our lost skill on arts and handicrafts; encouraging actual execution.

(c) the assessment of innovative work should not be left with bureaucratic science administrators, permanently anchored in abodes of files, or Institutions with emphasis on metaphysical concepts and publications of 'scientific papers, with no experimental data' Such administrators should be rotated between field establishments, and headquarters. Science administrators should be classified with a different identifiable grade.

Justifications for the above recommendation has been provided in Part 3, (page 322), sub Para's 3A and 3B and Chapter 18 (Page No. 469) narrating agro-industries, and events on Aeronautics and fluid flow measurements respectively, as examples, because of author's involvement. On such occasions, keeping Nation's development in view, consultancy from well known foreign sources should be preferred.

CONTENTS

PART 1

EVENTS INDEX

FIGURE INDEX

TABLE INDEX

INDEPENDENT INDIA

'The achievement we celebrate to-day is* but a step, an opening of opportunity, to the greater triumphs and achievements that awaits us. Are we brave enough and wise enough to grasp this opportunity and accept the challenge of the future?'

Jawaharlal Nehru on Independence Day, 15th August 1947

* at this point, author had desired an addition "to revive past glory, eliminate present evils, and (then continue) a step, an opening of opportunity

Author's view

After 62 years, the author wants to enquire what answer we have. This book attempts to analyze taking help of diverse religious beliefs; hypocritical noble concepts of humanism at the alter of selfish interests for power and wealth, history of feudal dynastic rules; our past, present governance and economic states, and the possible future. History currently written is mostly as a compendium of biographies of country's leaders when their noble utterances get published from time to time but not of any implemented actions, and not about mislead oppressed ones, living miserably mostly in rural areas, and also in city slums. This is an intentionally created illiterate slave society, with no mass movement against injustice done to them. The book is not on any specific subject creating our present situation. The main search is to understand the impact of these on our unacceptable situation mentioned above.

FOREWORD

It is well recognized that development and intensive application of science and technology is essential for any nation or society to increase its wealth and provide better quality of life to its people. However, equitable distribution of benefits from scientific and technological developments critically depends on the structure of the society and the State policies, which must ensure equal opportunity for all its citizens. Unfortunately, older civilizations, suffering from the burden of past history, which differentiated the rich and powerful from the poor, urban from rural and literate from the illiterate have not been able to build a truly equitable society where every citizen can lead a contented life. In some of the societies like the Indian society where the memory of the past and its long impact still lingers on, the illiterate rural poor depending totally on agriculture, continue to be exploited by the richer landlords. With limited land and no other avenues of earning extra remuneration combined with the poor agricultural productivity, the rural poor are desperately trying to survive below the BPL level. The rich landlords, princes and the neo-rich, continue to exploit the rural poor creating large inequity in the society. It is abundantly clear that if India as a country has to really shine, it has to totally abolish the rampant poverty in rural areas by providing the rural poor better education facilities, including vocational training and enable them to improve their earning capacity by establishing rural industries, which would necessarily require improved rural infrastructure such as roads and energy input. Initiation of a new ever green revolution for achieving better agricultural productivity, providing easy access to market both sell their products at a remunerative price ad timely availability of required inputs at a reasonable cost need to be ensured to enable agricultural community to be able to live a decent life.

Air Marshal SN Roy Chaudhury, a distinguished military officer and a highly competent technocrat who spear-headed the development of aeronautics in India as the founder Director of the Gas Turbine Research Establishment at Bangalore, for almost four decades, has written the book Restoration of split milk. The book is in three parts. The first part essentially traces the growth of civilization in India starting with the Indus Valley Civilization to the time India became an independent sovereign state in 1947. The author has brought out an interesting but not very well known fact about the discovery of flint by the primitive cave man which promoted the controlled use of fire for meeting day to day requirements, an undoubtedly significant point of transition in the growth of human civilization. The first part traces the history of India from the early times when the rural poor were oppressed by rich landlords and Princes, through the Mogul Period and the British occupation both of which further aggravated the widening gap between the so called elite and the illiterate poor class in the name of religion and caste.

The second part deals with the events leading to the partition of India into India and Pakistan based on religion through the clever manipulation by the British. The role played by great leaders of the time including Gandhi, Jawaharlal Nehru, Jinnah, Subhash Chandra Bose, Sarder Patel, Lord Mount Batten and others. India's freedom struggle is sketched as viewed through the eyes of the author. The partition resulted in large-scale massacre of both Hindus and Muslims as they were uprooted from their natural habitats. The effect of animosity and hatred created on both sides, resulting in large-scale misery, looting and destruction of people and property, following the partition continues to cast its shadow between India and Pakistan even today. The second part also deals with the state of India since becoming a sovereign Independent State, Rapid growth in population, continuing large-scale illiteracy, poor agricultural productivity and gross neglect of rural infrastructure, continue to bog down the entire nation. The author has also proposed a few solutions such as growing food using hydroponics technology, exploitation of bio-fuels, particularly Jatrope like plants in the vast amount of wasteland available in India or use of micro-algae in selected ponds or lakes for achieving energy sufficiency. There is no doubt that development of decentralized energy in rural areas across the entire nation is central for the improvement of rural infrastructure, providing basic amenities to people and establishment of rural industries which is essential for rapid and balanced development of the country and providing improved quality of life for all the people including the vast neglected rural masses.

In the third part the author provides a ring side view of the difficulties and problems encountered during the development of aeronautics in India, due to the short sighted leadership at the top level, which is a very common phenomena experienced in many developing countries where vested interests take precedence over technical wisdom. The narration of the story of vested interests which resulted in a serious setback in the development of aeronautics in the country is, to say the least, very regrettable.

Air Marshal Roy Chaudhury with his varied and vast

experience has closely knitted history and political turmoil in trying to understand the origin of rampant poverty and illiteracy in the country. Being very passionate about the subjects, he has forcefully expressed his opinions about the conduct and performance of both political as well as scientific and technical leaders of the day. Some of his comments, opinions and conclusions are to be controversial and may not be acceptable to all. However, I believe that all such opinions and comments need to be heard and debated for finding out the truth. The rapid uplift of the rural economy of India, must take the highest precedence, in our scheme, if India has to shine as one of the advanced nations where every citizen is assured of a comfortable, contended and peaceful life. This can only happen if illiteracy is eradicated, rural infrastructure is adequately strengthened, rural industries are developed and poverty is totally eradicated to ensure every citizen of the country enjoys a minimum acceptable quality of life. Air Marshal Chaudhury's book makes a very interesting reading on all these aspects of the national life in a bold, frank and interesting manner.

Sd/-

(Dr. U. R. RAO)

(Former Chairman, Indian Space Research Organisation)

THE BIG QUESTION

Originating as the first civilized human community, our current situation can be represented in Fig No.1

INDUS VALLEY CIVILIZATION ARTIC OCEAN MELTING

Source: Indus Valley Civilization – Wikipedia, the free encyclopedia

Can we reverse this?

The need for reversal is for three primary reasons. First, the urban-rural divide, with enormous socio-economic disparity, has virtually broken the backbone of the rural society of 800 million people, and therefore, the country's as well. Secondly, the impact of 'global warming' can be reduced effectively through bio-diesel, a product of micro-algae harvested in shallow saline (sea) water ponds, providing energy for rural development. (This soil less energy generation is still not successful, although much confidence has been exhibited both within the country, and abroad. The author believes that with dedicated research, this is feasible. The related important result is saving soil for food production to meet the requirements of growing population.)

Bio-diesel extracted from micro- algae harvested in saline (sea) water pond is the most efficient energy strategy for our country with 7500 km coastline. Canalizing to shallow saline ponds, plant can grow with a photosynthesis efficiency six times more than land-based plants. Not only the bio-diesel production can be much greater, a perennial source of pollution free energy will be available. This new decentralized approach to energy development can provide simultaneously potable water, with a suitable technology approach. This has been explained. Adequately funded, working hard with our surplus unemployed manpower, (including large community of young retired service personnel) emergence of a new India is not an utopia.

Finally, once the faith to be at par with developed nations is restored through God's gift of nature, reincarnation of the lost humanism will surface in this subcontinent, and can be a model for the world community to emulate.

The book has three parts. Part 1 takes us to the situation when the country became a free sovereign State, in 1947. Part 2 presents our current situation, elucidating the past heritage, causing the present. Part 3 suggests the solution.

Currently, ours is one among the poorest with regard to literacy and per capita income. Not only that, we are a weak, politely addressed by most as a soft nation. The Constitution declares the nation to be Secular with vast majority of Hindus, following Gita as their religion, legally accepted. It advocates *retaliation* when injustice is done. Gandhian concept is non-violent resistance with courage. Gita, with no Gandhian modification, is our religion. Poor we may be, but not having large disparity between urban rich and rural poor and losing self-respect.is our dream goal. Resolutely patriotic secular one nation should be our definition, with no compromise. *The book's aim is to justify this feasibility.*

In our current socio-economic situation, a new India needs to be born energizing our rural society to acquire two faces; one is agronomy. and the other, value added agro and the industrial products. The Constitution of India, suitably amended and *implemented* should be our guiding pole star to steer the nation to right destination in a clear sky. Currently it is not.

The initiation of the virtue of energized rural society has to be proved initially through the use of natural gas, operating decentralized co-generating (electricity and heat) systems when the research on aquatic bio-diesel and hydroponics food production activity will be carried out simultaneously to meet the future needs. Currently used energy systems, based mostly on coal, need vigorous research to capture CO_2 for further use e.g., for harvesting micro-algae to produce bio-diesel and simultaneously reducing green house effect.

To establish the above, for a subcontinent of more than 10000 years old, history becomes an unavoidable media, to germinate an apt driving force for country's development, particularly when a genetic strain has been retained, grossly perverted though, with an indestructible anchor with nature as the non-prophetic God. History tells us why we are in our present hypocritical deep-rooted socio-economic unhealthy state, when disregard to humanism has become a form of religion, for the high and the low alike. The most part of our history is the retention of our intelligent mind, even among the rural poor inspite of 4000 years slavery. That locked up asset needs an opportunity to make our country noble, through our appropriate rural development.

Over the years, since 1983, (initial plea to use flared away natural gas for rural development) the above strategy through decentralized cogeneration has been brought to the notice of all apex bodies; - the government, Planning Commissions, the Supreme Court, parliamentarians, - all mentioned in the text. However, lacking the courage to face the oppressed rural society with honesty, they are either evasive, or resort to hide behind impregnable bureaucratic shell, at time even misrepresenting the truth. Are they afraid of peasant's uprisings as had happened earlier in developed societies to establish justice and socialism, which our Constitution solemnly resolved to constitute

Independent India in 1947?

Gandhi sang *bhajan* highlighting two religions as under,

Ishwar Allah tere naam
Sabko sanmati de Bhagavan

Gandhiji might have felt that uniting these religious groups could bring about an united Nation. We have continued singing this with little success. Moreover, the country's Constitution has now formally accepts six religions, when many more and several non-religious cults are followed. It is necessary to update the Gandhian concept to create one Nation. The author believes the correct bhajan to sing to-day is,

Bhagwan sabi dharm ke naam
Sammilit shakti desh co de Bhagwan
Mano-vigyan banay karmasthan
*Ujala karey Bharat mahaan.**

Instead of singing Gandhi's *bhajan,* let us sing for the nation, when Pakistan will be knocking at our nation's door soon Recently the Prime Minister of Pakistan has declared 1000 years war, to release what is unquestionably our territory. Making 800 million rural people strong should be our goal, not the meaningless bhajan singing, providing no action oriented directive.

- Composed by the author

A CD singing Bhajan is placed at the back of the half folded cover page, conveying the core desire which the book has tried to establish narrating events over a period of 10,000 years.

- Undeniable is the fact that the end results have gone wrong drastically for our current 800 million rural people, living in an unacceptable condition. The book highlights the events leading to this condition, and should be read with an understanding mind. When truth, creating our present state, is narrated, it is so done to avoid repetition in our New India,. Two basic issues have been established. They are, Rich and poor divide since Indo- Aryan days (1900 B.C.), and our superior genetic intelligence, poorly exploited though. The narrations are 'Diagnostic Tools' and the author pleads that the book should be read in that spirit. The apparent 'negativities', though apparently subjective, are illustrations, to justify why we are in our present unacceptable state. They must be eliminated in our desire for NEW INDIA

- The narration has not stopped making remarks on what had gone wrong, which continues, the rectification and implementation strategy have been suggested.

CURRENT URBAN INDIA

City born Educated and Migrated Rural Urbanized literate but uneducated ladies, performing with equal efficiency

PART 1

Chapter 1

THE OVERVIEW

The Origin

The primary desire is to convey what we were, and what have caused leading to present dismal situation. There are several aspects we can still be proud of, and many more not to be. Finally, suggesting what can still be done to get back on rails of prosperity, reviving our genetically superior mental ability, skill and humanism. To compose a book dealing with these is difficult, but noble when, in general, about 1.2 billion people currently live in harmony, with the largest numbers of diverse cultures; - mostly good, but simultaneously a small despicable minority community with selfish perverted interests is trying hard to cause harm to the nation, conflicting with the original concept of humanism.

Indus Valley Civilization (made controversial by foreign historians) existed during 8000 - 6000 BC. That apparently disappeared mysteriously for 4000 years. There is no record of the missing period. Obviously, something had happened leaving no evidence. Such a sudden and complete devastation has remained as a mystery when several speculations are made. Each contradicts the other. Some talk about a great flood resulted due to ecological disturbances caused due to cutting down of trees to create fire, needed for the creation of civilized living. Everything got buried. On the other extreme, there are views on a strike of a massive meteor. The supporting evidence is objects, which could not have been created unless subjected to extreme heat, as may have generated through atomic explosion. There are yet other justifiable views that nothing of the sort as above had happened. If such a total annihilation had happened, it could not have mushroomed again with original attributes in a short period. The divination surfaced again in 2000 BC with evidence of continuity on several aspects with the earlier civilization of 8000 – 6000 BC.

There are evidences to suggest that people lived with God gifted humanism, with no caste and prophetic religious systems as practiced now by some. This book tries to take an account of happenings over a period of 10,000 years; addressing essentially what transpired during past 4000 years (2000 BC – 2000 AD).

Currently, the country is deeply buried in all kinds of socio-economic problems, whose origins can be traced to several dynastic rules. Transformation of mankind's way of life is interlinked with science and technology, which is recorded in the history of dynastic rules. Here one realizes the importance of literacy and education to judge the real events and fantasy.

RELIGION, SCIENCE AND TECHNOLOGY

Rig Veda-based religion gave birth to science and technology (S&T). Observing natural phenomenon, and meditating on them, laws of nature were evolved. Mankind started to ask 'why' on several things around him. The answers lead to many awesome technology which we admire e.g., pyramids. Scientific mind for the arrangement of the blocks of stone is the origin, some believe. However, the question is how these blocks were made? In fact, the origin is the observation that water *expands* when it is frozen. Nevertheless, do we ask, why? These observations lead to getting near equal large blocks of stones. There are several examples when the results of meditation of natural phenomenon are accepted as the gospel of religion when these are creations of God, - not man made. Can we achieve variation in photosynthesis processes at will, for different kinds of plants, - God's gifts, - in a laboratory?

This is not an academic book on science and technology, but accepts an undeniable fact that civilization grew with their progression, when the concept of religion has apparently remained static, often misused to achieve goals, different to what they were initially meditated for. History narrates these.

The current primarily materialistic self-oriented life style has been analyzed through several dynastic events, when the common strain had been the divide between the rich and the suppressed poor. Perverting the religious concepts to retain feudal way of life with a coat of hypocritical nobility, we have forgotten to distinguish the wrongs from rights. Tagore lamented the situation very aptly: "We are all kings in our country of kings" when kings can do no wrong. (Translated from Bengali). All make their own laws, as kings do. Indiscipline is no more a crime. It is taken as a perk of Independence. Laws are made to rectify but suggest no stern system to implement.

Highlighting deficient energy; scarcity of water, mindless S&T, feudal minds' non-implementable forward-looking plans, and degrading communal religions, the history of 4000 years has been used extensively as diagnostic tools to learn who we are now and why. Backed up with an apparent unwavering religious strain based on nature, the descendants of non-ethnic majority race of this subcontinent are essentially a product of the said period. This subcontinent began with a glorious past. A non-metallic 'heritage period' of about *2690 years, (1500 +1190 = 2690) began with Indo-Aryan race during 1500 BC, and it had ended up in 1190 AD to become a slave country till 1947. In between, the subcontinent faced many dynastic rules. They brought with them different religions, cultures and habits. Unfortunately, the noblest virtue of mankind, – *humanism,* - became the victim. The last was the British imperialism. The subcontinent was handed over to a few 'kings', educated in England, and their sycophants in 1947 to lord over millions of simple illiterate poor; creating the most irreparable damage, partitioning the subcontinent on 'apparent' religious lines. We have now two hostile Islamic Sovereign States, on either side of our large weak confused secular State. The two are now connected to Chinese main land, which is also connected to peace loving Tibet, recognized (by Nehru) as a Chinese territory, as a friendly gesture; but getting backfired in return. China is claiming now Arunachal Pradesh as their territory.

Since Independence, the country has been grossly mismanaged by feudal and corrupt governance trifling the provisions of the Constitution, particularly those related to rural people and their development. It was formally accepted on the 26 January, 1950. Based on 'OR' (Objective Resolution) presented by Jawaharlal Nehru on 22nd January, 1947, our Constitution follows, by and large, the British India Act of 1935; which 'scarcely desired to alleviate the distress of the predominantly underprivileged population of India. Except for a noble provision, namely PIL (Public Interest Litigation) keeping the poor in mind, the colonial rule continues. Typically, it is our noble minds show off. Has this law ever assessed any rural issue e.g., non-compliance of Article

243(G) of our Constitution, the current fundamental for rural development, although attempts have been made. This Article is an amendment of the initial Article 40. The parliament has never discussed this after introducing it.

SUMMARY OF DESIRABLE ACTIONS.

Undeniable is a fact that currently we live in a world of science and technology (S & T). Our society began initially with philosophical scientific concepts, now accepted as religion, and currently synthesized with metal-based world. Cross-fertilization since then, with the emerging world's industrial community, many changes have come about, some good but generally unsuited for our present rural society, where more than 800 million illiterate, - mostly poor live with the age old shackles. This situation needs urgent rectification, making use of nature's abundant unutilized gifts, through innovative S & T. Easier ones have been utilized for long since. Now the time has come to make use of the difficult ones. To do this, six essential activities need scientific evolution and *implementation.* They are:

a) Removal of illiteracy of rural poor and urban slum dwellers till the eligible age for casting vote.
b) Elimination of perverted religious practices; encourage non-hereditary religious societies; simultaneously ban communal religious groups, metaphysical but non- implemented thoughts and orations in public forums; encourage key note addresses, that can be supported only by achieved data.
*c) Have only*two political parties and members not permitted to cross over till their party is in power;*
d) Ban caste system.
e) Investigating and encouraging innovative science and technology-oriented activities even when originated by rural people e.g., not treating media report of production of as much as 7t/ha paddy as nature's freak, instead as creator's pointer to possibilities if related ingredients for enhanced harvesting are properly analyzed and used.
f) Continuation of S&T till successful as a certified commercial product for domestic use and trade.

g) *Practicing humanism faithfully.*

**Malaysia had several political parties. Now they have only two. One in power, other in opposition, essentially to set matters right and amending the flaws in the governance. The sole purpose is not to pull down those in power to wear the crown.*

A COMPARISON

We can have a maximum of 542 Lok Sabha seats (Art. 81 of our Constitution). There were 56 political parties, in 2008, eligible to contest for these seats. To be in power, the ruling party must have a support from at least 272 members. To bring about a progressive nation by rejecting / modifying the old ones, support of two third of the elected is preferred.

Each party has a manifesto, but not obligatory to follow after election. The elected members from various parties can join together and support a party with second largest elected members to make it a majority party with a desire to make themselves members of the ruling party. They now functions under the safe umbrella of the dominant party. A fair number of MPs are dummies and do not participate in any proceedings of the parliament but enjoy all the perks, in three ways. First, making a minority party form the government at a negotiated cost; secondly, getting remunerations and other benefits for being an MP; and finally getting a coveted appointment in the ruling coalition's hierarchy without any assessment of suitability, or competence. Finally, during any critical situation when the ruling coalition's continuity becomes doubtful, the dummy becomes a highly priced hero; - a saviour of nation's stability. What kind of electoral system have we adopted when a small political party winning just one seat can hold the whole nation to ransom, when the small party itself becomes fabulously rich for saving the dominant party. There are more than a dozen such parties with just one elected member. The root cause for such a despicable situation is our grossly defective election system.

THE CONSTITUTION

The preamble of our Constitution begins apparently with confused objectives. The nation solemnly resolved to be a "Sovereign Socialist Secular Democratic Republic". If one accepts what Oxford dictionary suggests, sovereignty and democracy need not co-exist. They can be poles apart. A sovereign independent nation can deal other nations, but need not be democratic. However, we add nobility stating, when needed, that ours is sovereign "*of the people*". What does this imply? Are we trying to confirm that the country belongs to people? But is it? Does it not belong to a few with hereditary strain? With our large rich and poor divide, where is democracy? Similarly, socialism embraces secularism (a non-religious strain) and needs no repetition. Thus, would it not be more proper and unambiguous now to say that ours is "socialist democratic sovereign republic", eliminating the contradictory frills? Let sovereign be an adjective to our republic only, till such time the evils of large disparity ratio, on all aspects of our National life is eliminated..

Presently, the list of unaccomplished promises, platitudes, and non-audited activities, excel the total of those honestly executed. Illiteracy and media have helped the creation of the adverse situation we are suffering from. On macro-activities, media could coalesce the manifestos of winning political parties, assess the audited achievements and non-performances, publish the findings for the common man to expose the realities of manifestos, and judge the virtue of our election system and governance, as practiced. After election in 2004, pledges of the current UPA government were published in two full pages of newspapers. Recently, a booklet titled '*Report to the People*' has been published. Do they tally? In the month of March, 2008, our prime minister, Manmohon Singh suggested about 'volume of good work' done during the last four years. The volume can be quantified, comparing with the manifesto, stating that the disparity ratio between rich and poor has increased during this period. Further, is there any accountability on Article 243(G) of our Constitution, the pole star for rural development? This was framed in 1992 when Dr. Singh was our finance minister. Perhaps it was his noble deed to amend Article 40 after 42 years.

ARTICLE 40

Our Constitution has 395 Articles and several amendments. For the governance of 82.7 % rural people (1951 census) out of a total of 361 million, only one Article 40 was formulated .for the governance of rural people. It was just one sentence.

"***Organization of village Panchayats – The State shall take steps to organize village Panchayats and endow them with such powers and authority as may be necessary to enable them to function as units of self-government.***"

Does it not imply that the remaining 394 Articles were written mainly for 17.3% urban people? Obviously, this interpretation is absurd. Yet the Constitution provides a confusing picture when the self-governing rural society elects the government for the entire nation. Why not the self-governing societies then govern their own affairs, except for common issues, such as finance, defense, and communications?. In our present governance system, the concept of gram Panchayats functioning as units of self-government is misfit. They serve two purposes. One, a source through which allotted funds for rural and agricultural activities, literacy programmes, and several others are siphoned away by the corrupt middlemen and leaders by retaining the hereditary caste system suppressing the poor.

Article 40 was first step of passing the buck to live as *'Sahibs"* in urban society, away from illiterate and unclean society, interposing the State Government in the middle, creating three parts out of one. One wonders, for whom the sovereign country was formed. Will it be improper to suggest that Article 40 was the foundation stone for rural and urban divide. Why a separate Article for rural people when majority of India lives in villages? Was not the very first resolution of All India Congress Committee adopted on alleviation of rural poor in 1886? Did we not go begging for their votes over 42 years, crying over their shoulders, promising improvements, and whipping off their tears since our Independence day in 1947? What did we achieve for the rural poor? What did we gain for the urban rich? Did not Jawaharlal Nehru confess at the end of his long reign that while the rich were getting richer, the rural poor were not becoming poorer? It was a true confession no doubt, but it could have been expressed more appropriately, stating that the poor was becoming poorer, when rich was becoming richer. Thus, the disparity ratio is increasing.

After 42 years, in 1992, amending the original one, Article 243(G) was introduced, elaborating 24 detailed activities. Will it be appropriate to suggest that Dr. Manmohon Singh and Planning Commission combined had formulated this? Narasimha Rao was the prime minister (1991 – 1996) when he was the finance minister. His first message to the nation was conveyed ritually from the rampart of Red fort that we need to fight poverty alleviation on *war footing*. Have we?

ARTICLE 234(G)

Out of 42 years (1950 -1992), the country was governed for 37 years by Nehru and his dynasty. (Nehru for 17 years, Indira Gandhi, his daughter, for 15 years in two separate terms, and her son Rajiv Gandhi for 5 years). The surprising fact is, did they not realize the needs as stated in Article 243(G) during 37 years?. It was felt afterwards when Narasimha Rao became the prime minister in 1991. While formulating this, did not the concern of their implementation without appropriate energy and other infra structural needs surface?

MANAGEMENT OF RURAL SOCIETY

A doubt arises when one peruse the current constitution of Panchyat Raj. Did the literacy, education and the competence levels of the managerial bodies of self-governments to look after the well-being of about 800 million (equivalent to total population of the USA and earlier the USSR) rural poor people (2006) receive consideration? If proper assessment was not made, there is a valid reason to doubt about the sincerity on rural development.

Since Independence till 1992, rural India was administrated by Panchayats at various levels. They were organised by 28 States, as desired by the Constitution, and functioned as self-government for 42 years (1950 – 1992). In 2006, we had a total of 2,38,439 Panchayats, - mainly Gram Panchayats (2,31,815.). They are manned by. 21,86,452 elected representatives, consisting of male (60%) and female (40%) representatives, inclusive of a small representation from schedule castes (SC) and Schedule tribes (ST)

25 Per Cent women in Panchayats are illiterate

The educational level of most women representatives in Panchayats is up to middle school or just above, a nationwide survey on elected women in Panchayati raj institutions has revealed. Almost one-fourth of the total women were illiterate. Their male counterparts fared better with just six per cent not knowing to read and write.

Source: Times of India, dated 28.04.2008

This amendment must have had approval of two third of the MPs, or more, as a major break-through for rural development, after 42 years. Did any parliamentarian ask why such a modification controlling the destiny of 80 % of the country's people was ignored for such a long time? Did they have the courage to question Nehru and his off springs? Did we sincerely believe that such a body could execute Article 243(G)?

An opinion down loaded from web site on 20.05.2009:

"The basic aims of development of rural areas cannot be achieved unless the rural development administration extends wholehearted support in the creation of various infrastructure facilities and provision of extension services. No specific mention about energy need has been made by any, yet unless the villages are appropriately energized, no real development is possible. The loopholes in the rural development administration that have come to surface during the last one decade need to be plugged in the 21st century.

An extract from 'India 2007' published by Publication Division, Ministry of Information and Broadcasting. government of India.

"In conformity with this commitment of the Government, the Ministry of Rural Development accords foremost priority to development in rural areas and eradication of poverty and hunger from the face of rural India. A number of new initiatives have been taken in the recent years for creation of social and economic infrastructure in rural areas to bridge the rural urban divide as well as to provide food security and to fulfill other basic needs of the rural populance.

The renewed emphasis on rural development is also visible in the commensurate progressive increase in the allocation of resources for implementation of poverty alleviation programmes. For the Tenth Five Year Plan, the allocation of funds for rural development programmes has been enhanced to Rs. 76,774 crore* as against Rs. 42,874 crore in Ninth Plan. An allocation of Rs. 24,480 crore was made for the Ministry of Rural development during 2005-06. The budget estimate for the year 2006-07 is Rs. 31443.62 crore."

*This allocation is consistent with our GDP of about $550 bn during that period, (Data Source: World Bank Development Indicator, Page 232)

A new ministry of Panchayati Raj was created in 2007. The plans and achievements are not known. The need to create a new ministry when we have already a Ministry for Rural Development, which was earlier a part of Ministry of Agriculture, makes it obvious that the progress is not satisfactory, even when fund is allocated following the set practice. The baffling fact is why then the large disparity ratio between rich and poor is increasing.

BEGINNING OF FREE INDIA

India became an Independent Sovereign country, in the divided subcontinent on 15th August, 1947, when Nehru became the prime minister, Lord Mountbatten continued as Governor General (equivalent to President) till 1950. Pakistan had become free a day before, on 14th August, 1947, when Mohammed Ali Jinnah became the President. Why Lord Mountbatten and a sizeable British army and administrators continued to stay back for three more years is not clear. Many key posts were still held by the British. The period 1947 – 1950 shaped the destiny of this subcontinent.

Nehru became close friend of Mountbattens. Thus he became a friend of Lady Mountbatten. A friendship between a man and woman can be very noble, - even desirable, There are several who raise alarm when this picture is presented. Different views are expressed about this relationship in British media too.. Those whose raise such alarm are the ones, in India and England, responsible for the germination of the most despicable history, now known as " Kashmir issue" – leading to the formation of Line of Control (LOC).. Through media they have succeeded to find a cover up, in fact. Now the subcontinent has become a land of 800 million illiterate rural poor Let us look at our selves for this situation, and make amends. Let us not waste our time on gossips, which we generally like. Let the fundamentals related to Kashmir State be the beginning before debating about the, cure of the recent cancer. Unfortunately, we seem to ignore the basics about the Kashmiri people while trying to decide who Kashmir should belong to.

Indian Summer:
The Secret History of the End of an Empire

Illustrated Biography of Jawaharlal Nehru. RBR INTERTIONAL

A picture of true happy friendship in public glare.

Guilty souls hide affections.

Two pictures of different nature have been left behind when Britishers finally left. They are shown below:

Fig 1 : Permanent Seal of British Rule, - Victoria Memorial at Kolkata

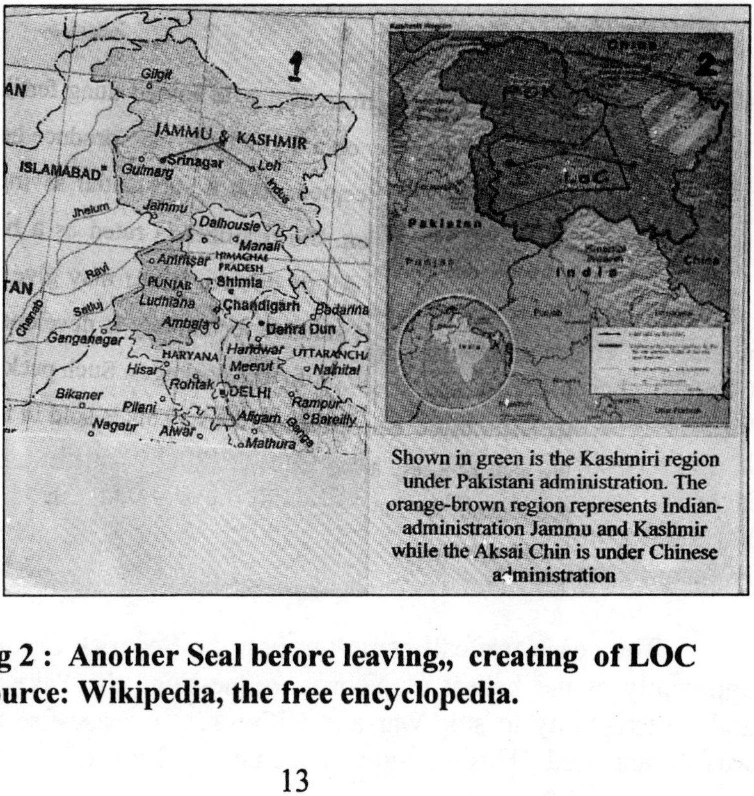

Shown in green is the Kashmiri region under Pakistani administration. The orange-brown region represents Indian-administration Jammu and Kashmir while the Aksai Chin is under Chinese administration

Fig 2 : Another Seal before leaving,, creating of LOC Source: Wikipedia, the free encyclopedia.

The service officers had a holistic mind for the welfare of the nation while considering LOC as can be seen from the picture below while attending a course at Institute of Defence Management, Hyderabad.

Service Officers during the course at Institute of Defence Management, Hyderabad.

The shaded Part 1 of FIG.2 is Jammu and Kashmir, which Maharaja Hari Singh acceded to India. On the East is China connected with Afghanistan through a narrow region, at the top of Kashmir. Part 2 of Fig. 2 illustrates the divided Kashmir, and the LOC. The creation of LOC is attributed to Nehru's desire for a plebiscite, when the defeated invading Pakistan Army was on the run to go back to their barracks in Pakistan.

The cease-fire call came through the Security Council, apparently at the behest of Nehru, requesting the Pakistani and Indian Army to stop war and withdraw. A cease-fire line was demarcated. This has now become the Line of Control

(LOC). The Security Council's directive brought back the defeated Pakistani army to LOC, with strength, when they refused to abide by the Security Council's directive, and refused to withdraw. The defeated Pakistani army standing now on legally Indian land (due to accession treaty) wanted Indian army to withdraw also. Where to? Since then these two armies are standing on either side of Loc, eye ball to eye ball, A fact not understood is when Pakistan Army refused to withdraw, why did the Indian Army not evicted them from our now legal territory?

Nehru's ancestry was of Kashmiri origin. He did not wish to take over a Muslim-majority territory apparently by force. He was keen on knowing the minds of the Kashmiri people. His noble fair mind surfaced much against the wishes of Indian army when the British General in command of British army, still in the subcontinent, expressed that after accession treaty, Kashmir was Indian territory. Here the confusion starts. Who motivated Nehru to rush to Security Council? It could not be Mountbatten because he had initially cleared the Indian Army to defend Kashmir against Pakistani assault after accession treaty signed. Nehru was still under the command of Mountbatten, serving as the Governor General. Who then motivated Nehru? Gossip begins here about possible influence of Edenwa over Nehru. This gossip is an act of passing the buck when the real culprits are several. It was a clever and easy way to divert the minds of common man, who loves such stories, both in India and England. They are littered on roads, discussed in private gatherings, much to the relief of the real culprits. It was essentially political in nature when LOC has changed this subcontinent. Much has been written about the main cause of our ruined financial situation in rural areas. Both the countries started buying expensive Arms and the poor started to become poorer.

Let our amusement centre around a developed rural society. There are this fact needs no elaboration. The initial goal on robbing the country was accomplished by British imperialistic rule to an extent as seen from the Table below;

British imperialistic rule

TABLE 1

	Per Capita Income ppp $	Literacy %	Population million	% Population below poverty line
Bangladesh *	2300	43	150.5	43
Pakistan	2600	49.9	164.7	------
India	3800	61	1,129.9	27 **
UK	31,800	99	60	17

Source : PENGUIN YEAR BOOK, 2008

* East Pakistan became Bangladesh in December 1971 as a Sovereign nation.

** per capita 2400 calorie basis. An improving trend is seen. The stated per Capita income differs from that stated in Manorama Year Book . It mentions $ 3700, a little more than Pakistan's.

England was poorer than India when they first came in 1609 as British East India Company for trade. The above table shows how the table was turned upside down when they left. Mountbatten was a man who's Curriculum Vitae certifies that he never lost in any mission. Did he win this time when he had announced at the very outset that his task was to divide the subcontinent?. Yes, he did after hammering in the death nail killing the golden goose, which made his country prosper.

Country's governance since Independence

The summary of our country's situation till recent days, is the resultant situation after 50 years rule of congress out of 62 years. The remaining 12 years were governed by the BJP for seven (7) years, and five (5) years by short duration leaderships. Thus, the country's present situation, good or bad, is the result of management of one party, viz. national Congress. The strategy was the same. Exploit the illiterate rural people, with noble platitudes, lock them up with agronomy, and make noble budgetary provisions only to rob these out through Gram Panchayats, the final recipients of the allocated budgetary funds disbursed by 28 State governments to benefit six lakh villages The norms for allotment and expenditure are not known. Apparently the desire is that rural people remain poor, with agronomy based economy..

Aftermath of partition

The country's problems after freedom shifted to military arena. The two diagrams depicted as 1 and 2, of Fig. 2 show how the nation jumped from frying pan to fire. This was an act of Nehru, with his unwavering desire for plebiscite, not a compulsive requirement when Pakistan wanted Kashmir by force. The accession treaty did not cater for a situation of forcible occupation by any. Plebiscite thus becomes meaningless then. It did mention about the wishes of Kashmiri people to decide, but not in a hostile atmosphere. When this was pre-empted by Pakistan and a war became a legally justified necessity, practicing nobility is a folly. With his ancestral heritage, it might have been difficult for Nehru not to have a noble face, but what prevented him to hand over the situation to Vallabhai Patel to decide? What we call India to-day, is Patel's creation. He got the non-cohesive and fragmented subcontinent under one umbrella. He was very much in the run to be the prime minister but for Gandhi's preference for Nehru. Also, why in a hurry to draft a Constitution even before Independence, to be guided by Nehru's OR (Objective Resolution) closely following British India Act of 1935. The entire situation was confusing, to say the least. Now the nation had to defend itself against the defeated enemy! The vanquished has become victor with only a seventh of our population. After the creation of POK, the entire Northeastern region of Kashmir has become vulnerable (Refer Fig 2) and needs several military outposts.

Our nobility has cost us much, the same way as what happened in 1191 A.D. when Ghazni was defeated by Prithiv Raj, in the first battle of Terrain. Badly wounded, he managed to escape, leaving behind his wounded soldiers. Prithiv Raj provided help to reduce their sufferings, and then allowed them to withdraw. Ghazni attacked next year and defeated Prithiv Raj; took him as prisoner and brutally murdered him. The Muslim dynasty was established in our country, when forced conversion to Islam was almost total.

British followed worst barbaric act. After defeat during first freedom struggle, (May 10, 1857) and revived imperialistic rule, thanks to our princely States and educated social elites, the elected poet emperor Bahadur Shah Zafar was sent to Rangoon as prisoner because he declared the eviction of the Britishers. His three sons were beheaded and their heads were kept hanging at the door of court, with a prominent placard stating "Never try again". We followed this religiously, thanks to Gandhi.

Muslim dynasty was in quandary, invited Babur in 1494. He was a warrior but no land to rule. Babur using his skill to dismantle the Muslim dynasty and become the ruler of the land. Babur founded the Mogul empire in 1526 after Ist battle of Panipat. Our noble mind has created a situation when Pakistan's illegal claim on Kasmir has made our more than their total population living below poverty line. There is no denial of the fact that the 'Kashmir issue' is the main cause for this situation. But can we not solve this, making the poor strong? Should not that be the first step to adopt?

If we had adopted suitable approaches, as stated in Annexure 1, making this vast population strong, the situation would have been different. We have more Muslims than Pakistan has. Are they ill -treated? Claiming Kashmir on the basis of Muslim majority population is a folly. They were not always Muslims. Earlier, it was a Buddhist country. Sanskrit was their language. Moguls came and left after creating their hallmark, the Shalimar garden. The polite beautiful people adopted Islamic religion then of their free will. It was not forced on them. The tourists flocked in that heavenly place because no one was bothered about religion. It was a personal faith, period.

Current comparative global situation (Year 2004)

TABLE 2

Country Population Million	India 1,079. 721	China 1,296.500	Pakistan 152.061	Thailand 62.378	Singapore 4.333	USA 293.50 7
Surface Area (sqKm)	3.3 Million	9.6 million	796.1 thousand	531.1 thousand	608 Sq. km only	9.6 million
Total GDP.$. Million	691. 876	1,649,329	96,115	163,005	106,181	11,667, 515
Per capita earning ,$	640.79	1272.13	632.33	2613.18	24841.39	39753. 03
PPP GDP $ million	3,362. 960	7,123,712	325,513	510,268	118,226	11,628, 083
Per capita, PPP GDP ,$	3116. 73	5494.5	2169.2	3130.40	27494.4	39618. 68
Population Growth,%	1.4	0.6	2.4	0.6	2.0	0.9
Literacy rate. Adult male	65.8	96	61.7	96	98	96
Same, female	61.5	88	35.2	91.5	88.6	89
Energy use, per Capita kg Equivalent	508.8	903	459	1,227.9	5560.7	8250
Electricity use, Per capita, KwH	356	827	351.9	1448	6795.4	12 .399
CO2 Commission (metric ton per capita)	1.1	2.2	0.8	3.3	14.7	19.8
HIV (%age 15-49)	0.9		0.1	1.5	0.2	0.6

Are we proud about what is presented above? Endless platitudes continue promising development, when increasing disparity ratio between urban and rural societies is the reality. Should we not make efforts to rectify this?

The issue to judge now is how developed they (Arabic Muslims in Pakistan) are in a society they have created since Independence. That should be the criterion, not religion based numerical numbers, to decide whom Kashmir should belong to. The order for cease-fire and the line disengagement (now known as LOC) was initiated by the Security Council. It should now decide, based on humanitarian ground, to whom Kashmir should belong to for development. The author believes that if we succeed to make the Nation as a whole, not urban society alone, as China has done, the solution will surface automatically.. If not done, the creator of this planet may have to take charge to reshape this.

Currently our assessment is based on borrowed military muscle power at the cost of poor. Establishment of military posts at hostile terrains, at altitudes varying from 5000ft (Srinagar) to 14000 ft (Laddakh), 17000ft (Chushul and Fukshe) and sustaining them is difficult and expensive, to provide creature comfort air lifting from bases at ground level is risky, needing skill and courage, to say the least. Flying between alleys with twists and turns, with lofty mountains on both sides, was done with a patriotic feeling not realized sitting in air-conditioned offices. During winter, the temperature up there is between *minus* (-) 25 to 45^0 Centigrade

Orpheus C119G Jet Pak

When the author was busy to enhance the muscle of the Gas Turbines for various applications, another officer was working overtime to make arrangements towards the well being of warriors posted in the hostile areas like north-east of the LOC and the eastern boundary adjacent to China. The history of development of arduous airfreight of men and material coupled with fatal accidents makes one realize how 'stupid' human beings can be, to satisfy the selfish interests of a few. Does not the table above prove this? What is the real reason for the long drawn fights, and heinous terrorism, resulting untold miseries, not only to the honest, hospitable, and the beautiful people of Kashmir but the entire subcontinent? The germ may spread and cause harm to the world's humanity.

The initiation for Orpheus Jet Pak has a long story. In 1955, the IAF purchased a few Fairchild C-119G from the USA at throwaway price, because they were phased out by the US air force. The author was then posted at Air HQ. His unshared office of Additional Director Technical Services (Plans) was in K block. Across the road was H Block – the powerhouse. At the furthest end, on the first floor was the office of our Chief of Air Staff (CAS). The office of Director, Policy & Plans- then Air Commodore Pinto, the most loved, respected, and a competent fighter pilot was on first floor. To go to his office one had to go past the office of the then Director, Operation (DOP), then Group Captain Idris Lalif. Did not meet him then, but heard that he was a terror. Crossing the curtained door of the DOP's, the author walked tiptoed, to reach the wooden staircase to go up.

CAS Air Marshal Idris Latif visiting GTRE in 1980

When I met him, much later, I was amazed. I was expecting to receive an aggressive looking CAS. I met a most pleasant looking person ,extending his hand said, rightly observed "naya suit silai kar liya ? (Have you stitched a new suit?) At that time, the author retired from Air Force and became a civilian Director, after 1979, through open selection by UPSC.

Air Marshal Latif was appointed as Air Attaché in Washington DC. He came to know about Fairchild C-82, fitted atop a Westinghouse J-30 jet engine, providing a thrust boost of about 1600 lb. The saga of Jet Pak began through this chance reading. There after Steward Davis Inc agreed to install J34 engine (3400 lb thrust) on our C119G Cargo aircraft, purchased earlier. The success of test flight of prototype C119G Jet Pak lead to ordering about 70 modification kits to convert C119G as J34 Jet Paks providing 3400 lb additional thrust. Yes, it did make all the difference in the Defence scenario in Kashmir and Laddakh. More troops could be injected and looked after.

Air Marshal Ltif had a checkered career. He was appointed as our countries Ambassador to France. Had a long tenure. He patronized indigenous S & T. He wrote most encouragingly on the development of GTX engine, during his visit in1980.

He also wrote an extremely encouraging letter, from France, when the author was awarded J. Om Prakash Bhasin award in 1984. (Page 467 refers)

GROUP CAPTAIN JACOB CHAKKO

A contemporary of the author, did his post graduate studies at Ecole Nationale Suprerieure de L' Aernautique, in Paris, France...Chakko was associated with Jet Pak activities, and became fully competent to make Orpheus C119G Jet Pak providing 4850 lb additional thrust. This he did, and gave a new life to the Packet Squadron, and also to the Jawans guarding the nation keeping vigil from various planned points. Technologically, it was a very praise worthy activity. He did not receive any recognization, - may be because it was not a file pushing activity. The author wishes to recognize his and test pilot Wing Commander Phillipose's activities as examples of excellence of team work of profession, and courage, serving the Nation.

Group Captain Jacob Chakko

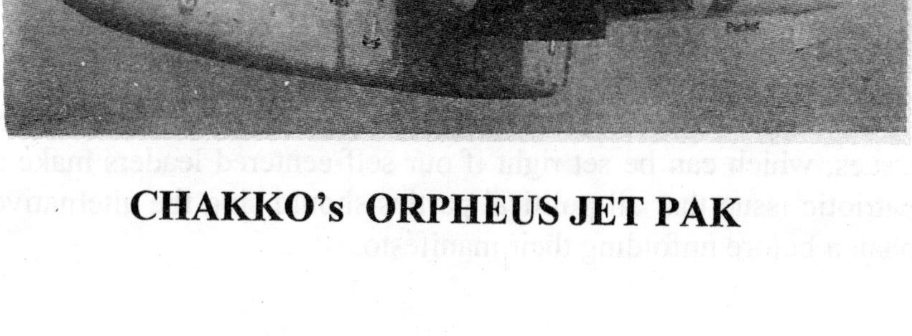

CHAKKO's ORPHEUS JET PAK

THE ESSENTIAL NEED

There is a justified need to bring out a pamphlet highlighting the differences between the two (what initially promised and what actually achieved, audited and then whetted by the President and parliament) and suggest rectifications formulating proper agenda and discussing in the parliament in a civilized manner, and not making uncivilized pandemonium, as commonly done now.

A non-erasable scene has been imprinted in author's mind. On one occasion, a lady MP walked down to the well of the parliament with a huge bunch of papers, hurled them at the face of the Speaker and walked proudly back to her seat. Assuming that some picked up the papers and walked up and reciprocated her action, what would have been the scene in the Parliament? The act would be rated as one grossly degrading to our noble Indian womanhood, amounting to assault. The most appropriate action would have been a demand for open house apology, or get expelled from the Parliament.

In some part of our country a highly knowledgeable and patriotic bourgeoisie society germinated, casting aside our Brahamanic mal-practices A noble and educated society, Brahmo-Samaj, was formed by a Bengali reformer Raja Ram Mohon Roy in 1828. How few know that Mughal Emperor made him his Ambassador in the UK soon after.? Does that not prove that religion was never an issue? Rabindranath Tagore was a member of this new enlightened society. This noble creation could not find popular acceptance when they were rated as 'Anglicized' Indians, because of their knowledge of English and civilized way of life.. Earlier, Buddha also could not get a mooring in our country. Only hereditary Brahmanic cult flourished.

The above is an illustration. There are several similar issues, which can be set right if our self-centered leaders make a patriotic issue that all political parties should sing the alternative bhajan before unfolding their manifesto.

ELECTION SYSTEM

We have opted for adult franchise, with no condition on literacy. It is a clever way of retaining sovereignty of hereditary system, keeping democracy at bay. We say very rightly that India lives in villages, even now after 62 years of Independence, but not as a part of the largest democratic society that we claim as ours. The illiteracy of poor rural people is pathetic, - a willful crime that the nation has carried forward since about 1500 BC. We adopted formally our Constitution in January, 1950, and leaders are elected mostly by the rural people, believing what was told to them during election campaign. May be, they do not believe the leaders any more, but they know about money's relationship with vote. Visiting a cotton growing village community, in the northern part of Karnataka, the author held a group discussion with village Panchayat members on rural development. The participants were both young and old. It was a very lively discussion. The old member, the village pradan, was sitting quiet. The author sought his opinion on the approach plan. He said that if elections were held every year, the development would happen. Everyone agreed. Meeting ended.

ASSESSMENT OF GOVERNANCE

It may not be difficult to gather information on what was achieved after elections. Systems exist in our Constitution, but what good are they for the illiterates. We have an Election Commission. The past manifestos must be available in its library. It should not be difficult to compile data on what manifestos had promised prior to election, and what actually was achieved. (Ref. Art. 151). One may hazard a guess that in all these manifestos, a pledge* would have been made towards rural development, and poverty alleviation. In the national interest, an apolitical independent research group (not a commission) can be formed to compile the statistical data on the above for last three governments. Two sets of documents need be scrutinized; (a) the manifestos of the winning parties forming the governments, and

(b) the audited reports, vetted by the President and considered by the Parliament, as desired by the Constitution.

*This was done, in one the three resolutions, during the very first session of the Indian national Congress in 1886.

The Constitution of India

ARTICLE 151

"151. Audit reports – (1) The reports of the comptroller and Auditor-General of India relating to the accounts of the Union shall be submitted to the President, who shall cause them to be laid before each House of Parliament.

(2) The reports of the comptroller and Auditor-General of India relating to the accounts of a State shall be submitted to the Governor[***] of the State, who shall use them to be laid before the Legislature of the State."

With comparative (manifesto vs. actually achieved) information published, and made known to gram Panchayats, even the illiterate rural poor may get to know the real face about our adult franchise. A demand for literacy will emerge. Without education and public accountability, the present system loses the virtue of our claim to be a democratic society. Such accountability is equally important for academic and scientific institutions, financially aided NGOs (non-government organizations) with self-assigned tasks made known to the government to get aid. Knowledge on implementation will receive the much-needed thrust, if quantified achievements and falsehoods are made public.

However, does the government have the courage to institute an assessment body suggested above?

PRESIDENT'S PLEDGE TO NATION

On 16th February, 2006, the Parliament was informed eloquently (Para 25) by the then President about a path-breaking Information Act, 2005, empowering every citizen of our republic to know about the implementation of government programmes, thus inducting transparency to reduce corruption. This noble platitude remained encased within the circular walls of the Parliament, strangely not pursued, even though announced by the country's President himself addressing the Parliament. Is this a legal Act that he proclaimed? Where has this been incorporated? Has this ever been implemented to analyze any major event, pulling the country down? There are several aspects that come under the purview of this act.

PUBLIC MONEY: TAX SYSTEM

Similarly, a mere statement that only about 10 % of the country's urban population pays direct tax, and no tax is levied on raw agro- products does not make the urban people any nobler citizen. Rural people should know that they are paying indirect tax, on value added agro-products whenever they are buying commodities from shops, although not paying any direct tax. The large rural people are sustaining the nation in two ways; first producing raw agricultural products, and then paying indirect tax on their produced raw materials, value added in urban areas. Our indirect tax amount is greater than direct tax. The finished products are often four times the cost of raw products. This differential is distributed among the middlemen and profiteers whom Jawaharlal Nehru wanted to hang from the first lamppost! Were they? They live in urban societies, as nobles. Needless to highlight that the nation is surviving because of the efforts of illiterate rural people, and rewarded with poverty. In developed societies opposite is the trend. Direct tax is more than indirect tax. The obvious need is to correct this situation. The book suggests the solution.

One likes to recall what Rabindranath Tagore wrote in his book, titled "Letters from Russia"

Moscow

20 September, 1930

In Russia at last ! Whichever way I look, I am filled with wonder. It is unlike any other country. Are rousing everybody up without distinction. Throughout the ages , Civilized communities have contained groups of nameless people. They are the majority—the beasts of burden, who have no time to become men. They grow up on the leavings of society's wealth, with the least food, least clothes and least education, and they serve the rest. They toil most, yet theirs is the largest measure of indignity. At the least excuse they starve and are humiliated by their superiors. They are deprived of everything that makes life worth living. They are like a lamp stand bearing the lamp of civilization on their heads: people above receive light while they are smeared with the trickling oil.

GANDHIAN ERA

1930 was the Gandhian era to fight for the common man. The then President spoke in the same vein, in 2003, the same year when the disparity ratio between the rich and poor had increased to about 10, but the USSR became the world power with competence-based equality in all spheres of activities.

PRESIDENT'S MANTRA FOR RURAL DEVELOPMENT

DH News Service Ahmedabad: March 29 writes,

Mantra for progress:: Kalam

"It is a known fact that president APJ Abdul Kalam's heart beats for missile technology and children. Today, as he visited

Gujarat to take part in convocations of the Indian Institute of Management, Ahmedabad, and the South Gujarat University, he made it clear that rural development is also one of his topmost priorities.

In a speech that left the IIMA pass outs at the 38th convocation captivated, Dr Kalam emphasized the need for rural development saying that the country cannot progress unless rural development takes place. In Surat, at the South Gujarat University's convocation he described poverty as the country's biggest threat. It's time to provide urban facilities to the villages, he added. He wanted the pass outs to pay more attention to villages. Dr. Kalam mentioned that a time when the WTO is posing a threat to diamond and textile industry, emphasis should be on rural development to a make up for the losses.

"We are facing three types of problems- religious, ideological and economical – and we need to handle these", he told that IMMA students in his address titled "when will I sign a song for India?" Dr Kalam also suggested that the students conduct research into the core competence of India. "we have many religions and many cultures. How do you manage a billion people? Isn't managing a billion people core competence", he posed a question, himself replying in the affirmative. Dr. Kalam's title for the address was based on a question posed by young girl in Ahmedabad about four years ago where she told him that her brother goes gaga over America and as to when will she be able to sing for India?

Describing how the world progressed during the early 20th century from human warfare to mechanical warfare and beyond, the President observed that in today's world we are facing ideological that we are facing religious animosity", he said. Mr Kalam did not miss out on making a mention of the war in Iraq and went on to day that one cannot ignore what is happening in the world. The effects are felt, he added."

A fact cannot be ignored that we are never short of platitudes. The above address at IIM, Ahmedabad, may be an exception if the announcement made by the media on PURA (Annexure 4) from the Rastrapati Bhavan by Dr. A.P.J Abdul Kalam on 25.1.2005 is a truth and can be verified visiting the three successful PURA villages. Dr. Kalam is still active, and people will respect him if he discloses the names and locations of these. If this cannot be done, it is the worst form of crime committed from our nation's noblest temple.

PURA Accountability

. Some account of PURA is available in "Penguin year book, 2008, pages 173 – 177. However, these pages provide little in quantified terms about three successfully implemented PURAS' comparing with *urban facilities* as announced earlier in January, 2005. Does a Vallam Periyar PURA model near Thanjavur include these facilities? Can anyone indicate what Vallam Periyar PURA'S provide? Is it different to what suggested in Article 243(G)?

PURA is a noble desire, no doubt, if only the basic calorie intake for all is a confirmed fact. Otherwise, it is a cruel populist gimmick for the rural poor, — that too from the highest quarter. Our noble desire for the rural poor has been stretched to an extent when PURA would be a thin line between urban and rural societies. Yet no body knows what his plan of action to achieve this was! Annexure 1 suggests an approach. There may be other to accomplish similar nationally desired end. Let us illustrate them in quantified terms, and debate to evolve the best in the national interest. Our most unfortunate habit is to herald undefined action oriented platitudes. We are addressing poor illiterate people. They understand numbers, not wise words.

The author is a retired service officer. Platitudes sound hollow till actual implementation. The country suffers from a fallacious syndrome. The country's cure is to get rid of this, legally, as a part of PIL (Public Interest Litigation). PIL court should form a separate wing of Supreme Court, for quick disposal. Orations of Platitudes without a quantified implementation plan should be treated as an illegal act.

FIG. 3

POVERTY LINES

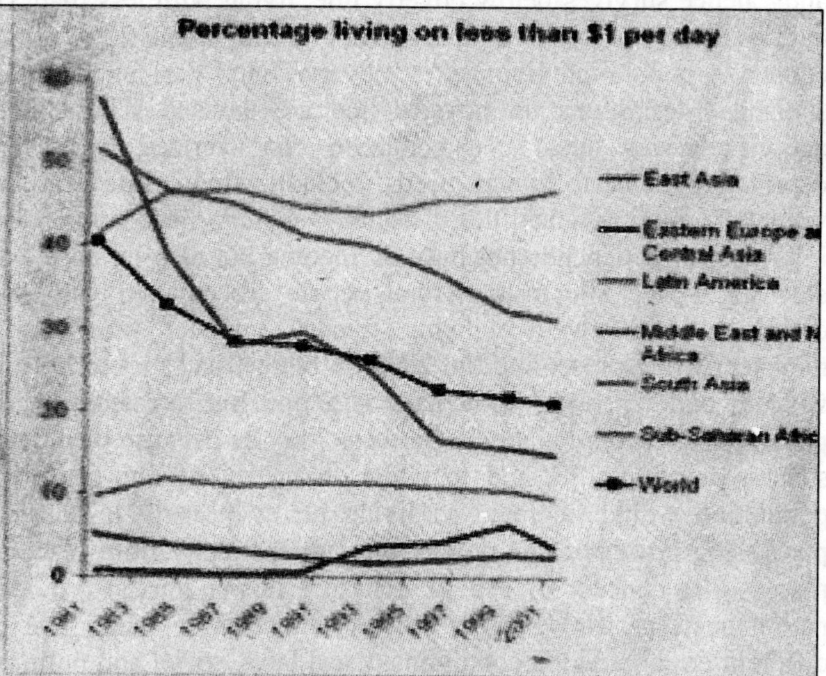

The percentage of the world's populatio living on less than $1 per day has halved twenty years. However, most of this improvement has occurred in East and South Asia. The graph shows the 1981-2001 period.

Source: Wikipedia, the free encyclopedia

Our country is a half baked knowledgeable verbose society. We herald the deficiencies to be rectified but not suggest any possible implementable solutions. Accountability is sadly lacking in almost all activities. The society thus gets moorings for feudalism leading to massive corruption in all walks of life.

Fig 3 above indicates that India is one of the poorest nations, and hence survives below poverty line, living with less than $1/ day. If dietary based norm is adopted, currently about 22 % of our country's population live below poverty line. Various kinds of statistical definitions on poverty line are devised. The United nations defines this, - "a condition characterized by severe deprivation of basic human needs, including food, safe drinking water, sanitation facilities, health, shelter, education and information. It depends not only on income but also on access to services." The 800 million rural people are covered with that definition. Our award winning finance minister (now home minister) while presenting the 2008-09 budget had picked up this wisdom and conveyed as a part of a one line presentation on poverty, but did not elaborate further. May be because then, with such a definition, he had to admit that 75% of our country's population would be rated as living below poverty line. The purchasing power of one dollar varies dramatically from place to place. The concept of PPP (Purchasing Power Parity) provides partial answer. However, it provides misleading values due to different environmental conditions, fiscal laws, social and political structures. Such definitions make the poverty line a function of regions where people live, fluctuating with the local prevailing market forces. Yet the body's demand on dietary needs remains reasonably invariant, depending on natural conditions. Let the fundamentals, based on safe drinking water, the dietary needs, and health be our basic parameters, to measure the poverty line. Let this be defined as * "expenditure required for a daily calorie intake of 2400 per person in rural areas and 2100 in urban areas. This expenditure is officially estimated at Rs.229.9 per capita in rural areas and Rs.264.1 in urban areas at 1993 - 94 prices."

•**SOURCE**: Glossary, Statistical outline of India, 2004 - 2005 Tata Services Limited

The other needs, though fundamental, should be added thereafter, to determine the quality of life. Poverty and quality of life should not be clubbed together in poor societies, as done by the United nation's definition.

POPULATION BELOW POVERTY LINE

TABLE 3

.POPULATION BELOW POVERTY LINE					
	2007	*1999-00*	*1993-94*	*1987-88*	*1973-74*
Number of poor (Mn.)					
Rural.........	*170.5*	*193.2*	*244.0*	*231.9*	*261.3*
Urban	*49.6*	*67.1*	*76.3*	*75.2*	*60.0*
Total..........	*220.1*	*260.3*	*320.3*	*307.1*	*321.3*
Poverty ratio (%)					
Rural.........	*21.1*	*27.1*	*37.3*	*39.1*	*56.4*
Urban.........	*15.1*	*23.6*	*32.4*	*38.2*	*49.0*
Total..........	*19.3*	*26.1*	*36.0*	*38.9*	*54.9*
Upto 1993-94,revised data based on the Expert Group headed by Dr.D.lakdawala, Planning Commission, as accepted by the Govemment in 1997.					

Although one must accept that the country's rural poverty situation is improving, the rate of improvement in urban areas is much faster compared to rural areas during the last twenty years, adversely diverging. This confirms not only the fact about increasing disparity ratio, but an urgent need to develop the other side of the rural coin. In addition, the fact about the number of people below poverty line in rural areas deserves serious consideration. 170.5 million (2007) people below poverty line in rural areas are about the same as the total population of Pakistan.

If one adds what media reports, the overall canvass of the country is certainly gloomy.

Times of India, 23.2.2009 (One year ago)

Elight out of 10 Children are underfed, say NGOs

Rs.51,000 ($51X10^{10}$) (Cr Allocated to NGOs, No Record of Spending

Himanshi Dhawn

New Delhi: The slew of development schemes of the UPA hasn't made any change on the ground. The budget for child schemes increased from 2.20% in 2003-2004 of the Union budget to 5.35% in 2008-2009. But between 1998-1999 and 2005 – 2006, the number of children suffering from malnutrition went up from 15.5%

To 19.1% while the number of kids under five which anaemia rose from 74.2% to 79.2%.
The proportion of rural population unable to access the required 2,400 calories a day climbed from 75% in 1993-1994 to a record high of 87% by 2004-2005. Razia Ismail of India Alliance for child Rights said: "Eight out of 10 children are underfed".
In its draft report, FORCES a national network advocating child rights – described the ICDS as a "failure". As of September 2007, ICDS's supplementary nutrition scheme reached less than half of the children between 0.6 years. The report card in the education sector looks grim. "Far from the promised 6% of GDP, the combines expenditure by the centre and state government fell from 2.9% ion 2002- 2003 to 2.84% of GDP in 2007.2008".

LEAKY FLAGSHIPS?

- ***Rs.50,000cr allocated for flagship schemes in 2007-08 transferred to bank accounts of NGOs, autonomous bodies and district authorities.***
- ***Govt. has told CAG it was not aware of actual spending by these organizations.***
- ***CAG report says money from Social and Infrastructure Development Fund diverted to cultural programmes like celebration of 150th year of First War of Independence.***
- ***Of Rs.20,000cr collected under Universal Service Obligation Fund in 2003-08 for subsiding rural telephony, only Rs.5,000cr has been spent.***

43Rs.30,100cr National Rural Employment Guarantee Scheme
Rs,13,100cr Sarva Shiksha Abhiyan
Rs.8,000cr Mid Day Meals Scheme
Rs.6,705cr Integrated Child Development Scheme
Rs.11,842cr JN National Urban Renewal Mission
Rs.7,400cr RG Rural Drinking Water Mission
Rs.40,900cr Bharat Nirman
Rs.12,070cr National Rural Health Mission

Are the NGOs under-fed? Alternatively, are they causing what they are moaning about? It would be interesting to learn about the NGOs efforts to remedy what they are rightly lamenting about.

PRESENT SITUATION

It is not known for what end use our government prepares the expensive and valued NSS (National Sample Survey) reports. If this is done to improve upon the rural society, a commendable objective is achieved. There are a few thousand government funded NGOs having social workers. They believe that rural people are not really poor. There are some who suggest that rural people are planning to buy Nano cars! This is a happy news indeed. However, the NSS reports depict a different picture altogether.

TABLE 4 **QUALITY OF LIFE:** NSS SURVEY. Report on Village Facilities **(July – December, 2002**

NSS Report No.4 ***Report on Village Facilities,***

Highlights

- ***4646 villages were surveyed in the 58th round of the NSS.***
- ***By 2002, more than three-fourths of India's Villages had access to electricity.***
- ***Non-conventional forms of energy were available in less than 12% of Indian villages.***
- ***55% of India's villages got their drinking water mainly from tube-wells or hand pumps.***
- ***Tap water was used for drinking in about 18% of villages.***
- ***Only 30% of Indian villages has any kind of drainage system; the major types were the open pucca and the open katcha systems.***
- ***76% of the villages had irrigation facilities, mostly in the from of tube-wells.***
- ***Cooperative societies existed in 30% of Indian villages and self-help groups in 24%.***
- ***Government development programmes for provision of drinking water and construction of approach roads were operative in 60% of villages.***
- ***Literacy campaign/ adult education programme was in force in 37% of the villages.***
- ***Post offices did not exist in over 78% of India's villages.***
- ***Only one- third of all villages were within 2 km of a telegraph office / PCO/e-mail facility.***
- ***Pre-primary school facilities were available in 66% of India's villages in 2002 compared to only 39% in 1991.***
- ***72% of the villages had primary school facilities in 2002 compared to 67% in 1991.***
- ***54% of the villages were more than 5 km away from the nearest primary Health centre and 27% were more than 10 km away from it.***
- ***Only 10% of the village had a medicine shop and only***

20% had a private clinic or doctor.

The 10th and last two items, listed above, are relevant in what follows:

Why did the medicos refuse to do their one-year internship in rural areas? For example, in the 'Report to the People' by the UPA government the first recommendation made on health is quoted below:

"National Rural Health mission launched; accredited social health activists - ASHAs – in all villages in 18 high focus states; 1.73 Lakh selected and being trained; 4 Lakh by 2007-2008".

No details on accredited activities are mentioned. No reason offered to qualify as high focused States. Are they the States having higher stakes for the government of the future? If the above is still our rural health mission , it is estimated a total of 5.73 Lakh ASHAs should have been employed by now. That is, virtually each village will have services of one ASHA. When the excited deliberations on medico internship were going on, why no mention on the above support service was made? If so done, would the medico internship not favorably considered with such helping hand? Has this scheme been dropped? Or, have the trained 'ASHAs' also deserted after being trained and gone to foreign lands with better job prospects?

Should not the NSS report begin with a mention about the dietary status of rural people? If so done, the NSS report gets correlated with what stated there after and the budgetary allotment.

NSS REPORT

National Sample Survey (NSS) is conducted by the Ministry of Information & Implementation. Such surveys are made at intervals of every five years. They provide information on quality of life, assuming, as it appears, that the basics needed for healthy survival are solved. The current one (2007) is due, but not formally published by 2009. The summary of the previous one ending (2002) has been indicated above. Will it be improper to suggest that the current one is not published because the election was round the corner? Comparing with the earlier one, people will know what has been the performance of the present government. There is still time to publish, retaining the earlier format for easy comparison.

The improvement made since 2002, though not published are available in their Calcutta Office. Sample survey indicates not much change. The numerous expensive survey reports are not available to gram panchayats, although they should be the first recipients.

Some indications about the recent one are available in the text. In our country's situation, the dollar related economy and PPP (Purchasing Power Parity) measure on poverty line are meaningless. To begin with let us assess making use of NSS reports and then add on the other aspects to determine the quality of life we aspire for the rural people as well e.g., PURA. Three successes from Rashtrapati Bhavan had been announced on 15th January 2005. There cannot be any doubt on this information, Let us take them as model. But we need to know in quantified terms .about the achievements of these.

In this regard, dogs and human beings are similar. An under-nourished dog will meekly run away if chased. The same dog, if fed well, will bark back and chase, making the same man to run for his life. If a poorly dog were left underfed, it would slowly die, in a neglected corner. Not only it becomes a cursed stinking object, it starts spreading dangerous, often fatal diseases. Our largest democratic society has much to learn from such life process.

We know that about 20 % of our foodstuff is wasted, but solution to prevent this. We have a food-processing ministry. FDIs (Foreign Direct Investment) came with great expectations but returned with equal disappointments. Even with success, where is the money for the poor and those below poverty line to buy this? Besides, in our vast country, the food habits are different in different parts of the country. Differences exist in other countries too but not to this extent.

The inactive society, primarily with a culture of 'words of wisdom', has to be modified, with an action-oriented one to solve the country's problems. Words of wisdom should follow, not precede, as done now. We seem to count eggs before they hatched. It is easy to express wisdom but difficult to practice. We are in a metaphysical world of wise words only. We are still in a Banana syndrome after 61 years of Independence. In the recent days, Rahul Gandhi is expressing need for a change; but he stops there. It would be more proper to know what he has in his mind. Has he got any constructive, quantified plan?

POOR AND POVERTY

While poverty is no sin, it tends to degenerate a society, when the poor loses his self-respect. A poor man's plight satisfies a rich (not wise) man's ego of self-esteem. The total number of poor people in the world far exceeds the rich. With unequal competence, the existence of rich and poor is a worldwide unavoidable social phenomenon. However, poverty is not. Going by the head counts of those who are below poverty line (dietary based), our country leads, second only to African countries. To assess the reason why the country is in the current unacceptable shape, considerations on our origin leading to British imperialism, and finally the partition of the subcontinent are necessary. In spite of 1000 years, and several dynastic rules, a basic strain, though not laudable, has survived. This inherent quality cannot be denied. The future hope lies in reverting back to the original concept of humanism, but improved.

The desire is to know what corrective steps must be taken to get out of our present condition. Unfortunately, those who can improve upon the lot of the poor believe that any expressed (not implemented) intention to do this is an act of nobility and deserve high national reorganization in return. "I" factor of the prime motivation but not for solving the Poor's rightful claims. Many sitting on high pedestal go to the extent of raising false hopes, for their own benefits. Other than falsehood, they even resort to corrupt means to rob the food and fund meant for the poverty alleviation and literacy. They receive media publicity if hauled up by law, and then freed on bail. Thereafter, they go about as benevolent social elites. Members of Parliament, ministers, commissioners etc., with garlands of scam round their neck, move about as honorable citizens for years. The bails provide them time to organize evidences in their favour when finally they face the courts of law.

The social degradation is galloping. We learn about a kind teacher providing an anti-pregnancy pill to the victim of a gang-raped schoolgirl, but not about actions taken against the criminal students. A happy situation for all. The victim with a shattered soul for life, is safe from future possible social predicaments, the threatened teacher is safe from assaults by the criminals, and the criminals go about to find the next prey, now carrying anti-pregnancy pills! The custodians of law and order get accelerated promotions for reduced crime rates statistics. Can there be any better social order?

All these have to change with an active and proper judicial system. We say, 'justice delayed, justice denied'. If this is accepted, by our judicial system, denial of justice is universal.

The following overview is essentially to highlight four features of this subcontinent;

It was the earliest nature based civilized land, with proper understanding of natural phenomenon sustaining life; Such understandings germinated through deep meditations of 'Rishies' Four fundamentals can be identified as under;

1. It was a land of plenty with competence based social structure, when the caste system existed to identify persons needed to sustain different kinds of activities. Society's management was not hereditary Militancy was secondary to activities of mental faculty;
2. It was a land of princes, and peasants; not a nation. Land owned by Princes, leased out to villagers and communities, who paid tax in kind or coin. Private armies were kept to collect taxes;
3. The Princes often fought with each other and services of peasants to fight were often demanded, when they did not know what was the issue;
4. It was the most invaded land with hardly any collective resistance The invaders plundered at will, and retuned with their booty, which included, at times, inhabitants as slaves.

Reader's Note Sheet on overview.

CHAPTER - 2

ANCIENT CIVILIZATION AND RELIGION

Origin of civilized mankind

Much has been written about the origin of mankind. The most contemporary primitive societies are Neolithic who practiced agriculture, made pots, weaved textile and worked on stones to make tools. Prehistoric man probably formed first primitive societies about 250,000 years ago. However, did they live in caves? While many conjectures are made based on fossil evidences, a doubt surfaces on what caused the transition of a primitive cave dwelling man to live now in well-constructed houses. What happened first? Ability of initiating controlled fire leading to the basic forms of current civilization, or primitive societies could exist without controlled fire, when mankind lived with earthen sun baked pots. In summary, the author believes that the primitive cave man discovered *flint – a sedimentary rock composed of microcrystalline quartz and chalcedony, when the seed of civilized mankind was planted.

* Safety match discovered in 1826 B.C. in England by John Walker

His discovery of flint was made by a cave dweller, while chipping rock to make his tool. If one accepts this, one can conclude that this cave man had an inquisitive scientific mind. Why spark was coming out from one kind of rock and not from others? He could light up dry leaves, oil oozing out of plants, and then logs of wood at his will. There after the cave populations were protected from wild animals, scorpions, snakes and they came out of the caves. Will it be an inapt statement to suggest that this cave man, discovering flint, was the first scientist for our mankind to create the first civilization, - the Indus Valley Civilization? Great cities got established, making use of fire from wood, for building large and small dwellings with burnt bricks, cooking food, lighting wax candles for domestic use, and limitless other activities, including a cigarette lighters now using flint stone. Since then, *Agni* – the fire became our God. Could this be an example of our religion, described as a hymn?

About 300 sites have been discovered till now. It would appear that many more unexplored sites exist to suggest that this civilization was widespread having both rural and agricultural societies.

MAHENJODARO AND HARAPPA CIVILIZATION

The physical presence of ancient civilization of India was discovered at Mahenjodaro and Harappa by Sir John Marshal in 1920 A.D., the then Director General of Department of Archeology of India .and his colleagues. At these places, the urbanized community lived in big and small houses. Some of them were built with burnt or semi burnt bricks. There was no caste bias, as evident from the large bathing places, where everyone could bathe.

LAY OUT OF A CITY OF MAHENJODARO

A thought surfaces. What did they wear at that time. Cotton, is an easily grown natural product. Did they know how to weave at that time? There were well laid out streets, (seen in the middle) and storm water drains running along side as practiced now in modern urban habitats. In most of the houses, there were bathrooms. The emphasis of cleanliness is evident. The black canal at the right hand corner is the sewage drain running beneath the streets.

'Free Street', Mahenjodaro City

Source: India, Dorling Kinderslay Ltd, UK.

Mahenjodaro City

Harappan city, a few miles away, was similarly laid out. It would appear that a centrally controlled Indus Valley Civilization existed and was spread over a large area in the northeastern part of our subcontinent. The picture above proves that our origin was not only the first but socially noble with no hereditary caste system.

The excavations are not complete. Money is the main crunch. Many believe that information on much of our past civilization still remains buried. These sites are now in Pakistan.

Seals

Although writing was not in vogue, the officials of East India Company gathered many seals. Some of them are personal seals. When carefully deciphered they suggest that the people lived with basics very similar to what exist today.

Indus Valley Seals, United Nation collection

PHASE 1 OF OUR CIVILIZATION

It is difficult to guess where we would be today if the primitive man did not ask why spark was not emitting on all occasions while working on stone to make weapons. The discovery of flint hard rock by the primitive man was the initiator of our civilization. Can anyone suggest an alternate approach for the initiation of civilization?

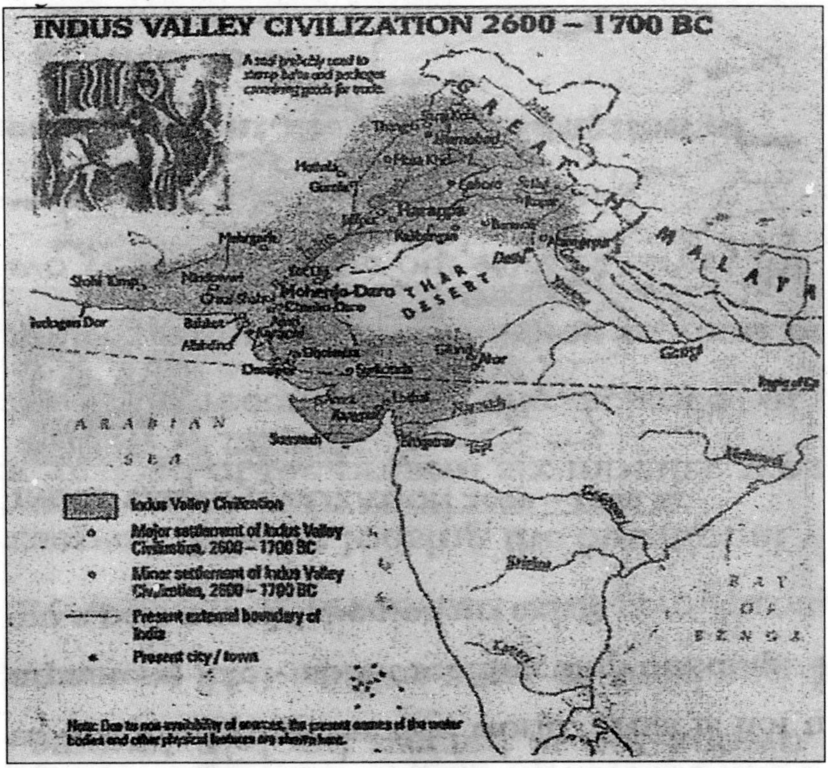

Spread of Indus valley civilization

Source: Monorama with handbook

Note: The date for this civilization varies suggesting 3000 - 1500 B.C. Author believes in what is stated in the map.

Phase II Of Civilization

Could Archimedes (287 – 212 B.C.), Isaac Newton (1642 – 1726) Marconi (1874 – 1937), Rutherford (1871 -1937), Edison (1847 – 1931) and many others (Refer Annexure 2) be rated as the creators of Phase II of modern civilization, when Phase 1 should be described above as Flint aided Indus Valley Civilization. Phase III may be in the offing after Feynman spoke about " many vacancies at the bottom".

The beginning of dynastic rules

A chronological account of dynastic rules is presented as under:

1. The earliest civilization of mankind (8000 - 6000 B.C.)
2. The missing period of 4000 years (6000 – 2000 B.C.)
3. The Indo – Aryan amalgamation, Vedic Indian heritage era (1500B.C. – 1190 A.D.)
4. Muslim dynasty (1190 – 1526)
5. Mogul dynasty (1526 – 1706)
6. Mogul - British rule (1706 – 1757)
7. British imperialism (1757 – 1947)
8. Sovereign Indian rule (1947 –

Mankind and religion

The civilized and organised existence of mankind became disciplined through religion. Secondly, our present unacceptable situation is also due to perverted applications of noble religious concepts of the past. This evil got imbibed into religion when the noble knowledge based religions got transformed to communal religious groups with primary emphasis of each is on acquisition of wealth and power.

RAMAKRISHNA PARAMAHANSA

ONE GOD

People assembled to get his blessing. There was some demanding a priority to get his blessing. A fable about Ramakrishna Paramahamsa is proper to narrate that our sages could illustrate that the religions are private choices to decide to reach up to one's God and humanism. He explained to the congregation of different religious faiths that let us assume that God has arrived to bless and waiting on rooftop. Now people started to climb through properly built staircases, some used ladder, and some climbed an adjoining tree with a overhanging branch reaching the roof. When people reached the roof, a saintly man did not distinguish who followed which path. He blessed them all equally.

"RACIAL DIVERSITY

Then the peoples who came to India represented various racial types; and with the material at our command, it has been attempted to appraise the different types of Humanity which came to be established on the soil of India, and how they reacted towards one another. The present work is concerned more with the mind and the spirit than with the body and the physical environment of the people of India- how they were enabled to think and act and find out for themselves a consistent world of ideas and of behaviour which have their value not only for the Indian Man, but also for the whole of Humanity. Consequently, it is not so necessary to dilate upon the physical bases and aspects which came to characterize Indian life and civilization in the different area within the country. The great fact remains that peoples of diverse origin came to the country at different times, and they settled down beside one another; and entering into a sort of great understanding or comprehension amongst themselves, they jointly built up the culture we are accustomed to associate with India: they built up 'the Wonder that is India'."

SARVEPALLI RADHAKRISHNAN: FORMER PRESIDENT OF INDIA

He was one of our most eminent educationists cum philosophers. As editor of the Board of editors, he writes in the preface of the noble compendium "Cultural Heritage Of India" about 'Wonder that is India' (The Ramakrishna Mission, Institute of Culture, Calcutta)

Hinduism is an assemblage of wisdom of many *rishies* for a noble soul and clear vision, and fearless strength against evils. Those who had the good fortune to listen to Dr. Radhakrishnan's Gita lectures on Sunday mornings, at Beneras Hindu University, will have no confusion on our practicing a perverted path, and the reasons why Hinduism, as practiced now, has reached such low depth.

Belur Math Shrine (1897) , Kolkata

This was built by Swami Vivekanada, the famed disciple of Ramakrishna Paramahamsa,. Ramakrishna having forsaken his brahmin heritage, preached unity of religious faiths and altruistic values of all people. Swami Vivekananda carried forward his Guru's universal concept of religion; made his landmark speech in 1893. to a spellbound assemblage at the Parliament of religion on universal brotherhood in Chicago, On return, he had built this unique shrine, which resembles a church, a temple, or a mosque, depending on from which point one views at the shrine

Factual narration of events over the revived 4000 years, with a prelude of about 6000 years, is difficult. Even a 'His-Story' abbreviated version has to be long and at times controversial. Unlike Egyptians, the people of this sub-continent had been poor writers in the past. Hindus follow non-prophetic Rig Veda,(Veda means knowledge) having more than 1000 hymns, mostly related to nature's precise occurrences. Thus, we have:

a. The terrestrial gods, such as Prithivi, Agni, Brihaspati (Prayer), and Soma;
b. The atmospheric gods, such as Indra, Rudra (lightening), Maruti (wind) and Prajanya;
c. Celestial gods such as Dyaus, Varuna (vault of Haven, Usha (dawn), Surya, Mitra, Savitri, and Vishnu, all associated with the most glorious phenomenon of nature. viz., Sun

Egyptians, similarly civilized in early days believed in Sun (AMUN) God, - built Temples of Amun. Nobles added this to their name; viz., Tutankhamun.

Although Rig Veda list is long, there is no hierarchy of gods. People could choose any god and worship to suit his mind and soul. There is no prophet. However, they believed in all of them with respect. One can find that a Hindu going past any temple will show devotional respect, do 'pranam'(with clasped hands), head bowed, not even knowing which specific god is being worshiped there. He has his own favourite, but he respects all. Such an open mind to religion makes Hinduism so tolerant to other religions. Perversions are also common. People offer money to get blessings on lottery tickets. Before going to race course, performing puja (worship) seeking God's blessing paying a sum as *Pranami* (a token sum put on the tray with a sacred lighted candle) is also not unusual. The priest brings his tray to the devotees who places his hands for a moment over the sacred light and then place his/ her palm on head as a proxy blessing. The rates for all services are prominently displayed in popular temples, and paid accordingly. Currently our perverted Hinduism is thus confirmed.

Integration Of Aryan And Indus Valley Civilization (1500b.C – 1190 A.D.)

Sometimes, after a lapse of this unaccountable period, Mediterranean derivative Dravidians had settled in the fertile and prosperous North Indian, around 2500 B.C. Living peacefully, Dravidians had concentrated on philosophy, astronomy, cultivation, building strong houses, rearing domesticating animals, etc., Dravidian is the name of a language, spoken by the Mediterranean people, and not any race, as commonly believed.

Around the same time, merry making fair-skinned nomad Aryans, with no formal religion, settled down in Central Asia. Their origins were not known. Some believed that initially they had resided at Artic region, In pre-historic times, this was a pleasant place with spring like weather all round the year. With adverse change of weather, the region became inhabitable due to extreme cold. Then they traversed southwards. Hitler believed that Germans were Aryans. They were looking for a permanent place to settle down. The fertile land of this subcontinent attracted them. Several intrusions were made, through Afghanistan, but they were repulsed by the dark skinned Dravidians. Finally, the Aryans won because of their better weapons and stronger physical strength. They were greatly surprised witnessing the civilization of the land they won over. Although they did not establish any dynasty, they wished to get themselves similarly civilized, adopting the culture of the land. Socially they got themselves accepted and inter-marriages became common. This may be the reason why people of northwestern region are generally fair. They encouraged to develop Hinduism to a greater height. They tried to 'sell' the Indus Valley culture as theirs, retaining and encouraging the fairer Dravidians, to enhance their knowledge but they lost out finally. Aryans slowly decayed. All our great epics were written post Aryan invasion, based on folklores, prior to Aryan invasion. The Indo-Aryan culture can be regarded as the foundation of the now formally accepted Hinduism. At the same time, it would not be proper to ignore that the seed for the civilization was the Vedic (meaning knowledge) religion, conceived much earlier.

Indo-Aryan race

The integration of Indo-Aryan took some time to settle down. Several princely States, big and small were created. However, they were not friendly to one another. The Aryan conquest and conflict with local tribes did not create destructive and exploitive ambient. One of the reasons could be that Aryans had no settlement of their own. They even fought among themselves. They wanted to settle down, and end their nomadic living. This desire helped this subcontinent to develop. Thus, their embryonic practices were improved as if these were theirs. Religion, agriculture, organised family lives, arts and crafts received encouragement, but *not on martial art.* The priority was on philosophical knowledge and looking down on *martial art.* This was rated as an inferior element of learning and created our 'slave subcontinent'.

Early religion

Vedic religion became a cohesive structure, when earlier it was practiced in a disorganised manner by many *rishies*. Rig Veda was composed. Women had a dominant role. They participated and were by the side of their husbands in all-important decision-makings, besides being the final managing authority in their own extensive domestic affairs. Political science had not evolved at that stage. They got developed, but the emphasis was still on philosophical way of life. Vedic hymns continued to worship personal divinities. They are deified representatives of natural phenomenon; e.g., Dyaus (the Heaven), Prithvi (the earth), Surya (the Sun), Usha (the dawn), Agni (the fire), etc. Some princes with noble heart annexed vast track of this subcontinent. 0500 BC–1200AD is regarded as our heritage era.

CHAPTER - 3

HERITAGE AND EARLY CIVILIZATION

A brief account of ours and contemporary heritage of Egypt may provide an introduction to what follows. The main search is why we are in our non-acceptable present state. The issue highlighted is that both Indian and Egyptian subcontinents developed themselves through observations of natural phenomenon, though not identically. Egypt to-day is far better off on literacy 71.4 % vs. India's 61%, and per capita income of $5,400 vs. *$2700. Unquestionably, assuming we started from similar civilized state, why are we so far behind?

Source: Manorama Year Book 2009 *Earlier stated $3800.

Geography

Geographically speaking, Indian sub-continent is well protected, by sea on all sides, except the north where the mighty Himalayan range, with sloping extension on either side separate this from the rest of the world, except for a few famous passes through which India is linked with Central and East Asia. The northwestern ranges are not very high. There are many passes, the most used is the Khyber Pass at a height of 3400 ft. (about Bangalore height). Foreign invaders, including Muslims used this pass. Between 1001 and 1027 AD. Mohd Ghazni made as many as seventeen great raids on India. Although his mission was to spread Islam, he indulged in looting palaces and desecrates temples. Enormous caravans of booty and slaves were taken back to Ghazni. Then we have several passes connecting with Afghanistan. The most used pass was the very wide and the least hostile Bolan pass, connecting with Kandhar of recent notoriety. It is through this pass numerous invaders came, and created havoc to the northwestern regions of the country. Notably, Moguls.

It is commonly known that both Moguls and Muslims coming through Afghanistan and from Ghazni respectively. Both follow Islamic religion, but they were not the same. Those who came from Ghazni, believed that the salvation of this country of 'infidels' was to convert whole of this region into an Islamic sub-continent. On the other hand, the Moguls tried, till Auragzeb's regime, for integration with Hindu culture. The harm and suppression done by the British imperialism to the cultivators and craftsmen have been described in detail in subsequent Chapters. Christians also believed that this subcontinent has no future unless it was converted into their faiths. But they did not succeed to shake off the minds of Hindus from their belief on Rig Veda with more than 1000 hymns. Gita, a chapter of Mahabharata epic was composed much later. It is more acceptable because Rig Veda was a difficult text, but Gita was down to earth composition, and advises a man about his surroundings, the good and evil, and advises on his proper responses. The basic form of Hinduism is related to natural phenomenon, which mankind could feel and touch, physically and mentally, because their existence lie in a close knit unit. It is this integration of humanity and nature in various shapes makes Hinduism so acceptable by all, in their own ways of life style. It is this basic equation that a person has with nature makes Hinduism so resilient, yet tolerant to other forms of religion. Why Bhagavadgita is acceptable to common man is seen from what Gandhi said about this universally accepted epic;

" When doubts haunt me, when disappointments stare me in the face, and I see not one ray of hope on the horizon, I turn to Bhgavadgita and find a verse to comfort me and I immediately begin to smile in the mist of overwhelming sorrow. Those who meditate on the Gita will derive fresh joy and new meanings from it every day."

Politically, India was never a nation, or a federation, with a central authority. Yet a common cultural theme originating from Rig Veda ran through the arterial of this sub-continent. In summary, the sub-continent was culturally united, but materially antagonist with one another. They all had a common desire to live a princely life, exploiting the cultivators.

Historians of the West believe that Egypt's civilization is

as old as 5000 B.C., earlier than Indus Valley Civilization. The geography of Egypt was totally different. It is a country built on either banks of the world's longest river, Nile, 6650 km long, ending at lower Egypt, (Alexandria), The starting point is generally taken as Nubia, the treasure land ahead of upper Egypt. While we dread flood, they pray for this, because flood brings fertile Alluvium soil on the banks of this river to help growth of agriculture. River Nile is the life of Egypt.

Other than the fertile riverbank, it is a country of desert. It was a feudal country with hereditary system far more perverse than ours. They believed in retaining Royal blood with in the family orbit. But in Egypt, organised living places were built for the workers, designers, and the Controllers for the construction of Pyramids, Sphinx, palaces at Laxor, the Nassar dam and lake etc. Regular records were maintained about their work, holidays, payments, and so on. But we have none. The children were trained by their fathers as a routine social obligation to fulfill the religious faith, Egyptians had. They did not fear dead, because they believed that it was a part of life cycle phenomenon. The son was trained to help the father for his sojourn to next phase of life, and possible reappearance to the life he had left behind. In contrast, the social status of the artisans of India was not known.

The fundamental difference was while Egypt was one nation, Indian subcontinent was not. Both were feudal and primarily agriculture dependent societies, but in Egypt the working class was organised and looked after. Indian fragmented feudal Princes were indifferent to the working class, peasants as well as artisans. Both had temples, but in Egypt, the high priest was the king himself. We have a separate class as priest who were often the advisors to the Princes. Egypt initially following Sun (Amun) God, had no class distinction and later also following Islamic religion We lived in fragmented lands and on top of that had graded caste system, non-hereditary initially, and now hereditary. The only superiority this subcontinent could claim was about its superior knowledge on natural phenomenon leading to scientific derivations and hymns linking with God.

The archeological development differed because of differences of religious beliefs of these two civilizations The Rig Veda hymns developed different concepts of God's elements. Many beautiful Temples were built to worship these elements. Egyptian religious concept believed in reincarnation of life. To safe guard their treasure to continue their earlier life, big Pyramids, and caves were made and sealed for kings and rich first at lower Nile areas, and later in upper Nile mountainous areas, near Laxer. (The author has visited these) Unfortunately, those who built these, they robbed these treasures, afterwards. A robber's colony had came up for this purpose.

Earlier discoverers of ancient Egypt felt that these were built employing massive slave workers. About a lakh workers worked on three hour shift, for 10 years, with scientific ingenuity to complete the Gaza Pyramid, for example. The ingenuity of their scientific mind can be illustrated from what narrated below. Having decided the highest solid rocky point of the desert, to be safe from the floods of the Nile, the designer needed a perfectly horizontal base. They did not have a 'sprit level' instrument. Having approximately chipped the rock level they created a mud wall at the boundaries of the semi prepared base. Then they cut narrow parallel channels at intervals and poured water. The watermarks after evaporation of water from of the channels provided the craftsmen to work on to get the perfect horizontal solid leveled base to erect the Pyramid. As the work progressed, they kept checking the horizontal level adopting this method. There were several similar ingenious approaches they had adopted to lift the heavy stones to higher levels. The exact process adopted, -- the ramp, or lever – is still debated. No pulleys were used, because these were discovered much later by the Romans.

The craftsmen's village at Deirel-Medina existed during 1504 -1492 B.C. around the time when Rig Veda was composed, during Indo - Aryan era. The Egyptian workers who had built Pyramids were those who would otherwise be sitting idle during their single non-harvesting periods. Thus, people of Egypt were generally employed round the year. They followed a set norm on employment based on their competence. We also progressed in building our structures of heritage. But do we not know how many unemployed youth participated to build up the heritage? With little activities on this, presently the emphasis has shifted to building structures in urban areas.

Four conclusions can be arrived at to justify the present differential situations, narrated earlier. They are;

1. Egypt was one cohesive nation with no caste barriers between the people. Indian subcontinent was just the opposite.
2. Egypt looked after their competent craftsmen in an organised manner, when the work forces in India were undisciplined rabbles.
3. Except for Roman invasion, Egypt did not have so many invasions and robbers as India had.
4. Egypt had a statutory law for educating their children

The Western and Northern regions

The geo-political situation is different with Pakistan on the west. The northern Himalayan countries are boiling; China's railways link with Tibet and roads to Pakistan; and hostile eastern provinces including Bangladesh make the geographically secure situation a questionable issue. This land has different but defined climatic conditions in different regions. It is separated partially by Vindhyas in two parts, at 'tropic of cancer' running through the middle (23° latitude), the most fertile land in the world. Socially, it was a country of diversity where people from five (historically estimated) different origins came and settled down. They did not fight and a non-ethnic tolerant race generated and settled down in village communes. With time, a few urban society got established, as trade centers, and the situation started changing. But it remained as an agricultural society till recent days. There are two possible solutions. A scientific break through similar to first green revolution, and/or increased irrigated land.

Napoleon said that 'army marches on stomach' It is immature to think of becoming a super power with 800 million hungry rural people, more so when the hunger is willfully created for selfish and hereditary class interests.

Some view that the main cause to germinate our large soft nation is due to our non-prophetic philosophical religion, leading to a feudal, divided and corrupt land. This helped Arabs, Turks, and Afghans, invade and plunder, taking away vast treasures of gold and jewelry. The unprecedented looting of Somnath temple in 1000 – 1026 A.D. by Mohamed of Ghazni. is well known established fact

MUSLIM DYNASTY

Our slavery since 1190 A.D. was initiated with Muslim rule in this subcontinent. The genetic strain of Muslims who came with Arabs was different to the non- cohesive Indo-Aryan people then living in this subcontinent. The land was ruled by feudal rich suppressing the poor, with an obnoxious caste system, including untouchable shudras. Slavery of peasants in a different form had existed even when the Muslims came. It was easy to convert the poor to adopt Muslim religion by force, and some, particularly the shudras, adopted this willfully when Muslims did not have any caste system. If flint, mentioned earlier, was the beginning of our civilization, the Brahamanic caste system was the initiator of our society's degradation. It was a knowledge based country, no doubt, but with total disregard to humanism.

This persists even to-day, but to a much lesser extent with literacy and education, in urban society. With increasing demand on performance and competence, the caste barriers are crumbling, but not among 800 million rural people, practicing the only profession, - agronomy, in addition to managing non-remunerative cottage industries. Their products are displayed and sold at a bargained price on urban pavements. One characteristic feature is that the products are skilled handicrafts not needing any conventional energy. This is not available in any case.

The conversion and destruction of earlier temples were Muslim's main goal. The whole of the subcontinent came under their control for a period of about 325 years (1200 – 1526). There is not much to show, or talk about this reign, except the construction of 'Dhai Din Ka Jonpara' at Ajmer and *'Qutub Minar' at Delhi. as a victory memorial, by Qutub ud–din Aibak during slave dynasty. It was completed by Altamash. In the final stages, Persian architects joined, and an Indo-Islamic architectural culture developed. with the accession of Alauddin Khilji. But the Muslim architectural supremacy continued, although many of these was designed and built by the craftsmen who had created earlier the rock cut temples. Many ornamental mosques were also made by Hindu architects, using materials of raged beautiful temples. Surprisingly, they took pride to herald these as symbols of their valour. Close to Qutab Minor, one can see the evidence of their poor ethical mind when one finds many stone curved figures are disfigured. Such acts are baffling. What kind of mindset motivated such destructions? The fact to recognize is that the invaders, since 1190 A. D. had ruled treating Hindus as slaves after the great Indo- Aryan period.

*An alternate story is Qutub-ud-din Aibiak built this to please his daughter who wanted to see sunrise unobstructed. If this be true, one has to admire two facts. One, the inquisitive minded young lady's love to learn how the sleepy silent world wakes up at sunrise. Or, could it be her astronomical inquisitive mind? Secondly, about her energy to climb. Author had climbed up in his younger days, up to the last storey, which was built at a later date. The climb in dark bat infested steps was not easy; - at times scary. Now, the adventure is restricted, but earlier the time taken to climb and come down were fitness tests for the young.

There were many in-fights during the Muslim dynasty. A notable event was the reign of Razia Sultan in Delhi. (1236 – 40), the first lady to rule this subcontinent. None of the few paintings of that time shows women with burkha. Vijayangar Empire was founded in 1336, during Razia Sultana's reign. Luckily, the Mohallas did not raise their heads then, but her ability to steer through rough water deserves admiration.

Qutab Minar (Height 72.5m / 382 ft)

The histories of reigns of Muslin dynasty were more about the several rulers and little about the people they ruled. The most notable character was their casteless society. It began with an excellence on architectural structure, - Qutab Minar -. aided by the creators of earlier heritage era.

An unhealthy question surfaces. If destruction of Hindu temples was the Muslim's pre-occupation, and now condemned, why so much commotion on destruction of one mosque, Babri Masjid, apparently built over a destroyed temple of Rama? Its existence is uncertain. To begin with why destroy this not very frequented Mosque, even if the fact about the earlier existence of a temple is correct? Having found none, it would appear that a decision has been taken to build two,- one mosque and one temple, side by side. The conflict will start again. Mosque will be to prey Allah, but which God for the Hindus? Shiva, Ganesha, Vishnu, or Goddess Kali? A commission will be constituted. But who will be the Chairman? From BJP, or Congress? Or, one from the numerous cults after a bitter fight?

Only an uncivilized mind can justify this. What are we trying to prove or gain? Are we trying to prove our valour over the minorities, within the country when we could not do this in 1192 fighting with Muslim invaders? And continued to be slave since then except for a short but glorious period of Shivaji lead Maratha rise of about 100 years to get rid of the Moguls(1659 - 1761).

INDO-ARYAN CIVILIZATION

Muslim Dynasty followed the earlier Indo-Aryan era .when the subcontinent gave birth to several spiritual epics, structures and noble people whom we revere even now. To quote a few, Vedas,(Compilation over a timeless period), Rig Veda (1500 B.C.), Upanishads (800 -500 B.C), Buddha (623 B.C.), Ajatashatru (551 -519 B.C.), Mahavira, et al were born in a land of several spirituals reigns. Non-prophetic religions were evolved mostly through inquisitive observations of natural phenomenon, e.g., mankind's basic nature, other living beings' behaviors, and growth of plants where solar energy played a key role. Simultaneously, the skill germinated to give shape to mental perception They created temples of many thoughts. The art of 'fresco' painting was another innovative creation. The rock cutting skill, the creation of many beautiful structures and temples are now the main tourist attraction. The beautiful features and objects make many to appreciate that these were made of stones, bricks mud and sand. Steel and many other materials were not identified and used. It is difficult to compare metal-based creative mind of mankind with that which used non-metallic materials. The key issue to ponder is whether such transformation has changed the mankind. to be better or worse. There is much to be said for or against. For example, in the earlier days, the southern hemisphere was richer than the primitive northern part, before the advent of industrial revolution. Thereafter, the condition has been reversed. One can see this happening in our subcontinent

STONE BASED-CULTURE :

Countless temples, palaces, and monuments are embodiments of our early prosperous socio-economic prosperity, and also our unassailable technological skill using primarily stone as the raw material.

Mamallapuram

The 8th century Mamallapuram, the rock-cut temple on the banks of Bay of Bengal.

SUN CHARIOT IN ORISSA

This Temple was built in the 13th Century It is a reflection of the architectural brilliance of Vedic India. The long chariot, still a tourist attraction, has 12 pairs of ornamental wheels, all but one not damaged. This is shown below;

One unbroken wheel of Sun's Chariot

It is now a UNESCO world heritage site. There are many conjectures about the location of this temple. Astronomy and Mathematics received much attention during that period. The Sun temple was established with an astronomical calculation that the solar eclipse would happen on top of such a temple. And it did happen, but several eminent astronomers of present times believe that it was a mere coincidence. Yet several astronomical scientists had converged at Konarak to witness this prediction. It is worth recalling that a statue of Aryabhata, the most famed astronomer and mathematician was erected in 460 A.D. Space craft was named after his name. But more importantly, he was the first to discover that earth revolves around Sun, and not otherwise as was believed earlier.

The Hampi monolithic chariot (14th to 16th century) is another example of the rock cutting skill, now one among 582 UNESCO world heritage sites.

Hampi monolithic chariot

Vijayanagar empire (1336 A.D.) in Karnataka flourished during the reign of Tughlak in Delhi.

While the industrial revolution came about with the advent of steel production and its use, through steam engine, the heritage age can similarly be proud of the skill on rock cutting, erecting magnificent temples, fine arts and crafts, and also for the intellectual pursuits. So beautiful are the architectural beauties that some feel that they are frozen religious hymns and poetries. Indeed a cluster of pillars of some temples, each capable of producing different nodes, could produce a desired musical tone, striking these with a stick. The pillars function as if they are strings of a musical instrument. We marvel these, but do we know, or try to know how these have been created. Is there any search for the acoustics of stones? Ragas are regarded as timeless. It is not known whether stone pillars functioned the same way as the modern string instruments are functioning now. An undeniable fact it that our scientific minds and technological skills were no less alert during pre – industrial days.

These caves and temples were created in various parts of our subcontinent. Some are mentioned below:

- Mukteshvara Temple
- Khajuraho Temple
- Ceiling Temple
- Tanjore Temple
- Rock cut Image of Gommateswara and so on.
- Much had happened during this time. Two prominent examples are presented below.

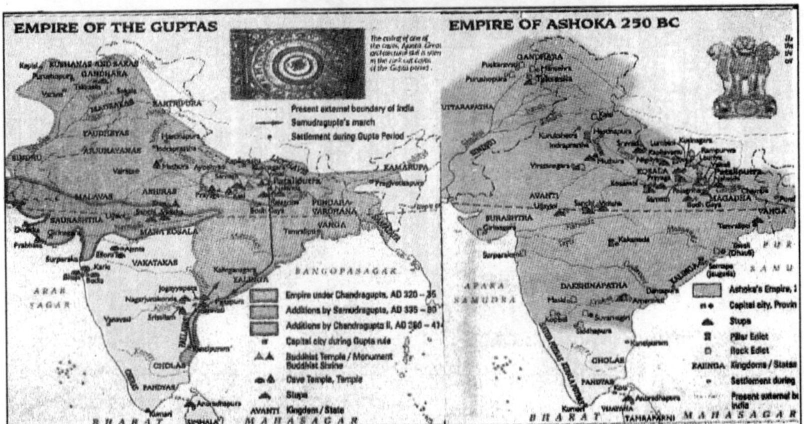

GUPTA DYNASTY
599 B.C. Birth of Mahavira

EMPIRE OF ASHOKA
563 B.C Birth of Buddha

One can see Kashmir was an integral part of Ashoka's Kingdom. Gautama Siddhartha Buddha, the founder of Buddhism was born in Nepal. He had established a monastery in Srinagar. The serene and beautiful ambient suited his doctrine. The first convention on Buddhism was held there, when deliberations were made in Sanskrit. It is pertinent to mention that Muslims had not put their first step by then in this sacred land. They came much later.

AJANTA AND ELLORA CAVES

Ajanta caves (200B.C. – 650 A.D.)

Ellora (500 – 1200 AD)

There are 29 Buddhist caves at Ajanta. They are known for their magnificent paintings. The 34 Ellora caves are more famous for their sculpture. These are not natural formations. Each has been hand -carved prayer halls, of Buddhist, Hindu and Jain faith. Ajanta caves were excavated during 2nd and 7th century AD. About 130km apart, Ellora caves are dated between 5th and 12th Century.

Painting at Ajanta caves

Apsaras

Inside these temples there are exquisite carvings and fresco paintings. Pictures below are from Ellora caves.

Exquisite carvings and fresco paintings at Ellora

Ellora pillar

Ajanta cave layout

The magnitude of work done can be judged from the visitors below.

The caves are numbered from right to left. Among Ellora temples, cave No. 16 is the most attractive one. The Kailasha temple is the largest single monolithic rock excavation in the world.

The most intriguing part is why they came to select these rocky area.; and what motivated them to work over a period of 10 centuries to create caves of two different cultures. While the Ajanta cave creators were devotees of Buddha and developed fresco paintings, the Ellora Caves excel on architectural religious monuments mostly of Hindu religions. If viewed in totality, it can be a venue for research study on formation of volcanic rock and people with creative minds for fine arts and crafts. Some link that such rock formations are linked with the very origin of the our earth's creation; There exists no volcano in this area. With C-14 tests, it may be interesting to learn the origin of these rocks, besides the excellence of these activities.

DEGRADATION OF VEDIC RELIGION

Initially the Vedic religion was learned by heart and passed over from generation to generation. It was learnt by students from their Gurus (teachers) over a period of 12 years, reciting hymns every day composed by Sages. Some question the feasibility of such a practice. If this had actually happened, there is no reason to doubt. The memory power is generally high. Does not a grandfather of 80 and above, recalls events to tell to his grand children about his early days? 12 years apprenticeship is long enough a time to memorize the hymns and transmit to the next generation. The gurus were strict to examine the learning. They would ensure also the correct accent with no missed words during recitation of hymns. Even today, if a learned institution is invited to perform 'homa' collectively, (a religious practice by lighting fire,) one observes that they recite in perfect effortless harmony.

BRAMANIC DERIVATIVE

Although claimed to be a derivative of Rig Veda, the main evil of the of present time is the hereditary Brahmanic caste system. The priests do not go through rigorous learning process of the past. There is no training system. His only qualification is his genetic certification by his father and not mother (legally speaking), Some attempts are being made to eliminate these perversions.

AN EXAMPLE

Prosanto Mahalanobish although formally educated as a scientist, a tripos from Cambridge University, was a Sanskrit scholar too. But his interest on collection of data to drive at a sense of direction made him to establish the most famed Statistical Institute in Calcutta. in 1921. His economic 'top down' concept, in conformity with Nehru's, laid the foundation of our economic policy during our second Plan (1956--61). It was a debatable conclusion. The author believes that the conclusion was not faulty, the execution got mixed up with our age-old feudal minds, which lead to our notorious Article 40 of our Constitution for the rural people.

A fable is told about this famous statistician. After his marriage according to Hindu rites, he requested his just married wife to accompany him to go to the marriage register's office. Surprised, the bride asked him, why when they had just got married. The learned husband told her that the priest had performed the ceremony reciting the wrong hymn. It was for "Shradh occasion".(A ritual to pray for the peace in the mind of the demised soul). He had patiently gone through the function, because he did not want to embarrass the priest, and the guests. Registration was necessary to legally sanctify the marriage, he explained to his wife. (No documentary evidence exists for this event but popularly quoted).

BRAHMANIC RELIGION: Suppression Of Our Labour Force

The county's biggest damage has been initiated through our pre-eminence on philosophical mind, and undermining action oriented innovative ventures. Beginning with two classes, with wide differences between them, societies of elites and labour came up. The country got fragmented with a divide between luxury loving princes, zamindars, landlords, moneylenders, and poor peasants.

RIG VEDA

Rig Veda was the original religion followed by the Hindus. A caste system had existed. Initially it consisted of non-hereditary Brahmans, Kshatriyas, vaishyas, and shudras. The shudras were the most needed labour force. The change from original Rig Vedic to Brahmanic religious system made shudras, the main labour force as low caste untouchables. Further degradation has destroyed the labour (action-oriented) culture. We introduced a hereditary system. So ours is a learned, - at times fake, - philosophical society, with a divide between labour force and a community of metaphysical scientific society. With the arrival of Aryans around 1500 BC, this perverted divide continued, with various shades. The most nauseating creation is the untouchable shudra caste The present caste system has no link with the original religion. Religions germinate noble attributes of humanism. They are not to destroy this. When greed for power and wealth become supreme, religions take a back seat, or may even be eliminated altogether from the mind. Only the shell remains as an identity for membership of a community.

SIMILARITY IN RELIGIOUS THOUGHTS

RIG VEDA HYMN

(1) Indra's Greatness.
What poet now, what sage of old,
The greatness of that god hath told
Who from his body vast gave birth
To father sky and mother Earth;
Who hung the havens in empty space,
And gave the earth a stable base;
Who framed and lighted up run;
Whose power transcendent, since their birth
Asunder hold the heaven and earth,
By axles framed by workmen's art?
In greatness who with Him can vie,
Who fills the earth, the air the sky,
Whose presence unperceived extends
Beyond the world's remotest ends?
A hundred earths, if such there be,
A hundred skies fall short of thee;
A thousand sun would not outshine
The effulgence of why light divine.
The worlds, which mortals boundless deem,
To three but as a handful seem.
Thou, Indra, art without a peer
On earth, or younder heavenly sphere.
Three, god, such matchless powers adorn,
That thou without a foe wast born.
Thou art the universal lord,
By gods revered, by men adored.
Should all the other gods conspire,
They could not frustrate thy desire.
The circling years, which were away
All else, to thee bring no decay;
Thou bloomest on in youthful force,
While countless ages run their course.
Unvexed by cares, or fears, or strife,
In bliss serene flows on thy life.

(Muir – translation of Original Sanskrit Texts, Vol. V, p 133)

KORAN

Comparing the above with a sura of Kuran, as under, one finds the marked similarity of wisdom between the two. So what could be the reason for discord between the two believers? Other than ignorance, resulting from illiteracy, it is difficult to trace any reason. Perversion, with a greed for power and wealth, has found an ***easy inroad to our current situation.***

NO DISTINCTION AMONG GOD'S MESSENGERS

QURAN
SURA-2 (136)
The Heifer (Al-Bagqarah)
Say
We believe in God.
And what was revealed to us, and what was revealed to Abraham and Ishmael and Isaac and Joseph and the Tribes, and what was given to the prophets from their Lord. And we do not make any destruction between individuals among them. For we submit to God."

OVERWHELMING SIGNS OF GOD

And your God in one God: there is no God but The One, the Merciful.
Behold, in the certain of the heavens and the earth, and the alternation of night and day, and the ships that sell on the sea to profit the people, and the water. God rains from the skies. Thereby enlivening the earth after it has died. And spreading animals of all kinds therefore. And the shifting of the winds and the clouds.
Enslaved between the heaven and earth

The essential Koran by Thomas Cleary

Both Hindu and Islamic religions believe nature as a

creation of God. But humanism took different routes in people who adopted one or the other. The biggest mistake is to link religion directly with humanism. Religion trains a human mind to choose the path to humanism. It does not dictate which way to go. Oxford Dictionary states that it is a system of thought that regards humans as capable of using their intelligence to live rather following a religious belief."

An undeniable fact is all religions believe in God. The fact equally undeniable is that they are perverted by Brahamans in Hindu religion, and Mullahs in Islam. The author believes that our temples and mosques should be learning centers of religions and not practicing hereditary cults through priests and mullahs .

Communal religions are against the dictum of God. It encases the human mind, and therefore, the humanism. Religions are similar to getting vocational training from an institute. Thereafter, the trained mind creates different paths of his own choice.

Some communal clergy of Islamic religion train the mind to live and think in a finite way. It is not open ended. Hinduism on the other hand was not communal but divisively practiced religion. Although originally open-ended, it got perverted with a hereditary caste system conceived by Brahmanic religion. Both have become communal, but in different ways. One must hasten to add that what is practiced now in the name of Hinduism is a perverted form of the original concept of Rig Veda composed. during 1500 – 1000 B.C.

The fact is that while talking about Hindu religion, do we practice what is written in our religious scripts? What were our apparently Rig Veda following Hindus doing during the great Bengal famine in 1943? (Refer Rig Veda X 117)* Did not the rich shut the door at the face of hungry dying poor, and let about 3-4 million die on Calcutta streets. Churchill was pleased with this type of Hinduism, and gave away titles who suppressed the hungry poor. For him, it was a political revenge for 'Quit India'(1942) movement.

One would expect that religion would bring humanity together, although following different paths to reach God, or the creator of the precisely operational Universe.

Rig-Veda X 117

VI. HYMN ON LIBERALITY

1.The Gods have not ordained hunger to be our death: even to the well-fed man comes death in varied shape.
The riches of the liberal never waste away, while he who will not give fiber none to comfort him.

2. the man with food in store who, when the needy comes in miserable case begging for bread to eat,
Hardens his heart against him—even when of old he did him service—finds not one to comfort him.

3. Bounteous is he who gives unto the beggar who comes to him in want of food and feeble.
Success attends him in the shout of battle. He makes a friend of him in future troubles.

4. No friend is he who to his friend and comrade who comes imploring food, will offer nothing.
Let him depart –no home is that to rest in –and rather seek a stranger to support him.

5.Let the rich satisfy the poor implorer, and bend his eye upon a longer pathway
Riches come now to one, now to another, and like the wheels of cars are ever rolling.

6. The foolish man wins food with fruitless labour; that food – I speak the truth—shall be his ruin.
He feeds no trusty friend, no man to love him. All guilt is he who eats with no partner.

7. The ploughshare ploughing makes the food that feeds us, and with its feet cuts through the path it follows.

Better the speaking than the silent Brabman: the liberal friend out values him woo gives not.
(Rigveda .x. 117. Translated by R.T.H. Griffith)

UNIVERSAL CONCEPT OF GOD

How can we ignore that the energy from fearsome lightening of cloud was producing fertilizer, in fact, combining the different chemical elements in the atmosphere and rain this to prepare the land to grow food and plants for the survival of lives on earth in different forms. Rains are the main massive factory producing fertilizers. We supplement this making fertilizers in many other ways, but their origins are also through rain. Can man made fertilizer without raib grow food? So we pray for rain, Varuna, in Rig Vedic hymn, as an element of God. We are children of one God fed the same way. But as spoilt children, we fight in the name of God.

MOGUL AND BRITISH DYNASTY

The Moguls

Babur defeated Ibrahim Lodi, in 1526 A.D.(first battle of Panipat) and founded the Mugal dynasty. It lasted till 1707, when Aurangzeb had died. There had been several invaders earlier. They all came and returned with their booty. Moguls came to stay. Their dynasty was perhaps one of the most distinct and glorious period of the country. The Moguls practiced a central theme: one law and justice for all. It was administered by the Chief Qazi speedily and with no interference even by the Emperor. Ibn Hasan writes "Not only was the law one for all, but the punishments awarded were the same for high and low". Akbar, the Emperor himself did not absolve himself from law. He had said , " If I were guilty of unjust act, I would rise in judgment against myself." Birth and position had no consideration with the Mogul emperors in executing stern justice. Can we say the same in our present judiciary system? It has lost its dignity. The contemptible functioning is voiced from all quarters. Can there be any greater injustice to the poor when it refuses to accept a PIL writ without assigning any reason? Even a request at the highest quarter for repeal of Supreme Court's decision had not been answered. Why? The fear of unrest by the poor?

The early Muslims (during Slave dynasty of Qutab Minar fame, established in 1206 A.D.) and Mughals did not belong to the same genetic origin, although both practiced Islamic religion.

Muslim rulers of India were invaders from the west. They started coming since 11th century from Bukhara, Turkey, Iran, Yemen and Afghanistan. The immigrants from Afghanistan had generally ended their names as Khans. The most famous preacher of Islam was Khwaja Chishti, who arrived from Iran. Spreading Islam was viewed as a holy precept. The accepted fact is that most of India's Muslims were converted to Islam by the sword. Meaning the Indians were given an option between death or adopting Islam. This may not be wholly true. Most of the converts are poor peasants/ lower caste Hindu.. The higher castes were generally rich and had perverted concepts of the religion, thanks to Hindu priests. The practice against touching, not permitting to enter into temples, and several insults inflicted could have been the reason for large conversions. The fact remains that Muslims in India are converts of the same origin and genetically the same. They did not come from different parts of world. The Islamic religion bonded them together, generally speaking.

Adding fuel to the fire the British started to provide special privileges to Muslims. It was easier to be closer to Muslims because of certain social habits; e.g. eating meat, particularly beef. The conversion rate had increased because of special privileges, and more importantly, humiliating caste system. Unless one can prove otherwise, the origin is from the same source. The mother of Jahangir was a pious Hindu princess, the most favourite queen of Akbar. His son, Jahangir and grandson Shah Jahan, both continued to follow the wise policies of Akbar and brought glory to the country. Akbar's legendary tolerance on religion was survived by both. Jahangir, a happy-go-lucky, did not take any interest in the governance of the country. He left it to his wife, Noor Jahan (Light of the world) and she proved to be a very able administrator. She was responsible for expansion of the Mogul empire.

The grandson, Shah Jahan was known for his articulate behaviour, and a highly respected architect and builder. He had built for posterity the Taj Mahal in Agra, Red Fort and Jumma Masjid in Delhi to name a few which are regarded as examples of Indian heritage. He expanded the Mogul rule down south and put India on the world map. Several foreign trading establishments were set up. The search for Hindu - Muslim rift to justify the partition of the country draws a blank from the happenings of Mogul period. This raised its ugly head during British rule.

INDUCTION OF BRITISH

Realizing prospects of trade with our highly prosperous country a large body of merchants of the UK appealed which was acceded to by Queen Elizabeth, the then monarch of the UK, to grant a royal charter for trade on 31 December 1600. Jahangir was not initially enthusiastic but eventually agreed. The British arrived in 1609, with a royal charter to form British East India Company for trading in the East.

They remained as dormant traders till about 1764. Thereafter, they derived indirect benefit on several counts; viz. from the third war of Panipat weakening both Hindus and Muslims; the in-fighting among fragmented princely States, when the Mogul empire was falling apart because of intrigues among brothers to ascend to throne; the brave Marathas meteoric rise with a patriotic mission to throw out the Moguls out and its fall within a brief period. The British got involved with the country's governance in 1764, three years after the battle of Panipat, when Clive was able to obtain dewani (right to collect revenue) of Bengal, Bihar, and Oudh from Shah Alam, the then Mugal emperor. Then on, with their sole interest to plunder and loot, they indulged in every possible heinous activity, including accentuating religious divide between Hindus and Muslims as a tool to rule. A separate Anglo-Indian community emerged, - the only good thing that happened, not intentionally though. This highly religious, disciplined and courageous outcaste of the British came up of their own, fighting for their rights, at times against hostile attitudes of some misguided people. This small community has done enormous service to education, defense forces, and the poor. While Anglo-Indians still respect their English heritage, it is not reciprocated with an equal measure by the British. The situation is similar to Brahmins and sub-castes.

On the other hand, the British has done enormous and perhaps an irreversible damage to the poor and the nation. A brief comparison between Moguls and the British can provide enough evidence to this fact.

1. Mogul : Tried to bring harmony between religions, specifically between the Hindus and the Muslims.

British : Encouraged animosity between religions, providing special favours to the Muslims to suppress the Hindus.

2. Encouraged indigenous industry, Akbar personally reviewed the progress of imperial (public sector) and privately owned Karkhanas (industrial activities) on day-to-day basis in the afternoon. Every village had weavers to manufacture cloth and the volume of production met not only the country's need, but also the large export commitments. Along with the cotton, the dying industry flourished. So flourishing was the textile industry that an eminent historian remarked that from Orissa to East Bengal (now Bangla Desh) looked like a big cotton factory, when Dacca produced the finest cotton. High quality Silk and woolen carpets were made. The principal items exported other than textile, silk, carpets were pepper, indigo, opium, drugs, saltpeter, spices, sugar, etc. The skill of shipbuilding became a necessity for the large foreign trades with distant lands. With in a short period of about 180 years, the Moguls transformed the country to be the showcase, and dazzled the eyes of the West. Many European trading companies established commercial dealings with our country.

Their interest on arts and literature is seen form the fact that they got several Hindu books, **including** Ramayana, Mahabharata, and Gita translated in Persian **language**. Although Persian was the official at the court, Hindi and **Sanskrit** books were translated jointly by Hindus and Muslims academicians.

BRITISH : The legacy of rural poverty.

While the advent of the Moguls in India ushered in a glorious epoch of multi-dimensional development of humanism, and economic prosperity of the poor and the country, in a short period of time, the British who came in 1609 essentially to establish trade with the country, took a 'U'-turn and established themselves as rulers on the ruins of the Moguls and the Marathas assisted by the Muslim community and princely States. There were about 526 such rich and highly feudal states, almost the same as the number of our MPs (542 in lower house). They were often fighting with one another. As rich foreign traders, they found themselves as welcomed guests. Preferred friendly relations were established with richer princes. The British with technologically advanced weapons provided assistance to those targeted States who were more beneficial to their trade missions. In this manner, they started to become the masters of their 'friends'. Higher taxes were levied to pay for their services in coin and kind. The rural cultivators became poorer, though there was stark poverty.

The main difference was that while the Moguls tried to be a part of the country, the British came to rob a slave country, and make their country prosper. Aurangzeb (1658 – 1707) did not pursue Akbar's liberal policy on religion. His upbringing was poor. He was initially appointed as subedar of the Deccan by Shah Jahan. He was elevated as viceroy of Deccan. The poor health of Shaha Jahan helped Aurangzeb. He imprisoned his father, and fought and killed his brothers - He created Aurangabad, the second capital of the Mogals in 1681. He had done much harm to the noble Moguls, and inflicted his misrule, particularly towards non-Muslim subjects. He reintroduced jazis that was imposed for non-Muslims earlier, but abolished by

Akbar. He executed Teg Bahadur, guru of Sikhs in 1675. At that stage a peasants uprising had occurred, but ruthlessly suppressed. While one can understand an incompetent to suffer, but when done on community basis, it is incomprehensible. Till that, stage there was no Hindu-Muslim divide. The divide was between the rich and the poor, regardless of competence. During the last phase of his life, he had to witness his sons fighting for the throne. He died in 1707.

A common belief is that Mogul dynasty came to an end with Aurangzeb's misrule. This is incorrect. At that stage there were five more, the most powerful one was one in Delhi/Agra. (Akbar – Aurangzeb rule) They used to fight. The peasants were the worst sufferers, when the foods for the fighting soldiers were taken away from them. The Country was in quandary. It came to a halt. There were many small kingdoms They used to serve Mogul empires. One can see that the peasants had been at the receiving end since Indo-Aryan race, for about 4000 years.

MARATHA RISE

A short spell of respite came up on the horizon. Maratha's rise began with Shahaji who had a fort in Poona. He controlled over a small territories. There were many Hindu kingdoms in between these five major Mogul empires. Shivaji, (1646 – 80), was son of Shahji. He was the most courageous Hindu warrior, who fought with both Moguls and British, and annexed large territories. To begin with, he captured Torna in 1646. His ambition was to establish a Hindu Raj.

History of Shivaji, though short, is one to be proud of. His patriotic feelings surfaced when foreign rulers were treating the Hindu kings and his countrymen as slaves. He wanted to get rid of these tormentors. The oppression of Muslim and the English, who was slowly creeping in might have made him intolerant to their religions. He was a devout Hindu and, a valiant crusader of its revival. He wanted to create a large Hindu welfare State called 'Swarajya'. The task began with the merger of 24 Mawal regions, then administered by Deshmukhs. They used to fight, plunder and burning down the neighbours' properties. The people were fed up with Deshmukhs. With the concept a 'Swarjya', emotion of togetherness emerged. However, he did not get support from all Hindu kings. Many of them were serving the Moguls as their commanders-in- chief. None the less Shivaji managed to acquire and establish 'Swaraj' territory. The title of Chhatrapati was added to his name. Shivaji was duly crowned as the Emperor of the Hindu Empire. He had difficult times, even served under Aurangzeb, but with his clever mind, he overcame them.

Regrettably, the end was pathetic. When he was lying on the deathbed, all his ungrateful relatives were around fighting to get their shares , when his second young wife Shobhabai was quarrelling to get her son Raja Ram installed on the throne of 'Swaraj' Empire. He founded a Maratha Kingdom and died young on 3rd April, 1680.

THE COUNTRY'S TURMOIL

However, Marathas did not disintegrate. but had gone through a difficult phase. In 1689, Shambaji, son of Shivaji was executed. The leaderships were changing rapidly. The Shiks tried unsuccessfully to chip in, The Moguls were also going through a difficult period. The English traders, led by Robert Clive, were slowly getting involved, with their 'friendly acts' taking advantage of the country's turmoil, They started minting money.

Peshwa Balaji Rao I & II expanded the Maratha rule acquiring territories, which covered whole of the middle part of the subcontinent during 1720 - 1819. They tried to halt the British getting a foothold in India. But the English established their landmark, capturing Chandannagar defeating Siraj-ud-daulah, in the battle of Plassy in 1757. But for the all time notorious traitorous act of Mir Jafar, working as Commander –in-Chief of Siraj-ud-daulah, the English would have met a humiliating defeat. For his help the English, made him the Governor of Bengal.

The chequered history of Marathas under Shivaji's leadership has not received the due place in history. The Marathas were the first to stop the British, but failed because of there was no oneness within the country.

The Creation Of Hindu - Muslim Rift

The well-being of the farmers was farthest from the British rulers' mind. The Aryans had made the preparatory ground. The fragmented country came under the control of linguistic princely States. There was no cohesiveness They fought with one another, and with in their own states. There were conflicts between the two classes:. the princes, Zamindars, landlords, and their subjects, when the poor peasants were always at the losing end. The richer class had maintained a private cavalry. The villagers had to pay tax, in coin or kind, to the rich because land belonged to the rich. On occasions of drought seasons, caused by poor monsoon, villagers were unable to pay, yet the dreaded cavalry was let loose on them. They came and plundered. These inhumanities are folklores and need no elaboration. British grabbed this situation with both hands, and started controlling the non-cohesive richer class.

The strategy of British was simple. There were two-prong attacks. Create religious rift between the Hindus and the Muslims, and exploit the peasants through their richer rulers. The economic success of industrial revolution in the 18th century accelerated the establishment of British empire. This subcontinent contributed to the maximum towards this. The English ways of life became a status symbol, place of our basic culture, - not always through imperialist thrust. We embraced this new culture willfully, socially and mentally, giving birth to urban society, neglecting the rural poor. Only recently, an understanding on the grave danger is surfacing. This, however, is covered up with economic jargons, which few understand.

INDUSTRIAL REVOLUTION

Industrial revolution came about around 1830 A.D. with

the use of coal and steel, This had happened about 1000 years ago and after the heritage era. Eiffel Tower in Paris, is a marvel of structural engineering made of steel between 1887-89. The most important question to ponder is how this revolution had changed the societies of the world. Before industrial revolution, England was an agricultural society. Europe, the northern hemisphere was poorer than southern part. Generally speaking, the world lived on natural gifts of God and animal power. Annexure 2 provides a glimmer on the reason for the development of industrial society, when virtually every thing got changed. The southern hemisphere, below 300 latitude started lagging behind, mainly because of energy deficiency.

INDUSTRIAL REVOLUTION AND HUMANISM

Both cultures, not undermining Egypt's achievements, are standing to-day as relics of supreme technological ingenuity of pre and post industrial revolutions. A fact is apparent. The basic ingenuity and skill of human mind did not undergo a change due to transformation from stone to metal use. The availability of resources expanded many fold during and after industrial revolution. This helped to explore the inquisitive mind. For example, Eiffel tower was built as a test facility to understand and evaluate laws of aerodynamics by Alexendre Gustave Eiffel. For his successful scientific work, the first aerodynamic laboratory was established in 1912, in Paris. The searching mind had remained the same. If he was to explore the virtues of his inquisitive mind in recent days, he would have built a Wind Tunnel, not the Eiffel tower.

CHAPTER - 4

THE NOBLE FACE OF ENGLISH IMPERIALISM

It will not be an overstatement to suggest an organised Indian subcontinent was created by the English people. This might have been done as a need for their imperialistic rule. Earlier it was ruled by 520/ 540 non-cohesive Princely states. There were two classes. The rich Princes, living in luxury, were the owners of land, which were cultivated by the peasants, They lived simply in village communes, and pay taxes in coin and kind, through *village pradans* .who were short of mangers representing the princes. They all had a small army to assist collection of taxes.

The taxes were not uniform. Such feudal practice was accepted in a land of plenty, not only agro-products, raw minerals and precious stones were also in abundance. The village people were illiterate, but a religious mind grew through rural folklores, related to our epics, viz., Ramayana, Mahabharata. The episodes of our gods were performed on open stages, and were retold by mothers and grandmothers. Our religions got social acceptance mostly through such process and not through scripts. Superstitions and perversions got easy inroads.

SPREAD OF RIG VEDA

Rig Veda is the main part of Vedic religion. Some believe that writing was practiced around 1500 - 1000 B.C. A question surfaces; in what language?

The archaic Sanskrit of the Ayans was codified by the grammarian Panini in his treatise, *Astadhyay*. It is recognized as the most scientific grammar composed before modern times. There after Sanskrit became more popular.

The British rule had two faces. While the British imperialism ruled taking recourse to many unacceptable approaches. It had a knowledgeable group of administrator -

scholars with inquisitive mind. Sir William, Jones (1783) and Wilkins are truly the father of Indology. Asiatic society of Bengal was founded in 1784. Sir Jones became its first president. *English translation of *Bhagavad Gita* was completed in November, 1789, (about one hundred year before first freedom struggle) when almost simultaneously Jones translated Kalidasa's *Shakuntala.* It became so popular that five English editions were published in less than twenty years. We owe to these learned noble souls, the discovery of our heritage. The law book of Manu, titled as 'Institute of Hidoo Law', was published in 1794. The spread of Sanskrit to France and Germany was through activities of the Asiatic Society, when the study of Sanskrit was introduced there in colleges.

* Penguin yearbook, 2008 suggests 1850 by H.H. Wilson.

Max Muller delivered lectures at the Cambridge University in 1882 on "India: What it teaches us." He was first to translate Rig Veda in English. *He had felt that 'these earliest philosophical treaties will always maintain a place in the literature of the world, among the astounding production of the human mind in any age and in any country. Indian people are philosophical in nature'*

18th and 19th century brought about much changes in this sub-continent.

The British-India flags were installed at all places ruled by the Empire. To meet the needs of Imperialistic rule, the fragmented subcontinent acquired the seed to become one nation. The railways, - the first India train was flagged off on the 16 April, 1853, when it traversed a distance of 34 km from Bombay to Thane. Today, our railways cover a distance of 63,221 km, most were operational before Independence in 1947. Similarly, at that time we had only 2,144 km of roadways, There has been a phenomenon growth since Independence, covering a distance of 65,590 km national highways. Adding to these, the telegraph, Institutes of higher studies, and seafaring with emphasis on education got boost since the initial stages of the British rule.

Administrative scholars with genitive inquisitive minds, and those with a desire to rob the wealth of this subcontinent, to prosper regardless of fundamental damages done. This duplicity in British mind is seen even when they robbed Egypt. Several prosperous people funded expeditions to Egypt to bring back antiquities from that land. England was a poorer country than ours, but they had the unique noble character to accept good and innovative minds. That is why Gandhi had often said that his fight was with British imperialism, and not with the English people.

The author had a test of this in 1942, in India, and when sent for higher studies in the UK in 1956, and visits later. His most cherish memories are those when in England on several occasions. There is a marked difference, even now, in the behavioral attitude of uneducated Englishmen, in general, towards Indians people in England. But this is diminishing when Indian students are excelling the natives, in academics and other intellectual activities. The colour bar existed then, but considerably reduced among educated class.

ECONOMIC AND LITERACY DIFFERENCE

The British rule of 190 years began formally in 1757 and ended in 1947. The economic differences between the three divided parts of the sub-continent and the UK in the current summary situation have been indicated earlier.

Most tend to attribute the above enormous difference to our slavery to the British rule, missing out much of our past and 61 years of the misrule as an Independent nation. Out of 61 years, Nehru dynasty has ruled for 37 years, when Jawaharlal Nehru (17 years), Indira Gandhi, daughter of Nehru (15 years) and Rajiv Gandhi, son of Indira Gandhi (5 years) were the prime ministers.

If Sonia Gandhi's *de facto* rule is taken into account, then 61% of our Independent national life has been controlled by Nehru dynasty.

Now a new sun is trying to rise. Rahul Gandhi is being groomed to continue the dynasty. To what end? Has he any plan to remove the disparity ratio of 12:1 between urban and rural society (2004), and alleged massive corruptions at all levels?. Now when election is round the corner, one finds half page of popular New papers boldly print announcements of achievements, by various Central government Ministries. Nowhere any mention is made on audited money spent, comparing with the budgeted allocations. No where any quantified strategy is announced to remove the unacceptable situation of real India.

The numbers within bracket are the years ruled.

DIVIDED NATION: INDIAN CONSTITUTION

A notable fact needs mentioning is that these dynastic rulers have never acted to improve upon the rural peoples abilities beyond agronomy. Their main interest was to earn votes to retain their dynasty, through means, which lacked sincerity. In our first Constitution, we separated out the rural people, the nation's main sustaining force through Article 40. The rich and poor divide originated through this Article. The elites, however, woke up suddenly about their existence during election time.

CHAPTER - 5

BEGINNING OF FEUDAL RULE

Jawaharlal Nehru dancing with tribal girls

These girls were ferried from their distant homes for Republic day celebrations. This gimmickry continues. Recently, media has published Sonia Gandhi learning dance steps from tribal girls. There is no doubt that her action will make the tribal people proud and happy to caste vote for congress without even asking the progress made by the then Minister of State Dr. Rameshwar Oran in 2004. Was Mrs. Sonia informed by the panchayats about the progress made, on literacy, health and hygiene, sanitation. and other aspects as desired in Article 243(G). during the previous years before feeling happy to learn about dancing steps. If this was not done, regrettably, she had proved that she had mustered her father-in-law's Indian political culture well, and graduated to train her son, Rahul Gandhi, to retain the hereditary strain.

Nehru posing with dancers on Republic Day at Teen Murti

The initial apprenticeship had apparently been successful when he got 'poori sabjee as a late night meal and slept on a charpoy'. Presumably, his morning chores would have been accomplished in a nearby guest house, using four times more water. Then he exhibited his exuberance as shown below.

Rahul Gandhi with a child during his visit to Aminabad, in Etawah

On the other hand, if such activities were meant to know the rural life and get a foundation in his mind, to create a New India, the main desire of this book, posterity will remember him. But he is yet to announce his strategy. Annexure 1 suggests one. What is his? If hereditary is his only weapon, posterity will similarly condemn him as well.

The peasants sustain the society, but they received little attention, since mankind's present form of living after 2000 BC. At times, they had rebelled, but only when the situation came to an unbearable limit, and the disparity was so glaring that they had felt that the fragmented governance system needed a change. Are we approaching that limit, and if so, should we not do something in a collectively curative and not palliative manner?

History tells us that the peasant's rebellious movements in developed societies had not followed Gandhian non-violent principles. One recalls of peasant risings in Europe during 14th and 15 century; for example, the Jacquie of 1358, which lead to over 30,000 deaths, and English peasants revolution in 1381, which captured London for a short period. The main cause of rebellion is the feudalistic treatment . One may also recall relatively the French revolution of 1793, when the king was executed; the civil right revolution of the USA around the same time when India's first freedom fight was fought in 1857.

The result is the histories of America, Russia, and France where feudal filth was rejected and discarded with inhuman violence; and societies of justice for all emerged. In India, we emerged with greater suppression by the British, supported by richer elites, and even some intellectuals. It would appear that we are waiting for such an occurrence to happen in our country as well. when the rural poor will rise. The Naxalite movement is gathering momentum, beyond the boundary of Andhra Pradesh.

This movement has now spread to over 160 districts all over the country. It is becoming the single biggest internal security challenge ever faced by our country, when the extremists are trying to establish 'liberation zone' in core areas where they are dispensing basic state functions of administration, polling and justice. (Refer "Diminishing role of parliament" – The Penguin year book, 2008).

The only urgent counter poise is rural development shedding religious caste bias, and illiteracy; and simultaneously creating employment opportunities in rural areas.

DISTORTION OF SOCIAL ORDER

During the Era (2000 B.C. – 1190 A.D.), people though not cohesive, were not poor to the extent that they would die of starvation, or commit suicide. They lived generally happy with their own culture. They were illiterate, no doubt; but not devoid of knowledge on aspects, their life depended on, except on health and hygiene. There were many superstitions on religion. The only deficiency, the subcontinent suffered from was that it was not a land of oneness. On the contrary, princely States were antagonistic and fought with one another. For this, we paid heavily.

SLIDE DOWN

Although the origin of the history of this civilized subcontinent is dated some 8,000 B.C. i.e., about 10,000 years old, a dramatic change took place in 1192 A.D. The subcontinent of plenty where a tolerant non-ethnic race lived, was transformed in all aspects of life. A new beginning with different shades ushered in.

Prophet Mohammed was born in 570 AD. He proclaimed Islamic religion in 612 AD. Mohammedan era began in 622. Arabs were the first to spread gospel of Islamic religion, if and when needed, by force. They conquered Sind in 712 AD, and by 715 Arab empire were at its peak but did not move any further towards the East. It collapsed in 750. Muslims who came with the Arabs as traders pushed ahead. Sori, after defeating Prithivi Raj, the king of a northern province, in the second war fought at Terrain in 1192, established Muslim rule, which changed several hands till 1526.

The Muslim rule found an easy inroad to this subcontinent because of two reasons. First, the fragmented princely states offered no collective resistance. The in-fight, often social in nature, among the neighbouring princely States was the reason for Prithiviraj's defeat although on the first occasion Sori met a humiliating defeat. Secondly, due to our Brahmanic religion creating an untouchable shudra caste system, millions of shudras opted for Islam and Christianity, which had little caste system. It is because of this that there is a greater affinity between them. Our Rig Veda, the core part of Vedic religion, was no less noble. It follows a well conceived non-hereditary social science, similar to the present HRD system. But ruined with the introduction of Brahmanic hereditary caste system, getting support from rich princes, land lords, and money lenders.

The foreign invaders turned rulers did not believe in any of our religions, except Moguls, till the reign of Aurangzeb. They had an even mind and tried to harmonize the two religions, till the last phase of their dynasty. Wars of religion had been fought in England, Germany and France during 1562 – 98 AD, but our religious war was fought *before (1946)* and continued there-*after (1948)* when the political settlement based on religion took place. The religious wars in Europe did not end up dividing the nations. Ours did without assessing the minds of the countrymen.

A few feudal lords believed that this subcontinent was theirs, and decided on partition without even trying to know the minds of one millions of people, or heeding the wishes (on partition) of the man who fought almost single handed to get the freedom. God is making us to pay for that now. The country got further divided, and a third sovereign State, Bangladesh emerged. Some surmise that a fourth one is in the offing. The stage is all set starving 800 million people with meaningless huge expenditure since 1948, when the most notorious Line of Control (LOC) was forced on us, at the initiative of a few. They did not take into account the miseries of the left behind widows, their children, their profession aged, parents, and unmentionable terrorist related social atrocities when the country was divided.

RICH AND POOR DIVIDE

The rich-poor divide had been in vogue since the arrival of Aryans till the country's Independence. It continues even now, in fact, except in election times. Then the politicians go from door to door of poor villagers begging for their votes with all kinds of promises for their welfare. Once elected their minds get diverted to make the poor poorer, through means which made them richer.

Non-erasable facts prove that ours is now a feudal society, and not a 'socialist secular' Republic, as stated in the preamble of our Constitution. If committing all kinds of unethical and unlawful acts at will is symbolic to democracy, we can claim this attribute for our nation. We have merely learnt all noble words, but not how to practice them. These can be proved in all spheres of life, at all levels. Some illustrations are made in the text of this book.

SCIENCE & TECHNOLOGY

A rectification process has been suggested. The theme is to provide equal opportunities to all to develop themselves to achieve the national goal, without creating hurdles to others. A Fellow of Royal Society (FRS) is not merely one for the excellence of one's scientific achievement, this honour is bestowed for promotion and encouraging science as well. We do not place an FRS in that group. We believe that an FRS is a 'know all' scientific person. A vain self centered scientific community has emerged. They believe that what not known to them is not worth knowing. An unhealthy culture has developed. This is manifestation of perverted religious system. We owe this to Aryans, and the Indo-Aryan dynasty.

In our science parlour, a story of a 'crab's failed attempt' to get out of a box full of his associates is well known. The story is unfortunately true. If the country has to get out of the present trap, - the 'crab culture' has to be shifted in the reverse .gear .to get set to our basic deficiencies. The result of our present practice is seen in Annexure 2. This may have missed at least one name, who has contributed much for the survival of the nations. Even then, the generic situation of our poor contribution to serve the world community through S&T oriented innovative work will hardly improve.

BRITISH RULE

British came with Royal Charter of 1600 in 1609 for trade and formed East India Company. Robert Clive found the subcontinent a rich and fertile land for exploitation and robbing. Although his initial CV (Curriculum Vitae) within his own country was extremely poor, he proved to be a master strategist in our fragmented land, ruled by princes with poor humanitarian ethics. Their advisors were Brahmins, at times, to an extent that they were virtually the rulers. The humiliated subjects, both Hindus and Muslims were ill-treated. After battle of Plassey, on 23 June 1757, the dawn of British rule in India emerged.

With the intuitive mind of a genius, Robert Clive realized that if the wealth of this still unexplored subcontinent can be transferred to his country, it would be one of the richest in the world. But to achieve this, an appropriate strategy had to be devised. With his fertile brain, he worked out his approach. They were:

1. Selectively establish goodwill, and function as police force during the in - fights of the ruling princes;
2. Raise a Royal Indian army under British rule, employing poor unemployed Indian peasants, for whom the princes, landlords, and money lenders had little time.
3. Establish forts for safety and ports to ferry away the wealth to England, and simultaneously conduct trade with East Asian Countries.
4. To Create Hindu-Muslim divide was a formal strategic policy.(The English had no faith on either of the two religions. This is true even now.)

BEGINNING OF FUNDAMENTAL CHANGES

The British rule appeared after Robert Clive conquered Bengal in battle of Plassey, against the large army of the ruling *nawab.* For this, he had received help from the British army, who came with their artillery. In 1765, Mogul Emperor Shah Alam granted the East India Company, Diwani of Bengal, Bihar and Orissa. For the first time, the trading company became the ruler and could collect tax in coin or kind. This they did to an extent that a tragic famine occurred in Bengal in 1770. The conquest of Bengal gave the new ruler a direct sea route access to England from port of this province.

FIRST WAR OF INDEPENDENCE

Churchill (1874 -1965) was not born yet. Our first war of Independence was a failed attempt of the British to convert this subcontinent to Christianity. Ordinary people of this country, both Hindus and Muslims, were oppressed and treated as slaves by the British and their local rulers. This was the common denominator. When the self respect was hurt, the rebellious population fought cutting across the religious barriers. It was an anger against the *firangis,* who wanted to carry their domination over the slaves' sacred homes as well. In 1857, this resulted in the first war of Independence. This was the first and perhaps the last heroic freedom fight when the country's *masses* as a whole fought although it was yet not a nation. It was administered by British federation of big provinces and small and big lands controlled by 526 princes. The fight was semi religious and political, beginning with earlier revolt by sepoys. The issue was about the use of grease used in cartridges.

There after a new kind of approach for freedom following non-violent, non-co-operation and non-retaliation doctrine of Gandhi got injected. His success at Transvaal and Natal , in South Africa implanted a deep rooted faith of his approach. He had made a strict rule to submit patiently and without retaliation to insult, flogging, or arrest.

This doctrine was successfully tried out by Gandhi, during the salt tax rebellion. He advised his followers to follow the same approach, and succeeded to abolish the salt tax. Retaliation to inhumanism became a sin. Self-inflicted starvation became an act of nobility to atone the sin, or to prove self righteousness. Gandhi took such a step as an aftermath of Jalianbagh massacre.

REVOLUTIONARY APPROACHES

After the first famine in 1770; the brutal ends of Tipu and his children in 1799; beheading of three children of the last Mogul Emperor Bahadur Shah Zafar, in exile to Rangoon, after the first war of Independence in 1857 and hanging the severed heads at the entrance of the court; the great Bengal famine in 1874; the partition of Bengal to create Hindu Muslim divide by Lord Carzon in 1905; the Rowlatt Bill of 1918 (arrest and detention without trial); Jallianwala Bagh massacre on 1919; and several brutal acts on peasants forced indigo cultivation, to benefit from cotton and textile related activities established in England, - all combined, germinated a feeling for revenge more prominently among the literate groups in Bengal and Punjab.

The revolutionary approaches for freedom fight were spreading secretively throughout the nation. Some examples of dedication of the members of revolutionary group can be illuminating. The rebels raided and succeeded in 1930 capturing Chittagaon armoury. They held their position for two days. The belief on getting Independence through revolutionary movement continued, much before Gandhi's non-violent movement. Did not the British flee from Bengal to Delhi in 1911 after an abortive attempt to partition Bengal, bringing in fore the Hindu-Muslim divide?

During a Calcutta university convocation, on 1932, Bina Das tried unsuccessfully to gun down Stanley Jackson, the then Governor of Bengal. It is seen that two parallel approaches were being made. The armed operation included three ladies, one of them was Kalpana Dutt. She was sentenced for life, and imprisoned at Cellular Jail, Port Blair, Andaman.

Creation of violence for gain is a sin, - there is no doubt on that. But is retaliation to such an act also a sin, particularly when it enhances sufferings to the hapless? Here one has to compare the peasant/ mass risings in the northern parts of our world community with our philosophical and Gandhian approach. Which has benefited the poor more?

The notable fact is the revolutionary movement and Gandhi's Satyagraha movements were executed in parallel. Was this a mere coincidence, or designed to take the minds away from the revolutionary movement? Did Gandhi want to carry forward his success in South Africa to India's fight for freedom? His leadership and success at Transvaal bordering Natal to get the indentured labour employed in mines, their rights through Satyagraha movement provided a hall mark to this approach. There Gandhi made strict rules for Satyagrahas to submit and not to retaliate even when flogged, and insulted. Does not one find similarities to what had happened during the Dandi March to protest against 'Salt tax'? His success on this movement generated an unwavering faith on this approach in the minds of simple illiterate people. The revolutionary movement got buried. Did it not bury the dictum of Gita too? Here one has to compare the peasant/ mass risings in the northern parts of our community with our philosophical and Gandhian approach. What has benefited the poor more?

CELLULAR JAIL

There was no doubt that the British imperialism was shaken by the revolutionary movement. They fled away to Delhi in 1911 and established the capital there in two stages. They wanted to root out this armed movement, segregating public from those who still harboured the country to be free from the yoke of British imperialism through armed revolution. They created an impregnable jail far away from the main land at Port Blair, the capital of the largest Andaman and Nicober group of islands in Bay of Bengal, 13,800 km (8,710 miles) away from Channai. The southern most point of these group of islands (and hence of India) is the Indira point, only 2,250 km(1,377miles) away from the tip of Indonesia.

The sadistic mind of the British and the nature of brutal torture meted out to the prisoners can be judged, if a visit is made to this notorious jail. Other than administering daily flogging to mentally torture the prisoners, the cell for hanging was placed at a point that all inmates could see what their fate would be like, whenever they dragged themselves out of their cell with heavy chain around their feet to the balcony to get some fresh air. A record of the heavily chained inmates is maintained and displayed. That the movement had spread over the whole nation, more in Bengal and Punjab. is seen. They also prove the passion with which the intelligentsia wanted the nation's freedom. There is no mention of our rich elites. The nefarious acts of betrayal by our rich and elites can be judged, indirectly though. The absence of any record with photographs with other personal details and states they belonged to clearly indicate that the princes and the richer class kept themselves away from the revolutionary movements.

ROSS ISLAND

A visit to Ross island, separated from the main island by a short stretch of sea, can be a moving experience. A half of this island was divided to keep these intelligentsia as slave labours. They were brought to the other side in the morning, where the English lived in luxury, to do the manual work, and sent back to their poor quarters at sunset. While we have forgotten them, the nature upholds this inhumanity. The long roots of banyan trees have kept the relics of inhumanity still erect as proof of our pre-Gandhian non-violent freedom movement. The church, the ballroom, the steam-powered electric generating house, the living quarters of the governor and others are not allowed to crumple down by these trees, as if fondly embraced to show us now what freedom fighters had gone through, to be free from the tyranny of foreign rule.

A visit to these two places makes one wonder whether such sacrifices of intelligentsia were of any use. What did they achieve when the large disparity between literate urban and illiterate rural society was such that the much needed mass movement was erased through Gandhi's non-violent doctrine. There was no mass awakening against British imperialistic rule. A handful of the British stage-managed the situation so cleverly, that ordinary illiterate rural folk in fact, virtually the entire India believed that the rich Indians were their tormentors, not the British. The tax collections and other suppressions were done through the princes, zamindars, landlords, moneylenders, etc. For them, the British were noble people. The policing act between fighting among princes, and the creation of Hindu-Muslim divide were the main ploys very successfully executed when Gandhi's non-violent movement clicked well. Without any mass movement, no united patriotic feeling germinated. So we are, where we are.

The armed revolutionary movement was destined to be a failure without a mass movement. Not that this deficiency was not realized. Attempts were made to distribute secretively booklets of a few pages, mostly through school teachers and others small groups, but such attempts were exercises of futility, when the masses were illiterate, and no open meetings were possible with pro-British landlords, zamindars, etc. controlling their livelihood. Any attempt to spread this approach to peasants would have resulted in arrests, tortures, and kala pani voyage to Cellular Jail.

There is nothing in commonly accessible record to suggest that Gandhi had visited these national monuments. He might have avoided because a visit and a praise of their freedom fight would counter his Satyagraha movement. Or, he might have been prevented by the British. One would never know. A fact has to be accepted. Gandhi did not support any other form of mass-based freedom struggle. He wanted people to be peace loving and self-reliant. *Charkha* and protest against salt tax are off shoots of such a desire.

An account of events leading to British rule is found in one paragraph of 'Encyclopedia Britannica'. This is reproduced below:

"On the death of Aurangzeb in 1707, the decline of the Mogul empire set in with extraordinary rapidity. Ten emperors after Aurangzeb are enumerated in the chronicles, but none of them has left any mark on history. His son and successor was Bahadur Shah, who reigned only five years. Then followed in order three sons of Bahadur Shah, whose united reigns occupy only five years more. In 1739 Nadir Shah of Persia, the sixth and last of the great Mohammedan conquerors of India, swept like a whirlwind over Hindustan, and sacked the imperial city of Delhi, Thenceforth the Great Mogul became a mere name though the hereditary succession continued unbroken down to the time of the Mutiny. Real power had passed into the hands of Mohammedan courtiers and Mahratta generals, both of whom were then carving for themselves kingdoms out of the dismembered empire, until at last British authority placed itself supreme over all."

A paragraph from 'Encyclopedia Britannica'

Aspects of two valiant freedom fights against British imperialistic rule have been written about in the earlier parts of this book. They were the first war of independence in 1857 and revolutionary movements.

Bringing forward the end of this rule was done essentially to free India as of now. But this subcontinent also got divided, as India and Pakistan before they left in 1947. History will remember two key players. – Jinnah and Gandhi - to achieve this end-result. Much has been written about both. There were similarities even on birth and death, and on the basic ambition. But the end result was markedly different.

JINNAH AND GANDHI

TABLE 4

	JINNAH	**GANDHI**
Date of birth	25th December, 1876	2nd October, 1869
Date of death	11th September, 1948 ***Natural death***	30th January, 1948 ***Assassinated***
Ambition	Nation's Freedom Hindu-Muslim unity better elementary education	Nation's Freedom Hindu -Muslim unity self reliance
Departure to England	1892	4th September, 1888
Return	Autum, 1896	15th January, 1915
Profession	Bar-at- Law from Lincon's Inn freedom fighter	Bar-at-Law from Lincon's Inn freedom fighter
Initiation	Indian national Congress	Indian national Congress
Religion	Muslim	Hindu

An interesting fact to note is while Jinnah was away from the country only for four years, Gandhi way away for 27 years, visiting India for a short period in 1896. He had spent nearly 20 years in South Africa. He was greatly influenced because of his work there.

AN ACCOUNT OF FINAL DYNASTIC PHASE OF BRITISH IMPERIALISM (1906 – 1948)

To arrive at this point by 1906, the subcontinent had gone through several dynasties and events described in earlier chapters. The youngest Indian first barrister, nearly 20 years old, Jinnah arrived in Karachi, in the autumn of 1896 form London after completing his studies. The other two leaders arrived later. Gandhi came finally from South Africa in January 1915. Nehru, the youngest of the three had arrived four years earlier, in 1912. They all studied law in England, and were greatly influenced by English culture. Nonetheless, they were patriots with a common goal to get rid of the ungrateful and demeaning British rulers.

One may recall about our general belief that Gandhi got us the freedom, when his every day Bhajan (prayer song) is now sung every year on his birthday 2nd October, known as Gandhi Jayanti day. He is revered as the father of our nation.

But Bhaghvan has not obliged yet. We got our freedom without Hindu-Muslim unity. Instead, we started our fight even before the freedom, death of both Jinnah and Gandhi's soon after the freedom, and now as an endless fight between two sovereign countries, causing the chasm between the poor and the rich wider through arms deal.

At the very outset, the author has stated that a more appropriate *bhajan* would have been as under;

Baghvan sab dharm ke nam
sammilit shakti Desh ko de Bhagavan

We should sing this song to avoid the impending danger. The dark cloud is building up.

A fact not highlighted is that the freedom has become an inextractable thorn, particularly in our rural flesh. An account of this is necessary for the readers to judge what has caused the current ignoble situation.

HINDU MUSLIM UNITY

At the beginning of 1914 war, the prosaic version of Gandhi's prayer song was implemented by Jinnah, when Gandhi was yet to return from South Africa. He managed to achieve his desire for Hindu-Muslim unity through a formal Lucknow Pact. Within a month after the war being declared, 70,000 Indian troops had moved to different parts, and by the time war ended in 1918, a million had sailed to assist the war efforts in different parts of the world. Gandhi returned from South Africa via England in January, 1915 after being away from the country for a long period of twenty seven years. Jinnah was away for four years, and became a prominent leader in Congress.

Gandhi was not yet in thick of Indian politics, except that on arrival, he announced his sole ambition to serve a united nation. He was still an unknown leader in India, but his exploits in South Africa was talked about. During a Muslim League meeting on 30th Dcember,1915, three prominent leaders –Annie Beseant, Sarojini Naidu, and Gandhi sat with Jinnah on the same platform to support his unity move. An atmosphere of emergence of a New India was in the air.

Meanwhile, Congress demanded a price their sacrifices in war effort. It demanded an equal partnership with Federated English Empire. Jinnah was instrumental to achieve the impossible. He managed to organize both Congress and Muslim league to hold their annual meetings in Lucknow on the same date and at the same time. Jinnah presided the League meeting where he said, "India's real progress can only be achieved by a true understanding and harmonious relations between the two great sister communities". Without dwelling on details, a joint 'irreducible minimum' of reforms was agreed to and passed on to the government of India. This was recognized as *'Lucknow Pact'* whose credit was duly given to Jinnah. He was now recognized as the leader of Hindu Muslim unity. This was the first and perhaps the last noble formal Hindu Muslim united agreement placed before the government. Who was responsible to set it aside, it is not known.

CHAPTER – 6

MAHATMA GANDHI

Date of birth : **2nd Oct 1869**

Place of birth : **Portbandar**

Date of death : **30th January,1948**

Place of death: **Birla House, New Delhi**

During his preparatory phase, he set up in May 1915 an Ashram on the bank of Sabarmati river, similar to Phoenix Ashram near Durban, in South Africa, where he had created another farm, called Tolstoy farm. He named the farm in India as Satyagraha Ashram. People soon came to stay there. About 25 men and women took vows of truth, ashimsa, celibacy, non-stealing, non-possession, and control of the palate, and service to the people.

He started his Satyagraha movement to settle several local problems, viz, peasants were forced into indigo cultivation at Champaran; conflict of the textile mill workers of Ahmedabad with their owners;

Tax payment in Kheda district, et al. His first conflict with British at national level began with the introduction of the Rowlatt Bill.

JALLIANWALA (JB) BAGH.

The origin of the most inhuman act was the imposition of the Rowlett Act of 1918. The main purpose was to suppress the revolutionary movement. It denied the civil liberties, and permitted arrest, imprisonment and *detention without trial.* Are we not doing the same now in free India? Protesting against this bill there was a nation-wide hartal, observed by Hindu and Muslim alike. All shops and business institution were closed. Gandhi was arrested. This excited the people, and in an assembled crowd, a police officer was killed. Gandhi was shocked at such a violent act. He called off the hartal, which he had named as *Satyagraha* movement.

An unarmed peaceful people gathered at Jallianwala Bagh , which had an entry point and three narrow exit gates. It had a high boundary wall. Unprovoked, General Dyer, the army commander of Amritsar ordered to shoot. The adults, women and children were gunned down. When the rifle bullets were exhausted, he called for a canon. It could not enter the narrow entrance path. So a few were saved. Even then, Gandhi's own estimate was that 1200 people were killed, and 3,600 were wounded.

In the agitation that followed, more than 1 lakh people participated and got imprisoned. The sadist General was still not satisfied. He wanted the 'bloody' slaves to learn a lesson. He declared martial law, and mass arrests, flogging and imposed order of crawling on belly in some streets. His inhuman action was condemned almost universally, even by the British. Sir Valentine Chirol called the event as a black day in the annals of British India.

In the frenzy of nationalism, a mob burnt about 22 (?) police men alive. Gandhi was shocked. He undertook fasting for five days to atone the crime committed by the mob. His logic was "it is a million times better to appear untrue before the world, than to be untrue to ourselves". Was it also better to prove our spineless nationalism? Were we proving ourselves true to the world tolerating meaningless killing of unarmed men, women and children? What lesson did we learn? Even now, we follow Rowlett Act of 1918. Thousands are held in prisons without trial. Did not General Dyer have a laugh witnessing the slaves crawl on their bellies and later Gandhi fasting? Did General Dyer express any regret? On the contrary, he justified his action when his conduct was enquired into in London. In our country, we begged Gandhi to give up his fast, accepting the event as if it was our crime, causing unhappiness to his noble soul!

GANDHIAN NON-VIOLENT RETALIATION

Would it have been an illogical act to threaten a repeat of the first freedom fight of 1857, and teach the handful British to behave as human beings instead? Was it not an occasion to throw them out of the country who dared to impose illogical laws, indulge in brutalities, treat people as stray dogs to crawl on bellies?. If this was done, this sub-continent would have been free in 1920 itself, and be totally different to what it is today. No doubt, there would have been much violence. The British , which 'ruled the wave', were not men of clays. Their valour-cum-intelligence has been recognized all over the world.

The first freedom fight happened because they tried to tamper with the very fundamental embedded in every soul, viz., the religious belief even within the sepoys. Currently we are crying hoarse, heralding rightly about keeping 'all options open' against terrorism. What did the leadership do? If the present is right, the past was grossly wrong,

The sepoys of British Indian Army would have revolted if the leadership had threatened the repeat of 1857. There would have been massacre, but if executed under proper leadership, instead of confronting the vast numerical superiority of Hindu Muslim combined, the British would have been wise enough to offer truce and leave at that stage. Perhaps there would not have been any savagery then, and would have avoided the massacre in the future.

Instead, Gandhi called upon the people to take recourse to non-violence, burning foreign clothes, returning the medals to Viceroy and decorations. Thousands of urban went to villages to spread the Gandhian message of non-violence and non-cooperation against the 'satanic' government.

Author's view is, instead, if Gandhi had called upon the nation to get rid of such barbaric rulers from our holy land, the people would have achieved the goal for which he came from South Africa in early 1915.

BHAGAT SINGH

At least one young man did not see the rationale in Gandhi's reaction. To Bhagat singh, a lad of 15 years old, Gandhi's non-violence and non-co-operation was a great puzzle. He lost faith in this approach, and joined the revolutionary movement. He paid for his love for the country. He was hanged on 23rd March, 1931, a day earlier than what was decided by the court. What was his crime?

He accompanied by Batukeshwar Dutt dropped a bomb in the legislative hall from the visitors gallery. It made a loud noise, injuring some, but killing none. When people were running out in panic, they were found sitting quietly on the bench. They justified their act stating that the bomb was made to create noise only. When vocal noises were not heard to quit India, the loud noise would shake the British rulers to listen.

Bhagat Singh

Their plea was rejected, and the trial court's verdict was to 'hang them by neck till death'. The duo and another associate Rajguru took the verdict cheerfully. Even standing on the platform of gallows, they were cheerful, shouted in the name of Bharat Mata, refused black hood, put the noose round their neck themselves kissing the rope.

While there were protest from all quarters before and after they were hanged, no regret was expressed by Gandhi, because Bhagat Singh and his friends were revolutionaries, and believed that these cowardly foreigners should be dealt with equal venom and made to leave our country. Were he and his friends wrong to think that way? Anyway, they did not kill anyone, nor had any intention either. If they had, why they kept sitting and not run away?

Gandhi had carried out his famed Dandi March, just about a year ago, and became famous. when he achieved his goal of abolishing the salt tax through non-violent approach on our part, but the rulers behaved most violently, punishiing brutally those who came to oppose the tax. He had succeeded in South Africa through this approach. His creed was non-violence.

Gita does not support practicing this against evils even though, it is often said, he read Gita every day. Did he believe that through the same approach, practiced in South Africa, he would get the country free from the yoke of British Imperialism? Removal of a legislation on salt tax, or helping the indentured labourers, is not the same as saving the goose, which was laying the golden egg for the prosperity of an alien ruthless ruling nation, starving the vast population of a slave nation. Was he not aware of what happened before he finally came in 1915?

Gandhi started his work to cure the symptoms then on and not the causes for these. In South Africa, he was dealing with a local issue of Indian 'coolie' community, as every member was addressed as a 'coolie', regardless of his profession. They were addressed as a 'coolie doctor', a 'coolie lawyer', or a 'coolie labourer' Here in India, he was to solve an international issue. Patriotic mass movement was the only weapon to use. He did not believe in that if it resulted in violence. Was Quit India Movement not a mass movement? But it was a non-violent one, so acceptable to him!.

Non–violent freedom fight was his noble creed. This he tried to propagate as an universal approach for the weak to fight the strong aggressor. It was undoubtedly a novel approach, and he became famous. But in the final analysis, did it work? Gandhi's solution in South Africa did not last long. The situation reversed back to the original condition, soon after he left for India, not before he had visited England with his family for a few days, on his journey back. It was not a political stop over.

A fact needs highlighting at this stage. Getting freedom was no doubt the primary issue, but the simultaneous actions to improve upon the economic conditions, through energy development, and appropriate skill needed adequate emphasis. This should have been done when the Industrial revolution was transforming the world.

The emphasis should have been to make people literate and understand that their self-respect was trifled with, robbing the nation at the same time, getting the help of feudal rich of the country. Did his bhajan singing address the core issues? Poverty was not due to difference in religious followings. Why then make that the main issue in bhajan singing? Did the 22 famines during British rule happened because of differences in religious beliefs?

The British did not believe in any of our religions, but they played this card for their imperialistic rule, and our elites and rich danced to their tune. British believed in patriotic self respect. It should have been ours too as our trump card, but our minds got diverted in the wrong direction. Does bhajan singing germinate patriotic self respect? It may have helped to elevate the mind for universal brotherhood, no doubt. But at a cost in our situation.

GANDHI IN INDIA : DANDI MARCH on 12 March, 1930

This was the first mass movement act through 'salt tax' imposed by the British rule even when it was domestically produced from sea water. Salt is a daily necessity. He started his march from his Sabarmati Ashram with 27 persons and as he advanced towards the sea, it grew into a sea of humanity. They suffered brutal punishment of the British without any retaliation.

Satyagraha taught the mass to shed fear and they showed to great amazement even those administrating punishment. Such mass support threw the British rule out of gear.

SALT TAX MARCH FROM HIS ASHRAM

Salt tax march from his ashram

Source: Illustrated Biography of Mahatma Gandhi, RBC International, Delhi

He started his march from his camp on the bank of Sabarmati river with 27 inmates, and reached Dandi on 5th April,1930. A sea of people had joined him on the way He picked up a lump of salt from sea shore salt field, violating the law. They courted arrest and about 1 lakh people were severely beaten up, some died as a result. They were imprisoned. The Yervada jail was full along with Gandhi as an inmate

There were two notable mass movements for which Gandhi is regarded as father of our part of the divided nation. The first was the protest against the salt tax. The other was the non-violent 'Quit India' movement of 1942.

QUIT INDIA MOVEMENT

In 1942, during WW II, the British rulers made that declaration of India as a belligerent nation. The main reason was to make the Indians as gun fodder of the Japanese, when Subash Chandra Bose's INA had joined hand with Axis power and was advancing alongside. What the English rulers had in mind, was difficult to guess. Could it be their very clever mind expected double benefit to push India with in the fold of allied Forces. They had dealt with the 'springing tiger Bose' earlier and felt wedging INA in between, they would save themselves from the ruthless unsought of the Japanese. Roosevelt had been asking Churchill to liberate India at that time.

Gandhi objected to such an unilateral decision by the British. Many believed that we should have taken advantage of the situation and strike. Gandhi felt otherwise. His view was " We do not seek our Independence out of Britain's ruin. That is not the way of non-violence.." Many congress leaders felt that we could join but as equal partners. Churchill's reaction was that he would not become "the king's first minister to preside at the liquidation of the British Empire" The situation was getting increasingly restive. To quell the situation, Gandhi called for "quit India"- a non-violent step. He announced this on August 7 at All India Congress Committee. Muslim League did not participate.

The author then a student of Banaras Hindu University (BHU), took some part, mainly disturbing the communication systems. Sir Sarvapalli Radhakrishnan was then our vice-chancellor. Our able leader was Professor Koirala, brother of former prime minister of Nepal. By the end of 1st week of any month, most students are left with little money after paying the college fees and advance mess bills. With no prior notice, we were thrown out of the university, by the British soldiers, virtually penny- less. Had very close encounter when the university students were hunted and arrested. Luckily, we managed to escape. Life would have been very different otherwise. But the experience was good. Learnt an immense lot about rural folks, and to live without money for14 days! Rural people were helpful, when learnt about our university student status. Those days, only a few colleges existed. The students were accepted as good sons of the soil, although no less mischievous than what they are to-day. Only difference is their acts were very different. The elderly people often lamented and wished that they knew what was happening so that they could help. Obviously, the rural people are never in the mainstream of national activities. What we herald as national struggle, was an urbanite game for power and wealth, in fact, earning votes from rural poor whose only profession was agronomy. They wanted to know what was going on. They could not understand why students were harassed. They had heard about Gandhi, and his fight with the British rulers. What for, they did not know. Their grievances were against the landlords (Zamindars and money lenders). Even the students were not clear and able to explain. For villagers, the only issue could be that related to agricultural land, the share of harvested agro-product for the landlord, and tax to pay. When nothing was happening on these, and life in villages was peaceful, why were the policemen chasing the students? They were aware of leaders who would come begging for votes. Student's involvement was a puzzle to them.

At the university, we used to assemble at very early in the morning at Gandhi Chabutra – a huge stretch of land, between the rows of hostels and the impressive buildings of academics for different faculties. There a briefing was received from our group leaders on destructive activities mainly related to communication objects. For example, when finally, we managed to board a train, from Allahabad to Delhi, not a single telegraph pole was erect. The train passed through demolished railway stations. The train moved very slowly, when a pilot single bogey-detached engine was escorting the main train. Passing over a bridge over a main road, one could see through window that all trees were felled on road. The train stopped when the uprooted rail lines were needing repair. The train moved cautiously.

The impact of this movement created severs concern to the imperialistic rule, when the land transportation and telecommunications systems were disturbed almost throughout the country and paralysed. Only wireless messages expressing concern were sent out. Jinnah took no part in this.

FIRST ROUND TABLE CONFERENCE

To come to terms, a Round Table Conference was summoned in London. 89 members from all walks of Indian population were invited. Gandhi and other leaders in jail were not invited because they had laid down *Poorna Swaraj* as a condition precedent for the Round Table.

King George V inaugurated the first *Round Table Conference* on the 12th November, 1930. No tangible solution to the Indian problem was found. All that could be decided on was a 'new concept'- a federation consisting British administrated provinces, and states ruled by Indian princes. The rich and the neglected poor, mostly the illiterate peasants, would continue to live divided as before, since Indo-Aryan Dynasty beginning around 1500 B.C. *This has been a unique feature of this subcontinent, supplemented by occasional hypocritical promises for the poor's welfare.*

Although British rulers announced that this was a great and mighty decision, it was a failure, *in fact.* It only reiterated what was already practiced. This decision did not address the main issues for the country's unrest. The key problem had been and is poverty among the rural people. The history of India can be summarized as a result of three phenomena; (a) perverted religions; (b) willful suppression of the poor by the rich, making them live in dark and agronomy mainly; and (c) willful creation of illiteracy of the rural poor.

The key reason for the emergence of the past degenerated and present hypocritical society is because of the divide between the feudal rich and the suppressed poor. Even after 'Sepoys Mutiny' of 1857' (wrongly represented by British press, and detailed in later pages) three major famines in Bengal, notably the Great famine of Bengal in 1874; the carnage of Jallianwala Bagh on 13 April, 1919; enforced indigo plantation and innumerable barbaric acts against cultivators and artisans, there was no nationwide condemnation by the rich and elites of the country. There could not be any when all these activities were executed by the slave bureaucrats.

SECOND ROUND TABLE CONFERENCE

The First *Round Table Conference* did not achieve much. The act of civil disobedience was gathering greater momentum after the conference. The British realized that Gandhi had a tremendous mass support. His being in Yervada jail, there was little hope of getting any solution to the nationwide unrest. He and other Congress leaders were released on 26 January, 1931. A reconciliatory step was taken soon after his release. This was possible because at that time Lord Irwin was the viceroy, Like Gandhi, he was religious devout at the bottom of his heart. This similarity resulted in the famous Gandhi – Irwin pact.

Ramsay MacDonald, the then the prime minister, invited the Congress to send a delegation for the second Round Table conference. It commenced on 7th September, 1931. More than 104 members (as against 87 of the first) attended when Gandhi was the only one delegate from Congress. Gandhi had by then become Congress. He held meetings in London prior to the conference. They were received with mixed feelings.

Winston Churchill's venom against Gandhi was inexhaustible. He said, "It is nauseating to see Mr. Gandhi, a seditious Middle Temple lawyer, now posing as a fakir of a type well known in the East, striding half-naked up the steps of viceregal palace, while he is still organizing a defiant campaign of civil disobedience, to parley on equal terms with the representative of the king emperor."

The first Conference could achieve little because of agitation after the salt tax movement, the second was also a fiasco because of communal disagreements. Muslim league had already announced their 10 minimum demands. The minority community agreed with the League's demand only on one aspect; - viz., their interests should be protected. With announced preconditions, from various parties; viz., *Poorna swaraj* by the Congress; Muslim League's 10 demands; the minority community's partial alignment with Muslim League, the conference became meaningless when it was required to function as vetting apparatus on various diverse demands, and not a deliberating venue .to arrive at a long term implementable conclusions. Thus, the second conference also did not bear any fruit. The failure was essentially due to communal problems. Jinnah and Ahmedkar claimed control over such number of population that the Hindus became a minority! Gandhi, on the other hand, claimed that these claims could in no way be proved and they were unnecessary, when Congress represented all. The British knew the real situation, but did not try to correct any. Now Jinnah decided to quit Muslim League when there were divergent views expressed by the Muslim representatives. He decided to settle in the UK. Gandhi also retuned with no success, but had the opportunity to meet a large number of people, including Romain Rolland.

THIRD ROUND TABLE CONFERENCE.

Third Round Table Conference held in London in 1931 was poorly attended. It could not resolve and carry forward what was discussed in two earlier conferences. A white paper was published recording what were discussed during the conferences. The recorded verdict of British was that these conferences were great success when it was not. Jinnah was thoroughly dejected by the way, Muslim behaved with divergent opinions, and Gandhi's unwavering view that all these were of little virtue when the issue was liberation of country as a whole. Thoroughly dejected, Jinnah decided to quit politics and settle down in England.

LIAQUAT ALI KHAN.

Born in 1896, twenty six years after Jinnah, he got married in 1933, and decided to visit Europe for the honeymoon. He met him in London at a reception. Liaquat was equally educated, called to the Bar in the Inner Temple. But he did not practice law . He became a politician. He had known Jinnah since 1928. As a great admirer of Jinnah, during the first meeting itself, he requested Jinnah to return to India. Muslim League was in poor shape, he told him, "you must come back. The people need you. You alone can put new life into the (Muslim) League and save it."

JINNAH'S RETURN

In April, 1934 Jinnah returned to India, overcoming his belief of 'no hope' of Hindu – Muslim unity. At a meeting, soon after his return he spoke that "nothing will give him greater happiness than to bring about co-operation and friendship between Hindus and Muslims." There can be no doubt about this, when one recalls that his first political move was joining Congress in 1906, after a most successful career as an advocate in Bombay. He became the richest advocate. The brain behind the formation of Indian national Congress was Allan Octavian Hume, a secretary of the Indian government. The Congress was formed in 1885. The foundation stone of Muslim League was laid in 1906 but Jinnah did not join because it was communal.

JINNAH'S INDIA IN 1934

The events in his life are most illustrious. His date of birth is controversial. School record suggested as October 20, 1875, when he himself suggested as December 25, 1876, which is recorded in law society. Some sources suggest that Jinnah's ancestors were Hindu Rajputs from Sahiwal, Punjab. His grand father was Poonja Meghji, a Bhatia from Paneli village, and the family moved to Sahiwal, near Multan.

He had spent more time in India and England than in Karachi, where he was born. He was legally an Indian citizen when he had built the famous 'Jinnah house' at Malabar hills, Bombay (now Mumbai). Born and educated in undivided India.

He completed his Matriculation (some believe degree) from Bombay University. His second wife was about 27 years junior to him, fashionable daughter of his Parsi friend, Sir Dinshow Petit, a very influential person who helped to build Bombay to be a prosperous city. Ruttenbai (Ruttite Petit) was his very pretty lively daughter. They got secretly married in 1918, when Ruttenbai was only seventeen, and Jinnah was about 42. Diana Jinnah was the only daughter and she decided to live with her mother's Parsi family. Ruttenbai had died early. Jinnah once lamented that he did not have a son.

As the first Indian barrister, when he returned from England in 1896, he felt like a stranger in Karachi. He moved to Bombay in 1897 where he rose from rag to riches, as the wealthiest advocate practicing in Bombay's lofty Victorian-Gothic high court. He joined politics in 1906 at the age of 30 - a year after Lord Curzon partitioned Bengal. Muslim League was formed the same year. However, Jinnah opted for Congress not the League. He had felt that the League was too communal. Congress had a handful of Muslim members. There were only seventeen Muslim members out of a total of 756. But that did not bother him. He was keen on Hindu – Muslim unity, and made attempts to uplift the downtrodden Muslim and shudras. At that stage, he was perhaps the wealthiest member in Congress. The founder Hume had felt that a few highly educated Indian citizen could meet once a year to secure greater freedom, a more impartial administration. The Congress was formed on 29th December, 1885, with such a lofty purpose. Gandhi once said that that 'it was a matter of the greatest pleasure that the Congress was first conceived in an English brain'. Most of the founder members were people who had been educated in England. Gopal Krishna Gokhale, (not educated in England) was the friend, philosopher and guide to both Jinnah and Gandhi, Dadabhai Naoroji, the first Indian *elected* member for Central Finsbury, of British constituency whom Jinnah served in later years as his secretary. W. C. Bonnerjee, to mention a few, was the first President of Congress. There was a overwhelming appreciation for the English mind for initiating the formation of Congress. The Congress, however, did not follow wholly the objectives Hume had in mind. The first business meeting took place next year, when a resolution out of three was passed to alleviate the poverty of the rural poor. Unfortunately, as happened in England, the predominance was given to higher education, when poorer people received little attention. Professor Gokhale of Ferguson College of Pune got involved with politics in 1902. He joined Congress and subsequently elected as a member of Imperial Legislative Assembly. He readily realized the erroneous education policy. He proposed *'Gokhale Elementary Education Bill'* with full support from Jinnah.

The government of India, in 1908, was remote controlled from England, by the Secretary of State, assisted by the Council of India. In India, this government was led by Viceroy having an executive council of six members They took care of the destiny of 300 million, mostly rural people in an arbitrary manner. This was changed eventually, in 1909, forming a much larger Imperial Legislative Council having 60 members. 35 of them were *nominated members*, the other 25 were elected. Jinnah was happy to be a elected member with support from Muslim community. There were special reservations for *Mohammedans and landlords*. One can see what kind of nation the British had in mind. An illiterate society, controlled by a majority of feudal rich under their control, when the elected members in minority were mainly from Congress and Muslim league.

At that time, Gokhale and Jinnah decided to go to England for a holiday. What kind of holiday, Gokhale had is not known, but Jinnah kept himself very busy talking mostly with Muslim students, and joined Muslim League. Now Jinnah was wearing three crowns. One, a prominent leader of Congress; two, a member of Muslim League and finally an elected member of Imperial Legislative Assembly. Some even felt that in time to come he would be the king of India!

Gandhi was not on the scene then. He arrived in January 1915 from South Africa via England. In-between Jinnah with his candour earned much admiration within Congress. While in England, he had opportunities to meet several nobles. Even within the country after his return, he became a well respected man with no religious barriers. He joined in 1916, Home Rule League, founded by Mrs. Annie Besant in Madras. She became the Congress President in 1917. This League was initially founded by Lokmanya Bal Gangadhar Tilak in Poona. The league was widely accepted but it did not conform with the sinister plan of the British. . She was imprisoned but soon released. She resigned after a year, when she found that Congress was getting too much of a religious bias. Jinnah, then 40 years old, held the fort till M.M. Malaviya became the President in 1918. The League was not accepted by the Congress, because it was for *'self-government within the British Empire'* with a belief that the subcontinent would progress faster, as happened in Australia and New Zealand. Gandhi appealed during Congress session in 1930 for complete *swaraj with no link with British,* so that he could create a new kind of subcontinent, as he wished.

The author is totally confused about Gandhiji. He used to read Gita often, - every day, some say. But he defied the very fundamental of this noble script. His act to prove himself a Brahamachari, was so queer that even the inmates of Sabarmati rebelled. Rajagopalachari did not believe in his experiment. But he had illiterate masses on his side. He was a saint, nay God to them. None dared to rebel against his practice, even though commonly accepted as a social sin. He got away on several occasions, for acts, many were arrested. Gandhi was first arrested on 1922. He avoided acts, which would impose punishment of hard labour. When people of our country were made to crawl on belly, he took to fasting for four days to atone the crime against our people, like innocent killing at Jallianwala bagh.

Triumphant Gandhi had returned to India in January, 1915. from South Africa (SA), but with a sole desire to serve India, freeing the nation from the yoke of British imperialism. Now his battlefield was totally different, but he brought forward the legacy of his success in SA, and started afresh, using the well tried out weapon of non-violence, non co-operation, and non-retaliation with courage, fasting to atone crimes. He realized the realities of the country's situation, but gave no credence to earlier rectification efforts, by Annie Basant, Jinnah, and Gokhale. He wanted to begin with a clean slate - satyagraha as the nation's creed. Events in 1930s will prove that he did not allow any grass to grow under his feet. He wanted to carry forward his success story of South Africa for India as well. In the process, Jinnah lost his ground. None of his proposals to Congress to uplift Muslim and untouchable shudra with special Legislative power in separate areas, where they (Muslims) were in majority were getting support from Congress.

Gandhi nebulous efforts to tackle several ailments of the country, e.g. illiteracy that Jinnah was trying to eradicate through League, and autonomous provinces but Muslim majority with special Legislation power were not accepted by Congress. Jinnah resigned his membership from Congress. These deficiencies surfaced during and after the nation's freedom. The author believes that a team approach, was necessary to tackle simultaneously all other aspects, with allotment of responsibilities to his associates towards legislation to eliminate illiteracy, on unification of religions, agronomy development, health and hygiene, science and technology, poverty alleviation, etc .He had several able co-workers and administrators, e.g. Moti Lal Nehru, Maulana Azad, Sardar Patel, C.R. Das, Lala Rajpat Rai, C. Rajagopalachchari, Asaf Ali, Sorojini Naidu, Aruna Asaf Ali, Mahadev Desai, Miraben, Malavya, Nehru, G.D. Birla, to name a few at random. The efforts to get the country free from the yoke of British rule was noble, but not paying attentions to the tentacles of evils holding a firm grip on the nation diluted the nobility. In our the then still fragmented subcontinent, there was no law against efforts to set right such adverse conditions. Gandhi had good relation with the prominent princes. We started corrective activities too late, after freedom, when humanism had lost its value.

JINNAH TRANSFORMED

Jinnah's approach was diagonally opposite. He desired now a divided country, with a separate region for Indian Muslims, who according to him, belonged to a separate race, with different culture. Jinnah as the president of Muslim League was making an all out uncompromising effort to have a separate region for Indian Muslims, He did not believe in Gandhian approach.

In 1930, Gandhi moved the resolution in Congress session declaring 'complete Independence ('*Purna Swaraj'*) as the goal of Congress policy. The pledge towards this was taken by millions throughout the country on 26 January, 1930. But he was not sure what action to follow. At that time, Rabindranath Tagore had visited him at his ashram, established at the bank of river Sabarmati. He asked Gandhi about his next move. Gandhi was at a loss for the next step. This query created the seed for the Salt March starting on 12 March, 1930. Many may not know that the world famed poet Tagore was no less a patriot. He had relinquished, knighthood in 1919 conferred upon him by the British after Jallianwala Bagh massacre on 13th April, 1919 at Amritsar. There was mutual admiration between the two, although not always agreeing to each other. Gandhi, addressed Tagore as 'Kavi Guru', who addressed the former as Mahatma (great soul) when Gandhi visited Shantiniketan in 1915. These affiliations got stuck. Gandhi had sent his children to Shantiniketan. Nehru had also sent Indira Gandhi there, when she was young. For reasons not known, she could not complete her study there.

IMPACT OF ROUND TABLE CONFERENCES

The Dandi (salt tax) March established two issues. Gandhi proved to the country and also the world population about his concept of fighting imperialist power with a non-violence approach. Within a few weeks, he proved the great power of a handful of soil, from a salt producing area at the sea shore beach.. Hundred thousand men and women came from all directions, courted arrests. The British had to withdraw the salt tax The world community admired Gandhi's non-violent approach, condemning the British rule. Gandhi himself was arrested on the 5th May,1930 and imprisoned in Yervada Jail. Belying the hopes of the British that the arrests of Gandhi and large number of political leaders, will suppress the growing agitation. It generated a contrary effect.

CHAPTER - 7

PARTITION

The partition and freedom came about simultaneously for more than one reasons. Gandhi had proved the power of mass movement of non-co-operation in 1942 when Muslim League did not take part. The Japanese, along with Subhash Bose and his INA (Indian national Army) were knocking at the eastern door of the British imperialism in 1945; and Jinnah's claim for a separate State for the Indian Muslim 'race' contributed to this. Much against Gandhi's lone voice of protest, with little support now from his colleagues, the subcontinent got its freedom, divided in a confused manner, not knowing what exactly was the core issue needing such a drastic action.

One of the possible reasons may be the concern of the British getting trapped within Indian sub-continent when axis power was winning and pushing towards the West. The support from the Indian people and army was doubtful after 1942 non-cooperation movement. There was much uncontrollable violence and rift within the country. Furthermore, the INA under Bose joining the axis power to throw out the British added fuel to the British apprehension. They wanted to leave. The British parliament had decided in 1945, before the cessation of war, to quit India in 1948. Lord Mountbatten arrived in February 1947, advancing this to a precise date of 15th August, 1947, and declared this during his very first address to the nation after taking over as viceroy.

Gandhi was dedicated towards Independence of an undivided subcontinent with Hindu-Muslim unity. This was his main goal. Mountbatten's announcement puts a bucket of cold water on Gandhi's effort to have an undivided India.

The most puzzling fact is, why Gandhi did not resort to his proven weapon of declaring *fasting till death* if the subcontinent was divided. He did threaten such a recourse in 1946. Would such a step not be consistent with his historic march, starting from Noakhali, on November 7, 1946 till March 2, 1947, risking his life during the carnage in the eastern and western regions?

The contemptible British diplomacy was at its peak when having initially created Hindu-Muslim divide, (Lord Curzon's notorious move to partition Bengal in 1905. This was revoked in 1911). Mountbatten wanted all to believe that now the country was getting partitioned, at its own will! Without allocation of the regions for Hindus and Muslims, how the announced Independence was to be implemented! Was it possible to draw a line dividing the Hindus and Muslim sovereign areas? A fresh violence erupted. The unprecedented inhumanism, recorded in what follows, will be a blot in the history of mankind for all time to come. The end result of such a diplomacy, as seen in Figure 2, provides an indication on what happened thereafter, comparing with the English who was in a situation not much different to what we are now, before the Industrial Revolution during 18th century.

The above narration is mainly to highlight that our independent sovereignty has not brought about any significant change for the rural life. The present situation is no different to our past. It has become worst. Some examples have been cited in subsequent paras.

THE GENESIS OF POOR INDIA

One can readily see the difference of Moghul dynasty (till Aurangzeb) and British imperialism. The Moghuls tried to unify the Muslims and Hindus. They established world famous prosperous industries based mainly on cotton, and removed earlier laws imposed during earlier dynasties. Such measures helped land reform and improved yield from land. British rule acted exactly in opposite direction. Not only they de-industrialised the cotton industry, they established their own mills in England. Their clothes did not attract any tax. Thus created a huge market for their Lancashire clothes, when large poor Indian people started buying them at low cost. Although cotton industry was dismantled, some weaver continued to produce fine textured fabrics, using handlooms. They were far better than what the UK mill was producing. The richer section of the society bought these instead. To stop this, they ordered cutting off the thumbs of the weavers. The story of the British perversion did not stop there.

The Lancashire mills initially used organic indigo, to colour their fabrics. This ruined the garments made with mill produced clothes. Inorganic indigo, produced in India did not do that. Indeed, after a wash, the garments looked better. So the British imposed a law that about 15 % of the land used for food cultivation should now be converted for indigo cultivation. There was much agitation from the farmers, but no protest from our elite and rich community. Thus, the obvious happened. England prospered, when India got sucked into deep well of poverty; - but not all.

The rich princes who acted on behalf of the English, got rewards, and some honoured with titles. Soon railways and communication systems came up to speed up conveying cotton, food grains and minerals to the docks, where ships, now powered by steam engines, were ready to ferry these to England at a much greater speed. No wonder, a penniless nondescript Robert Clive, with a questionable character returned to his country laden with diamonds, precious stones, food grains, cotton, and what not. He was welcomed with open arms, and elected to join the elite society of peers. Now Lord Robert Clive became the initiator for England's journey of 'rag to riches'.

Skipping over several centuries, the Churchillion era (1874 – 1965) has been brought afore because that had been the crucial time to create our present situation.

WINSTON CHURCHILL

Winston Churchill was a born aristocrat. His father, Lord Randolph Churchill took no interest in him. Yet, young Churchill worshipped his father, but got nothing back. Churchill jr was disliked by most. With an indifferent impatience, his father decided that he would better be a soldier and sent him to Sandharsh, even though Winston had a high IQ and tremendous power of concentration. He liked it mo: e than going to Oxford or Cambridge. On one occasion, he expressed that there he might have associated with 'drunken scholars . He was not a bigoted teetotaler, nor an alcoholic. His drinking habit was as peculiar as his uncompromising patriotism. Though not an obsessive drinker, he just drank day after day, every day all through his life, and remained sober, till he died at the age of 90. His patriotic feeling was supreme, bordering on obsession. He could take recourse to any action for his country. Likewise, his hate towards India was absolute, - immoral and sadistic.

CHURCHILL ON INDIAN SCENE

World War II was declared in September, 1939. Churchill announced on radio in 1940, '*we shall never surrender. We shall fight on until the curse of Hitler is lifted from the brows of mankind. We are sure that in the end all will come right'*. And he achieved what he said against all odds. But not once had he expressed any gratitude for the supreme sacrifices made by more than one million sepoys (soldiers) who helped the British during the war. War ended on 14th August, 1945.

Joined (Queen's own) 4th Hussars Regiment in 1895, he at 22 was posted in India, became a Lieutenant in 1896. He had active field service for two years. He was captured by the Boars during 1899 – 1901 war, but dramatically escaped. This made him a public figure. He was elected as a Conservative M.P. in 1900. Then on he had a chequered career. He was the Pime Mnister during 1940 – 45, saved England during the most difficult period of WW II, but ruined ours, inspite of the country's contribution of million soldiers in the war effort of the British. This was also a crucial period of freedom struggle of India. Surprisingly, Churchill lost during post-war general elections. His losing the election was not per reverence, he deserved. Some even expressed impolitely that he was ***sacked***. But he bounced back as prime minister again in 1951.

He was a member of BUS (Bangalore United Service) club now Bangalore Club for three years, in the elitist ambient of little England in India. His vision about India did not go beyond the wooden dance floor (still existing) at the club, playing polo, reading books, and romancing with a beautiful English girl, who lived then in Bangalore. Back to England, she became Lady Lytton.

Why this romance failed is not known. But it provides an interesting side of Churchill's personality. He was afraid of rejection, or getting defeated. A lady whom Churchill courted for two years was asked why she did not marry him, her reply was if Churchill had asked her, she would have accepted him on the spot. But he did not. Then again, it may not be true. An English media, 'News of the World' reported it. Since it was read by both commoners and peers, many prominent people contributed to the editorial page, expressing their views on important issues. People read that also. Our illiterate rural folks are blessed with only one concern. Their primary objective was to find a way out of their poverty. A deeply concerned village assembly, discussing strategy to be placed before the gram Panchayat, is shown below;

Thinking hard: working out the strategy for survival
A deeply concerned Village Assembly

GANDHI AND BOER WAR (1899 -1901)

Gandhi's sympathy was with Boer. He had organised a volunteer ambulance corps for the British army, because he had felt that as a loyal subject it was his duty to help Britain. Wearing the uniform of the Ambulance Corps, he proved that Indians were not cowards, or soft as generally viewed then and even now. For his and other volunteers' selfless and courageous activity to bring back wounded soldiers from battle fields, the British Government had rewarded him with a war medal. He was warmly welcomed. and much respected in England for his work during the Boer war. There is nothing in record to suggest that Churchill had a brush with Gandhi at that stage. But this cannot be ruled out. The unfortunate British colonial mind surfaced soon after the success of the war. They forgot all the nice words of protecting Indian interests in South Africa. The Indians there were back to square one and Gandhi started his protests. Churchilll's colonial attitude and aversion to Gandhi, might have originated at that stage. His early career was to control the British colonies. His infamous utterance about Gandhi a naked fakir during the second Round Table conference (1931) is very much in record. Every human being, generally, has two conflicting minds. Churchill had exhibited that amply later on.

He left the BUS (Bangalore United Services) club with an unpaid bill of Rs. 13. This was written off as 'unrecoverable' sum. But he had built a beautiful house in England, with a brook flowing at the edge of his back yard garden. It is not the paltry sum but his miserly ethics, one recalls. As a service officer, even now, unless he pays all his bills, the clearance certificate to proceed to his new posting is not issued. An officer without a clearance certificate from his earlier unit is not allowed to join the new unit. To believe that he had forgotten to pay is being generous, but not before wondering how he had managed to join his new unit, and accepting a fact that parsimonious behaviour is a mental disease of many rich. Did this make him to call Gandhi a 'naked fakir'?

His inhumanism took an absurd turn during the Great

Bengal Famine in 1943, soon after the successful Quit India movement of 1942. Three million (some estimate four million) people perished during the famine. Inspite of two million Indians fighting men providing assistance towards Britain's war effort, many paying through supreme sacrifice, Churchill's reaction towards a request to supply food to Bengal, as recorded by Mountbatten in 1944, was that it would amount to "appeasement of the Congress Party". He expressed that *"I hate Indians. They are a beastly people with a beastly religion"*. Though food was available, it was sent to save starving people of Holland. Churchill was delighted to learn that peasants were dying on Calcutta streets, when there was no sympathy for them even from their own elites. Churchill, during briefing Mountbatten, in 1946, prior to his coming to India as viceroy, expressed that Indian was a '*fragmented subcontinent* of princes. (which was true), and beggars; with *no religion'*.

A digression may not be inappropriate. Gandhi's weapon on difficult occasions was to resort to fasting to atone. the crime of retaliation. His last one was in Calcutta, in 1946, during Hindu Muslim riot prior to partition in 1947. Why did he not resort to his weapon much earlier on this most inhuman situation? Would not that have saved the lives of millions?

Is not Europe, almost equal in size to Indian subcontinent, a fragmented land? Do the countries in Europe fly one flag? Why then British unfurled one Indian flag, as under, and had *one* Royal Indian Army over a period of about 200 years (1757 – 1947). The British came first to plunder and then to trade, not to rule. They got control over parts of India in stages since 1757 more because of the reigning Moguls' creation of degenerated feudal social structure, involving the English in privileged nocturnal offerings, under the 'attar' perfumed blankets, savouring the beautiful flowers spread out under the best cotton sheets; and more for the follies of indigenous people, than for their gallantry. (Raj by Gita Mehta – an acclaimed book by India Today) The pleasure loving Moguls, during their last phase of their dynastic rule made them the masters of some important territories, and then on they became the master of the whole of the subcontinent winning over the luxury loving feudal and lazy Princes. Was that the reason to rule under one flag? Was it to unify the fragmented subcontinent for its progress, or to make the robbery easier enforcing one law, yet not erasing the non-cohesive statehoods for their safety. If Gandhi satyagraha, the non-violent and non-co-operation movement can be regarded as an innovative strategy for the poor to fight against powerful imperialistic rule, the briefing of Churchill was an expressed master piece of despicable mind. His uncompromising love for his own country, and his colonial mind with sadistic and bitter hate for the people of this sub-continent .were in contrast to the average Englishman living in England. They were far more humane. In1960s, most illiterate/ uneducated migrated Indians were used for menial jobs, - cleaning roads, public places like airports. school compounds, hospitals, etc. But they were paid. They volunteered to take up these jobs, and were not forced as slaves. Do we not see similar sights, - sometimes even worse, in big cities in our country? Gandhi had often expressed that his fight was against British imperialism and not English people. The author endorses Gandhi's view, having studied in England.

There is a common saying, 'give the devil his dues'. The English people deserve to be complemented when they grabbed the opportunity our people had created for them. Our philosophical minded people, the Brahmanical perverted priests, the pleasure loving Princes, the treachery, and the rich oppressing peasants did not jell to create *one* nation with a patriotic flavour.

Even when the British did not believe in any of our religion, they supported Muslims community preferentially, and encouraged Hindu-Muslim divide during the formative phase of Imperialism. This creation was a Imperialistic necessity and not because of any compulsions of restoring harmony between different religious faiths. The seed planted was to acquire the booty, and not settling religious differences. Did the British rule ever tried to settle the meaningless conflicts between Hindu and Muslim? This they did not, because then they would not be able to rule, rob, and prosper *their* country. Gandhi tried to achieve this with his missionary zeal of non-violence, and paid for this at the end. He was assassinated on 30th January, 1948, by a Hindu fanatic, He suffered martyrdom due to ill conceived assessment. The murderer had felt that Gandhi was giving away too much to the Muslims. On the contrary, he was not giving away anything to anyone except his life's mission on Hindu-Muslim brotherhood. Gandhi' mission to bring about brotherhood between them had the same passion as Abraham Lincoln had to remove slavery in America. He was assassinated too, but left behind his imperishably statement, "*government of the people, by the people, for the people*". Can we say the same for our country? Americans adopted what Lincoln said. We express similar sentiments, but act exactly in an opposite manner. Gandhiji was also assassinated, but could he succeed in his country adopting what he sang all along his life, "*Iswar Allah tere nam, sabko sanmati de Bhagwan*". We sing this song on 'Gandhi Jayanti' day. But have we accepted his song? Gandhi Jayanti is performed as annual 'Shradh' (prayer for the departed soul) ceremony, for the father of the nation. No sooner this is over, people rush to continue what they had been practicing, erasing from their mind what they just sang.

Our Constitution reflects some similarity of Lincoln's mission. But we paid respect to his missions by 'partitioning' the subcontinent on religious basis!. And this was done with the approval of a majority of 99, against an opposition of 52 members of his Congress party, The British India flag continue to fly when we retained our hypocrisy, eloquently expressing the need to uplift the unacceptable living condition of the illiterate rural poor. They were never consulted though elites always shed crocodile tears about their miserable existence.

CHAPTER - 8

A CONFIRMATION OF GENETIC STRAIN ON TECHNOLOGY

British flag

SERVING UNDER BRITISH IMPERIALIST FLAG

The author had a short inconsequential stint to serve under the British India flag as a cadet in 1946, at OTS (Officer's Training School) in Bangalore. This School has now been converted as the ASC (Army Supply Corps), improved but retaining much of the original pre-Independence ambience. It was an unforgettable experience, when the school was training 300 British cadets, and only a Company of 90 Indian cadets, with options for IT (Indian troop) and BT (British troop) rations. Although all cadets, opting for the better BT ration, would eat in the same dinning hall, the Indian and British cadets did not mix. Even their living quarters (barracks) were different.

Author, Officer cadet at OTS, early 1946

However, this army school changed an initially reluctant Engineer with specialization in aeronautics, to be a reasonably competent Infantry Officer. But soon was transferred to (RIAF), Royal Indian Air force's ITW (Initial Training Wing), Coimbatore, at the initiative of the Commandant, OTS, Brigadier (pop) Talbot. He had felt that an engineer specialized in aeronautical faculty should be with the Air Force. Began again, with refusal of seniority claim due for the earlier phase, as a cadet to be an Engineering (aircraft maintenance) Officer with further training at Tambram, both in Madras (now Tamil Nadu).

All these Officers, except Razdhan at extreme right, did well, and held high positions. (Razdhan and the author had shared a two room block during flying training at Begumpet, Hyderabad). He, a very handsome Kashmiri young man, had unparalleled ability, - in sports, music (his memorable piano recital of classical music), maintenance of aircraft, and flying.

The author believes that he was way above all of us in any

field. He was doing something all the time, and that might have caused his unfortunate demise. As an 'Orderly Officer' in Jamnagar, he was playing with his revolver and inadvertently shot himself. One notable fact of the remaining six has been, they all chose technical administration after short spell of maintenance activity except the shortest one. He was the only qualified Mechanical engineer.

First batch of graduate engineers in Independent India's Air Force (Author - *The extreme left)*

(Commissioned September, 1947, a month after nation became Independent)

The transformation from being an mathematically oriented Engineer, to become an infantry officer (army), then an aircraft maintenance engineering officer(IAF), and then servicing as such, which included a brief participation during 1948 Kashmir war, getting trained to be qualified pilot, followed by a short spell as a teacher at the most prestigious technical training college (then run by the AST, UK), getting posted at Air Headquarter as ADTS(Plan), (Additional Director Tech services), further education at Cranfield Institute of Technology, UK, for a master's degree in aeronautical engineering (propulsion and aerodynamics), short spell of association with active gas Turbine designers in the UK, was the most memorable initiation period in the author's life. More so when assigned in AFTC to teach who taught the author earlier during pre-commission (cadet) days.

The jet era, supersonic flying and the maintenance culture were rapidly changing. The first batch to be taught included the second senior most technical officer, then Gp. Captain U.K. Nair. Though not grasping initially the continuous combustion burning operating cycle of a jet engine, the concept of mach number, the virtue of C4 blade, the wide chord's backward shifting of point of thickness chord ratio, etc., they tried really hard to learn the changing aeronautical S & T era.

The author learnt much from them in the beginning, and now, when they not once imposed their seniority. They were never late, and treated their much junior what was due to a teacher. They showed exemplary discipline standing up as the teacher entered the class! Unbelievable, but it is an unadulterated truth. The true value of service life, the virtue of working with juniors giving them their dues, to earn the same from them, and the discipline; - all got engraved through examples of much seniors. When getting harsh for poor performance, a leader must try to learn the reason, and rectify. Such lessons were gratefully learnt combined with much mischief and hard work.

DIFFERENT PATH: FOUNDATION OF GAS TURBINE TECHNOLOGY

THE VALUED SEED OF AERONAUTICS IMPLANTED IN INFERTILE SOIL

What follows skipping over a political era is essentially to provide a feel that this subcontinent need not have been what is now, but for what transpired between 1757 (battle of Plassey) and now.

This path followed by the author engineer veered to an

altogether different direction, when the first Gas Turbine Engine was designed and made in the country, leading to his becoming the founder Director of Gas Turbine Research Establishment, Bangalore(1961).

This episode has been elaborated in detail in Part 3 of the book. Everything was not sweet and honey. Most of it was quite the opposite; unethical, in fact. But it was also an opportunity for self assessment when faced with difficult situations.

An aspect of the author's life needs mention at this stage. While studying in Delhi (Hindu College), economics was his subsidiary subject, mathematics was the first. The meritorious professor of economics, (Dr).B.N. Ganguli (who became the Vice Chancellor) made a point, which stayed with the author all along. Teaching about the GDP (Gross Domestic Product), he had taught us that the focus of all agro and industrial activities should be towards making products of greater value (the GDP) per man-hour spent. He had illustrated this through examples. The clarity of his mind could not be missed by any. But in those days, the opportunities were few to practice what was taught.

This engine was made because of a well meaning harsh challenge thrown by Hon'ble Krishna Menon, our the then famous Defence Minister (DM) in 1958. The author returned then from England after his higher studies on Propulsion, and association mainly with Bristol Siddley Engine Ltd., (BSEL) UK. Our DM felt that it is only by making the engine the author could prove that government's money had not been wasted over a period of four and half years stay in the UK. The economic concept taught earlier was kept in mind while trying to figure out the approach to make an experimental engine. But the basic thought was to evolve .the strategy. A nucleus team was formed at newly formed the DTD&P (Air Force), with Dr. Nilakantan as its Director. From the very first day of reporting to him about the task assigned, he had felt that the nucleus team had to move over to a hardware oriented establishment. The name of No1 Base Repair Depot (BRD) came in mind. The author was posted there before, in 1947, and was recommended.

Author, Wing Commander. 1958

EVOLUTION OF STRATEGY TO MAKE THE EXPERIMENTAL ENGINE

Several suggestions were considered. A view received favorable support. The generally accepted strategy was to identify existing components to be used, as blanks, to machine out the desired components; concentrate on developing heat resisting materials getting assistance from Ordinance factories of DGOF (Director General of Ordinance Factories), and develop in house technology to caste Aluminum components. Aluminum casting was not done then in the country. The author got in touch with his professor, - Professor A. D. Baxtor, at Cranfield Institute of Technology, UK. He was one of the pioneers on Propulsion systems, both Gas Turbine and Rocket Motor. He felt that our approach was worth trying. He sounded optimistic, and happy; wished us good luck. The nucleus body moved to Kanpur.

VISIT TO THE USSR.

Till that time, the aviation industry in India was surviving on refurbished left over of the Allied Forces; the inefficiently damaged Liberators and Dakotas, Several crated fighter aircraft; and license production of Gnat, Ajeet and Vampire. They helped to form IAF, (Indian Air Force), shedding 'R' as was before, (R-

IAF.). Krishna Menon, our DM (Defence Minister) was generally believed to be a left leaning politician. He wanted our Air Force to be contemporary with Supersonic fighter aircraft. At that time, our Defence services did not have *any* military store from Communist countries.

The author was and is apolitical, what prompted our DM to send a small team for a preview on MiG 21 aircraft, in Moscow was beyond his comprehension. The two senior members were talking about Left, Right, and Centre orientations while returning to the CV (Central Vista) mess. Their discussions made no sense to the author then and even now. But excited with the prospect of 'seeing' at close quarters the World famous MiG 21! At Moscow, three of us were taken to an Air Force base in a small transport aircraft, all windows covered with Black sheets. Mind rebelled, but looking at that aircraft, the author's heart melted. What an aggressive looking beauty!

MiG 21 the basic version

Reaching the military base, almost leapt out of the air-conditioned Volvo Car, when one senior member pulled the author back. "Put on your jacket (fur lined) and the gloves". The author's surprised look, was answered "otherwise you will leave your palm skin behind on aircraft's body". The out side temperature was about minus 17^0 C. Inside the car, a small gauge registered the outside temperature. The comfort inside made one forget the hostile outside. We were appropriately kitted at the CV

(Central Vista) mess tailoring shop before leaving to meet such contingency. The author had felt grateful for the senior members' watchful eye.

While the two senior officers with jackets on were discussing with their counter parts outside, a civilian person appeared accompanied by a military man. I was informed that the civilian person, wearing a heavy long fur coat, would explain and answer, the militiaman will translate, i.e., he would be the interpreter.

The detailed learning process started from the front. Desired to learn, to begin with, about the control mechanism of the central bullet, at different speeds, and about the normal and inclined shock wave generations for minimum pressure loss at different speeds. Expecting a continuous flight speed dependent optimized movement of the central bullet, related with engine rpm, it had gathered three automatic stepped forward movements instead, with increasing speeds. The 'delta' wing and its incidence variations from root to tip, the yaw stabilizers, and a few other facts were enquired into, and answered through the interpreter, often translated incorrectly, but set right with 'da-da' vocabulary between the two. Not much was learned about the single engine, RD-11 F.

In 1960 winter, the Moscow city looked quite common. It appeared that New Delhi was better looking on the southern part. What strikingly more amazing was that people, both men and women were working in the open, wearing no visibly warm clothes. The women had their head covered with a white scarf tied down at the back of their head.

We had a satisfactory debriefing session with the senior leaders. Retuned to Delhi, at night wrote a very appreciative report in long hand, and gave to our senior most, marked secret. Instructed not to speak to anyone, gathered that the senior most had a meeting with our DM. I was eager to return to Kanpur but was asked to stay back in Delhi,

After two days, organised by our DM, a short meeting with our prime minister, Pandit Jaharwal Nehru, was held at the first floor of his Teen Murty house in the evening. He did not want our DM, Krishna Menon (Defence Minister)'s presence. He was more keen to learn about our impression on the USSR's aero-space technology, not asking anything specifically about MiG 21.

The author, the junior most, was the technical officer of the team. His very brief reply was that the 'blip', which could be heard on radio, tells all. With a faint smile he got up, went to the window overlooking the dark wooded stretch of land hidden behind the imposing house, as seen from the front. A sharp featured beautiful lady came in, indicated that the meeting was over, and we followed her. Later the author came to know that she was Indira Gandhi, working then as the social secretary to our prime minister.

Declining politely her kind offer to have tea, we got back in the car. We drove silently to CV Air Force Mess, close to raj-path. A two km long stretch of wide green land on each side of the road, could be reached through a small gate, although not commonly used, except by morning walkers. It was a pleasant place. to sit in a lawn close to the boundary wall. Returning. the author was sitting and thinking about the entire episode, and also about the work left behind in Kanpur. Our two senior members came and sat down.

A volley of criticism erupted asking why switched over to space technology when we had gone for a meeting on aeronautics. Why MiG 21 not phased in my reply?. Regretting my mistake, walked to the bar, which had just opened. The author drowned his sorrow there. What transpired in between the bar and my room, the author could not recall. The mess waiter brought a tray next morning and informed to get ready quickly for a meeting with the DM. Other members of the team were getting ready. Complied as informed, but was least interested. With the DM, an Air Vice-Marshall, and an Air commodore, on one side, a Wing commander on the other, an uneven battle was anticipated, to defend the previous evening's apparently out of context *blip* episode. Setting this possibility aside, the author's mind had decided to be silent and back inside the quilt on return; and then the Upper India Express to Kanpur in the evening. What transpired at the DM's office did not even register in mind, Returning, sitting in front with the driver, received a big thump on shoulder from behind; heard some one saying , '*your blip seemed to have worked'*. Replying 'thank you', adding with a slightly empathetic Sir, reclining more, dozed off. Reaching back, got under the quilt without changing. In the evening, picked up a taxi, and reached Old Delhi Railways station, close to Chandni C howck. Nizamuddin railway station was not functional then.

DESIGN AND MANUFACTURE OF FIRST GAS TURBINE ENGINE: GTRC – CF-1 ENGINE

Reached Kanpur, feeling amazingly fresh in a densely foggy early morning. Returning home, got ready to get back to unfinished work, on a two dimensional copy milling machine of the AMD. The author's task was to design and machine the diffuser for the centrifugal compressor. It was rated as the most critical part, and the task was taken up voluntarily. The tasks were well defined after freezing the design.

The competent officer, who became the director later on, machining the other critical part; - the turbine using a heavy duty milling machine of the BRD, using four stepped formed tools, and an optical dividing head, discovered from left over junk when the allied forces vacated after the war, which ended in 1945. Another most talented was machining the compressor designing a special fixture for a Sculford lathe of the engine section; Another team was making the can annular combustor; when others were trying to develop technology for aluminum casting for the 'elbows' leading to the combustors, and so on, keeping our noses against the grinding stone.

In between, our commanding officer had set a target. The engine should run on or before 1st April, 1961, - our then Air Force day.

Our first experimental gas turbine engine, shown below, ran early in the morning on 3-4 April in 1961. After several throttle settings and the required dry runs there after to remove residual fuels for satisfactory light up and slow running, the engine was coxed to run at a steady slow running state at a throttle setting. Flight lieutenant Suranjan Das, BRD's test pilot, was with us throughout the night. Standing at a corner, he quietly watched what was going on. He was a pilot by instinct and an engineer at heart. Pushed the throttle a little further to check the response. It obliged beautifully. Rushed to reach a telephone to inform the Commanding Officer, only to be greeted with his unhappy scorn, for the *delay of 3 days* from the assigned date. He had planned to announce much on the 1st April. Author felt sorry to let him down, although every effort was made by all to meet the target. The last minute problems caused the delay.

The author swallowed the scorn ungrudgingly realising the shattered ambition of a person who wanted to build the BRD, a service controlled centre of Aeronautics, parallel to a civilian controlled HAL (Hindustan Aeronautics Limited), in Bangalore. He desired a government controlled Indian Air Force Centre, similar to the DGOF for the Army. Towards such an ambition, a hear say suggests that he had our DM's support. To achieve this he had worked hard.

The author was happy to realise that we need not be short of technicians to make gas turbine engines. The recruited mechanics were converted as technicians for different activities. The author's learning, the useful exposure in the UK, and our apparent backwardness germinated a strong confidence to try and be on par with the developed countries.

To avoid audit objections, using Air Force facilities, it functioned as an Air Force unit, the head was now designated as O i/c, GTRC still with no inventory. A small sum of Rs. 30,000 (thirty thousand) was granted by CSIR (Council of Scientific and Industrial Research) and this was spent on salaries of civilian scientists, and technicians. With the BRD's support, even this sum was only partially used. The unspent money became a problem. However, eventually it was transferred to the GTRE's account when GTR-C became GTR-E.

The first who rushed to Kanpur from Delhi was Krishna Menon. Our prime minister came after a few days. Details of activities is narrated in chapter 3B..

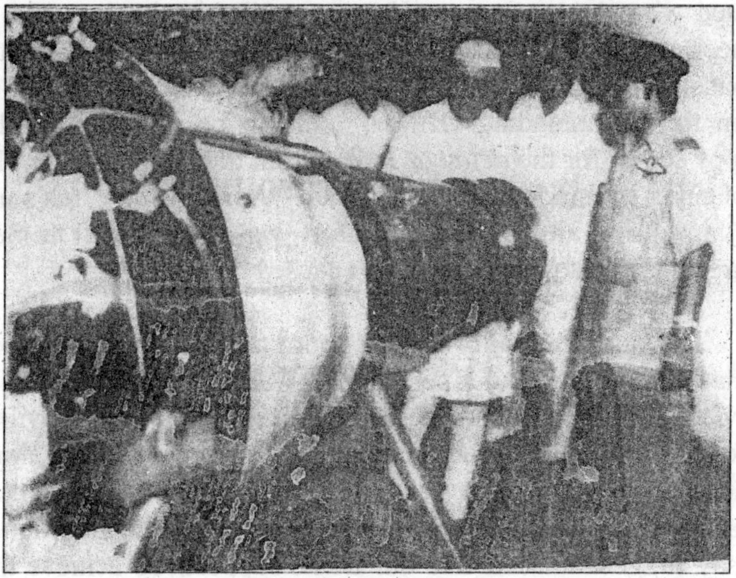

An experimental model of a Gas Turbine engine designed and built for the first time in the country, at No.1 Base Repair Deport, IAF, Kanpur. First run on 4th April, 1961.

Our Chief of Air Staff also visited us, and desired to know whether this could be developed for our jet trainer aircraft.

Moving towards his car to leave, our PM smiled but made no comment. Comments appeared in media, heralding "India can make it". That was perhaps the best and an appropriate one. Because this was made using common purpose machine tools and facilities, when the technicians are not specifically trained for the task. The training was done 'in house'.

The most critical lot was the physicists. A senior scientist came from the CSIR, who had subscribed Rs. 30,000 for research.

He wanted to know whether any scientific break through was achieved. The answer was in the negative; it followed the same continuous combustion cycle as in any gas turbine engine. He was shown a Gobline engine powering the Vampire aircraft. We explained the ingenuity of fabrication. He concluded that it was, in the final analysis, only an "iron mongery", with no new scientific achievement. It was a slightly improved version of Gobline engine with a can annular combustor. That was what he reported to Delhi, and this dampened the initial high spirit. Soon this effort was rated as a copy of Gobline engine.

A foreign journalist came to write about our effort as this was the first made in an underdeveloped country. but was discouraged on two grounds. First, no new science was involved. Secondly, it was a Defence project. His reaction was that all automobile engines following 'Otto cycle' were then 'iron mongery', and wishing us good luck, left.

All together, this activity provided the team, particularly its leader that people of this subcontinent *can achieve much, given an opportunity and encouragement.* And can be ruined too, if unfortunately gets trapped in an egoistic close minded and self centered environment. (More about this phenomenon in PART 3B.). It was realized that the skill needed to make our heritage beautiful edifices with stone material, could equally be diverted working on metals. This exercise proved that an unique character of having both agronomy and industrial cultures, as required, is feasible. Unfortunately, willfully this dual culture was not allowed to grow. *Article 40 of our Constitution provides the unworthy beginning.*

This was great moment in author's life. During the first meeting with Krishna Menon, the author had expressed his apprehension on shortage of trained man power to undertake this work. This got erased out. A genuine faith about the Indian genetic intelligence got imbedded. Not once the author had to ask any to leave the establishment due to incompetence Whenever a report of inefficiency of any reached the author, the search was about his misplaced venue of his work and attempts were made to find appropriate place providing guidance. It was not always smooth sailing. In general, a confidence to establish a Gas Turbine Institute germinated.

There is no inherent justification for becoming a slave subcontinent since 2000 B.C. till 1947 A.D. except that in a country of plenty, peasants did not find any need to resist when robbed. The conveyed massage was 'take what you want, but do not disturb the peaceful life.' This generous attitude made us what we were till 1757 when Mir Jafar was rewarded by the English for his treachery at the battle of Plassey, and made Nawab of Bengal. That was the beginning of our slavery, till 1947. Without a shade of doubt, we have become a weak nation, in all aspects of life, when 800 million rural poor are rated now, as 'they' and not 'us' by the urbanites, living in luxury, making use of migrated rural poor living in slums. An example of this evil may be appropriate. Bangalore is rated as a prosperous city. It has 526 slums, where migrated rural people come and settle; Their living is difficult, but far better than that in most rural areas. There are several Missionary schools, where children could start to learn. Though not free, it is affordable because of near 100 percent employment of parents.

AN EARLY CONFUSED MIND

Author's initiation of life was at the then East Bengal's (now Bangla Desh) prosperous village of Zamindars. There were two well managed schools, separately for boys and girls, only for the children of Zamindars. No children of lower caste were admitted. The author had an opportunity to refer to this unfortunate fact during the centenary celebration of the school. This is recorded in the proceedings published. The lower caste people lived separately. Treatment mated out to lower caste people was uncivilized, and feudal to core. Amazingly, the lower caste people accepted the situation as if it was their fated way of life. Otherwise, life in this village was peaceful and reasonably, progressive. Students from near-by villages used to come to study, found a place, living free, in a Zamindar family. The link with urban society was close when most of the children received higher education in Calcutta (now Kolkata).

Moving to Delhi in 1937 for college education was no hassle. The family had moved to Delhi around the time the British shifted the capital around 1911. Besides, the author's uncle held a rank of Major in military medical services, but resigned, responding to Gandhi's call for non-cooperation. He burnt his uniform. Professionally and also socially, he was a well respected citizen in New Delhi.

A similarity was noticed even in Delhi colleges. There was hardly any Muslim student. There was no Hindu–Muslim divide, in New Delhi, created by the British outside of the walled city of Delhi, now known as Old Delhi. In this part, one finds the heritage of Mogul dynasty's glory. The Hindu - Muslim divide is seen, but there is no conflict. A noticeable fact is these two Muslim dynasties existed in vastly separated lands. Journey from still existing India gate (Darya ganj, leading to Jumma Masjid and Red fort) to Kutab Minor had to be planned, when New Delhi was perched in between. Public transports were few. Horse pulled 'tanga' (cart) was usually the common community conveyance. This was generally used, but buses were plying in specified routes.

Does this separated living not prove that Islamic religion was also not a cohesive force. To begin with, the two streams of Muslims had also fought with each other. Those who came with Arabs were genetically not the same as those who came through Afghan passes. Khan was added to their names. History tells us about Hindu-Muslim marriage in the past and is practiced even now in educated urban societies. Such marriages are registered properly with no hassle.

FORMATION OF GTRE

In Delhi, a tug of war was going on, between the DTDP(AIR) and the DRDO, which was formally created a few years earlier. It took charge of all Defence oriented technology development establishments. They were then headed by the eminent Physicist, Dr. D.S. Kothari, our first Scientific Advisor. He retained his Delhi University post as the Head of the department of physics. Pandit Jawaharlal Nehru invited him to take charge of DRDO, with a symbolic pay of Re 1, essentially allowing him to make use of government facilities; otherwise, he was holding this assignment in a honorary capacity, in fact. The author was known to him, while studying in Delhi. While still in England, he received a letter from him advising to come prepared to establish a *research* center on Gas Turbines, and *not* making a Gas Turbine engine. The very first meeting with our Defence Minister changed the concept when he felt that both should be our goal. He was very empathetic about his view. He expressed that without a hardware in view, research was a rudderless academic activity. Thus GT*R* - *E* replacing '**C**' was a compromise solution of views held by Dr. Kotheri and Krishna Menon. The former wanted to retain 'C'. At that time, 'E' became a symbol of all the DRDO units, and thus 'E' qualified the embryonic formation to be a DRDO unit.

WAR OF ATTRITION

On return from England, the author was first posted to the DTD&P (Air). What narrated above followed an interesting episode. The DTD&P (Air) claimed that all aspects related to research, production, and inspection of aircraft should come under their purview. The author was allotted a room. A person entered, pulled a chair and sat down. With no introduction, he announced that he would be in-charge of all activities of mine. . When asked who he was and whether he was a Gas Turbine technologist, his answer was most perplexing. His reaction was that he had been invited by our DM to come to India from USA to organize Defence Aeronautics. He had seen many 'jet engines' in America, but could not name one. The author declined to report to him and reported to SA. There after we reported to one CCR&D,(Chief Controller of Research & Development). a highly competent Major General, working under SA. At Kanpur, reported to now AVM Harzinder Singh, who took charge of the DTD&P (Air) also. This office was moved to Kanpur. The invited Defence Science organizer also came.

PART - 2

CHAPTER – 9

PRELUDE TO CREATION OF INDIA AND PAKISTAN

The British rule lasting over a period of 200 years, (1757-1947) ended after partitioning this subcontinent in two parts. Common belief is that this happened because of religious conflicts between Hindus and Muslims. This being a defining event, it needs elaboration.

THE REAL ISSUE

The real issue was a fundamental difference between Jinnah and Gandhi on the path to follow to develop the nation. Jinnah (Muslim League) wanted a much greater and disproportionate share on *legislative* power to develop the minorities, - the Muslims and the untouchable '*shudra community*', with an emphasis on education at grass root levels. The author believes that it was the noblest thought if it could be implemented eliminating simultaneously communalism.

Gandhi did not want any differentiation on any ground, and wanted a new world order, following his saintly approach of non-violence and non-cooperation. and fasting to atone the disorder. It was the biggest ever experiment on mankind, needing unadulterated justice to wronged humanity, with no religious bias. He did succeed, but only partially when people like Jinnah stood at the other end. He believed that Gandhian approach was impracticable, and a sin. Such diverse and non-mitigating situation caused gravest harm to the subcontinent. The foreign ruler, supported by a community of weak and feudal corrupt hypocrites, took advantage of such a situation, to meet their ends. Finally, the subcontinent got divided in two parts. To-date about 1000 million illiterate rural poor exists in these two partitioned sovereigns. A third one, Bangladesh, the poorest of the three has surfaced in 1971.

CARNAGE BETWEEN HINDU AND MUSLIM

Jinnah's political life deserves mention at this stage. Could he be held responsible for the initiation of this unprecedented carnage between Hindu and Muslim? This had originated on the 10th December, 1946, suggesting initially as a possible exchange of population on *voluntary basis to provide a separate State for Muslim.* It was an impractical suggestion. So forceful eviction started in Hindu minority rural areas. Hindu, Muslim, Sikhs, and others lived in peace for centuries. The newly inducted concept of Muslims as a different race, and the desire to develop their culture in a separate place changed everything. Jinnah initiated this, when 90% of Muslims were originally Hindus, but adopted new religious faith. What transpired then on, excelled all the inhumanities committed by the British Imperialism. They happened over a period of time. But now this new concept began to spread like wild fire, particularly in Western and Eastern parts, where Muslims were in majority. The *tryst with destiny* sounded hollow.

Gandhi's return to India (January, 1915) coincided with when World War I was declared on 28th July, 1914. At that time, Jinnah was the most prominent leader of Congress. With Gandhi's arrival, Jinnah's ascend to be the leader for the country started to slide down slowly.

At this time, Congress and All-India Muslim League, were jointly demanding self government. In 1916, *Dr. Annie Besant had founded '*Home Rule League*' in Madras. This was accepted nationwide, but she was interned in 1917 because for the first time it was spreading to the mass. Jinnah took over. Released, she became the President of Congress. But soon resigned because she felt that the League, she formed, was getting intervene with religion. . M.M. Malaviya became the President,

*Dr. Annie Besant (1847 – 1933) was an Irish lady who took great interest for the welfare of Indian people. She established the Theosophical Society.

JINNAH – GANDHI

BEGINNING OF DIVERGENT VIEWS.

Under Dr. Besant, with Jinnah as a member, the objective was 'Self government *within* the British Empire'. Gandhi appealed for complete Independence, (*Purna Swaraj*) with no link with Britain. Such divergent views were discussed in a meeting. Jinnah objected stating that the meeting was not the forum to bring about such a change in the constitution of the League. In reply, the Chairman announced that if any member did not agree to such a change, he was free to resign .his membership. Jinnah resigned not only from the League, but also from Congress. He retained his membership with Muslim League. The tide started to change.

Jinnah had practiced law and in his time, he was perhaps one among the most successful ones. He believed in Legislative approach. He felt that autonomy of provinces having Muslim majority with existing boundaries and the country with a Dominion status as adopted for Australia and New Zealand would help to develop the country faster. But the past humiliating atrocities by the British did not carry the conviction. Gadhiji wanted a totally free united India, with his new non-violent social order. So convinced was he, that he did not patronize any other form of approach. Some believe that he has been a *sublime failure*. This is not true.

He achieved a sublime incomplete success of a new approach to humanity. In the changing world order, particularly in developed societies, whom we had started to imitate, Gandhi's saintly non-violent approach with no retaliation to wrong done has resulted into the creation of a noble but a weak nation. We have been so since 1192 when Prithiviraj, the king of the Northern provinces, was defeated by in the second battle of Terrain against Shaihabuddin, the first invading Muslim warrior. Other Hindu Kings did not response to his call to fight together. In fact, his commander-in-Chief was then fighting with another Hindu King! Defeated, he was taken as a prisoner and killed in cold blood. Thus, the sun of Hindu glory was set forever.

The non-cohesive strain and feudal attitude towards the peasants, and lower caste had been the cause for our country's present unacceptable situation. This continues. Prince Albert wrote, after 'Sepoy Mutiny':

The Indians are not a people capable of conquering independence for themselves, to say nothing of maintaining it. Since the days Bacchus and Nimrod, India has constantly been overrun and conquered by new races the Assyrians and Persians, the Greeks under Alexander, the Hiungnu, Tartars, Arabians, and others, down to the most recent times. The conquerors have brought under the yoke and oppressed the races whom they found in possession, but have neither rooted them out nor absorbed them; thus they remain intermingles, but without national coherence.

NEW RISE (Navuday)

SATYAGRAHA APPROACH

The difference between Revolutionary and Gandhi's Satygraha approaches was that while the former was secretive and armed, Gandhi's approach through Satyagrha was with the knowledge of government, and without the use of any arms, or any retaliatory action. Gandhi was more acceptable because our population, except the sepoys, did not know how to use the arms. The peasants did not fully understand the rational behind attacking the *firangies,* (foreign,- English people) when their tormentors were the Zamindars, landlords, and money lenders. The fair skinned *firangies* appeared to be nice smiling kind people. For the villagers, fair skinned people were superior and respectable humanity. In contrast to armed revolution in developed countries, the illiterate peasants were not a part of such revolution, although this was to get them out of their misery from the clutches of these *firangies,* and 'titled' nobles of Indian origin.

COMMUNAL FORCES

Although the nation is torn apart with *communal* religious concept, almost all people of the country are from the same non-ethnic origin. Did Jinnah import Muslims from other Muslim countries to form an Indian Muslim 'race' to claim a separate sovereign state? Did the Christians in India come from different origins? Who are these Hindu priests? Are they separately created by God in a mould, different to lower castes? If so, our priests should appeal to Him to change their defective moulds. Have they not proved themselves as utter fakes predicting great success of individual players and the team during the recent (2007) cricket world cup match? They returned with faces blackened. Yet the priests minted money with much fun fare before the team's departure. Why is it difficult to accept the unquestionable fact that all of us come from the same origin?. Acceptance of a different religious faith does not change the genetic characteristic of a person. No religious doctrine suggests formation of *communal* religious faiths. Yet a Muslim League, a Communal society, was formed in 1906 B.C.

CHAPTER - 10

BRITISH INDIA: THE ILLUSIVE NOBLE CONSTITUTION

While we tend to pass the buck to British rule for our poorly state, can we absolve ourselves from this? An unpleasant but true narration in British press tells, in Annexure 5, what really made the British rule us.

It is due to a combined impact of what stated in Annexure 5, and what narrated hereafter, this noble land is in a mess, It may be pertinent to quote Bertrand Russell, as under, to understand our country's situation.

"Between man and other animals there are various differences, some intellectual, some emotional. One of the chief emotional differences is that some human desires, unlike those of animals, are essentially boundless and incapable of complete satisfaction. Imagination is the goad that forces human beings into restless exertion after their primary needs have been satisfied. To those who have but little of power and glory, it may seem that a little more would satisfy them, but in this they are mistaken: these desires are insatiable and infinite, and only in the infinitude of God could they find response. Of the infinite desires of man, the chief are the desires of power and glory." - BERTRAND RUSSELL - on power

Bertrand Russell's view on Power

Are we victim of what stated above? The Preamble of our Constitution mentions nowhere anything about tolerance or otherwise to any *communal* religious parties. This is reproduced below. Yet the subcontinent has suffered, because of Communal forces, much more than what British Imperialistic rule had inflicted. Perversions to religion, practiced through self centric feudal minded leaders have torn apart the subcontinent, causing untold miseries to rural poor, and currently blissfully inactive towards grave danger, resulting from internal and external forces.

THE CONSTITUTION OF INDIA

PREAMBLE

"WE, THE PEOPLE OF INDIA, having solemnly resolved to constitute India into a [SOVEREIGN SOCIALIST SECULAR DEMOCRATIC REPUBLIC] and to secure to all its citizens:

JUSTICE, social, economic and political;

LIBERTY of thought, expression, belief, faith and worship;

EQUALITY of status and of opportunity;

and to promote among them all

FRATERNITY assuring the dignity of the individual and the [unity and integrity of the Nation];

IN OUR CONSTITUENT ASSEMBLY this twenty-sixth day of November, 1949, do HEREBY ADOPT, ENACT AND GIVE TO OURSELVES THIS CONSTITUTION."

GANDHI'S INDIA

After his arrival from South Africa, Gandhi had no plan in his mind except to serve the society. He was a totally unknown quantity in India, although some had heard about his exploits in South Africa. In India, his political 'Guru' was Gopala Krishna Gokhale, who was also the guiding force to Jinnah. Earlier he had met Gandhi in South Africa. He advised Gandhi to tour India in third class railway compartments, and mix with people with eyes and ears open but mouth shut. This he did faithfully and was appalled, to say the least, what he saw and heard. His mind was now clear.

The name Sathyagraha had it's origin during his struggle

in South Africa, with the same name, an Ashram was located on the bank of Sabarmati in May, 1915. That year G K Gokhale died. Almost in parallel to the revolutionary movement, which had started earlier, Gandhi had launched his freedom fight from this Ashram. The inmates took the vows of truth, ahimsa, celibacy, non-stealing, non-possession and control of the palate. Their sole duty was to do service to the people. While we, in one breath, refer to Gandhi as a saint, he had his inner struggle, on attributes related to a normal human being. His well known experiments, though not normal, to search himself as being a Brahmachari or not, confirms this. His son, Rajmohon Gandhi, described his father as below:

" THE GANDHI YOU MAY NOT KNOW"

Compressed here is the lifelong clash in Gandhi between attachment and detachment. We know what always won, but we do not understand him if we ignore the attachment, or the pain in his struggles to overcome it.

We have glimpsed the rare, but real, Gandhi who enjoyed the small pleasures of life: sailing on the ocean, music, delicious food, the putting together of words, the first-class compartment, a fine bungalow in Santa Cruz, and the company of his wife and children. Also real, of course, was the Gandhi who was a slave to his inner voice, his conscience, his destiny and the people of India."

Source: IIC Quarterly (Autumn 2007)

BRAHMACHARYA (CELIBRACY) GANDHI

Swami Vivekanand, the immortal Brahmacharya, wrote about cardinal guidelines about celibacy to Sister Nivedita, as under;

(a) self imposed self control; (b) control over sexual desire; (c) helping others to reach God; (d) not treating a woman an object of fulfilling sexual need only, but treating her as mother, sister, and friend.

Gandhiji's experimentation on celibacy was related mainly to item (b) only. Details of his experimentation are known, and need no exposition. Going by Vivekanand's norms, Gandhi was not a Brahmacharya. He was a normal human being, fighting simultaneously with himself.

THE CONFLICTING MIND OF THE NOBLE GANDHI

There were two. One, he realized that 'self reliance' at individual level could be a powerful non-violent and non co-operative instrument to fight for freedom. If one becomes self reliant, he was not violating any law. At the same time, freeing from tax payment, these would curtail the Revenue earning of the treasury. The concept of **'Charka'** use originated from such thoughts. This concept spread like wild fire. 'Khadi' use, replacing mill clothes, was easily appealing to the rural mass.

In almost all homes, the use of simple Charka became a symbol of freedom fight. But one needs other ingredients to live. Salt, for example. It was taxed even when poor people made this from sea water or when purchased. In 1917, Gandhi's first major political ploy was to break the salt tax law imposed on poor man for making salt to meet his daily need.

THE OTHER SIDE OF GANDHI'S MIND.

He abhorred the revolutionary movement; did not take stock of the work done by Jinnah to bring about Hindu-Muslim unity for getting the country's freedom; the legislative approach to uplift the minorities,- the Muslims and the large untouchable humanity; a formal legislation to promulgate literacy; restraining child marriage; and so on. Moving further down the memory lane, one recalls about the dismantlement of flourishing cotton industry; the indigo episode; dismembering the weavers; the resulting 22 famines, - all progressively reduced a rich subcontinent to rags. He took no stock of these. He was obsessed with his mental approach.

While unquestionably he was a saintly person, - a like of

his selfless honesty and courage will perhaps not ever be born again, but his apparent desire to emerge as the only leader for the nation, fighting on all fronts, did not address all evils, imposed by foreign rule. The concept of holistic mass based patriotism did not germinate in our still fragmented subcontinent. The illiterate people were 'followers' waiting for Gandhi call! He was a leader for the mass to respond to his call, and not a leader responding to deficiency the mass suffering from.

Gandhi's several acts are beyond comprehension. Jallianwala Bag massacre took place on 13 April, 1919. Gandhi returned from South Africa in January, 1915*. During his non co-operation movement in 1922, a protest procession in the town of Chauri Chaura UP, locked up 22 police men and bunt them alive. As a penance, he decided to starve for a few days. But why, when earliest about 1500 innocent people, women and children were gunned down in Jallianwala Bagh and General Dyer declared Marshal Law. He made people to crawl on belly to cross road, or to reach a destination. Apparently, he undertook this sacred step to atone crime committed by our country men. The author believes that it was a ploy to avoid KALA PANI voyage to Cellular jail, had he supported the retaliary action after Jallia nwala Bag.

Events, which followed, lead to revolutionary Bhagat Singh and his two friends to the gallows. But Gandhi did not try to fight their case, as a lawyer, nor expressed any regret. A just conclusion may be that this amounted to giving consent to wrong judgment, by the British rule, when they did not kill or murder any. They had only protested against the innocent killings. The paradox is, this assemblage was initially to express wrong being done to their revered leader, Gandhi.

* The exact date of his return is not uniformly quoted. Gandhi sailed from England, not SA, and reached India in January, 1915.

Gandhi lived, while in Delhi, either in Birla House, or in Bhanghi (Scavenger) colony at Reading Rod (now Mandir Marg).

He used to conduct prayer meetings at both these places. His living at Bhangi (scavenger) colony might have been to convey through his personal example, the irrational concept of untouchable 'shudra' caste. On few occasions when the author had attended these prayer meetings, accompanying his mother, he did not understand why no word of condemnation the hereditary Brahmanical religious system, which had created the despicable 'untouchable' shudra caste was uttered.

All that was done, he gave a new name to 'shudra's – Harijan, children of God. Are we all not? He elevated himself in the society, but did nothing to solve their real social and economic problems. During the prayer meetings, some would recite Suras from Quran. That had made some unhappy. Gandhi sang, "Ishwar Allah tere nam, Sobko sanmati de Bhagban……." But did such Bhajans moved Bhagban? Did the Hindu Muslim divide got eliminated?

Since the reason for the ailment was not eliminated, it is surfacing all over again, but in more harmful ways, It has become a political weapon. Two issues need mention. Gandhi had lived with rich Muslims and institutions. He stayed in the house of Maulana Muhammad Ali Jauhar (1924) and Agha Khan Palaces. In Delhi, he stayed at Birla house. But did he ever stayed in a poor Muslim house except once when he returned from Noakali carnage in 1946? Did he do that because of a fear about his safety?.

Other than Gandhi's dedication for Hindu – Muslim unity through his bhajan singing, he paid little attention to several social evils. They were no less important. He was a Hindu and read Gita almost every day. Was he not aware of perversions of his religion? Did he try to rectify them? Could it be that he did not want to upset Hindus, who were sold to perverted Brahmanic religion and become unpopular?

Hinduism was a highly knowledge based religion, yet now most perverted business oriented cult practiced by the Brahman priests. They became the embodiment of vices. ***Pranamis*** (money offered after the Puja), or ***Dakshina*** are essential parts of Brahmanic religion. Heftier the ***Pranamis,*** the greater is the God's blessings!. Poor untouchable 'shudras', incapable of offering ***Pranamis*** are not entitled for God's blessing, and therefore, not allowed to enter most temples. We all know whom ***Devdasies*** serve. Have we been able to abolish this perverted practice? We hold Seminars, of course, to high light this evil practice, and conclude with a customary valedictory address, which media publishes. ***Devdasies*** continue their services, to earn their living. Budhism and Jainism appeared because of superstitions and often immoral acts of Brahmanas. Although originated in our country, Buddhism (544 - 487 B.C) could not get a mooring here, essentially because of resistance offered by the priests. It could not spread in the Western countries, because of their own established religions. Buddhism is accepted extensively in the East Asian countries. China, Tibet, Japan, Thailand, Korea, Sri Lánka, Thailand, Myanmar, Singapore, and Indonesia.

The total absence of cleanliness and the accompanying noise at religious places where Hinduism is practiced are appalling. They are similar to market places; having middleman (priest) between the worshipping man and God. Even in Malaysia, - a predominantly Muslim country, going to a Budhist monastery is an unforgettable experience. Not only the peaceful ambience, all with no religion or caste bias, pick up a lighted candle and place at the alter, and quietly meditate, in pin drop silence. Can we compare this with ours? There is one place in India, which is comparable. Sri Aurabindo-ashram in Pondicherry provided a similar ambience.

One learnt that meditation is not a religious practice. It is a cult of searching mind, when the ***mantra*** is one; asking on any issue continuously **WHY** till no further answer was forthcoming except that of the Creator, - God. For such meditation, a quiet ambient is needed. One can realize the virtue of meditation when one tries and realizes that it is virtually impossible to stay on an issue when diverse factors distract the mind. Our ***rishies*** had gone ***to*** hills to meditate.

We have made our **'Dev-Stans'** as **'Pap Stanams'** (We have converted a sacred place into one of vice). The degradation is not limited to Hinduism only. Some one has recently remarked that there are two versions of Koran. One by Mohammad, other by the Mollahas. Christianity also suffered from aberrations, similar to Devdasi, yet it looks down upon other religions. But this book does not find a need to elaborate them when these are similarly exploitive in nature. The common fact is these practices results mainly because of poverty, illiteracy, and feudal perverts.

Gandhi Vs Jinnah

One of the two basic differences between Jinnah and Gandhi had been on the neglect of literacy of the rural poor. Jinnah retained his unwavering faith on ***Gokhale's Elementry Education bill.*** During a debate on Elementary Education bill at an Imperial Legislative Council meeting, in April, 1912, Jinnah's submission was, 'I ask, is it such an insurmountable difficulty to get three crores of rupees from the Imperial Exchequer? Is it such a great, gigantic feat to be performed for a country like India, with its three hundred millions of people? I say, Sir, that there is nothing in that argument. I ask the Government, I say "find the money- if necessary, tax the people. "But I shall be told that the people are already taxed; I shall be told that we shall be facing great unpopularity.... My answer is that you must remove the reproach that is justly leveled against British rule, namely, the neglect of elementary education. My answer is that it is the duty of every civilized Government to educate masses, and if you have to face unpopularity, if you have to face a certain amount of danger, face it boldly in the name of duty.....'

Gandhi continued his struggle to make India an Independent nation. But his dismal effort towards literacy is puzzling. What good is it to have an illiterate Independent subcontinent singing Bhajan during prayer meetings? Simultaneous to his struggle for freedom, should he not have placed an equal importance towards literacy and elimination of castes system? Are we not victim of such neglects?

The other was on Jinnah's demand on ***Legislative*** acceptance of the rights of the minorities. The author believes that so long the illiteracy and Communal forces are not Constitutionally (and hence legislatively) eliminated, both were anti-social and anti-national approaches. Secularism has NO relationship with Communal religious concept. If one cares to look into any Dictionary, the misconception will be removed.

Secularism has nothing to do with religion. But we grossly misinterpret this word. It means 'not subject to or bound by ***religious*** **rule**'. Our country, with so many religion, the only salvation is to believe in ***one God, one law and literacy for all*** Our Constitution should make this as the preamble replacing the present one At the same time make it clear that citizen can choose any religion to suit his faith.

The Dominant Mind of Gandhi

Even to-day several wonder whether it was proper for Gandhi to publicly announce, after Subhas Chandra Bose's win over Pattavi Sitaramaiah, as ***his*** defeat in general election for the Presidency of Congress for the second time. Did this not amount to telling the electorate that Subhas's 'direct action' approach to throw out the British was against his wish and improper?

Although hardly anything is currently talked or written about him, he was a young rising force, with tremendous mass appeal. He was elected twice in consecutive years since 1939 as President of Indian national Congress. He did not believe in Gandhian approach.

Born in one of the most respected and rich family in Calcutta (now Kolkata) he had a brilliant Academic career, stood third through open competition to be an ICS (Indian Civil Service)

officer, the .most coveted administrative post during British Raj.

But he resigned within a year the appointment and took a deep plunge in political movement carrying with him the humiliated Indian mass, impoverished by the British robbers. He did not pussyfoot his intention. He formed 'Forward Bock' within Congress in May 1939. He believed in direct action. His sole dream was to throw out the British from Indian soil. He was imprisoned, - as 'house arrest'. There was no protest from Gandhi inspite of his election as President by the members of Congress on two consecutive occasions.

SUBASH CHANDRA BOSE

This could have been the preparatory phase to send him to

Cellular jail in Andaman and get rid of him permanently. out of the way of Gandhian non-violent approach, which he openly disagreed with. He was a clever man. He knew what was being cooked for his disagreement with Gandhi

A new phase of his career began. He escaped on 17.01.1941 from his heavily guarded Elgin Road Residence, in Calcutta. He did not escape out of fear. He wanted to get the country free with the might of the country's mass. He knew that he would not get any support from Gandhi or Nehru. At that, stage there was no love lost between Nehru and Subash Bose. He took an extremely arduous route - through Kabul, Germany (where he met Hitler), Russia, and Bali. He reached Japan sailing in a submarine. He formed Indian National Army (INA) at Malaya, with a separate entity. Jai Hind was their slogan. It continues to be ours even now, slowly dying down. Japanese Army was then a powerful ally of the winning Axis power and wanted INA to merge with them, but he refused. Subash Bose's scheme was to march into India, along the Japanese Army, but not allowing them to replace the British Imperialism. Two events brought an end to such designs. Japan surrendered to Allied Forces after two atomic bomb attacks on the 6th and 9th August, 1945. These bombs were dropped at Hiroshima and Nagasakhi. Subash Bose's fatal accident soon after, on the 18th August, 1945 in an (controversial) air crash at Tyhoku, Japan., lead to INA's surrender to the British. It was disbanded.

The INA officers were tried for treason at the Red fort, Delhi. `There was wide spread protests against this decision. Pandit Jawaharlal Nehru defended the INA officers, and got them released. They were accepted as nation's heroes. It is difficult to predict what would have been country's situation if Subash Bose had not died. One possibility can be guessed. The country would not have the cancer of 'Kashmir issue', the sole cause for the country's current dismal financial and rural situation. What motivated him to flee from his own country, and create an Army in a foreign land to fight for his country's freedom, when the people of his country were with him?

CONFUSING ACT OF PANDIT JAWAHARLAL NERU

There are several views, particularly when Pandit Jawaharlal Nehru rushed to USSR soon after the crash. Why to USSR and not to the site of accident in Japan, taking help of USA? Is it not a common practice to rush to the site of accident? Why Russia instead? If Subash Bose had succeeded in his mission, whom would he have fought with? If he was successful, the author believes that inmates of Cellular jail would have been freed, and the English people would have replaced those inside.

Could it be Bose's house arrest had a tacit support from within? If he was allowed to continue, as the electorates had desired, the history of this subcontinent would have been totally different today. One should not doubt this possibility, when he could raise an Army in foreign land to fight the British in India. With support from Indian population, who had earlier elected him, he would have liberated India, with strength, and not as a benevolent grant of the foreign ruler. They not only had sucked the country, evil minds had germinated to create difficulties for the starving poor, and implanted deep rooted Hindu–Muslim divide. Super imposed we have become a feudal hypocritical society. Although the English rulers have left 61 years ago, they left a legacy, which is making the country's rural people poorer. The expenditure on 'Kashmir issue' is perhaps about the same as the British rule was robbing. Adding to this the corruption, one may conclude that per capita earning, at 1947 cost, of the rural people are now less, and suffering from depleted dietary needs.

JAWAHARLAL NEHRU

Jawaharlal Nehru had returned a few years earlier, in 1912, met Gandhi for the first time in 1916 during Lucknow Congress session. Both got involved with Indian politics ***after*** the first freedom fight of 1857. One can see there was a tremendous backlog they had to cover and set right. They were culturally different, and spent their times differently while in prison. Nehru devoted his time in reading and writing. His three books, - ***Glimpses of World History, The discovery of India, and his***

Autobiography are rated as classics; yet he was humble enough to write to his daughter on one occasion that he was a poor writer. That he was not is seen from the fact that all of them have been repeatedly printed (Editions); - 20 times or more. How few of our claimed 'best sellers' (claimed in small print) have even one reprint? Some claim this even before any could read the very fist sentence.

Gandhi spent his time studying and praying. And to learn how to be self reliant. He made a pair of sandals (Chappals) for General Smuts,(then Governor of South Africa and of Black Act notoriety) as a gift, which the General appreciated after 25 years use, stating that he felt not worthy to stand in the shoes of so great a man. He devoted his time operating Charka, reading Gita, and teaching Satyagraha to his prison inmates.

Gandhi's main preoccupation was, however, ***Hindu - Muslim unity*** to build a unified nation. One may summarize that the basic difference between the armed revolutionary and Satyagraha movements was that the former had placed the primary importance to get rid of British Imperialism fighting with force, Gandhi's weapon was through non-violence, non co-operation and non-retaliation. After salt tax episode and 1942 non-co-operation movement, the British ruler had no doubt that Gandhi had the country's people behind him. He was the shepherd who could direct the peasants the way he wanted. Even the students of academic institutions were in support of the movement. Unarmed they could stall the entire administration, as they did in 1942 movement. The British rule realized that the only way such movement could be made ineffective was to wedge the Muslims in between. This divides and rule approach worked. Hindu-Muslim conflicts became the routine of the national life. In the meantime, the Congress party started taking sides. There were moderates and extremists.

Jawaharlal Nehru had an altogether different background. Son of a famous and an affluent lawyer Motilal Nehru, he went to England in 1905 and admitted in famous public school at Harrow. After completing his studies at Trinity, Cambridge, and law, he returned to India in 1912. During his stay in England, he was greatly influenced by socialistic ideas; particularly by Bernard Shaw and Bertrand Russell. He had kept in touch with the happenings in India through his father, Motilal Nehru, who was an affluent lawyer and also a prominent leader opposed to English tyranny.

The exposures of Nehru and Gandhi were widely different. First, Gandhi took to studies not only the Gita (the translated version by Sir Edwin Arnold), he studied similarly Bible, Buddha's life, and chapters of Koran. Hinduism is an evolutionary religion when the earlier concept of worshipping individually the elements of God got merged with Aryan concept of Homa. The Vedic and the derivative Rig-Veda religion provide some idea about Hindu's very early concept of religion. (1500 B.C.) There were no prophets. Nehru was not overzealous about religion. His affiliation with religion did not go beyond his association of Gandhi.

Born to a Kashmiri family on November 14, 1889, in Allahabad, Nehru's religious leaning was never clear. One does not know whether he was an atheist. Gandhi was a Hindu, by birth, but he abhorred the caste system. Yet never rebelled against this publicly. He was also an atheist, in spirit, if one accepts that he believed that all religion is the same. There was an unity of minds between the two on one main issue; - to get the country's freedom out of the clutches of the most heinous and treacherous approach of British Imperialism. *Both were against revolutionary approach,* which was gathering momentum.

The British had persisted on two basic strategies. The first is the means to achieve the second. This was created through separate administrative bias between Hindus and Muslims communities, later receiving special privileges. Gandhi had been making untiring efforts to bring about harmony among the country men, regardless of their religions. This 'tug of war' was won by the British, because of aloofness of the Muslims to Gandhi's efforts, and the assistance received from the Princes, Zamindars, landlords who controlled the peasants.

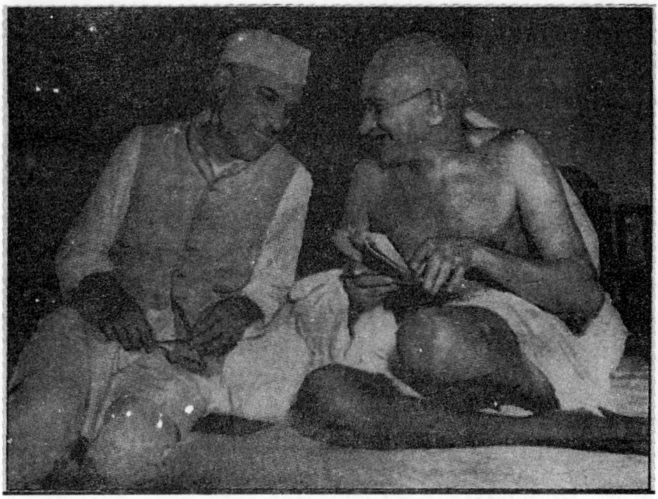

Nehru with Gandhi

ABSENCE OF MASS MOVEMENT

Though Nehru was wholly dedicated for the country's freedom, his approach was not directed towards getting freedom through country's mass movement. This became more apparent in the post Independence era. His long period of education abroad had created a mind for an Universal approach towards freedom of underdeveloped societies of the world. Gandhi's priority was wholly India-centric.

Nehru, like Gandhi, was stickler about cleanliness. He disliked Congress sessions, more for the unclean habits of the most congress members than their rudderless agendas. If India excels any other country, it is for it's unclean habits. Spitting anywhere, committing nuisance in public view, throwing rapping materials, cigarette buds, and washing trucks, cleaning clothes with detergents and taking bath in the same pond; - name anything which is highly punishable in a developed society is done in our country, as a perk of becoming a 'free sovereign (not Democratic) state of the people.'

There is sarcastic view about India. Here adults cannot even peck or sit close in public, but can commit all kinds of nuisance; whereas in the USA, the UK, or in any developed country, you can even kiss in public, but committing nuisance will attract heavy penalty. The moral guardians of our society believe that the concept of morality is incased below the waist, not above. Did not Gandhi try to prove himself following this dictum when he tried to prove about his being a true 'Brahmachari'? Yet the origin of all kinds of immorality originates from the top of our waist. Why not pay primary attention on the development of that through literacy, education and teaching?

NATIONAL FREEDOM STRUGGLE

Jinnah had differed with Gandhi on the basic approach to attain country's freedom. He believed in Constitutional approach. He had firmly believed that emancipation of the nation could only come through education. and maintained that merely singing prayer songs, and arousing their sentiments to take view on such an important issue was improper.

REFERENDUM

(A direct vote by the electorate of a country for a single political issue – Oxford Dictionary)

Even to this day, it is not clear to the author why the citizen of the nation was not taken in confidence about the proposed partition, making it clear that no decision would be taken without their consent. A system could have been evolved making it clear that partition might amount to eviction permanently from their legally owned homes, and going to unknown destinations with no guarantees on any aspect. But the call for a referendum needed simultaneous warning that any leader or any citizen of any hue opposing the *referendum,* would be dealt with severely. But who could issue such an order except Mountbatten? But how could he? The dictate on partition was issued abiding by the British Imperialistic ruler's decision on partition worded in such a manner that Hindu Muslim conflict would unavoidably result. But were they not compelled to take this decision, when the situation was getting worse by day, patronized by selfish evil minds.

Now Hindus and Muslims were trying to create their respective separate regions. Our previous three freedom fights did not involve the women. But referendum would have been involved the housewives, the children, aged parents, their land, business (and their domesticated loving animals). Now all would have involved. Congress members did not represent them. If a referendum, as stated above, was done then only Jinnah, his sycophants, and 99 political leaders of the Indian national Congress would have signed in favour of partition. The rest, without a shade of doubt, would have trampled it.

Ignoring the first freedom fight, which was against foreign aggressors, the fight for abolition of salt tax, or quit India did not involve the domestic lives of the freedom fighters directly. Partition invaded grievously the legal rights of individuals, which the English rulers must have given them. Were British Imperialistic rules for stray dogs? Was there no land occupation law? How could they then collect tax, through their employed agents?

Gandhi, Pandit Nehru, and Jinnah, in particular, were prominent lawyers. Could they not raise the legal issue of eviction when the first announcement on partition was made by Lord Mountbatten? They were far too busy to remain as revered leaders of the people! Were they not concerned about the plight of people, when Indian national Congress voted in favour of partition? Did the 99 Congress members who voted in favour of partition told about their consent for this to their family members?

The decision on partition was taken by 25 % MEN and not the other 75 % of the country's population. Krishna Menon used to say, 'a Sardar with all his ferocious looking 'manes' on his chin, roars like a lion outside, but when he returns home, he becomes a pussy cat .in front of 'Sardarni'. The surprising fact is on such an important issue, they kept women in dark. The decision on partition came as a holocaust. A referendum would have quenched it if the voice of women folk was sought for. A village woman would have barked and told her man "go to hell. This is my legal fortress. Don't dare to touch this unless prior arrangements on all aspects are made to their satisfaction." The puzzling fact is, why Gandhi did not think of asking Jinnah, Pandit Nehru, and Lord Mountbatten to hold referendum, before partition. What made Gandhi to confess to Louis Fisher that he was a 'spent bullet'? As a man of apostle of courage, what prevented him to let people know that he had requested for referendum before rushing to Noakhali to bring harmony there? What happened to his noble weapon of fasting for the people of the country? What prevented him to tell Mountbatten that unless the referendum was called, he would fast till death. When he was making such noble overtures to bring about harmony between Hindu and Muslim, why he could not tell that only after getting answers, the decision on partition would be effective, responding to peoples will. The nation had responded to his call for 'Quit India'. Could he not just ***inform*** the nation about the intended decision on partition, and possible consequences. The 'naked fakir' did not have to even make this a political issue, when it was not. It was a human issue related to women, children, old and domesticated animals. The situation then was aptly described as under.

Referendum would have saved the nation from having millions of hungry people. Can anybody guess how much money could have saved if there no 'Kashmir issue' and utilized to develop the rural society?

INDIAN NATIONAL ARMY (INA)

INA force was knocking at the Eastern door of this subcontinent. The British realized that defending this subcontinent would not be possible when the support from the local people would not be there. FDR (Franklin Delano Roosevelt) had been asking Churchill to liberate India, when he was making overtures to involve USA in the war in 1942. British government had been considering liberation since 1943. It had decided to liberate this subcontinent in 1945, well before 6th and 9th August, 1945, when the war ended, because of two atom bombs dropped in Japan on those two days.

Our leaders believed, and continued to believe that the nation belongs to them only. Each of them had started dreaming to become the 'King', or the No1 man of the liberated subcontinent, or a part of it. It was never a county of the people. Their possible sufferings were of least concern to the leaders. The Congress, a political party, had voted in favour of partition, little realizing that it was not a political issue. How a political party could decide on behalf of those when they were not even remotely associated with politics. The subcontinent became a venue of massacre of hundreds of thousands of people, uprooted and caused miseries to even more. Modifying the oft quoted Churchill's speech after WW II, one may say 'never in the field of human conflict was so much suffering to so many for the benefit of so few' .as happened during partition of this subcontinent, apparently because of difference on religions. There were several vested interests. Several fingers were in the pie. The result of their immature minds is writ large till the citizen of the divided subcontinents destroy themselves as slaves all over again. As matters stand, one should not dispel the possibility, when surrounded by Chinese through allies on all fronts.

Why Mountbatten had to go to Churchill, before coming to India, is not understood. At that time, Labour party, and not Conservative party was in power. He might have gone to his old 'boss' to pay respects. Churchill was the first Lord of Admiralty in 1939. Would not Churchill's briefing have been more appropriate advising Mountbatten to ensure that the country, which they had ruled for about 200 years and prospered, would live now in peace and prosper too. Or, could it be to work out a plan to get back the goose laying golden egg, after partition through the assistance of Jinnah, or Nehru as he would consider appropriate? The British did not come to rule with a missionary zeal, but a benevolent wish, at the final stage, would have been a good strategy keeping a good relationship with the subcontinent. The English left without a scratch, inspite of what happened on earlier occasions and partition. Gandhi admired the English people. His long association (1888 -1915) with them only, in England and South Africa, in one form or the other, developed a love hate relationship. He had said on many occasions that his fight was against the British rule in India, but not against the English people. His expressed view is shared by most in India. Are not the immigrated Indian people doing well in the UK.? No Hindu will like to go or settle in Pakistan, or in Bangladesh, except for business purposes. The divide between rich and poor in India has it's origin since Aryan days of about 1900 B.C. This divide has continued even now. The British exploited this situation, at times brutally, when our people helped them. The British came for trade. We made them our brute ruler and also benevolent friend for the country's good, but retaining their country's interest supreme.

From the above, it is clear that our political parties did not want a referendum to decide on partition. Jinnah had felt that a decree on divide should be issued first, retaining the existing formally accepted boundaries of the provinces. Feeling that if so done, the '*aam admi' (the common man)* would not be disturbed. The only change would be in the governance systems. He believed that the governance of TWO newly formed federations would be able to take care of the minorities. He just did not believe that an overwhelming Hindu majority would take care of the minority, when they had created *untouchable shudras*, defying humanism. The partition was done with feudal minds of a few more to satisfy their self interests than getting people of the country free from the yoke of humiliating foreign rules.

The author believes that the parting of ways came about more because of total lack of confidence Jinnah had on higher caste Hindus' towards the poor under developed Muslims, and the lower caste shudras. Their wellbeing and development to be equal would not go beyond cosmetic platitudes. Like English people, the higher caste felt that they were inferior and not worth bothering about. Jinnah was a very clever, ambitious, and clear headed man. When he was a member of both Congress and Muslim League, he tabled several proposals to bring about

Hindu-Muslim unity, and elementary education. But they received poor response from Congress. He realized that with massive Hindu majority, he would have to curtail his ambition to become a top leader in an united Indian subcontinent. He resigned from Congress.

These two stalwarts desired to achieve the same end, but in two different ways. Jinnah wanted the economically weaker minority people, - the Muslims and the untouchables, - to progress at their own will, efforts and with *constitutional* rights separately. Gandhi, on the other hand, wanted to take a holistic view, giving priority to unification of Hindus, Muslims, and shudras (Harijans, he renamed them), cleaning the minds of people, holding prayer meetings, singing devotional songs, and on occasions of conflicts, taking recourse to fasting to atone for any crime committed to and by others. Words of wisdom were plenty, but no clear directive to do anything to develop the society could be grasped. It was like going to temple, pray and come away hoping God will do the needful. In a way, Gandhi became the Pole star of the nation. He was a saint and a politician rolled into one. He was holding parlors with the highest authorities, all political parties, for the country's freedom, and simultaneously teaching the poor, to be self-reliant, which would not attract taxation. The great 'Charka' movement was one such. His defiance on 'salt tax' and production of clothes with self spun cotton threads were brilliant moves of passive resistance to foreign rules. But labour hour produced low cost items. There were several other activities needed attention. 'Khadhi' to-day is not what Gandhi had initially conceived for. Could it be that the literacy became a victim as a result of his initial concept. Gandhi exhibited little interest on this, even for his own eldest son. When he requested for permission to go to school, he preferred his son to go for vocational training instead. The life of his eldest son is not worth recalling.

THE ROOT CAUSE OF PARTITION

Gandhi's approach should have placed a primary importance to teach people about the ramification of partition.

The biggest crime, which had been committed, was /is not realizing that a nation is not a property of a few politicians. The issues are not political. They are related to the needs of the people. If Jinnah's faith on taking care of well-being of the poor minorities through TWO appropriate governances was to be accepted, Gandhiji asked why not through appropriate representations in ONE NATION's government? Jinnah, based on his past experience, believed that with a vast majority of Hindus, the minority which included also the large community of 'untouchables', would not get the required thrust for their development. The freedom struggle should have embraced *all, and not a few politicians.* With no priority in this direction, Gandhi's efforts over the years to bring about Hindu-Muslim harmony had been a meaningless exercise. His prayer song, "Ishwar Alla there nam, ..." which the country still sings on special occasions, has not produced any worthwhile result. The literacy and collective performance should have been our goal, not singing 'bhajan' led by a priest, and having 'sumptuous prasadams' there after.

Our urban society has learnt this, and moving ahead with education, and performance. This culture has to be ingrained in rural society as well, through literacy and developing two sides of a rural coin. The nation is presently in an unacceptable situation because the nation has retained the age old strain of illiteracy, perverted religion and Rich and poor divide. The text of this book deals with both sides of this coin in two different Chapters, since Independence. Agronomy and non-agronomical related issues.

The ruling prime minister, Churchill had realized the need to divide people, and made little effort to suppress the on going internal conflicts in the country. In fact, the British encouraged this with a noble face expressing that they did not want to get involved with local religious faiths. He knew what a partition of a non-defined non-homogenous community would result. The partition verdict was a generalized one, stating that Muslim should have separate regions to live. Were there any regions where Muslims were living separately? Did not the British see the obvious impracticality of their verdict, or was it a willful move to bring about a turmoil within the subcontinent, so that they could continue? Three leaderships with divergent approaches created what British Imperialism desired before leaving the country, placing Jinnah in the centre stage although he represented then only about 14 percent of our country's population, following Islamic religion. Gandhi tried his best to get Jinnah off his meaningless stand of Muslim as a different race. He met him 20 times but did not succeed.

There was some compulsions, which is apparent from Mountbatten's regret on Jinnah's demise. He had stated that if he had known that Jinnah would die in X months' time, he would not have partitioned the country. For him Jinnah was the Muslim community. Indeed he was, as Gandhi was for the country.

Gandhi could not sit idle watching the rapidly deteriorating situation of the country. He wanted to meet the Viceroy, but Lord Wavell declined to meet him. He knew that British were encouraging 14 % (approx.) Muslim's demand mainly to keep the Hindu and Muslim divided. This was the ploy for their desire to continue ruling of India now as before.

The nation's milk is not split because of religion. It was a chess game of individuals, high power politics and ambition. The rural poor peasants had no part to play. They were mere pawns. There is a divide in Christianity too in England, and conflicts between them was not uncommon. Supposing the Monarchy announced that Roman Catholics and Protestants should live in separate regions, would that not evoke a delirious laughter in their country? But nothing of that sort happened in India. Why?

Why did Gandhi not call for a referendum, similar to what he did in 1942, when the British announced the country as a belligerent nation, during WW II (World War II) without consulting people of the country? Was the proposal of partitioning of the subcontinent of any lesser indignity to the people of this country?. If the people of the country were told ***before*** partition, explaining what this implied, the country would have voted out the partition proposal. Admittedly the possible outcome, which had resulted due to partition, as stated below, could not have been predicted preciously, but an approximate estimate was possible, and this could have been made known to people.

The only person who could have done this, at that stage was Gandhi. That he did not consider as a necessity though baffling, had a justification. Jinnah had issued a call for all Muslims to launch "Direct Action" on 16 August, 1946. Jinnah was not happy about the manner the partition was to be implemented. The threat of "Direct Action" has been conceived since 1935. Now it was actually put into practice. It was a call for 'Strikes and Protest', as was done during 'Quit India' movement, which proved the nation's aspiration for freedom, even though, Muslim League did not participate. There was no violence then. But the call for 'Direct Action' generated this with such ferocity that the history of mankind will recall and write about it till posterity. Gandhi set up a camp in Noakali, the epicenter of violence, with just three persons: self, a stenographer, and a helper. He refused any police help, and walked, mostly bare foot on unprepared grounds, door to door to suppress the violence. He was 77 years old then.

Gandhi on his six month's tour visited 49 villages to quell communal rioting. If only he had called for a referendum, soon after Lord Mountbatten's announcement, his tour would have been far more effective, perhaps not needing. But could he single handed save the situation? His nominated heir apparent, Pandit Nehru of the national congress and Muslim League supporting the partition, he was helpless. He returned to Birla House, New Delhi, sick and tired to the extent that his life was endangered.

The carnage began at Noakhali where 80 percent of the people were Muslims. They started killing Hindus and outraged the modesty of women. In Orissa particularly the Hindu majority retaliated and began similar act. The scene moved to Barisal in

East Bengal. Now it was the Muslim's turn to take revenge. And finally the unimaginable carnage of brutality took place at Calcutta, when it was just recovering from 1943 famine. Almost simultaneously the same was happening in Punjab.

The people were compelled to vacate. In Punjab, an order was issued that they could carry with them only some clothes and nothing else. The trains were full, and people including mothers and young children started walking towards an unknown destiny of safety. A call for referendum from Gandhi was the only alternative to save these massacres. It had to be an unlawful call. But had not been his earlier freedom fight calls unlawful?.

AUTHOR'S PERSONAL EXPERIENCE

To rescue some close (mother's) relatives, the author had gone to Calcutta. They lived near Science college, (near Manicktola area) where savagery was at it's peak. The jeep could not move unless it had gone over the dead bodies thrown on the road. This area was known to the author. Ventured to march down in uniform, when the holster with a service revolver was visibly secured around the west. (The author had good training on small arm's use during his Infantry training at OTS, Bangalore).

This heroic jester was a wasted effort, because there was no body in the house. There was no one in the lane either to make an enquiry. The main road itself had only a few people moving about. Returned to Barrackpore, got a lift in a Dakota aircraft, to get back to Delhi. Sitting on a bucket seat, head dropped between two open palms. Recalled infantry training which taught never to be overwhelmed. But could not help wondering how this country, with so many religions and Gods, did not wake up to save the innocents including children. Some were chucked out from the roof, some thrown into hot oil. Women raped, and forced to marry the Muslims. Men were converted. What crime did these dead, - men, women and children commit! Where was God! Where were those wise men who told us that 'God is within man and man is with in God' The mind strayed back to Jallianwala Bagh.

Did not realize that a little over three hours had lapsed. Landing in Delhi reported the safety (assumed) of the relatives!. The neighbouring locality of Paharganj, bordering New Delhi, was in flame. From 'Gole Market', one could see huge smoke belching out. My uncle, a prominent physician, had transported a few Muslim families at early hours to 'Purana Qilla' (old fort), where a 'refugee' camp for Muslims was established.

There are several who believes that a call for referendum *before* would have brought Hindu and Muslim closer, when they would have realized that partition would mean uprooting their homes and every other things. In any case, it could not have been any worse than what narrated below. With partition, he did not succeed, nor that of Jinnah's who wanted to be the eventual ruler of the subcontinent. For the British the only option was to accept partition, when these two parties could not reconcile on any issue.

Due to partition, the generally accepted happenings were as under.

1. Ten million (100 lakh) people rendered homeless;
2. Twenty million (200 lakh) Hindus left West Punjab and East Bengal migrated to India; and eighteen million Muslims to Pakistan;
3. Half a million (50 lakh) people lost their lives;
4. 22,000 women were raped;
5. 220,000 people were declared missing

Were Hindu and Muslim that bitter against each other in 1946 that a call for referendum to consider partition would have resulted a greater calamity?. Even if a part of the above possible suffering was made known to people, a loud unified voice would have ranted through out the nation rejecting the absurd partition proposal. Was there any attempt made to let people know what was cooking for their future?

A typical scene of exoduses due to partition

Leadership carries a responsibility, other than receiving adulation, garlands, and princely living for most. They were playing with the lives of rural poor people. These people produce food for us to live, toiling hard on land. They save the country during war, and then, when the leadership makes plans to cause untold hardship to them, was this not a betrayal to the people of this country? Why was this possibility kept in a wrap as a secret from the people of the country? Absurdity of voluntary exchange of people, as was initially suggested by Jinnah, was talked about in high quarter, but the issue was not seriously considered. If the British were inhumane, our leaders were not any less to impose partition, without a referendum. Why our media kept mum before the partition? Did they support this too?.

That the partition would not have happened, if a referendum had a precondition that this would depend on the emerged will expressed by the nation. Partition without referendum was a political blunder of the highest order, to say the least. This is clearly seen from the current event when attempts are being made to uproot peasants from Nandigram, an unknown village, in West Bengal. Unfortunately our leaders felt that they were feudal kings, and the rest were their slaves, and could be ordered about as they wished. This is evident when partition was imposed on people without consulting them.

Nehru was already cleared by Gandhi to be his heir-apparent and the first prime minister of free India. This was done when partition was not in view. Gandhi, in his effort to avoid partition, offered Jinnah to be the first prime minister of undivided India. Jinnah declined. Although we make much noise about this noble offer, but Jinnah was wise enough to realize that Gandhi's nobility would hold no water in the parliamentary system being worked upon.

Jinnah would have faced 'no confidence motion' on the second day and lost, with humiliation. Whether Gandhi's offer to Jinnah was made with the consent of Nehru is not known. If this offer had the support of Nehru, it was of national importance. Earlier, partition proposal had the approval of both Nehru and Jinnah, after several deliberations. Gandhi's offer to Jinnah without Nehru's consent can at best be an emotional outburst to find a way out to achieve his mission, - Hindu Muslim Unity. Nothing more should be read, as commonly done.

In summary, the primary causes of such a catastrophic event are two:

1. Jinnah, heading Muslim League wanted *separate* electorate, while Nehru report wanted *joint* electorate. How could there be separate electorate for Muslim, when congress had many Muslim members, some were highly revered in the society for their eminence in knowledge and freedom fights. AICC had six revered Muslims as its president. Maulana Abdul Kalam Azad was it President for a record period of six years (1940 – 1946), which was the crucial period of our freedom fight. Normally Presidency is contested every year. Nehru had been President on nine occasions. How can any sane person accept a view that all Muslims were members of Muslim League. It was a political party, like AICC. They were not statutory bodies. Jinnah, with 11% Muslims as members of Muslim League wanted 30% share of legislative power. Nehru believed that this power should be

proportional to percentage of communal groups.

Undeniably both had merits. 14% legislative power would amount to nothing for the development of the minority group. Similarly, governance with ad-hoc allocation of legislative power will lead to unprincipled irrational demand.

A fact, which Jinnah ignored, was that the country had other communal religious parties too. Would they not ask for separate electorate and claim their greater representation in *one* government's ministries to look after one nation? Would that not cause difficulties to form the government?

The league boycotted the assembly, leaving the Congress in charge of the government, but denying its legitimacy in the eyes of Muslim.

Jinnah and Nehru in Jinnah's garden

Nehru receiving Lord Mountbatten on 20th Feb 1947

Mountbatten won over Nehru and his learned colleagues on the concept of partition. On August 12, 1946 Viceroy invited Nehru to form the interim government. He was then the President of Indian National Congress.

Jinnah declared "Direct Action Day" and Muslims started killing Hindus. Wherever they were in minority. The credit for initiation of killing and massacre should go to Surabworthy who was then the chief minister of Bengal, also holding the port folio of home minister. He started this in Calcutta on 16th August, 1946. He did not call out the police force to quell the violence. He felt that the number was too small to handle the situation. The country was still under British Imperialism, when Nehru had just taken over heading the Viceroy's Legislative Council. It is difficult to understand, why the Royal Indian Army was kept in barrack when an orgy of blood shed was virulent in the East and also in Punjab.

16th AUGUST, 1946

On that day an advertisement in Muslim League papers read:

An advertisement in Muslim League papers on 16 August read:

'Today is Direct Action Day
Today Muslims of India dedicate anew their lives and all they possess to the cause of freedom
Today let every Muslim swear in the name of Allah to resist aggression
Direct Action is now their only course
Because they offered peace but peace was spurned
They honoured their world but were betrayed
They claimed Liberty but are offered Thraldom
Now Might alone can secure their Right'.

The truth of the above allegation is difficult to judge. Some believe that Jennah's desire to develop these people was noble, but the other needs conflict with the concept of *Union of India.* What Jinnah wanted amounted to, in fact, having two nations within one nation, - a limited Pakistan' by leaving the control of Defence, Foreign Affairs, and Communications to the control of Union of India. He even spoke at this stage that 'I do not think that any responsible man will disagree with me, that we were moved by a desire not to allow the situation to develop into bloodshed and civil war..."

"Direct Action turned violent only in Calcutta. There were many portents of its nature in Calcutta. The Morning News, published from Calcutta and whose editor, Akram Khan, was a member of the Calcutta and Bengal Muslim Leagues, asserted in an editorial on 5th August that Muslims 'do not believe in the cant of non-violence.'. The conservative landlord Nazimuddin, often at odds with Surabworthy and his labour supporters, threatened: 'There are a hundred and one ways in which we can create difficulties, specially when we are not restricted to non-violence. The Muslim population of Bengal know very well what "Direct Action" would mean so we need not bother to give them any lead'. Muslims, according to Dawn's ......"

Jinnah did not want Hindu – Muslim conflict to turn into this kind of violence. He wanted a hartal, when he wanted the Muslim to know what his desire was. The Para above indicates that all Muslim were not in favour of violence. Jinnah himself, was against violence.

Mountbatten disclose the partition of India plan, From left to right, Nehru, Lord Ismay, Lord Mountbatten and Mohammed Jinnah.

Gandhi rejected the proposed partition proposal, and proceeded to Noakhali where communal riots were taking virulent dimension. Because of lack of information, Muslims felt insecure, thinking that in a country of vast Hindu majority population, they would be oppressed. Panditji was then working under Lord Mountbatten. If the Royal Indian Army was called out of their barracks it could have suppressed the conflict. A question keeps surfacing in mind is, was there no government existing then? Mountbatten had the destiny of the country in his palm. If wished he could have stopped the above savagery.

Other than the fear of increased communal violence, which had prevented Gandhi to call for a national referendum, the other probable reason could be that most in congress were now not interested. Having been suppressed over the years, now with the assurance of getting into power, the dormant genetic feudal Indian minds of his followers might have surfaced. They did not want to get involved into any more hostilities. They had served several jail terms, neglecting their families.

The country became a free sovereign State on 14th midnight. Pandit Jawaharlal Nehru, at the age of fifty eight was sworn in as the prime minister of free India.

JAWARHARLAL NEHRU

Date of birth : **14th November,1889**
Place of birth : **Allahabad, UP**
Date of death : **27th May 1964**
Place of death : **New Delhi**
Major Organization : **All India Congress.**
Religion : **Kashmiri brahmin.**

India became a partitioned sovereign state on the 14th August, 1947 midnight, when Pandit Jawaharlal Nehru made his historic address to the new nation;

Long years ago we made a tryst with destiny, and now the time comes when we shall redeem our pledge .....At the stoke of midnight hour, while world sleeps, India will awake to life and freedom. A moment comes, which comes but rarely in history, when we step out from the old to the new, when an age ends, and when the soul of a nation, long suppressed finds utterance...He talked about *wiping out tears of the poor and also hanging the black marketers and profiteers from the first lamp post.*

The oath taking ceremony

(Lady Mountbatten role not known. Was she representing the Queen?)

On 15th August, 1947, we got ourselves free from the yoke of British Imperialistic humiliating suppression of 190 years, with no fun fare, or jubilation. In which manner the change of batons to Pandit Jawaharlal Nehru and Jinnah was made has never been announced. The liberation was carried out in a hush-hush undeclared manner. But why? Could it be that Mountbatten wanted the liberation be done in a peaceful atmosphere? and he did not want any Hindu – Muslim riotous ambient on such a historical occasion? In India, people learnt about their freedom through a speech from Pandit Nehru, mentioned earlier, His speech made no mention of the horrendous past and regrets for the sufferings of and crimes done to millions.

JINNAH, THE FIRST GOVERNOR GENERAL OF PAKISTAN

Mohammed Ali Jinnah

Pakistan's 'Father of the Nation' & 'The Great Leader'

Date of birth : **December, 1876**
Place of birth : **Karachi, Sind, British India**
Date of death : **September 11, 1948 (aged 72)**
Place of death : **Karachi, Sindh, Pakistan**
Major Organization : **India National Congress, Muslim League**
Religion : **Shia Islam**

Pakistan was declared as a sovereign State, on the 14th August. a day earlier. During his inaugural speech as the first Governor General of Pakistan also spoke: *"You will find that in the course of time, Hindus would cease to be Hindus and Muslims would cease to be Muslims, not in the religious sense because that is personal faith of each individuals, but in the political sense as citizens of the State"*. He also made no mention on the ignoble journey to freedom.

What he said on religion is closest to what this book is about. His was not a deliberation with flowery eloquence, but a pragmatic utterance of hope for the future of this degraded subcontinent. Like Gandhi, Jinnah was dedicated for Hindu-Muslim unity till the time country got divided. Both grieved when this happened. Jinnah wept* witnessing the pathetic state of the refugee camp set up for Hindus waiting to go to India. Gandhi's camp in the East became bigger with time; packed with RSS and other similar communal parties. His visit to 49 villages trying to bring about harmony between Hindu and Muslim was in vain. There were too many mischief makers on either side. In the name of Gandhi and Jinnah, they committed every conceivable crimes. There are books describing them; e.g., 'Stern Reckoning' by G.D.Khosla. The author prefers not to include these purely because they will be misquoted and justify their misdeeds. Gandhi was assassinated on 30th January, 1948. Jinnah succumbed to his sickness on 11th September 1948. These two died soon after the partition, with a hope to end long struggle. On the contrary, the conflicts between the newly created nations began, soon after the partition.

* Creator of Pakistan* Hector Bolitho.

DEMOCRACY

Our Constitution makes our country as the biggest Democratic nation. The non-erasable concept of Democracy was defined by Abraham Lincoln: **"***government of people, by the people, for the people***"** **Can** our governance claim to be so to get the current tag of a Democratic society? The third element, viz. 'for the people' is sadly missing. Currently it is for separate groups of people, elected by people of different communal sects, for people claiming unequal shares from the whole. The success of US 'civil rights' campaign was due to acceptance of *equal* rights for all, - black and white alike. Religion was set aside while providing social privileges, and administrating justice. There is no communal consideration and 'quota' system.

The fallacies on several occasions in our country are monumental. How 'quota system' can help to enhance the knowledge of any? Will a student's right for admission with poor performance in common test make him more knowledgeable in the future with 'Quota' system? If the students of a particular community perform badly, the need is to create improved environment around them, and encourage to be more knowledgeable, and competitive. There are provisions such as *'national Commission for Backward Classes'*, but achievements of such an institution is not known. Year wise simple statistics on Backward class's performance can tell us much about the performance of this Commission. Passing the buck to the government is to hide the deficiency of several Commissions.

The best solution is to do what 'US civil right campaign' achieved. Let education be equally administered. Children will learn to compete, with no *'quota bias'*. To-day, America has risen from having Black slaves, to elect a Black President. The emphasis should be on education, not 'quota system'

A medical student, admitted through *'quota system'* will not be a better doctor compared to one admitted competing in merit test. '*Quota system*' is obviously harmful. But we adopt this. In highly competitive world of to-day, performance is the only criteria for progress. '*Quota*' system cannot help to enhance the progress.

IMPACT OF ILL CONCEIVED RELIGION

An experience is worth mentioning. Referred to about a case when two above average intelligent and educated boy and girl of different castes wanted to get married. The parents of both sides had happily agreed. But the brahmin relatives of the girl expressed some reservation, because the boy was a non-brahmin. The relatives came to discuss. They were asked, - heaven forbid, – if one of them needed blood to save his life, would they get this from a 'brahmin blood' bank? They left expressing regret for raising the issue. The same can be said about all inter religions marriages.

ABSURDITIES.

When we go to provision stores, vegetable shops, or to any well known (or, humble) restaurant, do we check about the source of supply of the ingredients, or about the caste, religion, etc. of the chef? The only truth is that we are all one God's or Creator's children, although we do not know or see Him. His creation of an orderly universe proves His existence.

Einstein (1879 – 1955) was a Jew by origin, but agnostic and indifferent to religion His God 'reveals himself in the harmony of all being, not in a God who concerns himself with the fate and actions of men'. He believed in such a God,

We feel and create Him through our minds, noble or perverse. Religions are expositions of noble thoughts originated at different times in different environments. We name them differently. With education, different religious Gods embrace one another, leaving behind the regional or Prophetic ones. It is only the mentally sick who holds on to his God undermining others. Such a person needs meditation, joining a group conducting social services to understand that same medicine is needed to cure the same ailment regardless of religion.

CASTE SYSTEM AND JUDICIARY

Is there any mention of a caste system in our Constitution? If not, will it be proper to state that our Parliament is *not* an assembly abiding by our Constitution, which provides the guide line for the Parliament to formulate the country's legal system. If this guide line is trifled with, should this not be dissolved to formulate a new proper one? Our Constitution follows the British Constitution, except for one addition, Viz. PUBLIC INTEREST LITIGATION (PIL) as a show of our noble mind. Again, judiciary has no time for the poor, unless it is formally approached through an advocate, and properly registered. PIL, as conceived in the Constitution, needs only a post card to proceed with. An example related to Rural development has been cited in the text (Refer: Dy. No. 617 / SC / PIL / 2002, dated 18th October,

2003) to prove that our judiciary system does not follow this added provision in our Constitution for the poor. The reason may be that when the Parliament does not care for the Provisions, viz., Art. 243(G) made for the rural poor, why should the Judiciary?

In Rig Veda, shudra caste was for the labour class, the anchor of the society. But the Brahmanical modification made them an untouchable caste to an extent that even if one crosses the shadow of a shudra, one has to purify himself taking penance!

With literacy these perversions can and are disappearing mostly in urban society. For example, in West Bengal it has virtually disappeared in urban areas, but persists in rural areas, due to illiteracy.

At the same time, such perverse modification has created a new social order. Designated SC/ST personnel enjoy some liberated standards, and reservations, (through 'quota' system), for admission in academic institutions, and for securing employment, mostly in government offices. Earlier, a marriage with in it's own caste was preferred. Now a liberalized social system accepts marriage within the first three castes, viz. Brahmanas, Kshatriyas, and Vaisyas, but not one with shudra caste. With the special quota system, the lower caste employee/ candidate for admission to any professional academic institution, has become a much coveted caste, specially for matrimony. A special matrimonial column in the media published that a lower caste employed boy is needed for marriage alliance with an educated beautiful, post graduate, brahmin girl. Media information (with reliability bias) suggests that now even the Christians are thinking of having a lower caste system in their religion to take advantage of the quota system. Caste system exists in Christian community. For example, some claim with pride that they belong to 'Saraswath brahmin' Christian community. They deserve their pride and do not need any help from the quota system. Enlightened, they opted for Christianity as their religion of their own choice. That is what it ought to be. Religion is a voluntary choice. With hereditary practice, we have messed up the initial religious structure of the country. Rig Veda was a perfect reversible non hereditary HRD system. The caste was based on profession practiced. For example, Parasurama was a brahman by birth, but because of his warrior like proficiency, he was recognized as a Kshatriya.

Let us analyse truthfully what are we trying to achieve with our current religious practices. Is it to ensure success of a political party with a reliable vote bank, or to rectify the result of our age old feudal system suppressing the poor? Or, are we trying to unify the nation as a whole, through literacy, and concept of one God for all, when people will choose voluntarily non-hereditary paths to reach up to him? .

Genetically deep rooted with nature, Hinduism based on *original* Rig Veda was socially constructive, and not destructive, with our present caste system. Rig Veda is accepted the world's oldest script on humanism since 2000 B.C.). But it is prone to degradation now, due to alarming illiteracy, particularly in rural areas.

Rig. Veda hymns were not acceptable to Kings, Princes, Land lords, and Money lenders. Although there is no hierarchy bias, peasants pray to God Varuna more. Rich Hindus chant the perverted ones now, on some religious occasions. They blindly repeat the Brahmans, conducting puja (worship) on their behalf. *"Putram dehi, Dhanam dehi"* - *not* the socially just prayer - *"Santanam* dehi, *sarbesu Dhanam* dehi" ('Give me son and wealth': - not socially just, - 'give me child (son *and/ or* daughter) and wealth for all). The Brahmanical feudalistic perversion is seen while praying to God for son only but not daughter. *Reciting* such degrading *Sutras* deserves to be eliminated *legally,* when in practice son and daughter are currently having equal rights on inheritance, and equally competent in most fields. Quoting 'mantras' which are legally differing from the socially accepted ones bring in unhealthy harmful duality in minds and societies.

Rig Veda is a difficult text for a common man to understand. Christian missionaries had no sympathy for Hinduism. Their view was that "Rig-Veda, at best, work of human folly and at worse the outcome of a diabolic inspiration". Does the above hymn on 'Indra' support the Christian missionaries' expression?

On the other hand, Gita, a Chapter of Mahabharata, - an epic composed much earlier, is a down to earth pragmatic guide to humanism, to decide on various alternative approaches, for one to choose from, on all occasions, including war against any evils. Thus Gita is the formally accepted as the holy script for the Hindus. It *is a philosophical derivative of wisdom of many learned sages,* providing alternatives to suit different situations. To build our neglected rural society, guidance of what stated in Gita may help to change our present 'soft nation' to acquire strength to fight against many social evils

So When Arjuna says, I will not fight", and sinks into silence, the Master smiles. Then Krishna speaks His words of wisdom unto Arjuna. "Weep not", the Master says to His beloved disciple, "but be a man, a master-man! Abandon weakness, O Arjuna! Stand up in courage! Stand up and fight!"

The Gita teaches that weakness is a sin. Shakti is a spiritual virtue. Will-power must be developed, and will-power must be both strong and pure. Wake up thy will–power; that is Gita's message.

An excerpt from Bhagvad Gita

. . . Beyond the power of sword and fire, beyond the power of the water and winds, the Spirit is everlasting, omnipresent, never-changing, never-moving, ever One.

Invisible is he to mortal eyes, beyond thought and beyond change. Know that he is, and cease from sorrow.

But if he were born again and again, and again and again he were to die, even then, victorious man, cease thou from sorrow.

For all things born in truth must die, and out of death in truth comes life. Face to face with what must be, cease thou from sorrow.

Invisible before birth are all beings and after death invisible again. They are seen between two unseens. Why in this truth find sorrow?

. . . Think thou also of thy duty and do not waver.
There is no greater good for a warrior than to fight in a righteous war.

There is a war that opens the doors of heaven, Arjuna! Happy the warriors whose fate is to fight such a war.

But to forgo this fight for righteousness is to forgo thy duty and honour: is to fall into transgression.

Men will tell of thy dishonour both now and in times to come. And to a man who is in honour, dishonour is worse than death.

The great warriors will say that thou hast run from the battle through fear; and those who thought great things of thee will speak of thee in scorn.

And thine enemies will speak of thee in contemptuous words of ill-will and derision, pouring scorn upon thy courage.
Can there be for a warrior a more shameful fate?

In death thy glory in heaven, in victory thy glory on Earth.
Arise therefore, Arjuna, with thy soul ready to fight.

Krishna to Arjuna, in the *Bhagavad Gita,* Chapter 2

Bhagavad Gita (Chapter 2), Gita Publishing House, Pune

It is seen Gita does not advocate non-retaliation as an universal weapon on all situations. It encourages valour in fact, to destroy the enemy, but. does not, however, advocate *initiation* of violence to acquire unlawful gains. Gandhi's non-violence, non-cooperation and *non-retaliation mantra,* and fasting is not accepted by some as the ultimate weapon. The basic doubt is whether by following Gandhi's non-retaliation on all internal and external issues, would we be abiding by the noble advices of Gita when. Hindus accept this as their guiding Pole star, legally accepted as well? Gandhi was a saint, - perhaps the noblest, but did he accomplish his missions? Could he eliminate Hindu-Muslim conflict singing his song: " Ishar Allaha tere nam ...". ?

Jinnah and Gandhi in happy mood

There are some who believe that his fasting to atone ***our crime*** after the Jallianwala Bagh and Chauri Chaura episodes in 1921 was a clever ploy to avoid a possible deportation for life to Andaman's Cellular Jail. As a lawyer he knew the possibility, when the entire episode began to protest against his arrest. He had to prove that he had no link with the violent activities, which could have been regarded as terrorist movement.

On one occasion, he had virtually got down on his knees to plead with Jinnah, ostensibly to examine Jinnah's troubling ankle. At the end of about 14 days marathon discussion on 'undivided' India, Jinnah complained about having some pain in his ankle area of his leg. Gandhi sat on floor, took the paining foot in his hand, to examine, while Jinnah was sitting on a chair. Though not true, under the circumstances, it almost amounts to Gandhi begging of Jinnah to give up his demand on partitioning the subcontinent.

A mud pack was sent as a cure. Jinnah set it aside with the same disdain, as he did on Gandhi's plea for undivided India during 20 sessions they had. However, Jinnah told Gandhi that the mud pack had helped to cure his leg pain!

Not only he did not succeed, he witnessed the worst possible savage Hindu-Muslim conflict, before he was assassinated. Had he been able to remove 'shudra' caste even though he had, at times, lived with them?

Controversies should be expected, when the text covers wide range of issues. Broad based humanism, believing in one God is a preferred approach for constitutional propriety, leaving religion to individuals to adopt as a private issue. This was what Jinnah stated also when he was sworn in to be the Governor General of Pakistan on 14th August, 1947.

Any controversy on religion practiced by any one should be condemned. But our society thrives on such practices. Even invited guests debate about the origin or birth of Rama, Hindu, Muslim or Christian debate to prove superiority of one over the other learning .their religions from the Priests, Mollahs, and Clergies and not from any recognized learned institutions.

Our subcontinent has been ruined apparently because of such nauseating religious discourses. Yet what is the real purpose? So long humanism is the eventual goal for national development, how does the origin of the past matter? A stanza of Koran, reproduced earlier, makes us to realize that we are ruining ourselves not abiding by the imbedded mind of one God for all. A hymn of Rig Veda, on 'Indra', has been reproduced earlier A comparison with a Sura of Koran may confirm that the great sages had at no times suggested existence of different Gods even though path (the other name is religion) to reach him may differ.

Are not the above two, embracing Christianity as well, saying the same about One God? Should not the United nation accept this as the law of universe, and announce this as it's pole star for all.

Rig Veda gave prominence to peaceful and not unruly group discussions as currently indulged in our Parliament.

"Assemble, speak together, let your minds be all of one accord. The place is common, common the assembly, common the mind, so be their thought united. A common purpose do I lay before you. One and the same be your resolve, and be your mind of one accord. United be the thoughts of all that all may happily agree".

No one can deny that the above is the goal we all crave for. Regrettably, we act derisively now, through various perverted social and religious communal units. Our Constitution mentions that "*The creation of pandemonium and unruly scenes as violators of constitutional values of citizenship and guilty of breach of parliamentary concept of the house.*"

Do we follow this? Parliament has become a mockery when we keep on harping on poverty alleviation on all occasions. but do nothing. In act we devise means to rob them.

RELIGIOUS OVERVIEW

BRAHMANI2002CAL PERVERSIONS TO VEDIC RELIGION

The origin of Vedic literature is the most controversial subject. There are theories, which range from suggesting that Vedic hymns are *Apaurusheya* (not made by man) and *Nitya (Eternal) composed* by ancient Rishis (Sages) at different times.

They composed four Vedas. The orthodox Hindus believe that Vedas are *anadi*, with a timeless beginning. Some, therefore, believe that the mathematical concept of zero (0) had originated from our religious belief. Hindus also talk about *Anantya* – the infinity.(∞), world's survival is between these two limits; 0 < world's existence < ∞. This limit suits an atheist as well, when not believing God, or creator, who is the ultimate in most (if not all) of our religions, - not Hindus only, when he enquires who created God, how and when? In our vast expanding universe, current knowledge tends to give credence to an atheist's doubt on the origin of God, but believing the fundamentals of the universe, we are eager to explore.

With time religion got soiled. The Brahmanical religious modifications originated because of greed for wealth, and security of their off springs, through perversions of caste and *hereditary* systems. How can a prosperous and respected Brahman's good for nothing son plough the field? The most nauseating one is the untouchable *shudra caste.* It is now a part of our Hindu religion. Currently practiced Bramhamanic religion is perhaps the most perverted one, although claimed to be one derived from Vedic religion. The 'drill', which a 'purohit' (priest) performs, is the one, which his client specifically wants to seek blessings of God. Different hymns are there for all occasions. With that in mind, one follows and repeats whatever is told by the priest. If one looks at the mid-drift of a prosperous priest, it becomes obvious where the offerings to God are getting deposited!

Children of brahmanic priest studying now in the USA to become IT professionals, not Rig Veda, relishing beef stakes (generally half done), hamburgers, and indulging in all kinds of practices which brahmanic Hindu religion prohibits. Believing "live as Roman while in Rome" is no crime to our Hindu religion now.

A brahmanic priest

RELIGIONS - PROPHET CONVEYED

We are told that prophets are sent by God to teach people about His intentions. Thus prophets are regarded as representatives of God. Islamic religion follows the dictums of a prophet as those of God's. Islam is an Arabic word meaning *"submission to God and peace"*. The religion demands compulsive followings of such dictums. Like brahmans, clergies, mullahs have also germinated perversions, in the name of Koran. We have Rig Vedic knowledge based Hindu's and Koran following Islamic people, on one hand, and most regrettably, followers of perverted religions evolved by ignorant brahamans and Mullahs. They are leading this noble sub-continent to total annihilation, in the name of religion.

Initially Hindus reached God through research on many of His creations, and not through any individual's wisdom. People occupied otherwise, acquired knowledge from such learned people. The *guru-sishya* system originated because of this. It has nothing to do with any religion. The splendor of natural phenomenon is described in thousands of hymns. There is no compulsion to accept any. It is open-ended individual person's overture of his mind. Thus Hinduism is a way of life one may like to follow. The Vedic concept is very similar to opting out to learn any specific subject in academic institutions. There is no compulsion to learn and practice any. It is a student's own choice.

Is there any mention about forceful conversion, or to suppress other religion in Koran? The word '*kaafir*' (non-believer) is more to convey the superiority of people following the Islamic religion, than to create animosities with Rig Veda following Hindus. They are not trained minds to choose paths to follow humanism. They are all after power and wealth, in the name of religion. The basic ailment the sub-continent suffers from is 'illiteracy and inappropriate education system to follow'

NON-ETHNIC RACE

Our sub-continent has been subjected to fluctuating cultures. Numerous invaders came and most returned with their booty. It is similar to what was experienced by Nubia, situated south of Egypt, and Abu Simbal temple. It was a treasure store of foreign traders, explorers, and people from Egypt too. The most prominent plunderer was the British.

During the era (2000 B.C. – 1190 A.D.), though not cohesive, people were not poor to the extent when any would die of starvation, or commit suicide. They lived generally happy with their own culture. They were illiterate, no doubt; but not devoid of knowledge on aspects their life depended on, except on health and hygiene. There were many superstitions on religion. The only deficiency the subcontinent suffered, till to-day, was that it was not a land of oneness. On the contrary, princely states were antagonistic and fought with one another. For this we paid heavily then and even now.

THE BEGINNING OF SLIDE DOWN

Although the origin of the history of this civilized subcontinent is dated some 8,000 B.C. or, is about 10,000 years old, a dramatic phase change took place in 1192 A.D. The subcontinent of plenty of various resources, where a tolerant non-ethnic race lived, was transformed on all aspects of life. A new beginning with different shades ushered in.

Prophet Mohammed was born in 570 AD. He proclaimed Islamic religion in 612 AD. Mohammedan era began in 622. Arabs were the first to spread gospel of Islamic religion, if and when needed, by force. They conquered Sindh in 712 A.D, and by 715 A.D Arab empire was at its peak but did not move any further towards the East. It collapsed in 750 A.D. Muslims who came with the Arabs as traders pushed ahead. Shaihabuddin, after defeating Prithvi Raj, the king of Northern Province, in the second war of terrain in 1192, established Muslim dynasty, which changed several hands within their dynasty, till 1526 A.D, when Babar established Moghul empire, after the first battle of Panipat. There after the British came when Mughals made a mess of their noble faces.

The Muslim dynasty found an easy inroad to this subcontinent because of two reasons. First, the fragmented princely states offered no collective resistance. The in-fight, among the neighbouring princely States, often social in nature, was the reason for Prithiv Raj's defeat although on the first occasion Shaihabuddin met a humiliating defeat. Secondly, due to our brahamanic religion creating an untouchable shudra caste system. Millions of 'shudras' opted for Islamic and earlier Christian religions, which had no caste system. It is because of this there is a greater affinity between them.

Our Rig Veda religion, the core part of Vedic religion followed a well conceived non hereditary social science, similar to the present HRD system. But it got ruined with the introduction of brahamanic hereditary caste system, getting support from rich princes, landlords, and moneylenders.

Much before that, a non ethnic race had settled down to create a glorious phase of our sub-continent. (2000 B.C. – 1190 A.D.). It continues to be this subcontinent's identity for excellence on knowledge on natural phenomenon, stone crafts, 'fresco' paintings, climatic conditions, and the universe. In between Aryan invaded during 1900 B.C. and overwhelmed the

Dravidians settled in North West regions. This invasion was a blessing in disguise.

The Aryans were nomads, originally from Arctic region when it had a pleasant spring like weather. As it became cold, they moved southwards and settled in central Asia. Aryans were surprised with the Dravidian civilization. They had a religion of their own, but soon it adopted the Dravidian culture, and briefly speaking, through the patronage of Indo-Aryan culture, the earlier Dravidian religion and culture got a definitive shape. This partnership was a boon to the existing religion.

The Dravidian race was, however, not proficient in martial art. It was a country of plenty of various resources, particularly in the northern part where the Ganges river flows, towards eastern plateau. People acquired a genetic philosophical mind set, which had an indifferent, if not a negative view on militancy. Closely observing the nature's phenomenon, and getting to know the fundamentals, a learned sect generated.

The biggest tragedy was the formation of about 520/ 540 indigenous feudal princely states, big and small as stated earlier. They were not friendly to one another. There were only two classes, - the ruling princes, and the exploited peasants who cultivated the land owned by the rich and lived in villages, paying tax in kind or coin. Taxations system was not uniform. Each state had a small private 'army' mainly to collect taxes. Rural and agricultural development was furthest from their minds Literary was viewed as a waste of time for the cultivators.

A managerial unit and a priest took care of book keeping, religious functions and rituals. The priests also managed a '*Pathshala*'- a sort of primary school, teaching elementary arithmetic (units different to what used now) and Sanskrit only to those belonging to high caste.

This knowledge based land got degraded and the poor became poorer progressively to our present state due to six basic reasons. They are:

1. Perverted humanism through distortion of the original non prophetic nature based religious concepts;
2. Prominence on metaphysical concepts in preference to action (experiment) oriented scientific activities; *communal* religious groups with hereditary caste system replacing *religion-based community*, and neglect to martial arts, even at the cost of the national integrity;
3. Energy deficiency;
4. Feudal princely states;
5. Imposed rural illiteracy and exploitation of agricultural society; neglect of rural development;
6. Improper social status to artisans and peasants

Undoubtedly, literacy is the basic need for all to understand various aspects, which control civilized living. We designate the extension of literacy as 'education'. This chapter below deals with education. This is essential to move ahead of our present unacceptable socio-economic situation.

CHAPTER - 11

OUR DEFICIENT EDUCATION SYSTEM

Renu Khator became the first woman of Indian origin to be appointed the president of the University of Houston, USA, and the chancellor of the UH system early this year. She will head a system which is considered one of North America's biggest with a faculty of 3,000 plus and over 50,000 students. On a recent visit to India, she talked to Meenakshi Kumar about the differences between American and Indian education system.

'You studied in India before moving to the US? What major difference do you find between the Indian and American education systems?'

While theoretical education is more strong in India, in the US, the emphasis is more on applied education. The other important difference is that in the US, education is more that is more holistic. The first two years are spent in studying liberal arts, irrespective of the fact that the students may opt for engineering or management courses later. Once the course in liberal arts is over, then they start taking classes in their chosen subject. It gives the students a wider perspective of things.

'Should higher education in India be privatized? Or is a public-private partnership a better option?'

I think public-private partnership in education is essential for India's future. The private sector has a vested interest in joining hands with universities to produce graduates with the skill set that they would need to keep them competitive in the global marketplace. It also needs universities to help with research. The public-private partnership in my mind is not about privatization of higher education but about having the private sector invest in enhancing the quality of education in universities.

Take the example of Houston University. Only 33 per cent funds come from the state while the rest are from multiple sources. Theses include direct research grants and contracts from government agencies and the industry; donations from individuals and foundations; and special appropriations from federal and state legislatures for projects of national or state priority.

During his studies abroad, the author had experience supporting what stated, answering the first question. The library and workshop were open for 24 hours, even on Saturdays and Sundays. One had to make his own experimental model, erect this with instruments, conduct experiments, study in library placing the book mark, where the book read was replaced. No purely academic thesis was accepted in favor of applied science. The theory had to have experimental support. Further, the research projects were mostly those sponsored by private enterprises. They funded the experimental activities.

This is the basic difference between ours and developed societies. Most of our prominent scientists are arm chair policy makers. Their instruments are verbose, metaphysical wisdom and pens. They do not build a laboratory to explore their innovative minds. Earlier, a mention has been made about Eiffel tower as test facility to conduct experiment on aerodynamics, and how the first aerodynamic laboratory was established in Paris.

Working in a workshop collaborating with technicians was not below their dignity. The author met Dr. Petter, the designer of several pioneering and successful aircrafts other than 'Saber killer' Gnat, at the floor shop, when he was working with another technician to devise a 'fool proof' design to fix the nipple with the steel cord providing extra strength, in addition to brazing the two together. He had left a word with his office staff to meet him there to keep his appointment, but had to be identified with the help of another similarly groomed technician.

When in difficulty, we import 'difficult' components from developed societies for all our high technology activities, yet the final product is claimed to be an indigenous product. We should cultivate an ability to understand and make a certified prototype of value added imported component, although it may not get into production for reasons of long gestation time to get into production. This may be because of non-availability of proper materials from indigenous source, high cost due to small production needs, and so on. To use blindly an imported system amounts to creation of a culture of unwise foreign dependence.

An example is worth quoting. China was helped by the USSR in their aviation industry. Due to some ideological differences, the USSR withdrew their support. But China could continue, because they had taken steps for such a contingency. During the 1971 war with Pakistan, the licensed production activity of the engine factory of the HAL came to a standstill, because of an embargo imposed by the UK on supply of the critical components of engine (B. Or 701 / 703) of Bristol Siddley design.

The nation's biggest mistake has been to believe that rural folks were incompetent to perform anything else other than practicing 'agronomy'. Whether this belief is a willful strain of a feudal society, since 2000 B.C., or to create a society of poor, migrating to urban society to carry out hard labour at low cost, is difficult to judge. Nonetheless, this anomalous situation is possible to rectify. if only our energy planning was linked with rural society's development. Chapter 16 on energy details the approach, which could have made our rural society strong.

UNIVERSITY AND HIGHER EDUCATION

India can be proud of having 20 Central and 215 State Universities, 17000 colleges, which include 1800 women colleges in 29 States. How many in rural areas? Besides, how much has been extended what presented in Annexure 2 through an Indian contribution? Is there one commodity, except textile, with a tag, 'made in India' in the international market, meeting international standards?

INDIAN SCENE

It is necessary to understand literacy and education are not one and the something. Literacy is the first stepping stone. to learn about his existence and rights as a fellow citizen of his country. Education opens up the vast spectrum of his God gifted ability to serve the whole world and beyond. In our country, we have removed the first stepping stone, in rural areas and to some extent in urban areas too.

India confers every years engineering degrees to 2 lakh (10^5) students, double of those from whole of Europe, 20 times more than in the UK. Persons are honoured in our country with honorary doctorates, not because of excellence of academics, innovative thoughts, or professional performances but for holding high administrative posts. Some receive such adulations from several universities, as ornaments added to their name, without any public citations. They then become the high priests to confer awards to the real ones, who had spent many years on research to write their thesis. Receiving such affiliation, they start belching out absurd metaphysical concepts, at times resorting to facts not achieved.

The literacy status of the country is a shame. However, to support the grossly adverse remark made, as above, a comparative statement may not be out of place. Thailand's current literacy is 92 %, when ours is 61 %. It was one of the poorest country in the world not so long ago. Now progressing rapidly through industrialization of rural areas.

SAMPLE STUDY ON ECONOMIC AND LITERACY DISPARITY

TABLE 5

Sl. No.	Country	Per Capita. Income ($)	Literacy
1.	Bangladesh	2,200	43.1
2.	Pakistan	2,600	49.9
3.	Vietnam	3,100	90.3
4.	India	3,700	61.0
5.	Indonesia	3,800	90.4
6.	Maldives	3,900	96.3
7.	Sri Lanka	4,700	90.9
8.	Philipines	5,000	92.6
9.	China	7,600	90.9
10.	Thailand	9,200	92.6
11.	Russia	12,200	99.4
12.	Malaysia	12,900	88.7
13.	Mauritius	13,700	72.88
14.	South Korea	24,200	77.23
15.	Taiwan	29,500	96.1
16.	Japan	31,500	99.0
17.	U K	31,800	99.0
18.	USA	44,000	99.0

Source: Compiled by author, data from Manorma, 2008

The above table should provide a convincing proof of our subcontinent's poor economic and literacy state; more so, as stated here after, about rural poverty and illiteracy with a disparity ratio of about 12.5 between urban and rural society. If one attempts to compare the income of an average *rural* Indian with those in the USA, one will wonder how the rural India survives! Our nation needs no more proof on our willful suppression of rural poor to have a prosperous urban society with scores of academic facilities in urban areas, but hardly any in rural areas.

SCIENCE CONGRESS

A question surfaces in mind. What for do we hold such assemblage incurring huge expenses? Such a science Congress was held in Bangalore on December, 2003, when our prime minister, Atal Bihari Vajpayee was the chief guest. A pamphlet mentioning the names of award winning scientists was distributed, the names of the eminent scientists appeared in two graded groups. On what basis the grading was done is not known. The achievements of these scientists were not indicated. Young scientists attended this occasion in a jam-packed large hall. When these graded eminent scientists filed past the prime minister, most attending did not know who they were except the name announced, but not what they had achieved so that the prime minister could announce that *Indian science was second to none.* The assembly loudly cheered, however. Was it that difficult to mention in a few words about their credentials? This can still be done. The Congress was more to herald names of individual scientists, and not their scientific achievements,

For example, Department of Science & Industrial Research (DSIR) had put up a stall exhibiting innovations under their patronage. Let alone the PM, not a single VVIP or a VIP visited this stall. The young students showed their interest. They came in large number. It was a great show of divide between carefully selected knowledge source (not all) and those aspiring to be knowledgeable, with security forces wedged in between, ostensibly to ensure the physical 'safety' of VVIP and VIP scientists! Or to protect the exposure of their ignorance if they had visited the stalls and got involved in discussion.

The drill followed was comical. From time to time leaving one person with each exhibit, the entire exhibition hall was evacuated whenever a VVIP was likely to come for inspection. Thereafter, when no one surfaced, the 'all clear' signal was given, and all managers of stalls were allowed in. The author had good fortune to attend many abroad, but never experienced one such. Invited, he had put up a working model* to exhibit a patented live fluid flow measurement system for domestic use with mechanical and electronic counters. It was an expensive demo and perhaps the most popular one. DSIR disbursed Rs.50/- to each for setting up his exhibit. The estimated expenditure to put up the stall on fluid flow measurement was about Rs.2500/-. What also not understood was the reason for a security measure for safety of VVIP scientists, when they were kept segregated from the rest. Who would kill or damage them?

SCIENCE EDUCATION

The Congress was held at the Bangalore university campus. Interaction with the visiting knowledge seeking students revealed an interesting fact. The average IQ (Intelligent Quotient) of the students was high. The author enjoyed the interaction with the students, trying to gather what subjects they were focusing their minds on. A most revealing fact emerged. They did not stray away from the set curriculum. The main thrust was on job prospects. Secondly, their minds seemed to halt, even on fundamentals. Some examples are provided, as under:

1. What is 0 (Zero) and infinity? Stand alone, can these be illustrated to a student if some desired to learn more. The number one(1) can be illustrated, raising a finger, but what about ' Zero'?
2. Is zero (0) a number? If yes, what would be answer when 0 is divided by 0, (0 ÷ 0)? Any number divided by the same number is equal to one (1). Is this true for 0 also? A check with scientific calculator will display that the answer one (1) is incorrect. Which is the right answer? If one (1) is the correct answer, which can this be mathematically established, should we not throw out the calculators?

3. We all accept $X^o = 1$. Why?

4. The famed and pioneering missile V2 missile was used during WWII, launching vertically, with a liquid fuel rocket motor providing 1.2 g ($F^0 \div W^0$ - 1)g* initial acceleration. Why? Why not 0.2, or 2.2? V2 was the pioneering activity

for the development of missile technology of to-day. A mathematical justification can be derived from the fundamental laws governing optimum launching acceleration, flight velocity, etc. The governing equation, derived by the author is as under;

$$(b \ln b + b)(F_0/W_0)^2 - b(F_0/W_0) - \frac{(1 - 1/b)(1 + C_1)}{C_2} = 0$$

graphically represented below when : $\frac{(1 + C_1)}{C_2} = \mu$

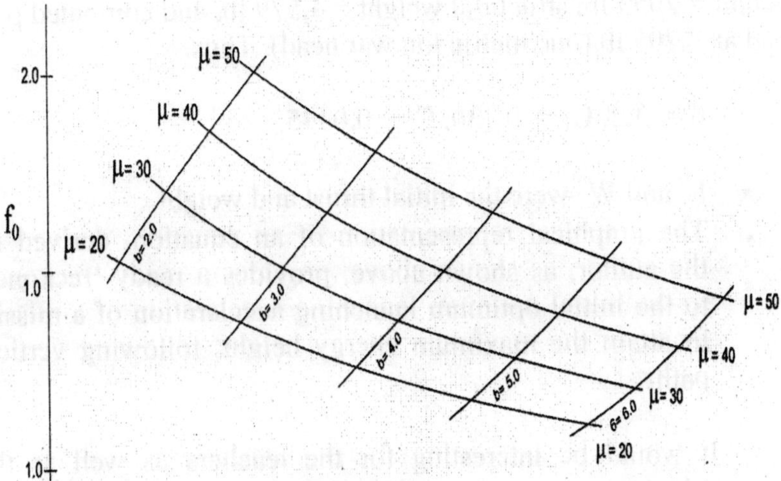

= 0

Graphical representation of governing equation

When b is the mass ratio, C_1 and C_2 are coefficients related to missile's features such as, C_1 is the ratio of structural and fuel weight, and C_2 is the Specific weight of the rocket motor, (Thrust per unit weight of propulsive unit).

The above example is to illustrate that basic motivation germinates from 'WHY'. A question surfaced why V2 was launched at 1.2 g? After all, any thrust greater than the weight of the initial weight of the missile could have lifted, when the duration (Range) would be a function of fuel it carried. The search began and the equation was derived. But this had to be verified.

This has been attempted with data available in page 390, Rocket missile and Space travel by Willy lay. For V2, the following information is provided;

F_0 = 59,500 lb, W_0 = 28,229 lb, We = 8,837. lb, .rocket motor weight = 2053 lb, structural weight = 4,579 lb, and computed pay load as 2,205 lb.(one metric ton war head). Thus.

b = 3,2, C_1 = 0.236, C_2= 0.0345,

- F^0 and W^0 were the initial thrust and weight.
- The graphical representation of an equation, derived by the author, as shown above, provides a ready 'reckoner' to the initial optimum launching acceleration of a missile to attain the maximum energy height, following vertical path.

It would be interesting for the teachers as well as the students to try and confirm the above without going to computer, when the human mind could function better than present day computer.

Another version of V2 missile, designated as A 10, had a mass ratio, b = 2.56. Assuming thrust and structural coefficients same as V2, the same i.e., μ = 35.6. One finds from the above graph, f_o = 1.4g. Actual was .(441,000 ÷ 188,090 – 1)g = 1.36g

What kind of Mathematical analysis was done by Von Braun

to determine the launching acceleration for V2 is not known from any text book/report. No doubt it was deduced, but not included in this text mainly to determine whether the basic can be worked out while studying rocket propulsion, and then on learning how our space craft is currently orbiting around the moon.

5. What is the weight of earth? (There are theories)

. Was this not a science Congress?. The five questions are to indicate that our education system often starts midway living out the basics as done by the calculator, starting with a confused answer. Solutions through elaboration of basics need not necessarily be the beginning of a science based treatise, but an indication of what left out may be an useful Para in the 'Preface'. Annexure 2 proves this.

The list tells the story of inquisitive minds and the resultant benefits to the society. The innovations listed serving the humanity does not make any mention of any Indian contribution. This may have been missed out, unwittingly perhaps, but the undeniable fact is that the number would be very few even if a conscious effort is made. An attempt to update this Annexure 2 will prove that what our Prime Minister had stated addressing the congress (i.e., India is second to none) was far from the truth then, and even now. The reason to highlight the basics is to understand that they are the seeds planted in mind. One may remove the seeds from a fruit, as an unwanted element, before eating the fruit, yet the discards may help to grow orchards. And feed many in the future. Has not the hybrid seed K58 proved that?

A defective approach to acquire knowledge without germinating an inquisitive mind may limit the development of a nation. In recent times a position paper on "Restructuring post-school Science Teaching Programmes" dated October, 2008 has been printed. It is a short but well composed document authoured by knowledgeable scientists representing our three premiere science academies of our country. The foreword brings out several important issues. They highlighted at one stage, "However, while infrastructure and other material facilities are essential for promoting quality education, how and what taught at different levels are also equally important." This most important observation will be more complete if 'why' is added before 'how' which provides the answer in real terms to 'why'. Is not 'why' the initiator of all science and civilization which follows? 'How' embraces more of technology, when 'why' is the seed in the mind, and 'how' proves the mind.

The spontaneity of Ramanujam, about the number, 1729, the smallest number which is the sum of cubes of two numbers, in two ways, tells us about an intuitive alert mind. What his friend Hardy had felt that it was an uninteresting number of a cab he used to come and visit him in the hospital, Ramanujam thought otherwise; and he viewed differently. There are many more similar 'whys' we ignore. Does our science study germinate 'whys' in the minds of the students?

Of course there is no set norm to create such a mind. At the same time let no mind becomes a machine, when the operational manuals are the text books. Let the employment opportunities, not science, be not the focal issue. Even at work places, an alert mind can do immense good carrying forward what the person is working on, asking 'why'.

In our proposed new India, we must free ourselves from the current practice of solving apparently simple situation through difficult ways. An example, often quoted, may be repeated to explain the above remark. A military convoy got stuck because the overhead bridge was too low by about 3 inches., and the convoy could not go through. There were much excitement because the convoy had to reach the destination in time. The best solution decided on was to excavate the road level. The nearby garrison was contacted, and the schemes were worked out to quicken the process. By the time the select team was about to commence the operation, to their greatest surprise, it was realized that there was already a clearance at the top and the convoy could easily go through. When the reason for this happening was debated about, a poor teenage boy sitting on the roadside, pointed his finger to the tyres of the lead vehicle. Soon they realized that the boy had partially deflated the tyres. Afraid of punishment, he ran away from the site, when some approached to reward him.

After the war, V2 missile was taken away by the USSR and the USA where competitively the space crafts were built thereafter. Initially the Russians won the race, putting unmanned Sputnik in space in 1957, orbiting around the earth. On ground we knew about its operation hearing the blips it was transmitting, Von Braun was then working in America, setting up a Space centre. Russians were again the first to place manned space craft in the orbit. Yuri Gagarin was the first man in space in Vostok 1, which was blasted into space on the 18th April, 1961. It became the Russian Air Force day. Thereafter, Neil Armstrong, the first astronaut set his foot on the surface of Moon on 21st July, 1969 (Apollo XI moon mission). 40 years later, our second to none nation is working hard to achieve the same!

The Para above can be summarized as under;

1. Nil-experimental motivation bookish education on science;
2. Absence of statutory compulsion on literacy; and education resulting in a poor economic state ; particularly in rural areas;
3. Nil desire towards value addition to currently used objects to make them more useful, and commercially competitive;
4. Academic institute's desire to confer honorary high academic honours to persons holding high government posts, without any scientific achievements to their credit, as ornaments, thus erasing .innovative thoughts and actions of others.
5. Metaphysical orations with no supporting data and publicity on daily basis through media making use of *employed* agents at tax payer's cost.

In contrast, eminent scientists abroad build research laboratories to explore the efficacy of their thoughts before heralding their dream based possibilities.

CHAPTER - 12

ORGIN OF THE NAMES OF TWO DIVIDED TERRITORIES

The names Hindustan and Pakistan needs amplification to realize that they have no religious connotation. Hindustan originates its name from river Indus. It was named as 'Sindhu' (meaning sea) because of vastness, then acquired a name Hindu because of phonetic problem of some invaders to utter 'S', and finally Hindustan – a land where people lived. It is a derived name from river Indus with no territorial gain, or formation by human being. It is a God's gift when five rivers with Himalayan origin meet. Most of the Hindu temples are on the banks of various rivers, or sea shores. That water is life was realized since mankind's civilization. Ponds are often parts of the temples when not on the bank of river or sea shore.

Pakistan is also a derived name, but with a different objective in view. People known as Hindus do not have a mind to forcefully acquire another country's territory. Vedic Hindu religion does not dabble with politics although, princes having conflicts with neighbouring states within the country were common. Muslim religion believes in territorial gains. True patriotic mind did not germinate among the vast majority of unfriendly Hindus, although we keep singing songs respecting Bharatmata. Are the shudras not children of Bharatmata? Is there any mention of the caste system in our Constitution? If not, why not ban this, designating it as anti-national. This has not been done because of two obvious reasons. The rich and powerful need cheap labour. And it is easy to fool them to get votes to stay in power. shudras are the most coveted citizen during election times.

The knowledge-based subcontinent was never a cohesive nation. Secondly, it was not militarily strong enough to defend the country. The subcontinent was an easy prey for the invaders.

FIG. 4

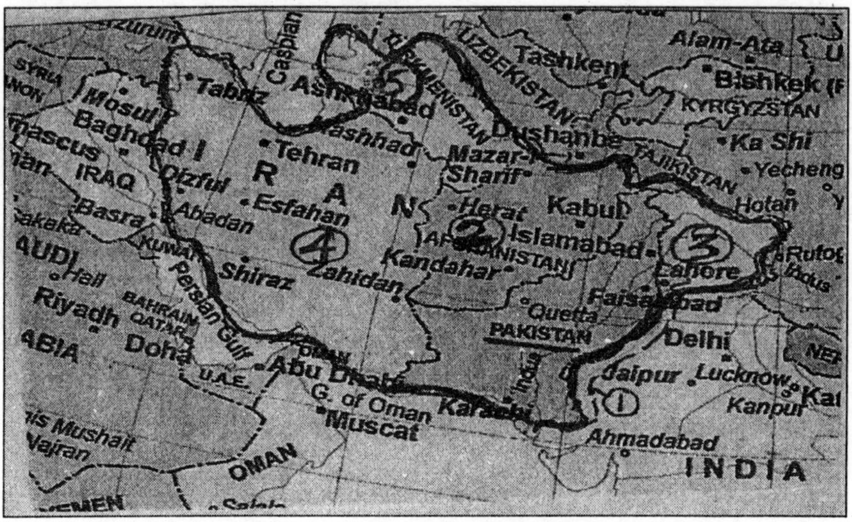

INITIAL CONCEPT OF PAKISTAN

Creation of name

The name of Pakistan was to create an Islamic territory, (territories shown within the red lined boundary). **P** for Punjab ;**A** for Afghanistan ;**K** for Kashmir; **I** for Iran; **S** for Sindh; **T** for Turkmenistan; **AN** is added to indicate as an integral territory, e.g., Hindustan.

Source: *Pakistan*, by Choudhury Rahaman Ali

The main purpose of the above grouping of Islamic countries is not known. Some conjecture that a creation of an united Muslim power controlling entire territories between Pacfic ocean to Red sea below 30^0 latitude was in view. India in-between was standing as a sore thumb in this grandeur plan to create a Muslim world.

Hitler tried to create one cohesive Aryan nation, conquering whole of northern part above China, stretching from Bering sea in the east to Atlantic sea in the west; thus annexing Russia, whole of Europe up to England. The details of his inhuman approaches are known. His non-erasable degraded act had created United nation (UN) instead, by Frankllin D Roosevelt, President of the USA on 1st January, 1942.

An Islamic union with a name, Pakistan appears as the desire then. It did not receive the support and was left with only one territory, between Afghanistan and a small part of Punjab. Claims on territorial gains in the name of religions is against the wishes of God. The author does not wish to predict who will be the eventual sufferer from the scorn of God.

CONTINUED HISTORY OF THIS SUBCONTINENT.

The earlier chapters have made an attempt to justify existence of the oldest civilized origin since 8000 - 6000 B.C.; about princely states controlling the subcontinent; rich and poor continuing divide originated since 2000 B.C.; early non-prophetic Rig Vedic religion; comparison with prophetic Islamism; one God; non-religion related humanism; evolution of perverted systems in both religions; Gita's directive for retaliation to evil; composition of learned Hindu religious texts; reign of Hindu kings (Ajatashatru Chandragupta Maurya, Ashoka, et al); incarnation of noble souls,- Buddha, Mahavira; illiteracy resulting poor economic States; education systems with absence of inquisitive mind; non-ethnic and Indo-Aryan race; rock cutting proficiency during heritage age; Islamic destruction of Hindu temples; Indo –Islamic ornamental architectural edifices treating Indian craftsmen as slaves; discovery of Harappan and Mohenjodaro civilization; industrial revolution; English translation of religious texts written in Sanskrit language; our progressive growth of metaphysical approach to science; origin of three partitioned hostile sovereign States. The above aspects covered over a period upto 1526 A.D. the end of Muslim reign over a period of 336 years, since 1200 A.D. Moghuls came and lost to British rule.

STATE DURING BRITISH RULE (1757 – 1947)

Currently the average paddy yield rate/year from 62 Mn. ha irrigated land is about 2 - 2.5 t/ha. Rain fed, 98 Mn ha non-irrigated land produces about 0.75 t/ha. This amounts to a yield of about 210 million tones/year, or an average of 1.3 t/ha/year, - perhaps the lowest in the world. (98 X 0.75 + 62 x 2.2 = 210).This estimate on our food grain production tallies with the generally accepted view about our food gain availability in the country.

The estimate on total agricultural land varies. The above suggests 160 million. Tata Statistical Outline of India (2006 – 07) suggests 178.6 million. The 'Hindu' survey of Indian agriculture mentions (in page19, 1999) that the cultivable land is 140-142 million, with little prospect of any further increase. What, therefore, is our future with increasing population? We are faced with two possible catastrophes - shortage of cultivable land, and water. There are two more, in fact. Poor literacy and inadequate energy.

RURAL EDUCATION

Now 'Netas' started invading rural areas seeking votes promising better living conditions in the future, not highlighting what science and technology had achieved, and could do. (There are two noteworthy omissions. First, Dr. M. P. Singh of ICAR (Indian Council for Agricultural Research) did not get due recognition for his work on K68 for wheat. He was no less a hero of India's green revolution.)

NEGLECT OF LITERACY

The other far reaching nationally damaging activity was the continued neglect of literacy in rural areas. The exact reason for this is difficult to understand, even to-day. On record, Jinnah was perhaps the only dedicated son of this subcontinent who tried hard to educate the neglected poor rural society when, he standing by the side of Gokhale, in 1916, pleaded with the Imperial 210Legislative Council; "I ask, is it such an insurmountable difficulty to find three crores ($3x10^7$) of rupees from the imperial exchequer?" He had to resign for asking such a question.

ELEMENTARY EDUCATION

The only other effort made when Rs. 22,268 crores (Rs.22.3 X 10^{10}, or about $5.0 billion) have been allocated to the Department of Elementary Education and Literacy for 'Sarva Shiksha Abhiyan'(SSA) in 2005 – 2006 budget. This includes fund allocation towards mid-day meal. Per capita, country is spending about Rs. 3/- per day to provide elementary education to 210 million (out of 330 million) children, in the age group of 5-14 yrs.($210 \times 10^6 x3 \times 365=23 \times 10^{10.}$ This suggests that most of the rural children should have been literate. But are they? Table below tells us the reality.

NSS SURVEY in the year 2004 – 2005 is as under:

TABLE 6

Age	Educational Level	Rural	Urban
Age 0 +	Secondary & Above (NSS 515) P.60 & P.63	10.2%	30.2%
Age 15 +	Secondary & Above (NSS 517) P.27	15.6%	42.2%
Age 15 +	Secondary only (NSS 516)	8.2%	15.3%

NSS: national Sample Surveys are conducted by ministry of statistical survey and Implementation, government of India.

FUNDAMENTAL RIGHTS AND DUTIES

Can we, from what presented above, claim that we are abiding by what our Constitution stipulates as our fundamental duty? Is there any law similar to what enforced on Singapore? Have we tried to rectify this default of fundamental duty? Where have Rs. 22,268 crores (Rs.22.3 X 10^{10}, or about \$5.0 billion) allocated to the Department of Elementary Education and Literacy for 'Sarva Shiksha Abhiyan' (SSA) in 2005 – 2006 budget been used?

ILLITERACY IN RURAL AREAS

An apparent reason surface to believe that illiteracy, let alone poor education, in rural areas is *intentional*. It is because of our legacy on social structure inherited since 2000 B.C. when we created our two distinct classes, - rich and poor. A brahamanical caste system, different to the original Rig Vedic one appeared on the scene These slowly developed two societies - urban ad rural Retaining the major modification to Rig Vedic class division was around the 'shudra' caste. The brahamanic system, making 'shudras' as untouchables may be regarded as the key cultural deprivation which has lead to our current unacceptable situation leading to breaking up of one subcontinent in three parts. viz. Pakistan, India and Bangladesh. The breaking up of the society was due to the need for the labour force sustaining the urban society.

Note: The difference between literacy and education is often confused. Literacy means ability to read and write. Education implies training on a particular subject. When Rs. 22,268 crores (\$5.0 billion) were allocated to the department of elementary education and literacy for 'sarva shiksha abhiyan' (SSA) in 2005 – 2006 budget, it was not clear who would be the recipients. We have many primary schools. These schools, if recognized by the government are entitled to get assistance including that needed for mid day meal. They go much beyond literacy levels with specified standards. The most unfortunate fact is there are very few such schools in rural areas. Even when they exist, far and in between, they are poorly managed. Children are often discouraged to go to school tracking long distances, and when permitted, it is mostly for mid-day meals. Literacy and education are in a complete mess in rural areas. The only organized activity is corruption. Visiting Jagdishpur, UP. when gram pradhan's son was asked why he had not gone to the school, he divulged that their school teacher teaches in three primary schools and it was not necessary to attend school regularly, when every one passes in any case. The teacher gets his pay of three teachers, from the office of the magistrate. An attempt was made to bring to his notice about this malpractice. His short answer was that he would look into.

The summary situation was that the villagers believe that it was more remunerative, if the children could find opportunity to migrate and find employments in cities. These do not require literacy.

LABOUR FORCE

The unskilled labour force keeps the urban society going. The employment avenue falls under two categories. Domestic and non-domestic.

DOMESTIC

With economic prosperity of city dwellers, the entire life style of urban people has undergone a dramatic change. There are two varieties. One, single bread earners, and the other, when both husband and wife work. It is difficult to say which is the preferred one, but in either case the demand for household help has gone up. There are two car owners, when both work. The demand for car drivers, with a duty hour for 11 hours, has become a necessity. With traffic jams and unruly driving, there is hardly any self driven car. For traffic offences, the car driver's license is endorsed. If fined, the owner pays. Besides, it has become a status symbol also. Then the school going children, the shoppers, attendance to social events, club goers, extra curricular activities, running errands, all together make the need for a car driver an essential part of even middle class urban domestic life.

DOMESTIC NEED

A household help is an equally important need. With our dusty roads, it is difficult to keep dust filtering inside the house. So sweeping followed by swabbing with a cloth soaked with antiseptic fluid is the daily routine to begin with. The next agenda is cleaning the utensils used for cooking and eating five course greasy meals, generally for four members. This has to be done to the satisfaction of the mistress. The filling of filtered water in bottles, making and serving tea in between are duties to perform. The clothes freshly washed has to be clipped with the cloth line for drying, and brought back in the evening, neatly folded and arranged for ironing. And so on.

Then, the gardener, and the security man at the gate, are essential components of several CEOs and senior mangers' household. Without these help, the present day urban society would collapse.

CONSTRUCTION LABOUR FORCE

With economic boom, satellite townships, with multi-storey buildings are mushrooming. They are self contained units, apparently with five star facilities .The construction and maintenance need sizable unskilled labour force. The migrating construction labour force live as nomads in temporary plastic sheet covered tents. Their children grow up playing on streets, with no schooling facility near by, and live with no civic amenities. Such labour force's main entertainment is listening music on battery operated music system and drinking after the day's hard work. The country's poor people consist of three groups. The poor rural people living on agronomy, the city slum dwellers, and labour force employed on various duties. Of the three, the slum dwellers are relatively better off. They pay no rent, no taxes, and children going to English medium schools mostly run by Christian missionaries. There are some run by benevolent organizations with no religious bias. There are thousands of NGOs, getting government aids. They are usually run by voluntary social workers, who are wives of single bread earners. Some are doing good work for handicapped children. Some are fakes. Ignoring that, they cannot fan out to distant villages. We have about 5500 big and small cities. Hence their noble services are limited. If not recognized, they receive no help from the government.

Increasingly a voice is raised about the utility of NGO and the financial disbursing agencies honesty. The view is this organizing agency is an income source for both.

Urban – Rural divide - Mumbai city (A morning scene)

A migrated rural youth going to seek work with his brother early in the morning. Photographed by author

CHAPTER - 13

WILLFUL NEGLECT OF RURAL SOCIETY

With the present style of living, our urban society cannot survive, without the help of migrated rural people. Assuming the rural society is developed, providing employment to those who are now migrating and providing the labour force mentioned above, will the urban society not come to a stand still? So why invite trouble to the urban society while developing rural society? Could that be the reason to keep Article 243(G) aside, and make the plough as the only appliance for the livelihood of 800 million rural people. Can a nation of about 1200 million remain as a democratic state for long, when north, west, and eastern boundaries are hostile? In such a situation, a programmed rural development is an unavoidable necessity. But are we concerned about this?

Uncontrolled underdeveloped rural society invites serious security risk. Now the illegally migrated personnel from Bangladesh will be-are, in fact, already filling up the gap on scarce labour force mentioned earlier. In certain areas of New Delhi, for example, virtually all household help are those from Bangladesh. They have built up a colony of their own. Our liberal society does not mind trading security risk with luxury in domestic domains. These illegal immigrants also acquire ration cards, at a cost and even the voting rights.

In Naogoan, Assam there used to be a vast stretch of shallow water. The local people did not know how to grow food (paddy) in such a land. But the illegally infiltrated people from Bangladesh, are used to growing food in such conditions. They soon made Naogoan a granary for Assam. The grateful people of Assam have absorbed them in their system even though it is close to Tezpur, - a military base, at the foothill of Arunachal Pradesh. Brahamputra river flows between Tezpur and Naogoan. People prefer living in Kolkata because of easy availability of domestic labour force from illegally infiltrated people from Bangladesh.

On 27th September, 2007, our Presidential award winning Finance Minister conveyed through media that the people of India would live like Americans, by 2035, but not forgetting to add 'perhaps not all'. This little exception will become the most important part for the fight in our parliament for special privileges on the basis of caste and sub caste. If living, as Americans do is the target of our FM, why not the concluding exception be replaced to read as 'if we eliminate the mention of religion, from our Constitution, as the Americans had done after the civil right movement. Incidentally, some Americans posted in India believe that living in India is an unbelievably cheap luxurious living, with a maid servant, a chauffer, a gardener, a security guard, cheap outings, and wining & dining in elite restaurants. These luxuries are unthinkable even for senior executives in the USA. The migrated Indians to America, or other developed societies know how hard the life is, without these help. There are several Indians who are already living with such luxuries and more, in India. Will these happy Americans/ Indians go and live in an Indian village with facilities as described in Table 1? If one well-known person ventures out to do this even for a day, he becomes a hero. Our media will herald in the front page, as if a great patriotic act has been accomplished.

Our learned FM would have made a proud India if he could ensure the past President's platitude of making urban-rural divide as thin line instead of 12 +, as of now, after 61 years of Independence. One would like to know what magic wand he had at his disposal to wipe out this disparity and take the country of 1.5 billon* people, (not all as he had indicated) to live like Americans in 2050.

*Assuming average population growth rate is reduced progressively to 1.0 % from our present rate 1.6 % *The author does not believe in such projections, unless justified in real terms.* A projection on population growth, by US census Bureau, is placed below.

TABLE - 7

POPULATION GROWTH

	Projections of Population in 2050
Australia	***24,175,783***
Brazil	***228,426,737***
China	***1,424,161,948***
Ethiopia	***144,716,331***
India	***1,807,878,574***
Indonesia	***313,020,847***
Japan	***99,886,568***
Nauru	***22,696***
Nigeria	***356,523,597***
Russia	***109,187,353***
UK	***63,977,435***
USA	***420,080,587***
Source: US Census Bureau	

The above table suggests that the average population growth rate will be reduced to 1% from the present 1.6% , that is, 27% excess of China's population. (refer third and fifth countries mentioned in the table above.)

Most doubting now, - may not be there to point a finger at our FM, that such predictions of living as Americans are well conceived absurdities. We are told about current 8 % GDP growth rate. Where? Why farmers are committing suicides at an increasing rate with booming economic progress?

RURAL ENERGY

Even if our FM could activate his mind to suggest what is needed to implement the 1992 amended Art. 243 (G) of our

Constitution for rural development, he will deserve another, perhaps bigger Presidential award. His prediction about our living standard similar to an American way of life will remain as a dream till such time rural society is suitably energized through non-hazardous pollution free energy approaches, and both sides of rural society's coin are developed through agronomy on one side, and value added metallic and non-metallic products on the other side.,

OUR HYPOCRITICAL SOCIETY

Announcement of such long term expectations do confirm the willful creation of our present unacceptable rural society. Is our current form of life style, in urban areas, feasible if the rural society gets developed and annual migration of more than two lakh/ year to urban society gets severely reduced? Where from shall this society get the earlier mentioned illiterate low cost labour force to live in luxury? *A totally reformed disciplined and hard working urban society needs be born.* Are we in a position to pay for the sins committed in the name of God over the last 3600 years (since 1600 B.C.)? Are we prepared to accept that Article 40 (1950) was a willful sin against humanity? and keeping it wrapped for so many years, prove that we are a hypocritical feudal society indeed.

MANMOHAN SINGH AS FINANCE MINISTER

Note: The sidelined part, particularly 'The unemployed youth in rural areas could be a force of destabilization' needs serious attention.

That he could not achieve much and needed to organize activities mentioned in Article 243(G) is seen from Table 7 presented early.

Our initial Art.40 for 'Organization of Village Panchayats' was brief, primitive, and not taking any notice of the changing world. It was one similar to asking a blind man to show path to another blind man. Table 7, after 42 years of its formulation proves this. The surprising fact is that the country took 42 years to realize this! All these years elections though *adult franchise* were taking place. Did not our leaders realize that they were getting votes raising false hopes in the minds of the rural folks? Financial allocations were made, but why the progress was so dismal? Constitutional provision exists for the Comptroller General of Audit and Accounts to submit the audited report to the President and Governors of States. After scrutiny, the report is to be submitted to the Parliament for taking a view on achieved performance. Was this done? If the answer is in affirmative, why our former prime minister, Rajiv Gandhi did expressed that when government allotted one Rupee for the development of the rural people, only 17 paisa reaches them. He did not elaborate where the remaining 83 paisa had gone. .

FUND ALLOCATION FOR RURAL AND AGRICULTURAL DEVELOPMENT (2004 – 2005)

The generalized rule for allocation of fund for rural and agricultural development is 3% of GDP, or 30 % of Revenue which is 10 % of GDP.

The sharp rise of GDP since year 2000, as shown in the Figure below, though laudable, has generated a two faced problem, when Banks were flooded with money. Loans were easily available, and could be serviced through 'disposable' money of employed people. Urban society boomed up purchasing/ hiring residential accommodation, buying cars, and other luxury items.

Simultaneously, a bleak picture was germinating in rural areas. The 3 % of large GDP increase could not be absorbed in primarily agronomy based economy . Rural Banks were also flooded, and some farmers took loan. But with their only agronomical activity, and no other employment opportunity, they got into debt trap, unable to meet the commitments towards Bank loan. The division between urban rich and the poor in rural societies and urban slums became worse.

Fig 5

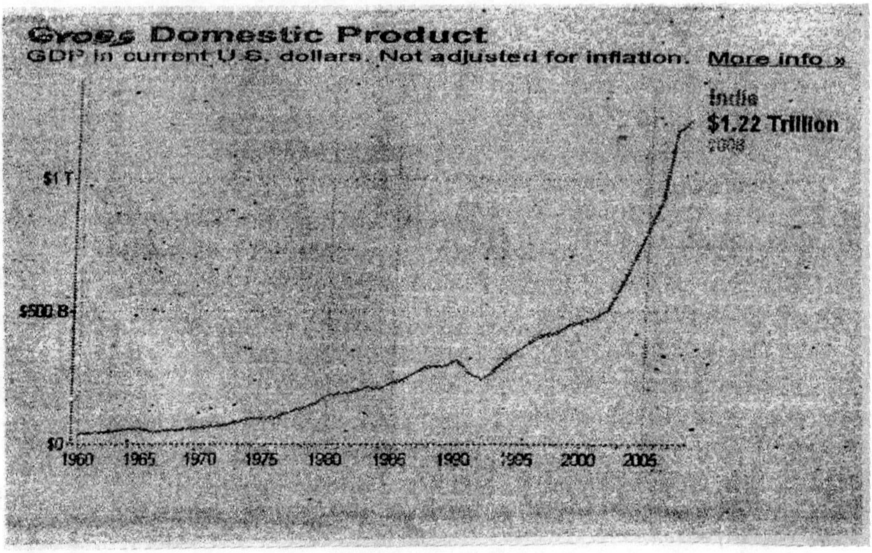

Data Source: World bank Development Indicator

CRORES FOR THE POOR GO UNUSED

DH News Service

New Delhi: Governments in power might claim to be dedicated to the uplift of the poor, but a latest parliamentary panel report exposes how money meant to be spent for the purpose remained unspent year after year.

The lackadaisical attitude of the Ministray of urban Employment and Poverty Alleviation as well as state governments in this regard has been harshly commented upon by the standing committee on urban development, which has even recommended possible imposition of penaliy on states failing to spend money allocated to them.

"Though the mandate of the ministry are urban employment and poverty alleviation and housing and human settlements, the ministry is precariously lagging behind in fulfilling the same...

(it) should seriously ponder over the issues as to why they are failing in the realisation of their mandates and objectives", the oummittee in its report tabled in Parliament said.

The report expressed deep conceell over the minstry surrounding Rs.458 crore between 2001-02 and 2004-05 as also by the fact Rs.1,320.70 crore was lying, as unspent balance with states and Union territories under various schemes and another Rs.132.61 crore with the implementing agencies like NBCC and Building Material and Technology Promotion Council.

The committee points of the failure of the states in spending allocated money, and said, "The government should explore the feasibility of imposing penal interest on the states / Union teritories if they fail to utilise the unspent belongs lying with them under various schemes with in a fixed time period".

The report also criticised the government for failing andrecommended imposing penal interest on states failing to submit utilisation certificates for the flagship Swarna Jaynti Shahari Rozgar Yojana (SJSRY), the only such scheme aiming at providing gainful employment to the urban un-employed living below the poverty line.

AGRICULTURAL LAND UTILIZATION FOR FOOD GRAIN*

Table below indicates the per capita utilization rate in years since Independence.

TABLE 8

Year	1950 – 51	1990 – 91	2003 – 2004
Tons / year *	0.14	0.22	0.20"

*Per capita yearly agricultural produce

The actual per capita consumption is 12.5 % less for reasons explained in the foot note of Table below;

TABLE 9

Agriculture					
. Availability of Food grains					
Net quality available					
Annual Total (Mn. Tones)			***Per capita per day (Grams)***		
	Cereals	***Pulses***	***Cereals***	***Pulses***	***Total***
1981.........	***104.8***	***9.4***	***417.3***	***37.5***	***454.8***
1993.........	***138.1***	***11.7***	***427.9***	***36.2***	***464.1***
1994.........	***142.6***	***12.2***	***434.0***	***37.2***	***471.2***
1995.........	***154.0***	***12.7***	***457.6***	***37.8***	***495.4***
1996.........	***152.1***	***11.3***	***442.5***	***32.7***	***475.2***
1997.........	***163.2***	***13.0***	***466.0***	***37.1***	***503.1***
1998.........	***147.9***	***11.7***	***414.2***	***32.8***	***442.0***
1999.........	***156.1***	***13.3***	***429.2***	***36.5***	***465.7***
2000.........	***156.6***	***11.7***	***422.7***	***31.8***	***454.4***
2001.........	***445.6***	***11.3***	***386.2***	***30.0***	***416.2***
2002........	***175.4***	***13.4***	***457.3***	***35.0***	***492.2***
2003.......(P)	***159.8***	***11.0***	***409.9***	***28.2***	***438.2***
87.5% of gross production, the balance 12.5% being provided for feed and seed requirements and waste, plus imports, minus exports and net changes in Government stocks.					

SOURCE: Statistical Outline of India 2004 -2005.

The above decline shown in Table 9 should create *alarm* because of two reasons. First, on one hand, the anticipated population by 2020 will be around 1300 million, on the other, the agricultural produce is on the decline. And, one well recognized citizen is insisting about our becoming super power by that time.

Dr. Manmohan Singh's concern about 'The unemployed youth in rural areas could be a force of destabilization' stopped with this utterance. Did he do anything further?

At that time, failing to get fund to initiate pilot plant, the author was trying to get UNDP's sanction for taking up six demonstration projects. The sad outcome has been narrated earlier.

The 9th plan makes an interesting reading to learn that we suffer from a genetic strain and we did not know how to come out from. Annexure 1 suggests an approach. Our past president suggested PURA (Providing Urban amenities in Rural Areas) without spelling out the details of the approach plan for success in three villages.

The 9th Plan's repeats what the AICC had resolved in 1886. Is there any doubt in our feudal mind, which had been exploited by other country and our rulers till now?

NINTH PLAN

Will it be wrong to suggest that ours is a dangerously rudderless verbose and not action oriented society. But our noble face towards rural society continues. One must admire our Prime Minister's persevered mind as indicated below comparing with what he had stated in 1992 as Finance Minister.

Ninth Plan (1997-2002)

The Objectives of the 9th Plan evovled from the common minimum programme of the Govenrment and the Chief Ministrer's conference of basic minimum services. The suggestions are follows:

a. ***Priority to agriculture and rural development with the view to generating productive employment and eradication of poverty.***
b. ***Accelerating the growth rate of the economy with stable prices.***
c. ***Ensuring food nutritional security for the vulnerable section of the soeoirty.***
d. ***Providing the basic minimum services of safe drinking***

water, primary health care facilties, universal primary education, shelter, and connectivity to all in a time bound population;

- *e.* ***Containing the growth rate of population;***
- *f.* ***Ensuring enviromental sustainability of the development process through participation of people;***
- *g.* ***Empowerment of women and socially disadvantaged groups (SCs, STs, PBCs and minorities):***
- *h.* ***Promoting and developing Panchayati Raj, Co-operatives, etc,:***
- *i.* ***strengthening efforts to build self-reliance.***

MANMOHON SINGH AS PRIME MINISTER.

(Times of India, dated 30.06.2004. May be compared with what stated in 1991 – 1992 as Finance Minister)

Although Dr, Manmohan Singh could not do much to implement Article 243(G) as finance minister, now as Prime Minister he has maintained his desire, as seen from what was published on 30th June, 2004. A comparison of his two utterances in 1992 and 2004.

Note:

1. His two views have been narrated in subsequent parts of this book. in Part 3 In an earlier Para providing consideration on 'Fund allocation', page 232, it was established that the increased allocation for rural and agricultural development, during 2004-05 the disparity ratio between rich and poor has increased. The obvious is starring at face, loud and clear.

2. To rectify this situation, he has pleaded for **decentralized electricity** for rural development. Rajiv Gandhi Gramin Vidhuti programme also recommendations such an approach, operating as a part of CIA (Central Elecricity Authotity, the functional component of Ministry of Power) to electrify each home, when the goal is poverty alleviation.

The author believes that electrification of homes cannot eradicate the rural poverty, nor can do much towards rural development. The answer in establishment of **decentralized co-generation systems**.

Recommendation has been made to the Government to seek expert's opinion on what stated in these two 'Notes' and on two divergent energy systems..

One must admire his mental perseverance since 1992 till recent time when he had been harping about development on poor rural people, yet achieving little. It is not that money had not been allocated. But the strategy for implementation has never been discussed and formulated. Should we not also admire the Congress who ruled the nation for 47 years, out of 62 years of Independence? What have we achieved for the rural poor and the country? An urban-rural disparity ratio of 12+ and volume of good work done as announced recently by our Prime Minister?.

TABLE 10

Procurement / support prices of selected commodities (Rs/ quintal)

	Wheat	**Paddy**	**Groundnut**	**Cotton**	**Sugarcane**
2001-02	**620**	**530**	**1,340**	**1,675**	**62.05**
2003-03	**620**	**530**	**1,355**	**1,675**	**69.50**
2003-04	**630**	**550**	**1,400**	**1,725**	**73.00**

Source: Statistical Outline of India, 2006

Although the procurement price had remained virtually the same, if one takes the inflation into account, the reasons for increased poverty and disparity ratio are readily seen. But there are conflicting assessment, as indicated below:

“India poised to become second biggest economy” Productivity Zooming: Goldman -- Times of India, 24.01.2007.

Then media publishes an opposite view, as under;

Economic boom hasn’t touched poor

By Mahiendra Kumar Singh / TNN

New Delhi: the boat may be rising but it’s not lifting everyone. Economic growth might have been spectacular since 1993- that is, post economic reforms- but it seems to have tricked down rather slowly.

A soon-to-be-relesed official report has estimated that poverty declined by a mere 0.74% during the 11 year period ended 2004-05. although there are signs of things moving a little faster at 0.79% between 1999-2000 and 2004-05, going by another measure, the number of people below poverty line may have remained unchanged.

National Sample Survey Organisation’s (NSSO) dinings show the number of people living below powety line (BPL) at 22.15% in 2004-05, compared with 26.09% in 1999-2000. in the same period, the county’s GDP grew at around 6%. This mismatch between growth and its distribuition is politcally worrying as it indicates a rise in economic disparities. Economists say uneven growth of tens leads to social unrest which, in turn, can cause problems for politicians.

Anyone consuming less than 2,100 calories in urban areas, and 2,400 calories in rural areas, is classified in the BPL category. The NSSO study also shows that poverty declined the sharpest in the poorer states. Leading them were Assam and the north-eastern states, where people below the poverty line decreased by nearly 4% annually, followed by Jharkhand (2.51% a year during the five year period), Chhattisgarh (2,15% a year) and Bihar (1.69%)

Apart from slow reduction of poverty, government is also worried over a lower decrease in poverty rations in urban aress compared to rural areas. BPL population in rural are

decreased 4.68% between 1999-2000 and 2004-05, which was over twice the pace of the decrease in urban centres, estimated at 2.12%. The trend of slower poverty reduction in urban areas, say economists, could be due to migration of poor from rural areas. But they wonder if that is the case, whether the rate of actual decline of poverty in rural areas is over estimated.

Times of India: 19. 10 2006

Comparing with what presented below and in earlier Para's since 2004, one wonders what the true face of our country is.

So why are we talking about charity? Apparently we held back the money to create a dismal situation in rural areas, so that we can show our government's noble face at an opportune moment, e.g., election.

Ms. Vandana Shukla/TNN illustratively wrote that ***'In India's Food Bowl, Farmers Commit Suicide in Droves'*** not only in just Maharastra, shockingly farmers are committing suicides in Punjab, long considered India's food bowl.An amazing 13,600 farmers, mostly involved in paddy, wheat and cotton cultivation, have killed themselves in the last decade in just two clocks of Andana, in Sangrur district. Suicides among farmer are on the rise. The government, of course, refuted such findings.

The findings, announced on Saturday, are in starck contrast to state government claims that there have been just 2,116 suicides in the corresponding period, that too in the "entire state" with 138 blocks. Those who have done the research say this figure is highly unlikely.

Inderjeet Singh Jaijee, convener of MASR, said, "The state government is under playing the magnitude of the Central government of the proble, it is because the central government does not want changes in budgetary allocation for the farming sector, what we demand is a census on farmers suicides, conducted by a neutral organisation".

Suicides among farmers are on the rise and there are

many reason for this,
Punjab's co-operatives minister admitted that "there are some suicides", but was quick to add, "The number of suicides has decreased from what it was during (the earlier) SAD government. .

"Most suicides are commited the day a farmer sells his last acre for food. Land holdings have st4eadily depleted. And 20% of farmers who commit suicide are those working as labourers on their own land. Those who do own land, have not more than 10 acres".

To rectify the above, the ploughs are taken out again forgetting the remaining aspects of Article 243(G).

Note: The two, controlling the destiny of the nation, direct the ploughing ends in different directions. While Sonia Gandhi's ploughing end points to cultivate the land, Manmohon Singh with his philosophical mind believes in ploughing the air – which he is used to since 1992. However, the end result for the rural poor is the same.

Sounding Poll Bugle At Delhi Rally

Congress Chief Blasts BJP

TAKING A DIG AT OPPOSITION: Congress president Sonia Gandhi and Prime Minister Manmohan Singh with ploughs at the Dhanyawad Abhinandan rally at Ramlila Maidan in New Delhi on Sunday.

It is difficult to understand how ploughs have appeared in the hands of those who are currently ruling the country. What message are they trying to convey? Is this to suggest that the country's future policy for rural development will continue as of before. Art. 243(G) will remain as an ornamental ploy, with a new Ministry of Panchayat raj to take care of this Article, for earning votes. An attempt was made to reach the hon'ble minister. The letter had reached him, I gathered, but he did not care to reply, in spite of three reminders.

While the primitive rural life style is retained, the political leaders, NGO's and the media convey that rural society is ***really*** not that poor. Why worry when only 22% (275 million – almost the same as in USA, or those living in our urban area) are below poverty line? One wonders for whom and why the NSS (national Sample Survey) reports on rural facilities are prepared. The urbanites are not interested about rural people beyond vegetable and food markets. The village Panchayats could derive benefits informing the rural folks where they stand, if. only they are aware about these NSS reports. Are these circulated to Panchayats translated in our national languages?

THE CRITICAL ISSUES

There is no doubt that Article 243(G) is full of well meaning activities. The basic need, though not spelt out, is to create two faces of a village community. One, agronomy, the other is the value added agro-products, and enterprises employing skilled technicians working on metallic and non-metallic materials. The emphasis should be to produce innovative competitive marketable products .The picture below (Figure 3) confirms that we wish to retain the first (original) face - agronomy , when the other face is willfully neglected. because then our age old social structure, the feudal rich and the poor divide, and vote bank will crumple.

Ploughing & preparing the soil for cultivation

Conveying seedling plantation
Photograph by author

Plantation

OUR ELECTION RITUAL

A media picture, shown earlier made many to think, whether the happy child got his exalted ride on the shoulder of the elite, because he had excelled in his school, or was this a mere show off about the exuberant nature of the elite, not bothering to learn whether he was going to a school or having enough food to eat? This must have been enquired, when our current status (2004 – 2005) NSS report No.513 suggests that the rural literacy is only 10.2 %. in the age group up to 14, even though funds had been allotted for 'Sarva Shiksha Abhiyan'(SSA). To make a child happy is indeed a noble act, and it will remain as his life long happy memory. The other part, that is vote earning ploy, *if true*, is vile.

OUR OFT REPEATED GOAL

Self reliant rural community might have been our apparent goal, while framing Article 243(G) in 1992, modifying the initial Article 40 of our Constitution, but we had never worked to implement this. May be this has happened because of non-availability of adequate appropriate energy. This and literacy are two *fundamentals towards rural development* We needed, to begin with an emphasis on both with no gender difference, followed by vocational training centers, managed by well educated Panchayats to *implement* in a programmed manner what stated in Article 243(G), and finally create centers of creative minds, to evolve a national strategy towards competitive trade and commerce.

In parallel, establish QCLs (Quality Control Laboratories) maintaining parity with international standards. Our desire to bring down the urban rural divide to a thin line, if genuine, deserves much more serious and honest planning *and* action, than what currently voiced but not practised. With our fallacious planning of our natural resources, and our poor energy situation, no desire can be more ignorant and absurd. The goal should be to talk less, and act more. Let us give up the set routine of organizing seminars in urban areas, to voice about rural people, (when no rural people participating) to get publicity. Currently, our nation's development is done through two acts, as under.

Act 1 in urban society:. seminar, Reception of Chief guest, Welcome address, key note address by Chief guest, tea break, departure of guest of honour, presentation of well prepared papers, lunch break, again well read papers when half of the delegates are half awake/ asleep, valedictory address, vote of thanks, *again tea break followed by cultural programmes*, and the grand finale, - *sumptuous dinner when a few are discreetly entertained with alcoholic drink* at a separate venue. No conclusion suggesting action oriented recommendation on follow up by a responsible body.

Act 2 in rural society:. Plough field since early morning, pray to God Varuna for rain; or sitting idle waiting for harvesting time, or making a rope to commit suicide, when the moneylender is knocking at the door .shouting intolerable abusive language.

Behold, nation is developed with Booming economy! So the government says.

NATION'S ADMINISTRATION: GOVERNANCE

CENTRAL GOVERNMENT

It may not be a commonly known fact that we have currently about 250 chairmen, commissioners, director generals, presidents, to look after various aspects of the country's needs, *in addition* to a council of 65 central government ministers, consisting of prime minister, 28 cabinet ministers, 28 ministers of state, and 9 with Independent charge, and their, secretaries, secretarial staff, personal secretaries, staffs attendants, drivers, and so on. They are Delhi based occupying accommodations built for them by the government, or get compensatory allowances, as HRA (House Rent Allowance). They manage 46 ministries, and 7 independent departments.(Total 53).

STATES

We have large and small in all 29 States and 6 centrally administered union territories. The biggest State is Utter Pradesh, with a population of 166 million.(2001). They are having similar support services, as the central government has.

MINDLESS SLAVE BUREAUCRACY

Creation of this class administrative agency was a part of the British rule. How else could the handful Englishmen control this vast country, with unaccountable diversities. A word of appreciation is due to the British administration. To select these bureaucrats, they introduced a system when aspirant candidates had to go through common tests. Gradation of merit was done through a common selection process, where religion did not play any part. Only meritorious persons were selected. This process of selection was applicable equally for all grades, ICS (Indian Civil Service,) - the highest administrative grade, to LDC (Lower division clerk). Selected ICS officers, initially on probation, were further trained in England. Retuning, appropriately trained, they had to go through punishment postings as magistrates in backward areas, before they could start climbing to the pinnacle, as secretaries to government of India. These 'know all' bureaucrats were posted to control the administrations of several state and central government ministries. These postings were done on consideration other than the requirement of knowledge to be dealt with. They were the 'know all' supreme, when the ministers were often the puppets, getting briefings from such secretaries. The ministers conveyed to the secretaries the direction of the governmental wind. This created a 'policy directive' for the clerks to grasp. . In fact, any issue needing consideration, was initiated at the desk of a clerk, and then the file started moving upwards, with additional remarks from intermediate officials before reaching the decision making levels. Thus 'file pushers' became an important element of administration. If a clerk did not want the file to move, knowing the mind of his superior, he could hold this back for any length of time. No query would be answered. The administration was flexible to an extent, when a file could obtain the final decision, in couple of hours; or not seeing the light of the day over a century. The 'under the table' culture generated, An approach to judiciary would make the case worse. Any government employment was a coveted job. Wealth and power were/are the two prime goals, not service to the society.

An undeniable fact is that within a space of about half a century since the first freedom struggle, our country's elites proved their instinct loyalty to our tormenter emerging as a distinct class, distancing from middle class intelligentsia, who in turn was not in step with the illiterate peasant and labour class. These three classes had distinctive features. Paradoxically, the poor were more loyal to the rich, because the later controlled directly the formers livelihood. The intelligentsia parched in the centre, could only form mutually admiring learned societies, hold seminars with three distinct parts; viz., the keynote address, the well-read papers, and the valedictory addresses. Usually these are prepared early, and they do not have any link with one another. The net outcome does not go beyond publishing a compendium with no finite action oriented conclusion. Providing fund towards such activities, the government wanted the intelligentsia to keep talking, but no sooner a proposal is made to implement anything new, the fund dried up. The employed intelligentsia served but did not create. They spoke in seminars. With high virtuous middle class morality, they became weather cock, mindless administrators (not all), respected scientists mostly with imitative minds, well-read learned professors, school teachers and clerks. The entire intelligentsia was encased in a huge infrastructure of 'government employment', with security of jobs and parks for towing the government policies, and more importantly, making in roads for foreign purchases, - thus the dependence on foreign goods became a permanent feature.

Earlier, the British domination was an era of diplomacy, viz. control over the rich princes, pamper the verbose non - functioning elites, and suppress by proxy the peasants, using the (despots – not all) middle class bureaucrats. The non uniform taxation systems were controlled through the princes to meet the needs of the British administration, and with little sympathy for the poor cultivators. They did not believe in literacy of the cultivators. Hence illiteracy happened on a massive scale - 700 million people were denied the light of growing science oriented civilization in the northern hemisphere, since industrial revolution. (Refer Annexure 5)

Even after independence the administration remained under British control for a while. The key posts were held by Britishers, but made little effort to suppress the carnage. The almighty iron man Sardar Patel, home minister, repeatedly complained to Mountbatten, with a new designation as the Governor General, that the police and the Army were abetting the communal riots. (30th January, 2009 The Statesman). We adopted the same as practised by the British rulers, but adding thoughtlessly new provisions to alleviate the economically poor and lower caste. For example, provisions are made to get admission in an academic institution even when in a common competitive test, an aspiring student from the privileged class performs badly.

RURAL MANAGEMENT

India has 6.39 lakh (0.639 million) villages, including uninhabited villages. According to the office of Register General of India, the number is 0.593 million. This number excludes some due to administrative reasons. Hence, it is safe to suggest that we are blessed with about 0.6 million villages, where 800 million people live, in an environment indicated in Table 1 and media published Annexure 4.

Item (h) of 243-(G) mentions about food processing and several items to be executed in rural area. They all require more heat energy than electricity. The Table below provides an indication on this, comparing the two. That an approach through a decentralized co-generated system is immensely superior and efficient to mere electricity supply, in our highly dispersed rural society, is evident, but not practiced. . Efforts had been made since 1983, to make the governance to understand this. But in vain. The energy ministry of the Central government rubbished this. The planning commission expressed about the paucity of fund. This aspect and the type of power generation system to be used for rural development has been discussed in PART 2. With supply of electricity alone, separate arrangement has to be made for generation of heat energy, needing additional energy source, - perhaps twice of that equivalent to electrical energy, and investment to organize this.

Note: Milk processing and Textile industries can be served wholly with a decentralized small Gas Turbine Engine. Sugar mill is known to be self sufficient burning biogases after sugar juice extraction.

CHAPTER - 14

WATER, FOOD, ENERGY

In the earlier part of this book, attempts have been made to present a glimpse of our society. Exact chronological order could not be retained because this subcontinent grew under different step parenthood, each had his own vested interests. The indigenous parents lacked brotherhood. They fought among themselves. But helped foreign rulers to get aid to suppress the neighbor. In a land of plenty of several resources, the initial non-ethnic societies became a tolerant philosophical, intelligent, but non-martial race. A subcontinent got developed with primary emphasis on a nature worshipping non-prophetic religion. The hungry world pounced on this land, ruled, and robbed with little resistance. If only this subcontinent was cohesive, militant when needed, without perverted religions and the genetic strain of luxury loving rich and poor divide, this subcontinent, - perhaps the world itself would have been different. A look at the fundamentals may help to assess our degradation, and prospects of revival.

WATER

BASICS OF OUR EXISTENCE

Sun

Light

$$6\,CO_2 + 6H_2O \text{ ---------}\Diamond\ C_6H_{12}O_6 + 6O_2$$

Rain water **Carbohydrate**

The existence of 0.03 % CO_2 in environs unpolluted air is assumed in the above process. Rain water provides the nutrients, similar to that from man made fertilizers, as needed for plant growth. The lightening provides the energy to make in the sky the natural fertilizer, which arrives as rain to make the mother earth pregnant and give birth to life saving green plants, categorizing them with scientific gradation of photosynthesis. Do we identify the influence of any religion in the above basic equation.? Can any religion modify this?

What buried below the earth's surface over unaccountable centuries, had also their origin above the earth's surface; and then aided by natural phenomena, created by God, got stored as energy source below the earth's surface. (Since we do not know about the origin of our planet, this may not be wholly true although generally accepted.)

This equation establishes the basics of our life processes. Not only that, the pollutant, CO_2 gets eliminated and the life saving Oxygen is released. God creates and sustains life the same way, irrespective of religion. *Rain Water, therefore, is life for all.* Hindus treat it like Shiva; when it can create, preserve and destroy. It is planet's greatest friend and foe.

Availability of non-saline pollution free water resources is limited but the demand for such water continues to rise steeply, making urgent need for an efficient planning and implementation of water resource programmer's appraisal, development, conservation and management. The creator is the same. Does not this fact prove that when we talk about different religions, we are belittling, unknowingly perhaps, God's basic creative power for survival of all. ,

INDIAN SITUATION

Ours is a poor agricultural society, with 22 % living below poverty line. Water is the basic need for such a society. Some indications are provided below on water requirement.

1. The water need varies on the scale of food production. The fragmentation of land with increasing population will need more water to produce the same per capita food. According to World Bank estimate, the water need will double every 21 years;.

2. Approximately 13,080 desalination plants are installed in 120 countries, mostly in Middle East. This water, devoid of nutrients, differs from rain water. Harmless for drinking but of no use unless nutrients are added to function as fertilizer for plant growth;
3. About 10 % improvement in irrigation efficiency, will double the drinking water supply for the poor.

One wonders whether our aspiration is to become a SUPER POWER by 2020 .have taken note of the facts presented above. \Apparently this feasibility was derived from group studies made by several learned bodies at the Department of Science and Technology. (DST), government of India, and other knowledgeable bodies and persons. An aspiration of this nature creates confusion, when currently we are short of all the basic elements required to live as civilized human beings, particularly in rural areas. These aspects are dealt with separately.

WATER AUDIT

An account on the availability of water in our planet provides an insight to our deficiencies, future difficulties, and what need be done. Hydrologic cycle provides an estimate. Out of the total, 97 % is saline sea water. The remaining, 3 % is fresh water. 75 %, that is, 2.25 % of this is in solid form (Glacier and polar ice caps). Those living on land of this planet depends only on 0.75% of fresh water. 70% of this, that is 0.525 % is used up for agriculture and plant life. The estimated remaining, 0.225 % is ideally available as fresh water flowing though rivers, and some gets collected in ponds. This gets further diminished due to three reasons: evaporation, ground water seepages, and floods when water flows back to sea. Assuming that these constitute about 65 %, we are *ideally* left with 0.146 % of fresh water. Much of this is polluted, and used to sustain animal life. Barely 0.1 % is available for human consumption.

Thus our target area is to try and make best use of 0.225 % of the total earth water. There are examples where human efforts have succeeded much to resolve their problems.

The hills of Malayasia provide fresh but not potable water in this region .shown below, except in Singapore.

Fig 4 Thailand

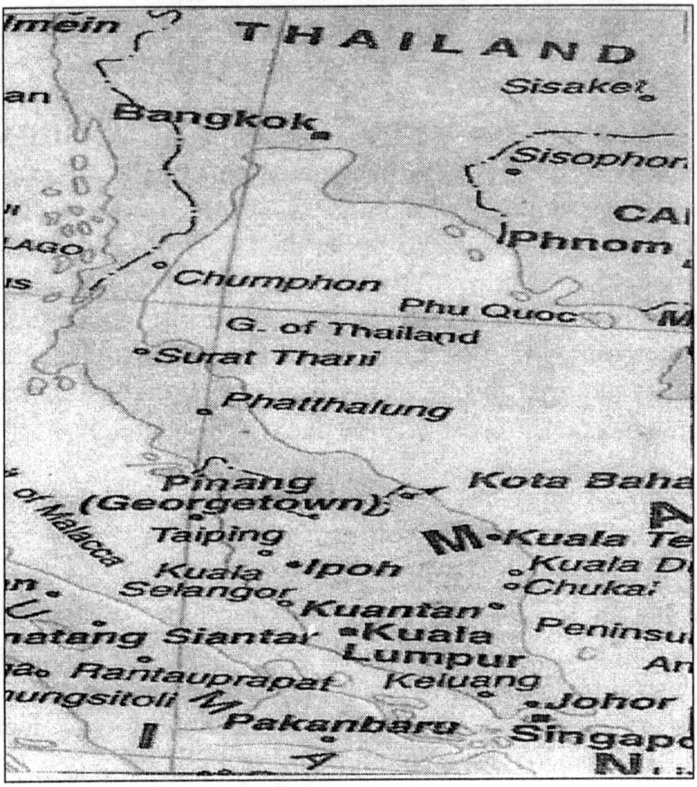

Singapore

2 NASSER LAKE

Population grew rapidly since the revolution of 1952. President Abdul Nasser took a bold decision to create a new dam. A new reservoir, known as Lake Nasser of 510 km length, originating from Nubia was completed in 1971. It has a capacity of 150 billion meter cube.

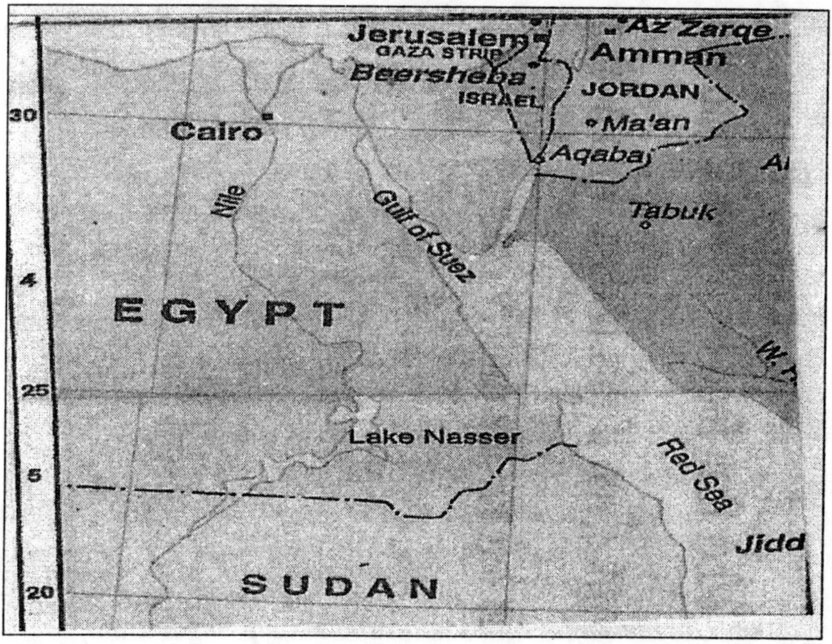

Nasser Lake

Source: CONCISE WORLD ATLAS, INDIAN MAP SERVICE

On its way towards lower Egypt, a massive hydroelectric project is established. To get the necessary fall across the turbine, a huge 'pond' is excavated. at Aswan. The author had the opportunity of visiting this site during the excavation phase in 1960s. It was incredible how such a huge pond was excavated out of solid rock with sheer manpower. Overlooking the work progressing down below, standing at the edge, was discouraged, because of whirling wind. However, taking precaution, lying on belly and crawling to the edge, the sight was awesome. It was similar to hundreds of ants meeting each other, transferring head loads and the emptied ones to a stream of men and women labour force, from bottom to top. There were two such streams on opposite sides. They worked often at ambient of 51^0C, in three shifts, living in congested dwellings. The controlling Ministry had been shifted from Cairo, and the supervisors were with the labour force.

It was an instance of exemplary leadership. To-day, most of the Electricity and sweet water in Egypt are from these two projects.

CANALS AND DAMS

In our country, several dams have been built to accelerate agricultural performance and to meet three needs, viz., irrigation and flood control, providing drinking water, and producing hydro-electricity. These are managed by a large number of government organisations.

- ***Nagarjuna Sagar Dam, Andhra Pradesh***
- ***Sardar Sarover Project build on river Narmada, Gujarat***
- ***Bhakra Nangal Dam build on river Sutletj, Himachal Pradesh***
- ***Gobind Sagar and Maharana Pratap Sagar Dam, Himachal Pradesh***
- ***Krisharaja Sagara Dam on Cauvery River, Karnataka***
- ***Tunga Bhadra Dam***
- ***Neyyar Dam, Kerala***
- ***Narmada Dam Project, Madhya Project***
- ***Hirakund Dam Built on Mahanadi River, Orissa***

Major dams and water reservoirs in India

Irrigation status has been discussed earlier. Punjab was an arid land and suffering from food shortage. They built a net work of canals. To-day it is the granary of India. The average yield of paddy there is about 4t/ha. On co-operative basis, most use tractors. But the national scenario is dismal. The average from irrigated land is about 2.2t/ha, perhaps lowest in the world. As regards flood, during rainy season, media provides information, yearly, on flooded areas, but not on measures taken on control. While we rate water as life, it creates insufferable damages to lives, countrywide. during monsoon time For example, Hoogly river mercilessly devour land and dwellings of the poor living on it's banks every year. Upper Assam gets submerged when Bramhaputra rivers' flooding water swirls down to lower Assam, as if to pay homage to Dispur, the capital of Assam. In summer, the subcontinent is thirsty. Yet with Nasser like leadership and motivated efforts we may get out of this predicament, creating three regional unconnected large lakes, designated with three names, e.g., Krishan, Jawan, and Manabica lakes respectively. One can be in the North-East area, off Bramhaputra river (2900 km) stretching towards West. Another in the central part, and the third one in the south. These three large lakes, with proper management. will get filled up with over flowing river water, during monsoon seasons.

The water will be retained even in summer season. Brahamputra and Ganges (2510 km) are perennial sources of water. Godavari (1450 km) orginating from Western Ghat is not. It gets charged with several tributaries, flows from West to East discharging into Bay of Bengal sea where the famed shore Mamallapuram temple exists as the crowning glory of 8th century, (Pallava Dynasty – 325/ 350 A.D.) It was an important trading port as well. One of the three suggested large lakes can be interposed in this (Godavari) river; when this may even be linked with Krishna river.

RAIN WATER HARVESTING

Water harvesting has been mentioned in Para 44 of the Budget for 2005 – 06. One reads about laws in the offing when sanctions for all new constructions in urban areas must have water harvesting systems. Is there a *plan* to create this culture in rural areas as well? Who will implement this? Has the work started? If so, what is the progress? Or, is this another ploy, or platitude to earn vote?

These three large regional lakes can individually be the mother sources to feed initially country's 700 water bodies with defined command areas and can modify our irrigation approach. We may now introduce agriculture as a coupled pond culture, as practiced in Thailand. For every cultivable land, a pond of suitable size is a compulsory element. The nation's water management may be reshaped as shown below:

1. Creation of three regional large lakes;
2. Irrigation system modified when pond culture has to be integrated with agriculture in addition to what is received on land through rain;
3. Organized rain water harvesting in rural areas, described in the following Para, mainly to meet drinking water needs in rural areas.

With such an approach, the major part of our 98 million un irrigated land may provide yield as if irrigated. South will be as fertile as Punjab. Other than cereals, other agro cash crops will be grown. Instead of interlinking rivers as a holistic issue for the nation, we should preferably approach this as regional activity. Our target should be, similar to Thailand, for an average annual yield of 4t/ha, or equivalent to take the first step to make a developed nation with two remunerative sides of the rural society's coin in energy deficient situation. This is discussed subsequently.

RAIN WATER HARVESTING IN RURAL AREAS.

Country's drinking water requirement is about 0.64 billion gallons* assuming a human body needs, on an average, 2 0 liter of sweet, preferably potable, water.(1200×10^6 x2)= 2.4 $\times 10^9$ litter), or 0.64billion U.S. gallons, (or 2.42 bn litrs) per day.(One U.S. gallon = 3.78 liters)

A fact perhaps not well known is that 1115 sq meter (12042 sq ft or approximately 120x 100ft) of land can collect 0.15 million (1.5lakh) lit. of rain water, if harvested ***annually***, suitable for drinking. Properly harvested, 41* people can have harvested rain water per day from standard '40 X 60' land.

* 1.5 lakh lit harvested from 12042 sq ft can serve 205 persons ***per day.*** 40 X 60= 2400 sq.ft can therefore serve 41 persons./ day. Village communes, administered by gram panchayats, may consider what follows.

A sturdy sheet of canvas (as used for making military tents) having a central hole, and twelve strong poles can provide for making a rain water harvesting system to provide drinking water in rural areas. Four poles are erected at four corners of the land and the other eight in the middle of the four boundaries. The sheet is tied to these to collect the drinking water from the central hole, draining in to a suitably sized tank with a locked cover. The water thus collected can be further filtered in each house. The filter can be made of three earthen pots. The first with layers of white clean sand, followed by one with charcoal pieces and the last one, fitted with a tap collects the filtered water. It is not a new concept, and had been in vogue long since. Now some add a pinch of chlorine to the top most receptacle of unfiltered water. Such systems are kept at a corner. A simple but sturdy device should be developed. Additionally, a testing system has to be developed to confirm that the filtered water as potable.

Such a tent like device for rainwater collection with filtering arrangement can be standardized, so that they can be mass-produced. The numbers of such systems to be erected at each village commune will depend upon the population involved.

The above is only a basic illustration. Several modifications need be made to make the system reliable and hygienic. Such a *properly* erected water collector can be used also for several other purposes; e.g., a community meeting place, amusement centers, literacy promotional venues, etc. They will replace, or reduce (often non functioning) tube well use, and thus ground water potential will improve.

Nation wide 'water harvesting' had been proposed for the first time during the 2005 – 2006 budget. This is a well expressed intention, provided the funds allotted do not simply create an additional cadre of more corrupt leaders, as is happening with the funds allotted for rural and agricultural development, and literacy programmes. We will soon know the plan and progress made during the next budget for 2006-2007. (No specific mention about the fund allocation for water harvesting has been made in the current Budget)

IMPLEMENTING AGENCY: RETIRED JAWANS

Here the Geological survey of India may identify the best locations to create the three huge lakes which will fill the excess flood water. If Egyptians could cut through solid rocks, our people are equally capable of making these lakes cutting through soils. There are several instances when big lakes have been made; e.g., one in Chandigar, at the foot hill of Simla range. Have not our jawans (and their leaders) climbed 70^0-sloped rocks at Kargil to defeat the well-entrenched enemy? Have not they (Border Road organization contingent) laid highest HTV (Heavy Transport Vehicle) roads under most hostile atmospheric condition? These three region with artificially made lakes, can eventually be the high land mark of our gratitude, for all time to come; named, suggested earlier, as Krishan, Jawan, and Manabica lakes. They can become centers for firing the minds of young for unity and national services. There are countries where flood control is a part of irrigation. Let ours be so.

The enormous excavated earth, with proper landscaping can create all kinds of designated parks at higher than water level, as venues of botanical learning and recreations (not holiday resorts). These lakes can function in the same way as Singapore to Bangkok piped water supply system, under SARWP scheme, meeting fresh water needs along the whole of

Indian subcontinent. Such a project will be of no less virtue compared to the on going connectivity road. (One does not know what progress it has made and at what cost).

A change has been introduced. The connections will be made only to villages having population of 1000 or more .Earlier, this road had been planned to connect villages with population of 500 or more. It implies that 3,64473 villages (61.43%) out of 5,93,616 villages having population less than 1000 will remain unconnected and suffer the way Table 7 has indicated. Approximately, 0.163 billion (163 million, about 14%, - the same as the total population of Pakist an) will be severed from the country's main stream and live as people did during early civilization.

Source: Compiled by author from data presented in INDIA 2007, published by Ministry of Information and Broadcasting, government of India.

J.M. Roberts, in his famed book, *History of the World* had aptly commented about our country's non progressing state comparing with ancient India. This is reproduced below.

ANCIENT INDIA

Even now, ancient India is still visible and accessible to us in a very direct sense. At the beginning of the twentieth century, some Indian communities still lived a sall our primeval ancestors must once have lived, by hunting and gathering. The bullock-cart and the potter's wheel of many villages today are, as far as can be seen, much the same as those used 4000 years ago. A caste-system whose main lines were set by about 1000 BC still regulates the lives of millions, and even of some Indian Christians and Muslims. God and goddesses whose culturs can be traced to the Stone Age are still worshipped at village shrines.

In some ways, then, ancient India is with us still as is no other ancient civilization. Yet though such examples of the conservatism of Indian life are copmmonplace, the country contains many other things too. The huntergatherers of the early twentieth century were the contemporaries of other Indians used to traveilling in railway trains. The diversity of Indian life is enormous, but wholly comprehensible given the size and variety of its setting. The sub-continent is, after all, about the size of Europe and is divided into regions clearly distinguished by climate, terrain and crops.

The above depicts how 163 million people still live when it could also be an account for their way of life in 1500 BC

DESALINATION

Finally desalination of sea water appears to be long term savior. The current status on desalination is indicated by Wall street Journal, dated 17th January, 2008, reporting that world wise 13,080 desalination plants produce more than 12 billion U.S. gallons of water per day. United Arab Emirates has the major share. The use of the Nuclear energy appears to be the most favored approach. However, a safe and economic strategy has to be worked out for transportation of large quantity of water over long distances. Currently, de-salined water is beyond the reach of countries like ours. In our highly dispersed locations of both rural and urban societies, transportation of de-salined water will be beyond the reach of most located away from sea coast. It is estimated that transporting saline water over 1600 km, or lifting by 2000 m cost about the same as desalination. Current situation world over is all coastal places will get into desalination system for perennial supply at a cost of about \$0.4 -0.45 per m^3, almost the same as available in Bangalore which gets potable water at tap, from Cauvery and Kammanahalli tanks, serving about 6 million people.

In addition to what river water provides, the solution for our country is what suggested earlier; i.e. through large lakes, pond combined agriculture, and rain water harvesting.

(Source: Desalination – Wikipedia)

HYDROPONICS history

The soil is not an essential part for food production. This fact was realized from early days, but not scientifically understood. So we stayed with soil based culture, even when there had been several instances when soil less agro-products had been possible with better nutritious quality. Hydroponics is a technology of soil less plant growth when the root is wholly or partially immersed in water mixed with nutrient to produce food. Soil provides no part in plant growth, except, importantly, holding the root firmly for vertical growth. If suitably researched, standard equipment set can be developed for house hold hydroponics culture, to get enough of all kinds of pesticide free vegetables. Commercial hydroponics cultivation can be 5 to 10 times more productive than what can be grown on soil; but special arrangements need be made. It can be a low cost solution with appropriate engineering approaches.

The greatest advantage is that what needs to be supplied at the root can be regulated. And hence the agricultural products can also have standards. If open water bodies are created through rain water harvesting, as subsequently suggested in the chapter dealing with this subject, then this approach for cultivation may make us free of problems during a draught season. An interesting feature of this culture is that the nutrient mixed with water` can/is drained and recycled. The opportunities became almost limitless, once two German scientists Julius von Such (1860) and W. Knops (1861) published the first standard formula for a nutrient solution that could be dissolved in water and in which plants could be successfully grown.

Now it was possible to grow several kinds of food when the roots are buried inside sand, gravel, charcoal, etc. which are inert media. These are required to be moistened with nutrients dissolved in water. An important fall out is the soil-borne pests and diseases are eliminated, so also the weeds. In our situation, when per capita soil availability is diminishing at every second, soil less culture becomes an important experimental science of Botany. Numerous hydro phonic units, some on very large scale, have been built in Mexico, Puerto Rico, Hawaii, Israel, Japan, and Europe. In the United States, recent survey indicates that in more than 1000,000 (one million) household hydrophonic units are operating.

In the West, expensive environmentally controlled green houses are constructed. It is interesting to find that USA having per capita 3 times more land than ours is currently doing more research on soil less cultivation. In India, hydroponics came late, -round 1946. The first experiment commenced in government of Bengal's experimental firm during summer that year, in Kalimpong, near Darjeeling. It did not gain popularity essentially because of financial reasons. Most of the experiments have been tried out in West Bengal. A manuscript, projecting the possibility of agricultural revolution through hydroponics, suggests possibilities as under

HYDROPHONONICS

TABLE 11

CROP	***Agriculture (Per acre)***	***Hydroponics (Per acre)***
1. Rice	***1000 1b (455 kg) 1.36 ton/ha)***	***12,000 1b(5454 kg) (16.36 ton/ha)***
2. Wheat	***1600 1b (727 kg) (1.8 ton / ha)***	***5000 1b (2273 kg) (5.66 ton/ha)***
3. Potato	***22,000 1b (10,000 kg) (25 ton/ha)***	***50,000 1b (68182 kg) (170.5 ton/ha)***
4. Tomato	***5-10 tons (12.5 ton/ha)***	***200 tons (500 ton/ha)***

Table showing possibilities through agricultural revolution

Soil based vegetables are still cheap, seasonally, but often grown on unhygienic soil conditions. These lead to several diseases. Yet there are deep routed social practices preventing such agricultural revolution. In spite of all the benefits mentioned, in West Bengal cities, - for example, in Kolkata, going to vegetable and fish market in the morning is an unavoidable ritual. It provides several benefits. Unintended morning walk; meeting neighbours and exchanging political views (Kolkata's unique culture of *two* persons generating three divergent opinions on the quality, type, size of fish and cost; and friendly conversation with the shopkeeper is a Bengali culture.) Walking down to market and returning home to discuss merits,(or demerits) on purchases made with the wife over a cup of tea is far more easier than looking after hydroponics.

Additionally, the NEWS paper has to be read. This is a must. How else to discuss the country's political and sports situation, in the office? So where is the time to look after Hydroponics.? There are several other reasons offered against hydrophonics. First, induction of a new generation of agronomists, and synthesis with low income group farmers. Secondly, increased labour required at domestic levels to attend to hydroponics. Hydrophonics can be a profitable occupation in rural areas.

If socially acceptable and successful, the required equipment can be made of suitably moulded plastic/ earth material, and much healthier food can be had at competitive prices. The important benefit through domestic hydroponics will be the release of soil to grow more soiled based cereals. Cereals can also be grown through hydroponics approach, but only if large commercial approach is made.

Hydroponics is a relatively new organized science, although practiced very successfully in isolated cases long since, in varied situations, without understanding the science behind it. Now the situation has changed. The science, and the equipments are available in market particularly in developed societies.

A long list of sellers of hydrophobic equipment is available in the American market. These, suitably modified, can be produced in our country, at cheap prices. The new Ministry of Panchayati Raj should add this as one more to the 24 items recommended in Art 243 (G). It can be a very profitable business for landless labourers. If socially acceptable and successful, much healthier food can be had at competitive prices.

Source : History of Hyro-phonics.19.12.2005

OUR CURRENT FOOD PRODUCTION

Current production of food and other basic dietary needs
(Balanced Diet – 2559 calories)
Food production (Totel-191.2x10^6 T)

TABLE 12

Item 1 Grain & Fish Production		
1.	***Wheat***	***65x10^{6}T***
2.	***Oil seed***	***24x10^{6}T***
3.	***Fish***	***5x10^{6}T***
Item 2-Horticulture		
4.	***Bananas***	***Ist in Global production***
5.	***Mangos***	***"***
6.	***Coconuts***	***"***
7.	***Potato***	***"***
8.	***Onion***	***"***
9.	***Onion***	***"***
10.	***Green Peas***	***"***
11.	***Pineapple***	***One among 10***
12.	***Flowers***	***"***
13.	***Spices***	***"***
14.	***Apple***	***"***
Item 3 – Milk Production – 75 x 10 6 T > USA's production		
15.	***Tea***	***0.8 x 10^{6}T***
16.	***Coffee***	***0.2 x 10^6 T***
India's Area		***3,287,263 Km^2***

Forecast Cover Reported	*770,000 Km^2- 23.4% of total*
Actual	*639,200 Km^2 – 19.4%*
Good cover	*357,700 Km2 – 10.9%*

An overall picture on cereal and vegetable production

CREATION OF A PERMANENT CADRE

Why not create a permanent cadre to deal with these appropriately? There is a ready made task force. The young retired jawans (soldiers) may be a major component. They will work in parallel with village Panchayatis. but not as a part of these. They will execute major projects for rural development. Such a body will not have any administrative power for rural development. Sitting together with village Panchayats, they will decide their responsibilities. They will never impose any authority over the village Panchayats but assist the executions of literacy programmes, sports, water management, health and hygiene management, road building, communication systems, etc. In short, they will be a helping force towards execution of these as budgeted for. No sooner the retired militia gets control, and not a helping hand, a new breed of feudalism will raise it's head conflicting with Pachayats.

The village folks will love and respect them so long they function as friends and not masters. We must learn from our mistakes in East Bengal and Kashmir. So long the retired economically better off than average villagers remain humble and help with discipline, to develop the rural community, they will do immense good not only to rural society, but also the country as a whole. The retired jawans should behave as school's headmasters, and not a commanding officers.

All jawans and several technology oriented ex-service personnel come from villages. About 60,000 service personnel retire every year at young age. The number of those, still in forties or fifties, and capable of hard work are eager to find employment. When one makes an estimate on the benefits which may accrue from the activities, mentioned above, the additional expenses involved to organize and operate, with less corruption, will be a mere pittance. The remuneration can be met following the standard norm as currently followed, viz. pay plus pension equals remuneration as received at the time of retirement can be adopted. Currently the justified pension amount disbursed can be utilized for the much needed nation building, through rural development.

The jawans are used to face difficult tasks. In fact, they like to face challenges collectively. An estimated 3.2 lakh ex-service men are currently unemployed. Out of this around 30% are still able bodied personnel, fit enough to handle many problems faced by villagers. If we decide to form such a corps through assistance of Resettlement directorate of Defence ministry, the three Defence services will be most respected in the rural areas. There will be an additional fall out of great virtue. Service personnel are mostly from rural areas.

A disciplined corps spread all over the country can organize sports and elementary military training in rural schools. The children love sports. This corps can be used for literacy programmes for the rural folks as well. These activities need not be regimented. There is a wrong perception about retired persons. They love to be near their family. But not sitting idle. The whole concept is to generate a vibrant rural society to come up to the standard of urban society and more, adopting the approach suggested earlier.

INDUSTRY AND WATER NEED

Talking about the origin of agriculture, and rural poor, we often forget that even the industrial society's growth would not have been possible without water. The European industrial revolution had it's origin through externally fired steam engine in 1765 by James Watt. The first precursor of steam engine is Thomas Savery's steam pump in 1712. Once the steam engine became operational, making use of Michael Faraday's discovery of electromagnetic induction in 1831, electric company generation became feasible. There after, England did not have to look back. It became the world power backed up by their science and technology oriented innovative minds. While the production of steel was the backbone of industrial revolution, the steam power was the heart. The basic element for progress remained mainly on water use. and energy development.

GLOBAL ENERGY SITUATION

The map provides why the southern region needs urgent innovative R&D activities to create a new social order. The primary emphasis should be to generate energy in a manner to provide equivalent to the prevailing deficient conventional resources, suiting the agronomy based rural societies.

FIG. 6

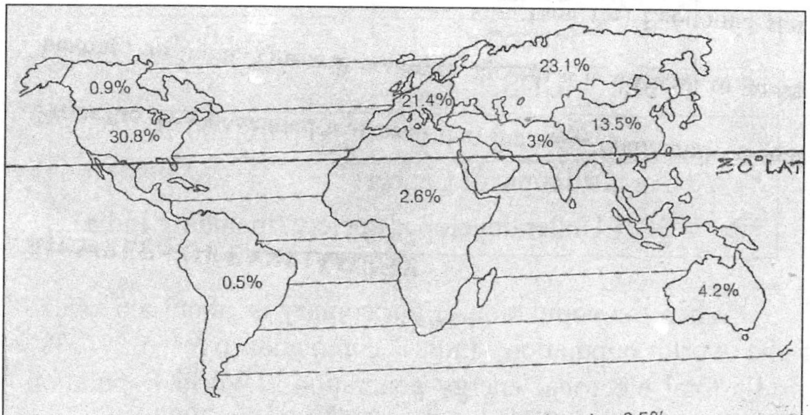

Canada 0.9% · United States 30.8% · Latin America 0.5%

Europe 21.4% · Africa 2.6% · USSR 23.1% · China 13.5%

Rest of Asia 3% · Oceania 4.2%

Recoverable coal reserves of the world.

Source: World Energy Conference Survey of Energy Resources, 1974.

Energy divide below and above 30^0 latitude

WORLD WIDE ENERGY RESERVE

Although the data presented above is 35 years old, the generic picture on energy availability in northern and southern hemisphere has not altered to any significant extent. The energy reserve situation is not man made. Can we, therefore, conclude that God wished that people in the southern hemisphere should be poor? But it was not so before the Industrial revolution.

TABLE - 13

Total global energy generation through conventional fuel

*	United State	25.9 %
*	Africa	20.1 %
*	USSR	21.1 %
*	China	11.5 %
*	Europe	13.6 %
* *	UDS	7.8%
Total		100.00 %

* Above the Tropic of Cancer

* * UDS - Under developed society (including India)

When the population of our country is about a 6th (5.75^{th}) of the world population, India commands over only 3% of world's total electrical energy generation,. (World Population – 6.79 billion, when India's is 1.18 on 7th January 2009.).

Characteristics of Indian conventional energy sources

Conventional energy sources such as coal, hydro, and nuclear are least suited to small energy generation. These are ideally suited for large power generations. Till recent days the power generation situation in India was as under;

Table – 14

Current central power generation in India

Year	2004		1980
	MW	% of total	MW
Thermal	74,420.82	65.13	18,678
Hydro	26,261.00	23.00	11,384
Nuclear	2,272.00	2.00	640
Wind	1,869.00	1.64	---
Natural gas	9,000.00*	7.88	317
Others	448.00	0.35	---
Total	1,14,278.82	100	31,019

ELECTRICITY DISTRIBUTION PATTERN

That there was a willful desire to keep the rural society under developed is seen from Fig 5 presented earlier (page 232), the media observation which followed .and Fig 7, indicating the pattern of Electrical distribution pattern. Yet it is commonly accepted that unless the rural areas are energized the urban rich and rural poor divide will keep on increasing, to what end, it is frightening even to ponder.

It is difficult to fathom the reason why such reluctance to develop the rural areas, and keep them locked up primarily with agronomy based economy .

Is it the genetic strain of Indo-Aryan era since 2000 B.C.? Do we sincerely believe that this country with 800 million people will survive long as Sovereign Nation?

The had been suggesting a solution through 'Decentralized Energy generation' since 1984. Any amount of persuasion at all levels has received no response. The Government believes in decentralized electrification and providing electricity in all rural homes to achieve rural development and poverty alleviation. Suggestions to get these approaches assessed through a competent body has no response.

This amounts to a poorly 19,500 MW for 800 million people in a manner shown. Most used up for energizing pump sets, and village homes remain dark at night. One can appreciate why the rural society is illiterate.

Fig 7

RURAL **URBAN**

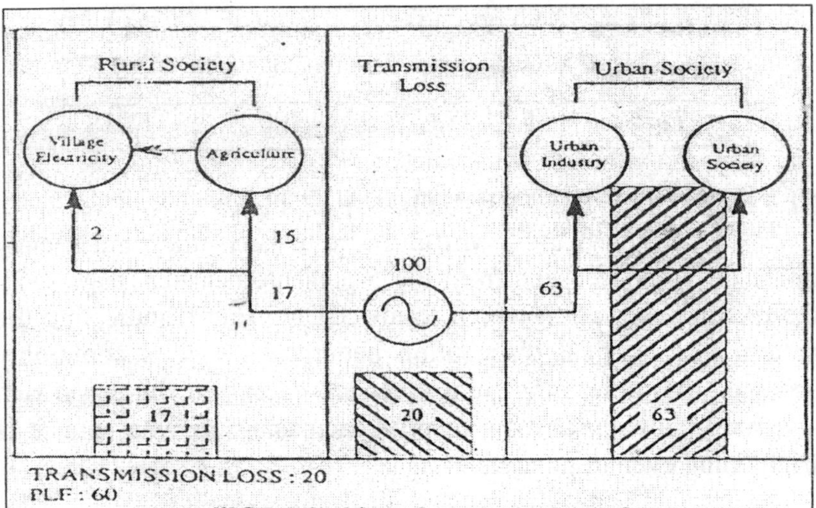

FIG II : ELECTRICAL ENERGY FLOW PATTERN

Electrical energy dustribution pattern pattern

Most commendable fact is the rural society is surviving in spite of the above situation. Not only they are feeding the urban society, they are feeding themselves too; -. though poorly. Even then, they are the backbone of the Defense and Para Military Forces. The tragedy is corruption is slowly creeping in such noble and disciplined services. However, indiscipline is appropriately dealt with.

A fact needs consideration. The marshal law quickly disposes off any alleged offence often within a month. The outcome of proceeding, - the punishment, for example, - gets vetted by the law ministry, before implementation. Not a single case has been returned for re-examination. If justice can be administered so very efficiently, in military services, what prevents the nation to adopt the same for civilian population as well? If so done, a disciplined nation will emerge. Currently the citizen are afraid of approaching the law, because of several well known reasons. The delay, the litigation cost through lawyers, wastage of prime time, and lastly not the least, the corruption are encouraging the wrong doers. Adoption of law similar to what is designated as martial law will eliminate them.

ENERGY FOR RURAL DEVELOPMENT

Keeping in view the future adverse possibilities, an innovative change in the energy situation in this part, below 30^0 latitude, is needed. Two reasons are apparent.

While water is life, the availability of appropriate energy is the diet for that life to grow with strength in agro-based society. The capacity of electric energy generation, is currently viewed as the index of progress of any country. This, based on electricity generation ***alone,*** is not valid for agricultural society like ours. A rich developed society in the Northern hemisphere depends mainly on electricity, when the required fresh and processed agro-product needs are imported from poor agricultural countries. The financial return from industrial products, needing mainly electricity is much more that from agro-based products .needing both electricity and heat energy. Our top down strategy, propounded by Nehru for nation's development, apparently advised by Prosanto Mahalanabish , did not realize that our current poor agricultural society of 800 million people, living on agronomy alone, cannot join the club of the rich, in urban industrial society, unless this society finds a way to earn more adopting an energy system suited to a primarily agricultural society.

To search such an energy system, studies were sponsored by the government. Much persevered efforts, spear headed by Total Energy Systems, with a sub-title 'Navuday' – meaning New rise,- were needed before government letters, authourizing the studies by SICOM (State Industrial Committee of Maharashtra), and formation of a high level steering committee were issued. The details of studies made were presented to the Steering Committee. Even though the quantified data are old, the pattern appears to remain the same when no change has been made in our country's management system.

AGRO-INDUSTRIES

The study was based on the use of natural gas, Naphtha and also alcohol, for processing agro products. Lower efficient simple engine provides for greater amount of exhaust mildly vitiated hot air as needed for several agro processing activities after electricity generation. Study confirms that heat energy needed can be met adopting Fig 8 approach Studies were made to establish this benefit. This is presented below

Ratio of heat and Electrical energy needs for Agro-Industries.

TABLE 15

Sl No	*Agro-based indsutries Products & Processing*	*Heat Energy/ Tonne B to (Equ.KWH)*	*Electric/ Tonne KWH*	*Ration (2) /(3)*
	(1)	*(2)*	*(3)*	*(4)*
1.	**Rice Par-boil**	**1.52 x 10^6 (475)**	**89**	**5.33**
2.	**Groundnut oil**	**10.48 x 10^6(3070)**	**438**	**7.00**
3.	**Sugar**	**20.68 x 10^6 (6060)**	**1066**	**5.68**
4.	**Paper**	**41.35 x10^6 (12120)**	**1333**	**9.09**
5.	**Textile**	**72.37 x 10^6 (21204)**	**6065**	**3.49**
6.	**Tea Processing**	**10.0 x 10^6 (2930)**	**500**	**5.86**

(1)	(2)	(3)	(4)
7. Milk Processing	0.45×10^6(132)	35	3.77

*** Note**

(1) With 25% efficient electricity generation system, ratio of heat / Electricity 3.0

(2) Expensive more efficient generation system has no obvious virtue in total energy applications.

Heat energy and electricity requirement

ECONOMIC BENEFIT

GDP per kWh can be much greater with agro-product. The electrical energy required to make an useable metallic commodity of the equal value is much greater than for an agro-product. Table 16 illustrates this.

TABLE - 16

Rations of

Industries		*Fixed capital to value added*	*Fixed capital to gross output*	*Net value added to gross output*	*GDP/KWH*
Major non agro industry group		*2.39*	*0.48*	*0.20*	*3.57*
Agro-industries					
1	**Soyabean processing (Natural gas fuel of HBJ gas Grid) in MP**	*34.2/90.02=0.37*	*34.2/264 =0.13*	*90.02 /264 =0.34*	*33.34*

2	**Paddy processing (Natural gas locally available in Assam)**	***41.5/148 =0.28***	***41.5/356 =0.11***	***148/ 365 =.0.42.***	***32.54***
3	**Paddy processing (Natural gas as available off HB) gas Grid**	***0.28***	***0.11***	***0.42***	***32.54***
4	**Groundnut Oil processing (Naptha as fuel in Karnataka)**	***32.6/70. = 0.47***	***32.6/205 = 0.15***	***70.0/205 = 0.34***	***14.49***
5	**Fish processing (Naptha as fuel in Maharashtra)**	***22.7/46. = 0.49***	***22.7 / 114.17 = 0.40***	***46.34/11 4.17 = 0.40***	***14.85***

SOURCE: Earlier Study made by SICOM, Bombey, in 1986/87, when the author was the nominated Principal Investigator. (Gov letter No. 45/322/86 – P dated 05.09.1986).

FINANCIAL BENEFIT THROUGH DECENTRALIZED CO-GENENERATION

Centralized cogeneration. operating in a programmed manner to meet other needs; as shown in the Fig 7 below. Two such units, generating 1 MW are used to cater for unexpected outage, or periodic servicing. A cross section of the power unit is shown below:

FIG 8

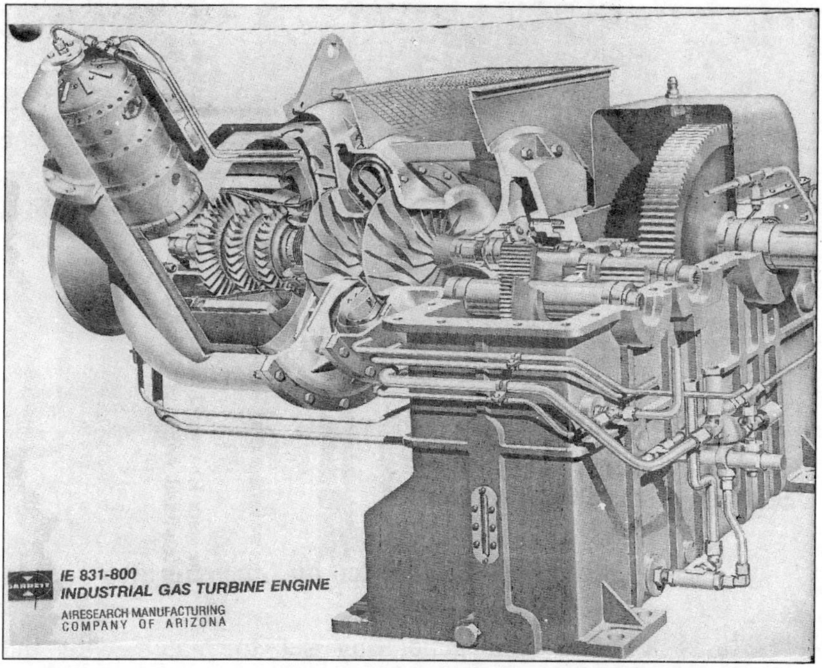

IMI – 800 industrial gas turbine engine

SOURCE: HAND BOOK ON IM 831 – 800 INDUSTRIAL GAS TURBINE ENGINE.

The generator is coupled to the large geared shaft on the right side. Air intake for the two stage centrifugal compressor is through a vertical intake, with air filter. The control panel is mounted on top of the generator. as shown below.

FIG 9

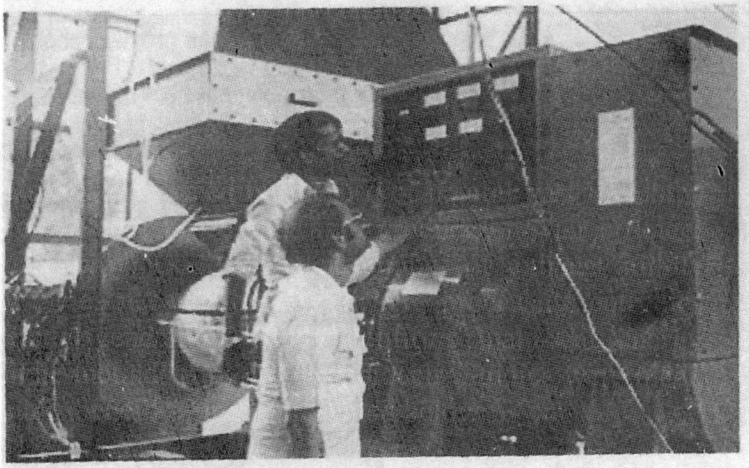

Source: Photograph by author

Control panel mounted on the generator

It is a fixed rpm generating set to match with the generator's need. The maximum rpm could be slightly adjusted although governed. The exhaust was the primary hot air of the ejector on the left. The ejector system could reduce/ adjust of the final exhaust virtually non-vitiated air to suit a specific need for processing agricultural raw materials.

AN EXPERIMENT ON CO-GENERATION

The 500 kW engine was bought by HAL, financed by DST (Department of Science and Technology), operated at Mandya sugar mill first with diesel fuel and then using alcohol, as a decentralized co–generated power generation system. The exhaust heat was attempted to dry the biogases which was burnt in the boiler. The experimental system was designed by HAL's energy cell. Operation with alcohol gave rise to a problem, when the alcohol had 5 % moisture. This produced a gummy substance within the fuel pump, and the driving shaft broke after a few runs. This needed replacement. Advised not to operate for long unless the alcohol was 99% moisture proof. This sugar mill did not have facility to remove the excess moisture.

FIG .10

Counter flow Biogas drier

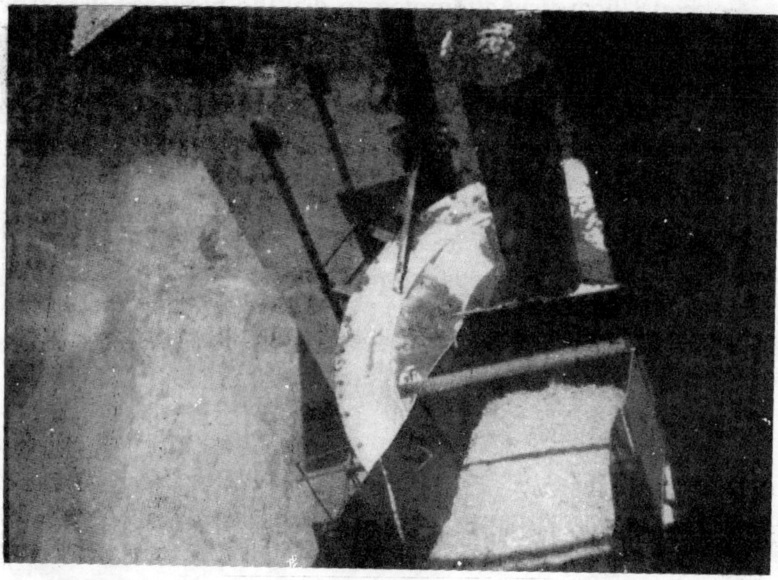

Baggase feed from the top to the Biogas drier

The vertical tall counter flow biogases drier was too small to handle the full load and the drying could not be done to the extent desired. Attempts to control the input often caused over drying and self ignition. It was difficult to control the amount of wet biogases which would meet the design requirement. Considering the fact this was the first attempt, and partial drying could be achieved, a new approach was being thought of, when biogases would be fed at the hot, but lower temperature ejector's gas outlet point. That is, the concept of counter flow would be revered.

This experiment could not be conducted when the supply

of alcohol was stopped. However, the exercise on the assigned objective of operation with a renewable energy source, alcohol - was satisfactory generating rated power. Co-generation was not a part of government assigned objective but attempted to gather data on co-generation. using an ejector to control the final varying hot air temperature. With the experience gained, a new drier was being worked upon, when the energy cell of HAL was closed down by the new management. Further the auctioned alcohol fetched greater revenue to the state government. However, the ability to use bio-fuel (diesel and alcohol) was confirmed, and it opened up a new dimension discussed in subsequent Para.

USE OF AERO GAS TURBINE

A fact needs be mentioned. When a fleet of aircraft is taken out of service, the engines are still useful for power generation. An engine of a fighter aircraft has many years of useful life for power generation. A fighter aircraft's engine is designed to go through extreme torture when in use, For example, to qualify the engine for aircraft use, it should be capable of operating six times, *in 20 seconds*, from slow running to maximum. This demands design skill to utilize both thermal and mechanical stress and fatigue properties of the metal used. Besides, such rapid acceleration and deceleration should not cause any instability such as 'surge' or flame out. But for power generation, it operates at a *fixed rpm* (revolution per minute). Overhauled, a time expired aero-engine can run for thousands of hours with no variation of generation properties.

The above generating set, IMI 831, is a derivative of an aero-engine (Garrett) which was under consideration for licensed production in HAL for a small Donier 220 transport aircraft. (This did not materialize) It was a single shaft power generating engine.

ESTIMATED CO-GENERATION FOR PRIMARY FOOD PROCESSING

The highly dispersed rural society can really boom up economically *if enough fuel is available to operate such co-generation systems*. The multi fuel engine shown above operates on fossil and renewable fuels. Studies were made, as under, to confirm the utility of decentralized cogeneration system. Fig 8 shows that such systems can provide large electrical energy and economic benefits in rural areas, With our current practice the disparity ratio is increasing rapidly as seen from analysis presented earlier

AN ESTIMATE OF NATURAL GAS NEED FOR RURAL DEVELOPMENT.

Ideally the generation need for rural development, consisting of six lakh villages, and 800 million people; is about 1,50,000 MW. For conditions stated below, the need is 1.224 bn m^3 of Natural Gas (NG) per day.

JUSTIFICATION

1 KwH = 3412 Btu/H = 0 .096 62 m^3/H wih 100 % generation efficiency. Hence with 25% gecneration efficiency, PLF (Plant Load Factor) , 10 % transmission loss, 1000 KwH (1 MW) will require 340.0 m^3 /H

Per day running continuously, 1 MW generation will need 8,160.0 m^3 /day of 24 hours.

Therefore, for 1,50,000 MW generation NG requirement will be 1.224 bn m^3/day. When our ideal NG production is about 22 b m^3 /day, even if we can harness about one 20th of our flared away gas, energy need for rural development should pose no problem. We don't need to run around foreign countries, which we love to do

Combined with a fact that we can use initially phased out aero-engine, (which we manufacture under licence), and make use of enormous useable wasted energy, rural development should pose no problem, ***provided we want this to happen.*** There are valid reason to believe that we do not want it in our 4000 years inherited way of life. This book provides enough evidence towards this conclusion. from events of past narrated, and also recent happenings, not narrated in the book.

Recent approach had been to request for a joint Parliamentary session to work out a strategy to implement Art. 243(G). Our Parliament is the apex legal authority, headed by our President.

This has been rejected. Finally, to get a collective view a subsidy of Rs. 5.0 lakhs had been requested for to approach our 1000 knowledgeable people to work out an acceptable implementable strategy. This has not materialized. That the Nation is going to face serious turmoil, unless we take care of poor agronomy based rural people, should have no doubt.\

ELECTRICAL ENERGY NEED FOR BASIC FOOD PROCESSING

ELECTRICAL ENERGY NEED
FOR AGRICULATURAL VALUE ADDITION
THROUGH
DECENTRALIZED TOTAL ENERGY SYSTEMS

TABLE 17

	Mn.MT	*Power (MW)*	*Rate for needing 1 MW*
A. Food Grain Inclduing pulses	*158.4*	*1100*	*20^T/Hr*
B. Oil Seed (Solvant oil extraction)	*13.1*	*218*	*200^T / day*

C. Cotton (Ginning & Spinning)	*8.5*	*310*	*100^T / day*
D. Sugar Cane	*173.0*	*192*	*5000^T / day*
E. Fishery	*0.30*	*60*	*25^T / day*
F. Tea	*0.65*	*452*	*1000 Kg/Hr*
G. Tobacco	*0.45*	*562*	*500 Kg/Hr*
Total		*2924MW*	

** Accounting for recent increased productin and a few other items need* ***for primary*** *value addition will be about 3500 MW. Total electrical energy required / year about 30 bn KwH/ year.*

TABLE 18

1. A PROFILE OF THE INDIAN ECONOMY SINCE INDEPENDENCE

	Unit	2005-06	1996-97	1950-51	CARG (%)
Demography*					
Population	(Mn.)	1,124	946	359	2.1
Females per 1,000 males	(No.)	934	927	946	—
Urban Population	(Mn.)	338	250	62	3.0
Birth rate	(Per 1,000)	23.8	27.4	39.9	-0.9
Death rate	(Per 1,000)	7.6	8.9	27.4	-2.3
Expectancy of life at birth					
Total	Years	65.4	61.0	32.1	1.3
Male	Years	63.9	60.2	32.4	1.2
Female	Years	66.9	61.4	31.7	1.4
National Income					
GDP (At factor cost)					
At current prices	(Rs. crs)	3,717,465	1,255,982	9,642	11.2
At 1999-2000 prices	(Rs. crs)	2,844,022	1,513,328	219,127	4.7
Share in Real GDP:					
Agriculture	(%)	18.5	31.5	55.4	-1.9
Industry	(%)	26.4	24.9	16.1	0.9
Services	(%)	55.1	43.6	28.5	1.2
Net National Product (At factor cost)					
At current prices	(Rs. crs)	3,267,371	1,104,902	9,233	11.0
At 1999-2000 prices	(Rs. crs)	2,515,372	1,329,251	206,493	4.6
Per Capita Income					
At current prices	(Rs.)	29,069	11,680	258	8.8
At 1999-2000 prices	(Rs.)	22,379	14,051	5,752	2.5

SOURCE: Statistical Outline of India, 2004 – 2005, Page 1

Note: The table above does not mention about rural population. However, from data presented above suggest the rural population (Country's population minus urban population), as under

INDIAN RURAL PEOPLE

TABLE 19

YEAR	2005 - 6	1996 - 7	1950 - 51
Rural population (Mn)	816	696	334
Disparity ratio*	10	6.05	2.25
Disparity ratio extrapolated, year 2100 : 13 (Current estimated Disparity ratio 12)			

* Disparity ratio – Per capita income based on GDP earned in urban area divided by the same in rural area.

Source: Computed by the author based on data presented at Table 11.

BENEFICIAL IMPACTS ON NATION BUILDING

The assumption made is non-pollutant bio-fuel will be available in due course of time. Much interest is shown on micro-algae based bio-diesel. However, much work is still to be done. Initially, the beginning has to be made using natural and coal gas. To achieve rural development to the extent when villages will acquire two faces, a fresh look at our energy policy need be made.

For example, we need to make serious efforts to:

1. Stop flaring of remaining natural gas, when much had already been so done in the north eastern part of our county.
2. Stop use of natural gas for centralized power generation.
3. Accelerate exploration of large reserve of coal gas in our coal belt area, and similarly impose a legal ban on it's use for centralized power generation to benefit the urban society.

The power generation has to be divided in two forms; - centralized Urban and decentralized rural. Rural society will now have agronomy on one face, the other literacy, vocational training, and energy based cottage industries on the other, not undermining the traditional skill based handicraft. Energy based cottage industries may take up outsourced manufacture of components needed for urban based industries.

At this stage the above may appear 'day dreaming'. However, efforts are being made long since as may be evident from what indicated below. As usual little interest had been shown to set up 6 such experimental units. Approaches were made to get assistance from NREL (National Renewable Energy Laboratory), Colorodo. USA. This is illustrated below:

RENEWABLE: BIO FUELS - NEW HORIZONS ON ENERGY

AN IDEAL NON-POLLUTING ENERGY GENERATION TO LAST TILL POSTERITY

Bio-diesel from aquatic species: approach through blue micro algae.

In the USA, the project focusing on liquid fuels from micro algae began .at Colorodo based NREL in 1982. Coincidently, the first plea to develop rural society using flared way Natural gas in Assam was made that year to establish 6 demonstrator models. There were several socio-economic and political compulsions. The technological considerations favored bio diesel. Some are mentioned in what follows.

Micro algae's are products of photosynthesis *six times* more efficient than in any other plant. It is the highest natural oil collector. Compared to bio-diesel extracted from various seeds it is many times more efficient. The use of bio-diesels needs hardly any modification to an existing diesel engine. If produced from aquatic sea water, the energy availability can be inexhaustible. The beneficial features are indicated below;

1. Mixed with fissile Diesel, even only upto 20 % (B20) the pollutant emission is reduced by about 65-70 percent;.
2. The filling station's equipment needs no change;
3. Large foreign exchange saving;
4. Self reliance;
5. Large employment opportunities for production of several ancillary equipment;
6. The harvesting could be enhanced in CO_2 atmosphere.
7. With iron as fertilizer, the micro-algae production can be enhanced significantly.

SALINE WATER POND SIZE .FOR CULTIVATION OF BLUE MICRO ALGAE.

NREL (*National Renewable Energy Laboratory*), Colorodo, USA has established that micro algal oil from 200,000 ($0.2X10^6$) hectare saline water pond can produce one quad (10^{15}) Btu/yr.

To generate currently produced one lakh (10^5) MW electrical energy, the ideal annual heat energy required is 7×10^{15} BTU/yr. This value has been arrived at assuming generating efficiency of 30 %, and a PLF of 0.7. Solar pond area required will, therefore, be $1.4X10^6$ hectare. The estimated deficient electrical energy is 2 lakh ($2 X10^5$) MW. Ideally $2.4 X10^6$ hectare of solar pond area can generate the deficient pollution free electrical energy for all time to come. To provide an idea of the magnitude, this area is equivalent to the whole of Run of Kutch whose area is 10800 square miles.

The additional benefits will be generation of pure sweet water @2400 liter/day /MW from the sea water; that is, 88 bbl liters/day, meeting the needs of quarter of our country's population. Ideally 6 lakh villages will be developed. The above estimates is essentially to provide what can be achieved form God's free gift of sea water and solar energy, growing micro-algae. A new era of Indian civilization will emerge.

CULTIVATION OF BLUE MICRO-ALGAE

The great Run of Kutch is a huge barren area in Gujarat state, jutting into Arabian Sea having a common northern border with Pakistan. A short war was fought with Pakistan in 1966, when Lal Bahadur Shastri was our prime minister. It has an area of 10,800 square mile (= $2.8X10^6$ ha) and theoretically this can be converted, with proper barrier, into a 'saline sea' to harvest green micro-algae which naturally grows. Keeping the earlier estimate in view, theoretically two (2) lakh MW can be generated.

The algal oil can be transported to our villages. A new nation will be created. To do so, the efforts needed will be tremendous, but not beyond human capability. Bhakra Nangal Dam, our biggest multi-purpose river valley project provides enough proof of our capability. Does not the great China wall prove about human capabilities? Did man think that one day a man will put his feet on the Moon's surface.? There will be one non-technological problems.

Run of Kutch gets flooded during rainy season for about four months; otherwise the top soil is dry and saline. This top soil is the feedstock of local salt industry. This provides livelihood for salt traders. This will not be disturbed. The anxiety about the salt traders are more than offset through desalinization of sea water to get fresh water, using waste heat after power generation when the concentrated saline water will provide for an easier approach to get salt for the salt industry.

There is another equally major obstacle. Migratory birds, especially the largest number of wading flamingos with long neck and leg, and pink or scarlet plumage come every year. The environmentalists may take serious exception if it is converted as a perennial salt-water pond (sea). The apprehension may no be real. With careful planning and regulating water depth the same which they are used to, the concern of the environmentalists may be satisfactorily met.

THE LITTLE RUN OF KUTCH

Rajkot, Sundernagar, Banaskantha and Kutch districts of Gujarat state surround it. The government of Gujarat feels that this area can be utilized for micro-algae cultivation, to begin with. A triangular shaped saline pond of about 550 sq. km (one sq. km = 100 Hectare) can be constructed building a 5 km long water barrier. If micro-algae cultivation is taken up in this saline pond of 55000 ha, about 3929 MW electrical energy; or, 47.4 million barrels* of algal bio-diesel oil and 1.729 million liters of potable water/day can be produced. A township of about one million people will soon become a center of several activities, mentioned earlier in Fig 3.

The prospects of employment will boom up. Value additions to agricultural products, creation of civic amenities, road building, educational facilities, and so on will transform this area. The eventual benefits will become a showcase for the nation as a whole. The 800 million people will wake up and not gather and wait for hours to hear meaningless platitudes in scorching sun. They will not have time to do so.

The political leaders will learn to implement the promises they make. One may go on mentioning endless benefits, which will sound like 'utopia' at this stage. Unless we act to develop our rural environment, the mass arising is a distinct possibility, as suggested by Dr. Manmohan Singh himself on two occasions during in 1991-96, initially as Finance Minister and then recently as Prime Minister. Other than expressing his concern, and pleading Scientists to develop Bio-Diesel, he did nothing else to eliminate the possible national calamity. His recent move to usher in n-energy in collaboration with USA will help urban society. He is apparently trying to go back to Nehruite top down concept for rural development. That it has not worked, needs elaboration. The author believes that a simultaneous approach for micro algae based Bio-Diesel and n-energy should have been made, while negotiating with USA. What America has in mind is seen from a letter reproduced below.

* (a) A barrel of 42 gallon diesel oil provides $5.8X10^6$ Btu. (b) 3929 MW generation needs $275x10^{11}$ Btu/yr. OR, (c) production of transportable 47.4 millions barrels (each containing 42 gallons providing heat of $5.8X10^6$ Btu/yr). 1 MW can produce 440 liter of sweet water, through desalination of sea water.

RECENT COMMUNICATION WITH NREL

Keeping that in view, and NREL's expressed desire to assist research even to private institutions, efforts were made to establish a link to make a start in our country. A copy of their letter (typed version) is reproduced below

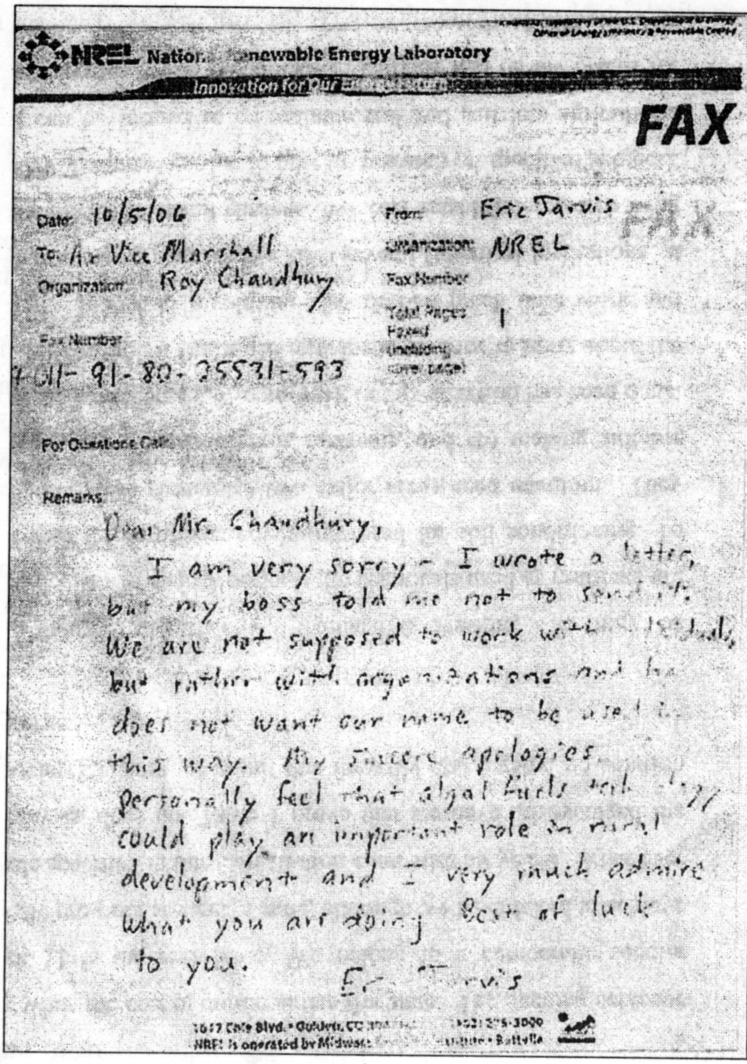

NREL National Renewable Energy Laboratory

Innovation for Our Energy Future

FAX

Date: 10/5/06
To: Air Vice Marshall
Organization: Roy Chaudhury
Fax Number: +011-91-80-25531-593

From: Eric Jarvis
Organization: NREL
Fax Number:
Total Pages Faxed (including cover page): 1

For Questions Call:

Remarks:

Dear Mr. Chaudhury,

I am very sorry – I wrote a letter, but my boss told me not to send it. We are not supposed to work with individuals, but rather with organizations and he does not want our name to be used in this way. My sincere apologies. [illegible] personally feel that algal fuels really could play an important role in rural development and I very much admire what you are doing. Best of luck to you.

Eric Jarvis

1617 Cole Blvd. • Golden, CO [illegible]
NREL is operated by Midwest [illegible] Institute • Battelle

Retyped for clarity

Dear Mr. Chaudhury,

I am very sorry – I wrote a letter but my boss told me not to send it. We are not supposed to work with the individuals but ather with Organizations and he does not want our name to be used in this way. My sincere apologies. Personally feel that algae fuels technology could play an important role in rural development and I very much admire what you are doing. Best of luck to you.

SEED BASED ENERGY.

Alternatively, the energy may be had from seed based agricultural products. Seed based approach has been worked upon by several countries. Soya bean, rapeseed, and corn based bio-diesel have been developed and used to operate diesel engines. Rudolf Diesel patented his Internal - Combustion (IC) engine in 1892, using vegetable oil, a renewable fuel. He had established many vegetable oil factories. They had to be shut down when cheaper fossil fuel surfaced at much cheaper cost.

Recently a committee has been formed by the government to look into the feasibility of producing seed based bio-diesel. Oil from seeds of jatropha trees is being actively considered in our country. Each hectare can deliver 3000 litre/year(15.7 barrel) of bio-diesel. Negotiations with D1 Oils plc. of UK has been under consideration to plant this on 5 million hectares of land to produce 15 billion liters (90 million barrels) of bio diesel.(The Energy World, February, 2005 issue).

Media information suggests that the plantation will be done along the county's 63,222 km railway track, and provide fuel to operate about 11,000 trains, which we have. If this order of self sufficiency is achieved, a significant amount of foreign exchange will be saved, besides providing employment to many. However, this railway track harvesting may not contribute much towards rural development, except for assisting trade and commerce needing transportation. There are, however, problems to face; viz., guarding these plants, when even oil from raw crushed jatropa seeds burn easily. Such oil will be a free energy source for domestic use for villagers living near railway track. On the other hand, refined oil can operate decentralized co-generating systems.

The exact amount of bio-diesel from jatropa plant is

difficult to ascertain. jatropa plants can be planted at the boundaries of privately owned cultivable land.

* Micro-algae cultivated at a 5 million ha solar pond, practicing harvesting once a year, will produce 55 times more of bio-diesel compared to jatropa plant seed based product. With increased photosynthesis one should not be surprised. This has been indicated earlier. However, a detailed justification is provided below;

COMPARATIVE ESTIMATE OF BIO-DIESEL

Saudi Arabia has formed a joint venture, D I Oils (UK) Arabia Limited. The first refinery in South Arabia was expected in the second half of 2006. (It ought to be operative by now). We are trying to establish a tie up with the British company .to sell the seeds to them, as reported. This will be processed in the UK. Attempts are being made to develop the processing plant in Mysore. Encouraging results on the progress made are available, when KSRTC celebrated world environment day by aiming for 5000 bio-fuel run buses by June 5, 2010.

COMPARISON BETWEEN MICRO-ALGAE AND JATROPA

Research has been conducted long since using micro-algae. At this stage, it is difficult to predict which of the two approaches can provide a better solution. If viable, both approaches can be adopted. With our deficient agricultural land situation, yet having a large coast line of 7500 km, the approach through the use of sea water trapped in natural territories such as Run of Kutch, man made shallow ponds, filled with sea water making channels etc., can provide a more permanent solution on energy. Further, if we succeed to make use of CO_2 emission from our major coal fired power stations, to accelerate growth of micro-algae we achieve simultaneously the much desired benefits towards pollution control of our environs. Jatropa plants can be grown in semi arid land. We have millions ha of such land spread all over the country, mostly in North Western region

Harvesting of seed is seasonal, generally once a year. But micro-algae can be harvested several times a year. As stated earlier with iron as fertilizer, the growth can be enhanced significantly. So the rule of thumb for blue micro algae growth may be the **USE OF IRON AS FERTILIZER.**

Beginning initially with Natural gas, (Fig.11 next page) the rural society can be transformed into townships to become a partner to urban society with little difference between the two. The migration to urban areas will stop. In fact, a situation for reverse migration from populous polluted urban to non polluted developed rural society may occur. (Fig. 13 placed at page 335 refers)

This section brings to fore what decentralized energy input can do to develop not only the rural society, but the country as a whole. At the same time, we need to realize that not only the divide will reduce, the nation's GDP shall grow significantly with increased earnings in industrialized rural areas, needing and producing varieties of Hardware Durables in large quantities. The demand on these and several other items, now beyond the reach of 800 million rural poor will increase many fold. These villages will produce these to support various other needs, not only for rural people, but also for urban societies. The products will have to meet international standards to compete with those produced abroad with a free trade situation. Combined with newer and better products of arts and crafts, foreign exports will find a prominent place earning foreign exchange, as has happened in China, South Korea, Thailand, Singapore, et al.

The rural Banks will now not be short of customers seeking loans. The situation described in page 232 will need a total revision. There will be no scope for surrendering unused money. The demand for loan will be from both new entrepreneurs as well as large private sectors exceeding those in urban society. Needless to mention that such a situation will not come about over night. The author believes this development will happen progressively in about 5/6 years, provided Government is serious about Rural Development. Currently it is not. Siphoning money from the fund allotted for Rural development is the goal in mind.

Fig 11

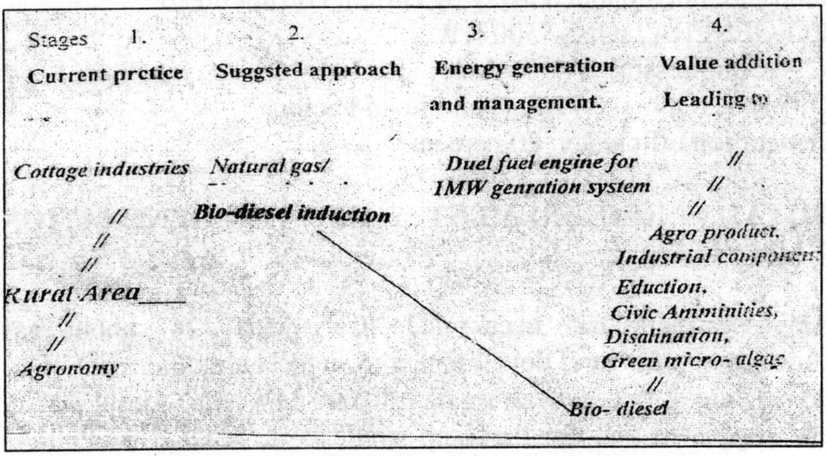

An experimental setup for bio-diesel induction

Fig.12

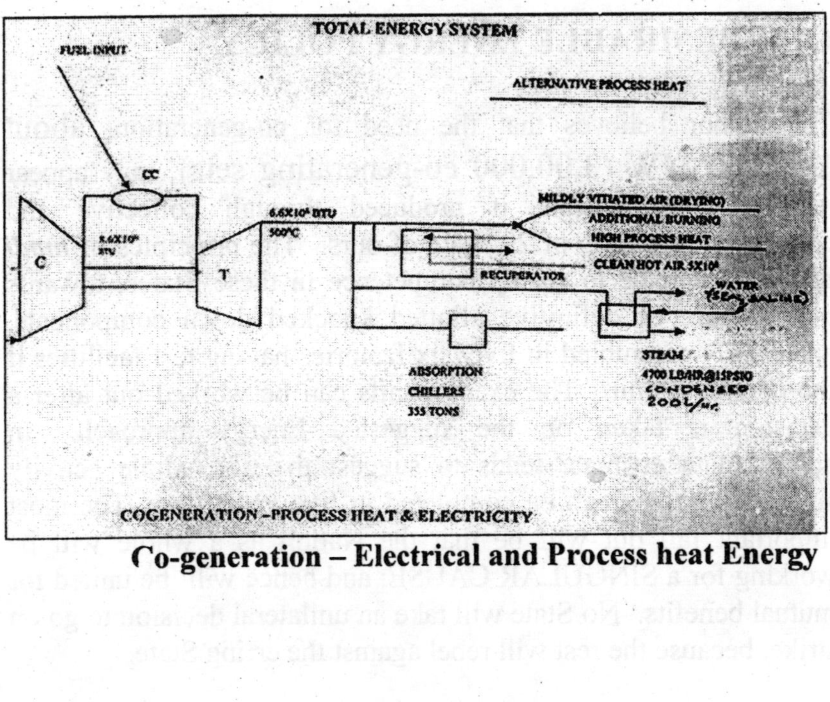

Co-generation – Electrical and Process heat Energy

CONCLUSION

The target set out is feasible, if properly planned and allocated funds are not siphoned away by current corrupt breed.
CO-GENERATION - 500 KW
C - Compressor; T - Turbine
OPERATION: 0.8 PLF, (Plant Load Factor)
Generation efficiency: 20 percent.

TOTAL REQUIREMENT OF CO-GENERATION CAPACITY

An assessment has been made (ref page 424) about gas consumption for rural development to suggest a requirement of 11 bn m^3 / day for co-generation of 1,50,000 MW. Dr. Abdul Kalam had suggested that the first step would be to have 7000 PURAs (refer page 461). To meet this requirement, on the basis of the above estimate, we would need to have 7000 MW co-generation units needing a mere 0.55 bn m^3 / day, when the flared gas is about 22bn.

OUR DESIRABLE ENERGY POLICY

The author believes that the need for co-generation, about 1,50,000 MW (3,00,000 co-generating sets), may appear massive, but feasible if produced through collective and collaborative efforts of 29 State of ours. The principles of ***modi operendi*** will be to set up competence in these States, towards manufacture of definitive allotted knocked down components, and finally assembled in five/ six factories having test facilities if the complete unit. The exact details can be worked out after a decision is taken on the suggested Energy approach. An approximate estimate tends to suggest that the whole activity suggested above, can be completed in five years time. The most important fall out will be that the Nation as a whole will be working for a SINGULAR CAUSE; and hence will be united for mutual benefits. No State will take an unilateral decision to go on strike, because the rest will rebel against the erring State.

JUSTIFICATION FOR

PART – 3

Reader's Note on Energy approach

THE STRATEGY FOR RURAL DEVELOPMENT

(VALUE addition ACTIVITIES IN RURAL AREAS)

Earlier it has emphasized that the country can develop only if the rural society's two faces are active. Currently we are using only one face. Agronomy is the only profession practiced, when the other face remains virtually blank. The main reason is because of severe shortage of appropriate energy. An estimate on electrical energy shortage has been presented in the earlier chapter, highlighting that that we need co-generated energy.

In our highly dispersed rural situation co-generation had to be decentralized. Small gas turbine based generation was regarded as the ideal answer. The problem was what fuel to be used. A visit without making any prior appointment was made to ONGC with an introductory letter from HAL, as it's consultant, on daily wage basis. The letter placed below provides an indication about the result of the visit.

...atural Gas Commission 157
...Bhavan
...248003

157

May 28, 1982.

Please refer to your D.O.letter No.HAL/CT/04-07 dated 28th April, 1982,

AVM Roy Choudhury met me on 18th instant. He also had detailed discussions with Dr.K.L.Goyal and other concerned officers. His study report on energy development of North Eastern Region is an excellent work. However it may involve commitment from State & Central Government Departments, in addition to finding out an agency for maintenance and operation of the generating sets, and building up consumer demand. We have, therefore, suggested to AVM Roy Choudhury to initially put up a small demonstration plant at a suitable place nearest to our producing field or gas trunk pipeline.

As far as ONGC is concerned, we shall be able to supply natural gas for this demonstration plant. All the other tie up including operation and maintenance of the plant is to be ensured by H.A.L.

AVM Roy Choudhury has appreciated this idea and has suggested a joint study for location of a plant in Eastern Region alongwith ONGC. We shall certainly give the necessary assistance.

I am forwarding a copy of this letter along with a copy of your letter to Shri Lovraj Kumar, Secretary to the Government of India, Ministry of Petroleum, as I am sure he would be very happy to note the efforts that are being made for the utilization of the gas. We will have to seek his guidance whether some funds could be made available either from the Department of Science & Technology or from Oil Industry Development Board.

Yours

(S.P.Wahi)

Shri B.K.Kapur,
Chairman,
Hindustan Aeronautics Ltd.,
Indian Express Building,
Vidhana Veedhim, Bangalore-56000.

Reply from Chairman, ONGC to Chairman, HAL

Gas Turbines are the unique in such situation when it would operate on any form of fossil fuel, e.g. diesel, ATF (Aircraft Turbine fuel), petrol (automotive fuel), naptha, natural gas, alcohol, at el. Natural Gas was the easiest transportable fuel. Hence it was selected for trial.

The following chapters illustrate how we can rescue the rural society, simultaneously the urban society as well. Activities are divided in two categories. Part 3A provides examples of value addition on non- metallic agro-products. Part 3B mentions about out sourcing components of high priced metallic objects, produced in urban society, in *energised* cottage industries in developed rural areas. The assumption made is rural society is energized .through decentralized co-generation, as explained in Figs. 10 and 11. The precarious energy shortage has been presented in the earlier Chapter.14

Although the new Chairman did not favour, the Hon'ble Minister showed interest. The ONGC office shifted to a new building (Samrat, a new hotel next to the Ashok Hotel). A beginning was made, when a Steering Group was formally approved with a government of India letter. (Reference: Office Memorandum, No.4/2/85 – EP, Ministry of energy, Department of Power, dated the 18th December,1985,) that is, three and half years after knocking at all responsible doors since ONGC's .letter of May, 1982. A very competent technologist, member thermal, CEA, was designated as the Chairman. The purpose is stated in the letter. Three other help came forward. They were:

1. Hindustan Aeronautics Ltd (HAL) who formed an energy cell and deputed four knowledgeable and dedicated officers. Another competent officer from GTRE came on deputation. An office accommodation was allotted.
2. The State Industrial & Investment Corporation of Maharashtra (SICOM), agreed to depute a team of professionally competent officials with thorough knowledge on business management norms, in addition to their technological understanding. This team was headed by an ex-professor of IIT, Madras (now Chennai), now

employed as a manager of SICOM

3. Fund was sanctioned to DNES (Department of Non - Conventional energy Source) to undertake study with regard to 'Decentralised energy Generation for Rural Development' through SICOM. (Ref: Gov letter No. 45/322/86 – PV dated 05.09. 1986.)

The well represented Steering group felt that initially a field survey need be done. at villages situated along the natural gas pipe line already laid. SICOM, Bombay (now Mumbai) and HAL team agreed to conduct this survey when the author of the book was nominated as principal investigator. One of our first visit was at Guna, in Madhya Pradesh.

VISIT TO GUNA, CULTIVATING SOYA BEANS

On arrival at District HQ, we were briefed about the District's undeveloped situation, and also about the adjacent notorious Chuman valley (ravine) of Phoolan Devi fame, We were told about Soya cultivation, instead of paddy, due to water shortage. Earlier paddy was grown. Our desire was to visit a village adjacent to cultivation. The recommendation was to visit Guna village.

Guna is located on the Kanyakumari - Srinagar high way, and connected to Bhopal through branched off road. The main gas pipeline runs through a district off the highway.

INSPECTION OF GUNA VILLAGE

Visited district head quarters to gather information about the village. The office was well maintained. But the condition of the village was awful. On record, there is a mention of a non existing primary school. The water supply was from a polluted well, although drinking water was supposed to fetch water in a water tanker up to a point, near the village entrance road off main road. This road was badly damaged, so water had to be collected from main road. Usually children did this chorus, waiting on road side, playing dangerously, when the arrival of the water tanker was uncertain. The economic condition could be judged for the clothes they were wearing. The inspecting officer is seen on the right side. He seemed to have collected a lot of data.

Collection of data on Soya Bean cultivation

The two cultivators are seen standing behind. Earlier, paddy was grown, but recent scarcity of water compelled the farmers to change over to Soya cultivation, needing much less water. The most intriguing sight was the happy children, wearing hardly any clothes. There was a big banyan tree near the entrance. Gathered that was the site for the pre-primary school. With no teacher, what could be more happy occasion.? The author wanted to take a group photograph. A little girl came running requesting to wait. And then ran towards her housed and returned with her little sister. The elder sister did not leave out her young sister in the group photograph. After the flash, the children came running demanding their copies. The girl still carrying the baby sister demanded two.

The survey team

Source: Photograph by one from the team members. The author second from right.

We moved in to inspect the village. This was done for a purpose. The survey team was to gather living condition of rural India. The contrast is presented.

Water deficient Guna village houses with stone-tiled roofs

Water flooded village houses with straw roofs

Top one is the Guna village. The roof was made using stone slabs. The bottom one is one in Assam. The roofs were covered with straw. Guna was short of water, Assam villages flooded with water grow paddy. So straw was available. Met the village pradhan. Learnt that the absence of School teacher was usual. Then expressed a desire to see the interior of his household. This was denied, stating ladies were busy with their household work, and it was not possible to disturb them.

LIFE OF A VILLAGER

All team members employed in HAL had left for Bangalore, to attend some urgent conference. Left alone in Bhopal city, visited the famous mosque, and also the land mark lake of Bhopal. Some information was gathered about the notorious gas leak and the after mirth. It appeared that poorer people not having proper shelter ran confused in all directions to avoid the killer gas. Some elderly people fell down, suffocated The ones with 'pucca' housing escaped shutting down the door and windows, isolating from outside atmosphere. They were saved. So now the endless misery of the poor initially affected began because of inadequate medical assistance. The endless battle for compensation commenced. Most claimants, deformed, have expired. There are the difficulties on identification. With negotiation in the hands of government, no clear picture could be obtained.

A desire surfaced to learn about the ways how poor villagers not directly involved with agronomy survive in this district. This search offered a chance encounter, revealing a story which is so very pathetic yet educative. After visiting the village, growing Soya beans, the team was told about a Soya beans oil producing factory. A visit there was decided on. Traversing past the gate of the Bhopal factory of notorious gas leak, towards the ('Surya Brand') Soya oil factory, near Sanchi,(Buddhist monastery fame), a column of women with large head loads of branches of trees, as shown below, created an interest. Why carrying such heavy head loads in hot afternoons?

The initially reaction was about deforestation. Could these stream of ladies moving in a file with such head loads causing deforestation, for their lively hood? But what was the outlet to absorb such bulk daily? Several possibilities, such as the feed stock to a char coal producing factory; a source to generate heat energy for the Soya Bean factory; or 'a mandy' to supply fire wood for domestic purposes came in mind.

Sanchi, (Buddhist monastery fame). Often known as Stupa, it was built by Emperor Ashoka in 300 B.C. Photographed by the author when the top end is missed

Women with head load (Photographed by author)

The driver of our taxi car was intrigued when was asked to stop ahead of the column of women. He was requested to find address of any of these ladies. Initially he was reluctant, and informed that these ladies would not divulge. He felt that being a government agent, they may apprehend that any conversation might create problems to them. When the intention to know about them was explained, he agreed to try. He walked along side, when the ladies refused to stop, and talked for a while, walking. He returned smiling, and conveyed that 0one lady had agreed for a meeting at her juggi (a slum colony) early in the morning, next day.

He got to know her name and was aware of the location of the slum colony. What gathered from the visit next morning was revealing. She had just returned collecting tube well water, 5 km away so that her two children did not become unwell. She was rushing them to school wearing the faded uniform, carrying their deformed school bag (was it more because of mid day meal, it was difficult to say), Then she wanted her neighbour, a Hindu lady, to bring tea, and a glass of water. Being a Muslim lady, she did not want my 'dharam'(religion) defiled. During the course of talking to them the previous day, our driver might have guessed and informed her about my religion.

She flatly refused when I wanted the water she had just brought. She felt 'Allaha' would not pardon her if she had agreed. She assured me that the water was the same as given, because this was collected at the same time. When asked, on her way out in a hurry to collect the branches of trees, why was she not trying to get employment as a household help, instead of roughing out as she was doing, her very clear and venomous answer was that it was far better to live with 'izzat' (honour), than hearing the obscene curses every day from 'be- izzaty' rich women. When confronted about the harm done by cutting down the trees, she was again very clear that the trees were their livelihood, and they cut only selectively, the old and dead ones, so that they grew better. Each tree of the wooded area was known to them.

They even fought with traders when they chopped the trees recklessly. Their mode of survival was to sell the head loads to the truck drivers, parked near the town below the monastery situated at a height, buy rice on return journey, and collect some twigs to cook food. She had no knowledge about what happened to the head loads there after. On the return journey a very short visit to the impressive but surprisingly desolated monastery was made. Then the oil producing factory was visited. The process was the similar as adopted by any other solvent extraction process, e.g., for ground nut oil. It was confirmed that the head load was not the heat source .for the factory. A separate contractor was supplying the logs of wood. The mind was not at rest, not knowing about the initial query which surfaced about the use of the head load.

'Surya' Soyabean oil

Photograph by author

VALUE ADDED HEAD LOAD

My driver came next day at the appointed time, Since the report about the GUNA village visit was to be written, the driver was requested to get information from the truck drivers. By this time, he was convinced about our mission. He agreed to do the needful. He managed to get the full information. The head load was sold to truck drivers, after hard bargaining done by the lady met at her 'juggi'. She happened to be the leader. These were delivered to a wood cutting (not saw mill) factory. There they are dressed, and cut to a size. Weighing, bundles were made. About 20-25 persons were employed. The vendors were waiting. Having paid the money, the bundles were taken away, and finally sold on footpaths, market places, etc. According to his assessment, these bundles would be costing at least four times the sell cost of the head load.

Listening to his investigative work, and thanking him with a small sum for his 'jal pani' (a token fees for services rendered), which he refused to take, a thought surface in mind for the welfare of these women working so hard for small earnings.

Dressed head load

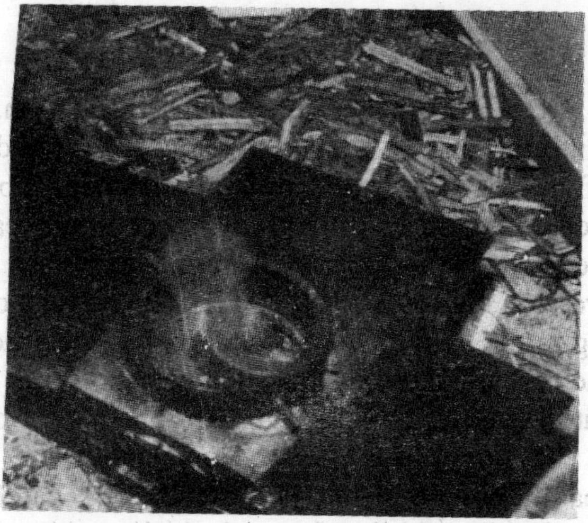

Wood burning chulla with swirling flame (Photograph by author)

Coincidently, the Hon'ble Minister for rural development was in Bhopal. Next day's newspaper carried the story about his emotional address about the rural poor, who were the main victim of the gas leak. He mentioned nothing about the compensation.

UNWELCOME BENEVOLENCE: LESSON TO LEARN

Why not set up a wood dressing outfit locally on a co-operative basis close to juggi. Barren land was available. The Delhi office, which had recommended the visit, had stated that if a de-centralized power generation scheme was decided on within a maximum of 50/70 Km, from the gas pipeline, ONGC might consider to supply the gas for 1/ 2 MW. generation system. Every thing seemed to fall in the right slot. Mentally excited I slept well, after preparing a briefing paper for the State government. Next morning, dressed a little formally, went down to lobby, and took just a cup of tea.

Our car driver came in time. in addition, wasting no time got into the car. He wanted to know about the destination. When briefly replied, government, he looked back, appeared surprised, but continued. The driver was by now a likeable middle-aged trusted companion. The flickering surprised look, made an impression that he was perhaps apprehensive about the purpose of going to the State government. He was requested to stop the car at the roadside curb. A detailed narration was made, explaining about the virtues on setting up a co-operative wood cutting outfit, near the 'juggi' for the development of the people living in unhealthy environment. He listened very carefully. but did not respond. Surprised, when asked about his view, he felt that before approaching the government it might be wise to talked to the lady 'union leader'. However, why not the men folk, I asked? His reply was that it would be useless, because they go to work, and whatever they earn, they spend drinking, and return at night to abuse and beat up their women, eat food and go to sleep. That appears to be the routine. In any case, the project was on elimination of hardship of the women.

Men folk would oppose this. They would not like their 'mute punch bags' having regular employment, in addition to becoming shareholder to an industrial outfit! His frank opinion shook my earlier enthusiasm. So what was to be done? He relied with typical politeness, " *Chote Mu se Bara Bat karna achacha nai, bhirbi mera bhichar me, phailay juggi aurat leader se bhat karna thik hoga*". (Small persons should not open their mouth, even then in my judgment, it would be proper to speak first with the juggi woman leader). I could see the sound logic. My enthusiasm was 'jumping the gun'. We anticipated that she would be on road with her head load. However, we were early. Therefore, we waited at the truck depots. Our driver talked with some of the truck drivers, who recognized him. They were obviously curious why he wanted to meet her in particular.

She had a reputation of being harsh, the truck drivers cautioned him. Finally, she arrived. Some truck drivers pointed her to our driver. I kept sitting in the car. She ignored, and got on with the sell bargaining, often in very loud voice, discussing from time to time with her colleagues. After settlement, wiping her face with the 'pallu' of her saree, she headed for the teashop with her friends. One could make out that she was in command. My driver managed to attract her attention. All she said that this was not the place to talk. Looking at the car, told the driver loudly, to come to juggi. 'Our shab is leaving tomorrow', but it would appear she did not hear the information conveyed. Obviously hurt, my driver retuned to the car, started and headed to return.

AN ATTEMPT TO ESTABLISH IDEAL VILLAGE.

With nothing to do, an attempt was made to witness an attempt made to set up an ideal village near Denkenal, Orissa. This was inaugurated by our then prime minister Mrs. Indira Gandhi. The poor villagers were carefully selected. A windmill was installed to pump out potable water. Land was allocated for cultivation. However, it was a total failure. All villagers left soon after the beginning for want of food. Enquiries were made to find out why no provisions for food were made, at least for two years to settle down, but no answer was available. Also no infra structure for cultivation was arranged.

Apparently, a Station officer could provide the details. However, he was untraceable. Some around blamed the poor for not being enterprising enough. One could see that land was fertile and some attempts were made, but obviously, food could not have been sprouted out soon after the land was ploughed. Detail planning was needed to habilitate them. This ideal village with specially selected poor was situated in a near deserted land, when at a distance a developed habitat in view. Mahanadi river was flowing at a distance. Detail planning was needed to make a success of such a noble thought. Where were the much talked about NGOs? Could not the government agency invite some, and ask them to camp with these villagers to help the 'ideal' village to grow under their guidance?. They could have told that the government their support would be withdrawn if they did not act to save such a noble project.

The broken down houses, a severely damaged windmill, a small lonely girl, a few stray dogs, and the inauguration stone with inscription stating the event were the only remains. The lonely girl refused to leave the spot, hoping for the return of her parents. She refused food offered, and did not want to leave. The village Pradhan was informed about the girl. With his assurance that he would take care of the child, the visiting team left with a heavy heart. Ideal village it was indeed! Was it a vote-earning stunt, wasting huge public money and considerable effort?.

Lonely girl in an 'Ideal village' waiting for her parents (Photograph by author)

No word was exchanged until we reached hotel. A request that he should have lunch with me was declined. He informed that he had his home food, in his Tiffin box. Then asked what time he should come next day to go to the Airport. When informed about the desire to go to juggi instead, and being a Sunday, he could come at an appropriate time, he could not believe what he heard. He wanted to say something, but he was not given a chance Informed that best would be to talk tomorrow.

Next day. before reaching the juggi, I could sense that the

driver was eager to talk. Sitting inside the car, I had a briefing session, before starting. He started with an apology, for misguiding me yesterday. Ignoring that, I told him about the development of the juggi, the school, the vocational training centre, - every thing about my dream project. Reaching there, I requested the driver to go and find out about her availability. He obliged. Took some time to return, and informed me that she was having a meeting inside, but had stepped outside to learn from our driver about the plan on setting up the co-operative wood cutting mill, and the possible advantages, which would accrue. She would come to meet me, to discuss after a few minutes. I opened the car door to get out as she approached, but she stood at the opened door, our driver by her side. She conveyed all the imponderables. To begin with, much money would have to change hands to acquire the land, even though apparently the land was government's and could be had at a token price for such use, Then the gas pipe laying, setting up the factory with a generating set and distribution of electricity, although theoretically can be arranged through government funding, much private money would be required to get the fund released and get on with the work going.

Socially it might appear the proposal was noble, but bluntly told me that it was clear to her that I was trying to be a 'neta' controlling the slum labour force to eventually get elected as MLA/MP. *Apka matlab muje pahley roj puta chalgeeya tha, jub up mere ghar ka pani magatha.* (your design was obvious on the very first day when you wanted to drink water from my house). Your desire to become a Neta here was a useless effort, she said. (It was apparent that she had the characteristics of a Union leader) She left, making a sign to my driver to follow her. I signaled him to go. Again, he took a little time to return. Approaching, he could hardly control his smile. Sat in the car and reversing, he set course to return. Then, when out of sight of juggi, he burst into laughter. What he then told me was amazing.

The woman leader told him that there was no doubt that the project was good, but it would not see the light of the day. because of reasons, she told to me. The best solution was to *initiate her* as the one making the proposal, because she knew all the ropes. All Ministers, and other leaders were known to her. All that was needed was to recommend her to the DM (District Magistrate). Any proposal of this kind had to pass through him to reach the government.

My driver had apparently asked her, where from she would get the 'private money' she had talked about. She conveyed that the 'Private money' might cause problem with police, etc., but there existed an 'exchange rate', and she was already in command of that. *'Yowhi rate se Desh chalta hay'* (The country was moving on that rate). He was about to continue, but I cut him sort rather harshly, almost shouting at him, - *bakbas bandh karo,* - and asked him to take me to DM's office. Reaching there, I handed over my hand written project proposal to the Secretary, who had initially directed us to Guna village. He wanted me to sit down and tell him about the visit. Declining, I told him that I was in a rush to catch a fight. Returning to hotel, I settled the hotel bill, and paid the driver whatever he told me was his due. 'Adab' and he went away without a word. I wondered whether I had over reacted believing her narrated utterances! Perhaps he had also believed her, and wanted to tell that when I had cut him short not very politely. Could it be I was so upset when my dream was sunk into such a filth.

I reached Bombay (now Mumbai) late, because the fight was delayed. To my very great surprise, my colleagues from SICOM team members were waiting at the lobby. It was quite late at night. After checking in, we shifted to my room, and ordered some food for all of us, through room service. I told them about my visit to oil producing and the sight seeing including the unintended discovery of Sachi monastry, blanking totally about the 'head load episode'. Although not within our purview of our assigned task, I again reiterated that, our task was to find out about the virtue of 'de-centralized power generation' and the resultant economical benefits only. We may stray out to learn about literacy situation, but nothing beyond. We were not social workers to uplift the social aspects, but to generate *means* to do so. Continuing, we had to now decide in which direction we move next. HBJ (Hazira to Jagaspur in UP) gas pipeline had reached up to that point in the East. The question was, do we go Eastwards first, and then go Westwards finally. We decided to go eastwards right up to Assam, where gas was flared away.

MANMOHON SINGH AND RURAL DEVELOPMENT

The coincidence of timing for the amendment of Article 40, leading to Article 243(G), when he was the Finance M inister, leaves little doubt that a Congress party led continuity of old strain of divide between rich and poor, without a break, would be retained, but now with an apparent noble face. This is seen from his utterances quoted hereafter.

MANMOHAN SINGH AS FINANCE MINISTER

The alarming disparity which was increasing in Orissa would have caused national concern. Realizing the gravity of the situation, Shri Narasimha Rao had himself addressed the nation from the famous rampart of the Red Fort, on the Independence day of year 1991 that rural development should be taken up on *war footing*. Next year he mellowed down to state that rural development should be our primary duty. Narasimha Rao in his full five years tenure (1992 – 1996) could not find the strategy to launch the declared war.

That the rural situation needs urgent rectification had been felt by his Finance Minister as well. He echoed, stating *'unless this was done, he apprehended about a force of destabilization by rural youth'*. Our media had published what had stated about rural development, as under;

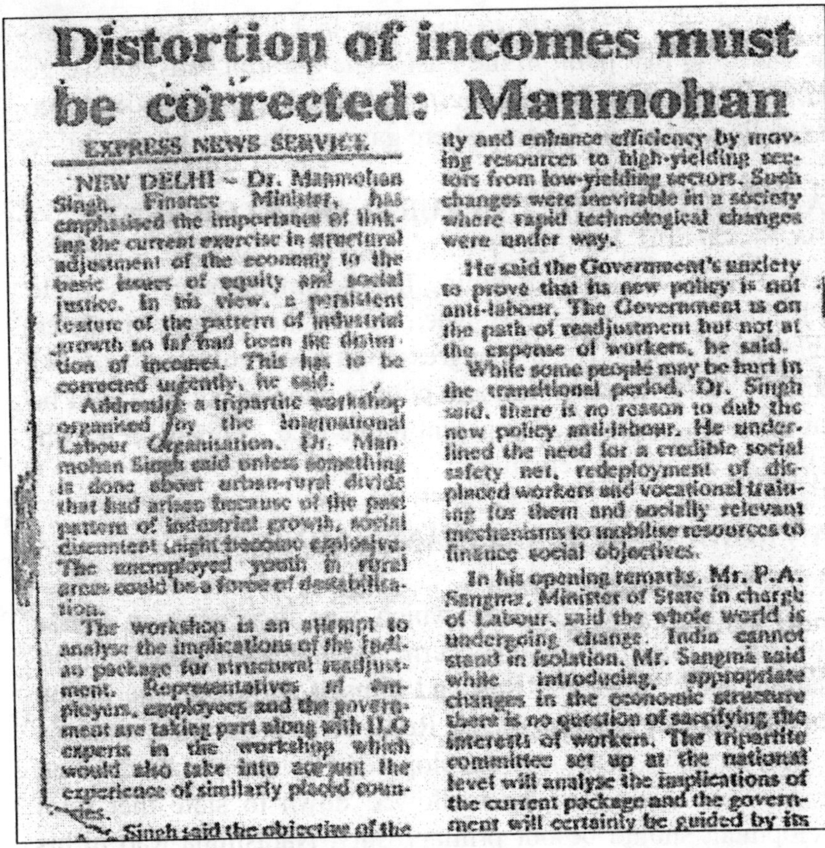

Distortion of incomes must be corrected: Manmohan

EXPRESS NEWS SERVICE

NEW DELHI – Dr. Manmohan Singh, Finance Minister, has emphasised the importance of linking the current exercise in structural adjustment of the economy to the basic issues of equity and social justice. In his view, a persistent feature of the pattern of industrial growth so far had been the distortion of incomes. This has to be corrected urgently, he said.

Addressing a tripartite workshop organised by the International Labour Organisation, Dr. Manmohan Singh said unless something is done about urban-rural divide that had arisen because of the past pattern of industrial growth, social discontent might become explosive. The unemployed youth in rural areas could be a force of destabilisation.

The workshop is an attempt to analyse the implications of the Indian package for structural readjustment. Representatives of employers, employees and the government are taking part along with ILO experts in the workshop which would also take into account the experience of similarly placed countries.

Singh said the objective of the [...]ity and enhance efficiency by moving resources to high-yielding sectors from low-yielding sectors. Such changes were inevitable in a society where rapid technological changes were under way.

He said the Government's anxiety to prove that its new policy is not anti-labour. The Government is on the path of readjustment but not at the expense of workers, he said.

While some people may be hurt in the transitional period, Dr. Singh said, there is no reason to dub the new policy anti-labour. He underlined the need for a credible social safety net, redeployment of displaced workers and vocational training for them and socially relevant mechanisms to mobilise resources to finance social objectives.

In his opening remarks, Mr. P.A. Sangma, Minister of State in charge of Labour, said the whole world is undergoing change. India cannot stand in isolation. Mr. Sangma said while introducing appropriate changes in the economic structure there is no question of sacrifying the interests of workers. The tripartite committee set up at the national level will analyse the implications of the current package and the government will certainly be guided by its

Distortion of incomes

The above clipping is a verbose undefined expression of wisdom. For example, he did not state what kind of structural changes he had in his mind. True, this is needed but without any definition, it is a metaphysical expression. The only real value of the above is what stated about the unemployed youth. in 2004. Will it be improper to link Naxalite movement with his expressed view on unemployed youth?

One must admire Dr. Manmohon Singh's persevering metaphysical mind on his expressed views, now as Prime Ministe

PRIME MINISTER TALK ABOUT RURAL DEVELOPMNT

Time News Net work.New Delhi.

Prime Minister Manmohon Singh told chief Ministers on Tuesday that he wanted to decentralize spending by transferring funds to district and local governments. At a meeting on decentralization he said the nearly 17,000 crores spent on rural development each year isn't yielding the result it should Most CMs demanded greater discretion in spending.

"Our strategy must unleash the productive of our agriculture", said Singh, traversing the range of technological possibilities, the Chinese model of rural business hubs, *decentralized electricity, even turning the disadvantage of low-input agriculture into the advantage of high-value organics farming. This can only happen if local communities have the deciding voice.

The PM suggested that poorer districts could get grants not tied to specific schemes to give them more room for creative solutions to beat poverty. Can it be done? Panchayat raj has to be "the medium to transform rural India into 700 million opportunities, "he dais, asking CMs to become" Champions of decentralization".

The system has to be institutionalized, state finance commission awards on funds should be honoured- funds should be transferred in time, with no diversions permitted. There is a need to make course corrections and involve Panchayats in ensuring access to basic services such as health and education. The use of IT could radically alter governance and service delivery.

****IMPORTANT NOTE: The author believes the major defect in our country's energy policy begins with a mistaken belief that 'decentralize electricity' is the answer for Rural***

Development. The answer lies in accepting 'decentralized co-generation', *as the legally accepted policy for Rural Development. The Government refuses accept since 1884.'*

The mention about 'decentralized electricity' is apt if only this means "decentralized energy'. Electricity alone cannot 'unleash' productive potential of our *agricultural society*. Besides, can we have small-decentralized viable electricity generating units to suit our highly dispersed rural situation? Can Panchayat raj with their massive illiteracy and education transform six lakh villages of rural India as centers of employment opportunities with electricity supplied to rural homes? Without mention of possible approach paths, the country may be lead to blind allies. Without employment opportunities, can we stop our rapidly diminishing per capita land holdings? *The average land holding was 2.3 ha (hector) in 1970. It has reduced to 0.5 ha now.

By 2012, the estimated population will be about 1300 million people (assuming population growth rate reduced to one per cent from current 1.4). In addition, the food demand will increase to about 265 - 300 million tons, from our current production of about 200 millions. If that happens, the solution may well be to barter our Sovereignty with USA perhaps, for their security to fend our poverty. Should we not take up Hydroponics as our Nationally accepted food production culture at domestic levels.

*Source: Rural Development by Dr. Satya Sundaram (page 184).

MAKING MANMOHON SINGH'S VISION VIABLE

The pivotal issue is decentralized energy (not electricity). Unfortunately, the difference between the two is often missed out. For example, when we speak about Nuclear energy, we mean Electricity, in fact, generated out of such energy. Even if this is feasible, two obvious unacceptable situation will give rise to. We will have nuclear generating units littered all over the country. Secondly, where from we will harness knowledgeable people to manage these. The most confusing utterances are about decentralized electricity and his intended resignation if Nuclear deal had fallen through. Neither are pro rural development, and feasible solutions for execution of Article 243(G).

The author believes that the solution to our situation can be through what depicted in Fig. 12 and what stated in Part 3.

AN OBSERVATION ON MISSED ELEMENTS

An aspect on rural and hence the country's development need be highlighted at this stage. The book has tried to trace the history from Indus Valley Civilization till present times. Narration of the period 8000 B.C till 2000 A.D may not have received the due justification in a book addressed for rural development. **The author wants to clarify that development of mind is just as important as providing 'improved quality of life'.**

The fact often missed out is that even after 4000 years slavery, we are able to think at par with developed society is because of the genetic strain developed during Vedic era. The kind of rural development this book wishes to germinate is not only for 'Roti, Kapra, Mokan' but simultaneously developing our original creative mind. Otherwise, whatever development we may achieve will be based on second hand knowledge as currently dished out through our text books. We must learn to ask 'why' to excel, competing with developed societies.

The book has many 'negativety' which may create some unhappiness. The author wishes to explain that those are not subjective opinions. They are to narrate, with examples, why our country is currently in a totally unacceptable state. We are victims of these 'negative' occurrences and should be avoided in the New INDIA.

PART – 3

RURAL DEVELOPMENT THROUGH AGRO AND NON-AGRO BASED ACTIVITIES

CHAPTER 15

PART 3A

VALUE ADDITION THOUGH AGRO-INDUSTRIES.

The assumption made is the availability of non-polluting transportable fuel to establishing decentralized co-generation systems, when their operations will be done in a programmed manner through a microprocessor.

Three examples are narrated on the use of de-centralized energy to prove how rural society can be developed through value addition done locally instead of done in urban areas, because of the urban energy pull.

ASSUMED ENERGY SOURCE

Utilization of two gas turbine based decentralized 500 kWh x 2 = 1 MW co-generated energy

Utilization at 0.8 PLF (Plant Load Factor)

Transmission loss is not accounted for.

EXAMPLE 1

Rice milling (Paddy harvested by three villages, each having 500 people)

Such an energy set up would run a 20t / hr. rice mill for 10hr/day *during day time*, (8am – 5pm, lunch break 1 hr) needing 625 kW when the surplus 175 kW out of 800 kW capacity will be utilized to meet other civic needs e.g. at health centers, schools, and small cottage industries. The evening shift for 6 hrs will be utilized for domestic and street lighting as may be needed for 1500 people (each village having 500 people), when the residual heat ($10.9X10^6$ Btu/hr during this period (Ref. Fig. 11) will distill, or desalinate sea water in villages near sea coast. and provide for about 2,500 kg, or liters of sweet (distilled water) This will be enough for 1500 people. (Ideally, a human body discharges 1.7 liter of water/day.) The remaining 8 hrs can be utilized to energize agricultural pump sets and other need still 8 am in the morning, During this period utilizing the residual heat from the generating sets, paddy could be dried in a fluidized bed drier from 20 to 12 per cent moister ideally needed for processing in a rice mill. Thus the entire capacity of 800 kW (PLF 0.8) is made use of, operating non-stop. Gas Turbines function better non-stop, more so at fixed operational rpm of the generator.

ANALYSIS OF ADDITIONAL BENEFITS.

An analysis of resultant benefits, comparing with present state 1 of Fig.2 will readily bring out the significant socio-economic benefit which de-centralized 1 MW co-generation result. This estimate is not complete when other associated elements are not taken into account. For example, each Ton of milled paddy produces 0.06t of Bran. Through solvent extraction process, 18 per cent of this can be fibrous oil. De-oiled Bran, with addition of appropriate vitamins, is pet bird's feed, and can have export market. Additionally, 0.04t broken rice can be used to make pre-processed food to make Idly or Dose. Alternatively ,the broken rice can be used to make highly priced 'Rice Wine'.

380A summary of annual products from a 20t Rice mill is listed below;

TABLE - 20

1.	**Total paddy processed**	**(20X10X365X0.95) 69,350 t**
2.	**Rice @ 0.7/t**	**48,545 t**
3.	**Bran @ 0.06/t**	**2,912t***
4.	**Broken rice @ 0.04/t**	**2.77t****
5.	**Husk @ 0.2 t**	**13,870 t**

All activities mentioned above need considerable amount of heat energy. particularly for item marked with * & ** The value addition from these is taken into account in Table 6.

PADDY DRYING

Currently, the general practice is to sun dry. This practice causes wastages for two reasons. Birds come to eat and pollute. Secondly, an unexpected rain makes the paddy wet. Sun drying process is labour intensive, and not cost effective when this practice tends to increase the broken rice during rice milling. The correct drying is certified by an expert who chew a grain to assess.

Paddy drying (Photographed by author)

20T/hr paddy drying from (generally) 20 percent to 12 percent moisture needs 4.48 x 10^6 Btu/hr. Co-generation provides for all the heat needed in a fluidized bed drier. An instrument as used to measure the moisture of saw dust in a wood board manufacturing factory can be used, with a little modification.

RICE WINE

Rice wine (Photographed by author)

That the bottled wine is from Rice is seen from the label attached on the left side bottle. Cost $ 5 at a Singapore in a well known wine shop.

This wine is crystal clear and scientifically made. It is totally different to cheap 'toddy' which the rural folks buy from illegal breweries and often get. into serious health problems, at times even fetal. Currently the broken rice is used to make the pre-processed food, e.g., Dosa and Idly mix. The total broken rice produced is estimated as 2.77 million tons,* annually. The price difference between the two kinds of value added products is difficult to assess. The ex-factory price of rice wine could not be ascertained. The retail price is high. It is a favorite drink in Japan and East Asian Countries.

* Broken Rice production, based on total rice production, : $69.35X\ 10^6\ X\ 0.04 = 2.77X\ X\ 10^6$ t/ year

EXAMPLE 2

This study was done, in 1983, at the behest of Shri K. H. Patil, then a well known Co-operative Minister of Karnataka government.

Gadag situated in the Northern upper part of Karnataka grows cotton. With several value added activities, e.g. ginning, cotton seed oil extraction, spinning mills, colouring the yarn as cottage industries using a 'charka' like appliance, hand and semi-power looms, towels making, etc., and several homes operating as business centers selling the woven apparels, it is not only a thriving city, a situation of over employment has been created. Earlier it was poor village, growing chillies and garlic, sent to Bangalore markets, fetching little money. To-day it not only has primary education facility, it has colleges teaching humanitarian subjects upto degree standard, an engineering college, and health and hygiene facilities.

Spinning mill at Gadag, Karnataka, Photograph by author

This spinning mill was operated with a diesel power generating set when the humidity control is done separately. A co-generating system as shown on Fig. 12, can be an alternative with additional advantage that the dependence on grid power at night for domestic and street lighting will be eliminated.

At that time, the Co-operative Minister was from Gadag. That helped. But the basic features projected would have not changed if the Co-generating system, what this book trying to promote, is accepted, keeping in view the energy deficiency in view. It is seen how the value addition to raw agro-product if locally done, a wholly agronomy based rural society can be developed to acquire urban facilities, removing the underemployed situation.

An example of a family unit may be appropriate. After receiving the cotton yarn from the Cotton Spinning Mill, the grandmother colored the thread with the grandson in her lap. She used a 'Charkh' like appliance as shown in the picture below;

Grandmother coloring the threads, with Grandson in her lap (Photographed by the author)

The coloured thread was carried to hand looms to make variety of products, - well designed high quality cotton 'saries', bed spreads, bed covers. etc. Such thread was to be feed stock for semi power loom. Unusable threads were used for making towels of various sizes. They had good export market.

Handloom (Photographed by author)

There were sales counter a these places. The daughter-law, and the son take their turns to man these, and also sending the children to schools with their Tiffin boxes. The entire operation including watering the 'Tulshi' and a few flowering plants was done with quite efficiencies.

An interesting feature is the 'dead and dried' cotton sticks were carefully preserved in stacks. They were used as fuel for cooking food.

A very interesting portable handloom was exhibited at the Institution of Engineers, Bangalore.

Photographed by author during an exhibition on handloom model in northeast

Later the Hon'ble Minister accompanied the author when the team visited Pavagoda, a severely caste ridden village. He was the translator. What conveyed moved the villagers to such an extent, that the team was compelled to stay back, and hold a meeting at their community hall, next morning. They all came; the hall was full. Was informed that the sitting was divided, caste biased, on either side of the central passage. Expressing gratitude, the author began stating that let there be an exchange of people in the rows on either side. There was an indication of hesitance. The author sat down. The miracle happened. They exchanged their seats! Without complementing, the author unfolded his views about co-operative efforts on value addition; literacy programmes; vocational training; drinking water; setting aside caste bias in Panchayats. Our Hon'ble Minister did not speak. Sweets and fruits were then freely distributed as breakfast.(the author was told that earlier the distribution was done separately}.

When we left, our car was loaded with flowers. The author felt terribly ashamed for creating false hopes in the minds such simple trusting people. A lesson was learnt, however. This was the way, political leaders earn votes and the country's governance is executed. on falsehood and with nil accountability. The concept of untouchables is fragile, and this was amply demonstrated. At the same time, the author was wondering whether the laRige gathering was because of the presence of the Hon'ble minister, or the suggested casteless approach. evening before.

On way back, late in the evening, visited a large rice mill at Tumkur. It was making non-edible bran oil, through solvent extraction process when the time expired bran was the feed stock, - some came from other rice mills, Shri Patil kept company all through. The team members were taking notes. They were a competent lot.

EXAMPLE 3

SUGAR MILL

Sugar cane is a product of highly efficient (C-4) photo-synthesis process. Next to Brazil, India is the second largest sugar producing and exporting country in the world. Mandya, situated in a district in Karnataka State, grows sugar cane and paddy alternatively from the same cultivable land for a good scientific reason for paddy cultivation. After harvesting the canes the left over short stubs are set on fire. The field is now having porous charcoal. It helps the growth of paddy.

A sugar mill, as a government undertaking, was established. Soon a few other private sugar mills also came up with demarcation of 'command' agricultural areas for supply of raw stock to the sugar mills. In early 60s Mandya was a poorly village, when it had no place to take a brake on the way to Mysore. To-day it is a flourishing township, having sugar and rice mills, described earlier. It also has now schools upto pre-university standards; collages for humanitạrian and Engineering studies, poly-techniques, employment opportunities, amusement centers, hotels and restaurants.

The conversion of sugar cane to sugar needs lar

ge amount of energy. This is self generated. The excellence of nature's gift is seen from the fact that a sugar mill does not need any external energy source to produce sugar. After crushing the sugar cane, the (wet) bagasse becomes the fuel for the boilers tc generate steam and this generates the power needed to crush the cane. The cane juice is then converted into crystalline sugar and the left over is known as molasses, often stored for alcohol extraction. The residue, commonly named as 'spent wash' is highly pollutant, with Biological oxygen demand (BOD) of about 60 – 65000. This can be treated to generate Hydrogen (H_2) as 'green' fuel. Again, although the feasibility has been established, further research is needed to establish and purify this.

There are two ways Hydrogen can be used. It can generate captive power. Or, produce Hydrogen fuel cells. They are now rated as the future totally pollution free energy to drive automobiles. Although the net heat value of Hydrogen per lb is 2.76 times more, (51,623 Btu compared to Gasoline's 18,700), it is about 60 times lighter than Gasoline. Thus to get the same heat value one of the biggest problem faced is the weight of the Hydrogen fuel cells. Much work is going on in developed countries to overcome the problems; e.g. Balard in Canada is the leader on Fuel cell development. A fuel cell of 3.5 kWh capacity has reached a stage to be sold as a commercially viable product.

Germany is working in collaboration with Ballard, when Sigen in the UK is active in this field. We prefer to live with the pollutant, lagooning this in large ponds, or letting this out into a nearby stream. Both are highly unhygienic practices; when soil around becomes toxic and unusable for cultivation. This often percolates through soil to wells. Water from these are used by rural people and get unwell. Dysentery is the common disease. Our unhygienic mind baffles most. Yet solution lies in getting Hydrogen to remove the pollutant.

A motor cycle was running around the campus of Bana ras Hindu University using Hydrogen as fuel. Some preliminary work was done at the MCRC (Murugappa Chattier Research Centre), Chennai. Characteristically, an eminent scientist was elected to co-ordinate and study this development and report in about 4 months time. If this has been done, the author has missed this. But what most significant is, one does not know whether any activity has been recommended and what is the current status on this new encouraging energy front.

The country has 243 molasses based distilleries producing about 8000 kl of spent wash effluent/day. Hydrogen (H_2) production and use can be useful research areas, and should receive attention. With rapidly increasing fossil fuel cost Hydrogen fuel cells are currently the targeted R & D activities to provide automotive power in developed societies. For rural development, Hydrogen fuel can provide supplementary energy for decentralized co-generation.

The analysis presented above is related to year 1999 – 2000. The summary theme is that rural 'coin' should have their both sides equally active, so that the illiteracy and massive unemployment will be eliminated. No doubt a significant change in our Constitution and social order will be required eliminating the caste based reservations.

An indication on what Dr. Manmohon Singh tried to propagate is shown below. To begin with, the need is to establish experimental units as shown in Fig 11. Attempts had been made since 1986, but with nil success.

Four major reasons surfaced coming in the way of taking up six demonstration projects dealing with different raw products. The treatment infrastructures for these are not the same. For example, wheat processing and down stream production of commodities need different approach to frozen fish processing for export. Non-availability of Natural Gas, although initially agreed to. Paucity of fund allocation by the Planning Commission. And finally about executive body.

The author's approach to form one comprehensive body was not acceptable. Citing the example of the GTRE, making a humble beginning, did not carry the conviction, yet it was perhaps the most appropriate one.

The core concept which the book wishes to propagate is illustrated in the Figures 12 and 13.

These two diagrams expose the relevance of the key strategy the book has addressed. With acceptance of decentralized co-generation the enormous locked up competence in rural area will find opportunity for application, in multitude of activities. The rural areas will become the hub of activities, eliminating totally the unemployment situation. The author firmly believes, based on work dome earlier, that the rural society will then excel what has been achieved in China.

The rural society of China earns more foreign exchange than urban society's efforts.

The author had been making efforts to get this prospect assessed, comparing with Government's strategy on Rural electrification since 1984, but met nil success, inspite of a senior level Steering Committee's recommendation.

The author believes that at this critical juncture when the Nation is facing real danger internally, and from external sources, keeping the 800 million rural people locked up with agronomy based agronomy is a willful anti-nation activity.

The author has, therefore, pleaded again to our Appex Institution for an assessment on Rural electrification VS Decentralized energy generation, as presented in Fig. No. 12 as the key to the solution for our Rural Development, inviting a world known foreign Institution, to bail the Nation out of the present predicament. The assessment should cover all relevant socio-economic aspects.

THIS APPEAL IS IN THE NATION's INTEREST

The core concept which the book wishes to propagate is illustrated in Figs. 13 and 14 presented in the next page

FIG. 13

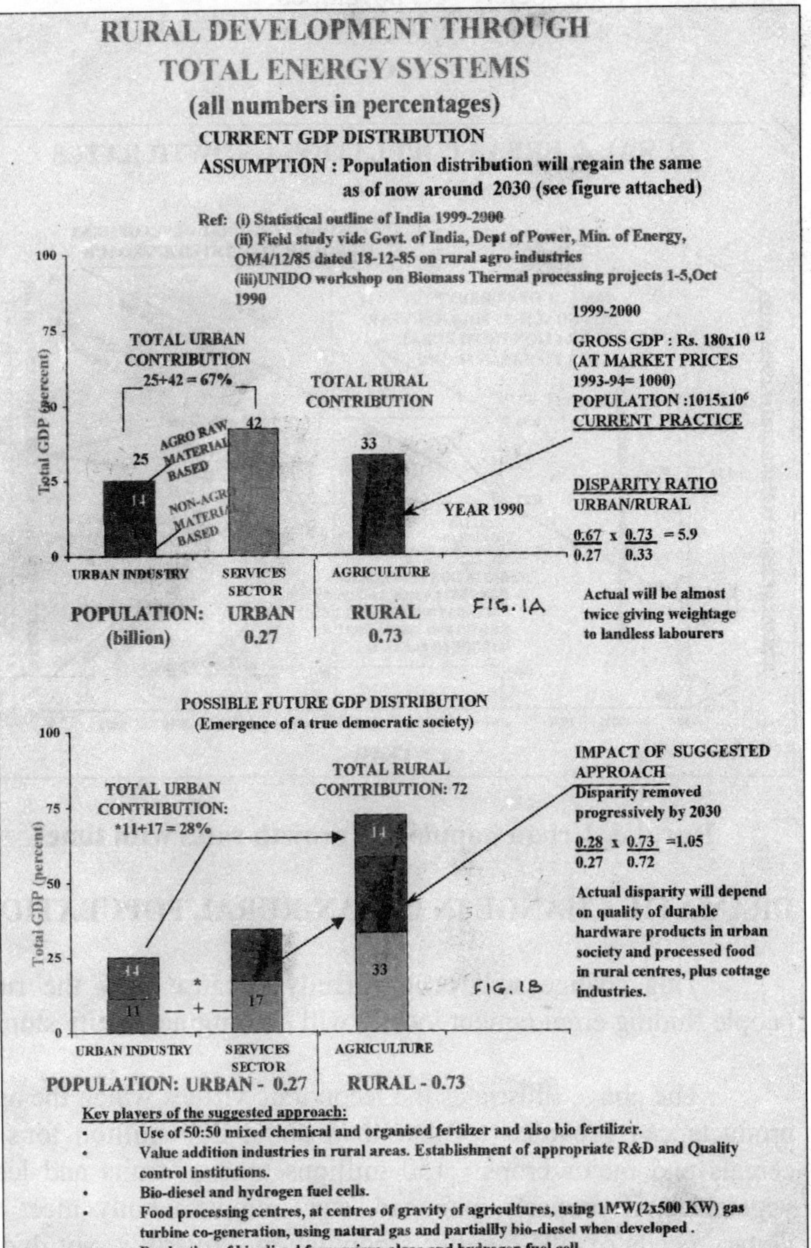

Rural development through Total Energy Systems

Resultant Impact on population distribution when the other face of rural society gets developed.

FIG. 14

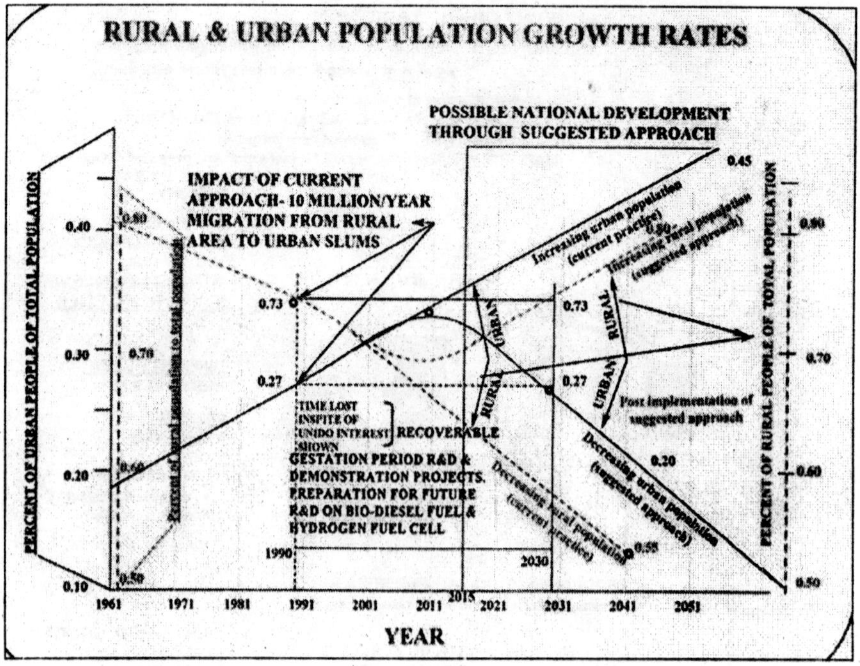

Rural & Urban population growth rates with time

DRAMATIC CHANGE IN URBAN-RURAL POPULATION

This change will occur mainly because now the rural people finding employment locally will not migrate to city slums.

The above illustrates the economic virtues which the ago-products can provide. Other than about 200 million tons of cereals and major crops, 150 millions tons of fruits and leafy vegetables, if properly managed, can almost wholly meet the dietary needs of the country's population. Poverty is not due to the food shortage. The real issue is massive unemployment. Most of the neutrinos food staff is beyond the financial reach of the rural poor.

JUSTIFICATION OF DECENTRALIZED ENERGY GENERATION.

A simple analysis may justify the above. Ignoring the additional benefits, the rural ex-mill price of whole rice, can be about *Rs. 8.6 per kg.* (taking into account, cost of energy, 70% conversion, and 4% broken, when the procurement price of paddy is Rs 5.60 / per kg). The retail market price in city is Rs. 20 - 25/- Kg. and more. Who earns the differences of Rs. 11.4 - 16.4, and what for? Can we justify such earnings by those whose physical exercise does not go beyond the effort of eating what is produced though the toil of the peasants in the field round the year. Even a poor urban labourer pays this amount, unless bought from the PDC (Public Distribution Centre) with a ration card, at the ration shop. Is this the definition of "sovereign democracy'.? Often a malpractice is indulged. The ration cards are 'sold' to middle class, when the poor benefits getting some cash in hand after purchasing 'ragi' and the middle class benefits purchasing rice at low cost from PDC meant for poor people. Exploitation of the poor to get economic benefits has become the creed of those who are not poor. Estimates on massive scale pilferage with full knowledge of the governance have been provided in an earlier Para.

If rice mills are established in rural areas, as described earlier, and sold by the village cooperatives, will that not eliminate much of the rural-urban divide. This is illustrated in Fig 10, sub FIG 1B sub para 1A is our current practice. Combined with the central budgeted revenue, elimination of pilfered money the face of the rural society will change.

ENERGY SOURCE

Fig 7 provides an indication that the country, with a disparity ratio of 12:05 between urban and rural society need not be so, if decentralized co-generation energy is used, as shown in Fig 12.

PART 3B

RURAL DEVELOPMENT THOUGH NON-AGRO BASED INDUSTRIES

The narration of this Chapter needs explanations. There are several reasons, GTRE needs a critical look as an example how our action oriented establishments tends to be non- functional. GTRE's arrival to Bangalore was to be a close-by R & D unit to the newly established Engine Factory, also to conduct such design and development work whose production should be possible using the infra structure which was being created at the New Engine factory. The goal was:

1. To prove our basic genetic intelligence, and confirm that we can rise overcoming difficult circumstances, to meet the Nation's aspiration to be one free of foreign dependence.

2.To establish a partnership with aircraft design office.

3. To create an Institution to serve Aeronautical activities, Marine propulsions, multifuel power generation systems, and providing help to our energy deficient subcontinent.

4. Build high technology core competence to assist other R & D activities. Move to Bangalore, initially was much against the wishes of our the then ,large hearted, currently not much talked about Defence Minister, but accepted only when the wide perspective in view could be explained. Differences between Aircraft and Engine designers are common, scientifically justifiable, when both are creating FORCE, but vectorally opposite and equal in steady state of flying condition. The similarity ends there... With a deep rooted National interest, decisions were taken to cope with such situations. At the very out set, the author would like to explain that such differences were wholly technical in nature, but not in the National interest.

The essential fact to realize is that GTRE grew as one body to germinate activities, not only in the field of aeronautics, but in other fields as well, with no discord. The seminars held at GTRE, an example placed at Annexure 3, prove this. Finally, the author would be most grateful if an alternate quantified implementable strategy was suggested by any.

AERONAUTICS AND AEROSPACE TECHNOLOGIES & RURAL DEVELOPMENT

Having dealt with the degraded religion; perverted hereditary caste system; illiteracy and education; the unique heritage of excellence; the foreign dominations; the freedom fights; dismal situation on corruption; massive pilferage of allotted fund towards literacy, rural and agricultural development; poor state of agronomy, malnutrition of children; energy, water, and other associated aspects; local agro-processing; to move over to write about a high Science and Technology subjects, viz., aeronautics and aerospace technologies, may appear incongruous.

The main thrust is to build up the rural community, possible only through greater wealth generation in rural areas beyond agronomy. The activity on aeronautics provides an example that given the necessary support and encouragement the country can achieve much, making use of the inherent genetic intelligence of this country's people, though economically poor. This part is written essentially to confirm the prospect of getting back on rails of prosperity, the knowledge based developed society hurtling on earlier, and why it is not now.

DIFFERENCE BETWEEN AERONAUTICS AND AEROSPACE TECHNOLOGY

The difference between aeronautics and aerospace technology needs an explanation at this stage. In the final analysis, unless the per capita income in rural society is significantly improved, the country's several ailments cannot be removed.

Staying focused on rural development, one can summarize that aeronautical activity needs many more relatively lower level of technology oriented persons, compared to aerospace technology based activity. Both needs, however, fool-proof competence. and innovative mind.

For the nation's security, both aeronautics and aerospace technologies are used, but in different ways. Both are expensive, and take longtime to develop. The big question is which can serve our society more, eliminating the deficiencies dealt with earlier. Although no statistical data is available, aeronautical sciences, particularly the Gas Turbine Technology can serve more towards rural development than aerospace, and at lesser expenditure. If agricultural rural society's development is achieved through Gas Turbine based decentralized co-generation of Electricity and residual heat, a *strong* action oriented literate and educated fully employed nation will emerge. Aerospace technology needs far more articulated labour force, but cannot provide direct benefit to large rural mass through employment.

A manned aircraft provides for *direct* man to man relationship in many ways. A spacecraft provides for *indirect* link for the entire world's population, even when unmanned. The most important contribution can be learning about earth's resources. and climate; with infinite possibilities in the near and distant future exploring the space. In our present situation, we need to learn about these. Manned spacecraft is not dealt with because the long term possible benefits are still to be explored and confirmed.

INITIATION OF GAS TURBINE TECHNOLOGY

A brief reference about the first indigenous Gas Turbine was made earlier, in Chapter 8 essentially to indicate that our agricultural based subcontinent could rise to be at par with Northern hemisphere industrial competence from grass root level, with proper patronage. There are several who believe that the Southern part below 30^0 latitude is poor for three reasons. First, we are short of conventional fossil fuel based energy resource.

Secondly, our agro-based life style is not conducive to germinate industrial aptitude. The earlier mentioned working model of a gas turbine engine was made to prove that this view by people, influenced by the industrial revolution, is wrong. Indeed, the remark by a noted scientist cum technologist, then heading

NGTE. UK reaffirmed what was established in 1961 when the first experimental model of Gas Turbine engine was successfully designed and run. The author was asked to be his guide when he came as an invitee to our Science congress. He was keen to see our country. Greatly impress with the skill of our technologists, making delicate artifacts with stone, he expressed his unreserved faith on the country's ability to make gas turbine engine.

Thirdly, we also suffer from several self-generated genetic strains, - one generally designated as 'crab' mentality. We do not like a contemporary to excel. We like to scheme and make efforts to pull him down, instead of helping and making efforts to help him to climb to a greater height. We like sharing fabricated negative views, and spread. As a result we go for foreign products.

V. K. KRISHNA MENON

After the country's Independence, a debate on the governance approach to make the nation strong through capitalism, or through communism – a system following principles of Marxism – surfaced. Jawaharlal Nehru, the nation's nominated leader by Gandhi, an intellectual, got himself in a confused state of mind. The emphasis of nation's development through rural development, or making the country strong through industrialization before rural development were the two factors weighed heavily in his mind. Jawaharlal Nehru has met Krishna Menon in England, when he was working hard as Secretary (1929 – 1947) of the India League in the UK. He had joined the Labour party. Was a popular labour leader and politician. Was elected Borough councilor of St. Pancras, London, and conferred the freedom of Borough. The only other person so honoured was Bernard Shaw.

V. K. Krishna Menon

He was a highly literate person, worked as an editor for Penguin and Pelican Books. He was one of the founders of these two publishing agencies. After Independence he became the country's High Commissioner during 1947 – 52, and thereafter became our minister for Defence in 1957. Whether he had held an independent charge of this Portfolio was not clear.

AUTHOR'S RETURN TO INDIA

After a very satisfying spell of learning, the author returned back, not knowing what to do. While still in England (Bristol), had received a letter from Dr D.S. Kothari mentioning about country's desire to establish a Research centre on Gas Turbine; and the author should come prepared to establish this.

Dr. D. S. Kothari was an eminent Physicist, teacher, and Head of his subject's department in Delhi university. He was invited by our Prime Minister to look after Defence Science. Now he had two offices miles apart. His new designation, within the orbit of officialdom, was 'Scientific Advisor to Defense Minister', commonly addressed as SA, receiving a pay of Rupee one only. It was, at his choice, an honorary appointment, in fact. This arrangement was necessary, to be regarded as a government official, when he could exercise some official powers and use

Government facilities, viz. transport. He did not shift to a government accommodation, in New Delhi, and retained his house allotted by the Delhi university in Old Delhi. His office there was an isolated small building in the campus.

The author's encounter with Krishna Menon, the legendary person was through Dr. Kothari. Accompanying him, entered the chamber of hon'ble Defence Minister. Customarily saluted, and stood awaiting to receive his order to sit down. He was busy examining a file, and did not respond for a period which appeared to be an hour. For a Squadron Leader, it was difficult to take initiative. Eventually heard a voice stating, "there are many empty chairs. You need not keep standing". He said this without lifting his eyes from the file. The author sat down next to SA.

Now looking up, he said that he was going through the author's dossier. Added he said, that he would believe what all file contained only after an indigenous engine was made. Shell socked with this remark the author's spontaneous reply was - "it cannot be done, Sir. There is no material, no infrastructure, no trained technician, - nothing." Glaring straight he now spoke with raised voice,- "yes, it can be and has to be done. If you had felt so conclusively, why did you with your family(wife and a 6 year's old son) spent nearly five years at tax payer's money in England? Why did you not return? India has every thing. Go round and search, and make that engine".

Helplessly, the author looked at SA. The assigned task by him while still in England, was to establish a '*research*' laboratory on return. But he did nothing to ease the confrontation. Instead signaling to follow him, we made our exit from the 'horror chamber', dazed. SA's office was almost next door. He was a mild man. But his advise was still more impractical. He said, 'make a small engine, and then it will be alright'. How to explain that it was far more difficult to make a small engine. Without saying anything, I left through the rear door of the suffocating 'south block' which had another name; - 'the mad house'.

On return from England, I had to report back to air headquarters. This I had done a day before. Wrote the customary report on activities in the UK, filled up other forms, applied for family accommodation, assuming a posting in Delhi, from where I had left to go to the UK sailing in a P & O ship from Bombay.

Out of the 'mad house' walked to near by 'K' block, thinking about what action should be taken now. Decided to request for a posting to an Air Force unit, and be out of the absurd situation being forced into. Reaching DTS (Director of Technical Services)'s office, received a posting order to report to DTD &P (Air). Never heard of this new animal, I mused. Enquiring from Director's p.a. learnt that it was a new directorate to take care of technical development and production of aircraft, located at a place next to the office of Chief of Air Staff in 'H' block with a fence in between. I also gathered from him that promotion to next rank, 'wing commander', had been recommended by the director, and was being considered by the selection board.

The name, DTD & P (Air) sounded interesting, so decided to *explore* (as if the posting order is something, which could be changed if not liked!). It was an unimpressive hutment with asbestos roofing. . Resigned to my destiny, I walked in. Close to entry, on the left side was the office of the Director, Dr. Nilakantan. A not too wide a passage lead to the rear end. The offices were. mostly on the right side of the passage. Peeped in and saw some old senior friends. Nair (Armament), Krishnan (Electrical), Srinivasan (Signal), and some more, Reached the end where an empty room with a dusty table with couple of chairs, was waiting for me to set up my office.

THE BEGINNING

Three more talented and all educated abroad up to master's degree soon joined. Now we began discussing what transpired earlier at the "mad house". Reported to Dr. Nilakantan, and the rapport was instant, even before we spoke. Without asking who I was, or the purpose of this unannounced intrusion, he offered me a chair to sit down. Such a courtesy wiped off the unhappiness which was building up. I felt perfectly relaxed. Narrated the 'story of my life' from Cranfield Institute to SA's advice. He did not interrupt once. At the end, he stated that my activity should begin at a hardware oriented establishment. Enquired if the author had any suggestion. Having worked earlier there, promptly suggested BRD, Kanpur. (No. 1 was affixed afterwards when more BRD's came up). He stood up, extended his hand which I grasped with both hands, when he said, " let me try, but you should consider DM's desire".

Retuning to my room, the team was told what transpired. We got on to thinking seriously how to make the engine. Several suggestions were considered. A view received favourable support. The generally accepted strategy was to identify existing components to be used, as blanks, to machine out the desired components; concentrate on developing heat resisting materials getting assistance from Ordinance factories of DGOF (Director General of Ordinance Factories) and develop in house technology to caste Aluminum components. Aluminum casting was not done then in the country.

The author got in touch with his professor, - Professr A. D. Baxtor, at Cranfield Institute of Technology, UK. He was one of the pioneers on Propulsion systems, both Gas Turbine and Rocket Motor. He felt that our approach was worth trying. He sounded optimistic, and happy; wished us good luck.

MOVE TO BRD, KANPUR, 1958

With a name GTRC (Gas Turbine Research Center), the nucleus body moved there. With that name, it was not clear which component of Ministry of Defence would be it's controlling authority. Arrival at Kanpur was the most refreshing experience. Other than round the clock buzzing activity towards establishing an Aircraft Manufacturing Unit (AMU), everything looked the same. There was a welcomed smile from all. Credit must be given to the nucleus team, now slightly expanded. In no time they became a part of the Depot, and at their own initiative, started to build the center. There was unreserved support from every Department of BRD and AMU.

Group Captain. Baljit Kapoor, Chief Engineer, AMD

The Chief Engineer of AMD needs a special mention. His first posting was to work with the author in 1949. But he worked more with the Commanding Officer's 'hobby' and designed and made a light weight aircraft at Kanpur. Also studied aircraft design at the Cranfield Institute of Technology,UK.

The first meeting with the same Commanding Officer of BRD, after 10 years, was most encouraging.

Group Captain- Harjinder Singh, Commanding Officer No.1 BRD

He spoke as if he was now talking to the same officer who had served under him, as a pilot officer in 1947. The only difference was the smiling encouraging expression. He said, 'I want the engine made', adding 'I know you can do it.' During my first posting, in 1947, he had reservation about graduate engineers becoming maintenance engineers. But he had changed his opinion soon.

He was a unique personality. He had started his carrier as a 'howayee' (Aircraft) sepoy, and virtually built up the technical faculty of the Air Force single handed. He did not attend any flying academy and learnt flying at the station he commanded, taking lessons from other pilots, posted in BRD. The coveted pilot's wing was, however, pinned on his uniform during a passing out parade in Ambala, then the only flying training school. The author accompanied him on that occasion. He was a strict disciplinarian, retired as Air Vice-Marshal, one among the few at that time.

With collective effort and support, the team began it's venture for unknown. All that we had was a conceptual strategy. The center was allotted an empty large store room, and nothing else. Adding to our owe, a very noisy compressor was located just outside. Our discussion had to be synchronized with the compressor's 'On' and 'Off' sequence. The story of technology development, self learning, and in house training given to selectively recruited furniture making carpenters, utensil making, sheet making workers, cast iron molders, oxy-acetylene welders, and skilled workers was an unique experience for all. The most important motto was 'never give up'. Everyone designed and worked systematically.

There were serious differences, at times, e.g., adopting then practiced Can combustors, VS a Can annular combustor which was finally accepted. Gobline engine had Can type. The early models of Avon also had Can type The decision making was simple. Try both and accept the winner. The other approach was to work with the recruited technicians. The carpenters became pattern makers, utensil makers became aircraft grade certified sheet metal workers, the oxyacetylene gas wielders became argon arc welders suited for aluminum wielding, and fitters learnt about the importance of fits and tolerances, making use of micro-meter and vernier caliper. The dimensional tolerances were now referred in 'thou' (thousandth of an inch), instead of 'Ek/ Tho Suth'. The concept of advanced technology as used in Aeronautical engineering was getting the needed acceptance. Everyone worked to make the designed components meeting the specified tolerances in 'thou'. The universal metric system came in being much later.

Last but not the least was the unbelievable speed of conversion of the empty hall into a reasonably acceptable office complex, with separated single row of cabins with curtains, chairs and tables. The raw material was the empty wooden boxes heaped at thc other end of the store hall. The furniture making carpenters, now patternmakers, did not want to loose, it would appear, their earlier skill. With name plates fixed, and a long coir mat running in front of all office entrances, a new feeling of dignity and confidence started rising on the horizon. Beginning with one table, with shaky legs, and *four* chairs, most with one hand rest missing, for *six* scientists, this transformation was done most gratefully by the 'tarkhans' (carpenters) we hired to make them pattern makers. The team of six soon became twenty. We were lucky to select such talents. Yet the fact was that all were from one dusty Kanpur city only. They were barely literate.

Since no married accommodation was available within the campus, the one allotted outside to the author could not be any better. It was a vestibule barrack type, but with a larege lawn in front. What more, it was right across the most famous colonial 'Cownpur Club' retaining much of the pre-partition 'shahib' disciplined culture.

The scientific staff members were accommodated in the officers' mess. The author was apprehensive about their stay in the officers' mess. Will they jell with the air force officers? In a recent birth day party of one retired senior officer who was then a junior officer staying in the mess, recalling those early days and my apprehension then, spoke highly about this 'bunch' of young scientists. He expressed that they got quickly in the rhythm of service life to an extent that it was difficult to make out any difference other than that they were not in uniform. The rest did not require any special arrangement. They were local people.

All together made the Prototype and commissioned. More details are written in the subsequent Paras of Part 3, to provide an unique and comprehensive account on the development of gas turbine technology for the benefit of rural society as well.

Pandit Jawaharlal Nehru, our prime minister came to witness. Moving towards his car to leave, he smiled but made no comment. Comments appeared in media, heralding *"India can make it"*. That was perhaps the best and an appropriate one. Because this was made for the first time in an underdeveloped country, using common purpose machine tools and facilities.

PRODUCTION OF THE DEMONSTRATOR

Shown below a group photograph of dedicated persons who worked with no time limits. It was true example of service before self.

The Dedicated Team At No. 1 BRD, IAF, Kanpur

(Most sitting in the front row, the author in the center, and those sitting below on floor and few others came to Bangalore to set up GTRE, absorbing technology from the most helpful HAL's Engine Factory, expanding rapidly during 1962-65).during next three years.

With a name GTRC (Gas Turbine Research Center), it was not clear who to report to. DTD&P or officer commanding BRD? Most interesting feature was no one asked. We could work as we liked or required. One notable technological break through was the making of a circular blank of Rex 448 heat resisting material for the first time in India, to manufacture the Turbine disc. This was done at an ordinance factory, Cassipur, West Bengal, under DGOF..

GAS TURBINE RESEARCH CENTER, KANPUR

With collective effort and support, the team achieved the targeted goal. The center was allotted an empty large store room, with heaped up packing cases at one end, and nothing else. Adding to our owe, a very noisy compressor, installed inside a small enclosure, was located just outside; facing our store house. Our discussion had to be synchronized with the compressor's 'On' and 'Off' sequence. The story of technology development, self learning, and in house training given to selectively recruited furniture making carpenters, utensil making sheet making workers, caste iron molders, Oxy-acetylene welders, and skilled workers with hand tools, - the expensive one was a file, - was an unique experience for all. The most important motto was 'never give up'. Everyone designed his tool and worked systematically. There were serious differences, at times, e.g., continuing with the then practiced Can combustors, Vs a Can *annular* combustor which was finally accepted. Gobline and all other engines had then Can type. The decision making was simple. Try both and accept the winner. The other successful approach was the engineers working with the recruited technicians. Soon the carpenters became pattern makers, utensil makers became aircraft grade certified sheet metal workers, the oxyacetylene gas wielders became argon arc welders suited for aluminum wielding, and fitters learnt about the importance of fits and tolerances, making use of micro-meter and vernier caliper. Everyone worked to make the designed components meeting the specified tolerances.

Last but not the least was the unbelievable speed of conversion of the empty hall into a reasonably acceptable office complex, with separated single row of cabins with curtains, chairs and tables. The raw material was the empty wooden boxes heaped at the other end. The furniture making carpenters, now patternmakers, did not want to loose, it would appear, their earlier skill. With name plates fixed, and a long coir mat running in front of all office cabins, a new feeling of dignity and confidence started rising on the horizon. Beginning with one table, with shaky legs, and *four* chairs, most with one hand rest missing, for *six* scientists, this transformation was done most gratefully by the 'tarkhans' (carpenters) we hired to make them pattern makers. The team of six soon became twenty. We were lucky to select such persevering talents. Yet the fact was that all were from one dusty Kanpur city only. They were not even Matriculates, but very eager to learn. There were endless events of very hard work, failures, and rework with no fixed working hours.

The married accommodation allotted to the author could not be any better. It was a vestibule type barrack, but with a large lawn in front. The kitchen at the rear, was separate connected with the main building through a covered passage. What more, it was right across the most famous colonial 'Cownpur Club' retaining much of the pre-partition 'shahib' disciplined culture. It had a nice small swimming pool. The author was familiar to the club facilities, when posted earlier in 1947.

The scientific staff members were accommodated in the officers' mess. They deserve credit. In no time they became a part of the whole system. The rest did not require any special arrangement. They were mostly local people.

A SHORT BREAK IN THE AUTHOR'S ACTIVITY ON EXPERIMENTAL MODEL

While settling down with work, a call came to report to DM's office in Delhi. With apprehension, entered and saluted almost at the threshold. My previous experience was still in mind. But felt a little courageous when two respected senior Air Force officers were seen sitting inside. This time Krishna Menon seemed to have changed. After confirming that the author knew them, he asked the author to sit down. Smiling, he said that he was happy learn about our on going effort to make an engine. Then asked whether the author had any knowledge about (Mikoyan – Grevich designed) Russan MiG 21 aircraft. The reply was a truth, and nothing but the truth. "Heard of it but no knowledge" was the reply. While studying at CIT (Cranfield Institute of Technology), UK, in 1956, had learnt about Supersonic intake. OSWATITCH pitot intake was one innovative solution for supersonic aircraft's intake. Gathered then that this approach was been tried out in MiG 21 and earlier in English Electic P1 supersonic aircraft since 1954. It was a system to break the normal shock though a system of inclined and normal shock to reduce the pressure loss at the engine intake at high (supersonic) flight speed.

INDUCTION OF SUPERSONIC FIGHTER.

Our 1948 war with Pakistan was fought with Tempest, – a

subsonic fighter aircraft powered by a piston engine coupled to a propeller . It was perhaps the last designed most powerful fighter aircraft propelled by a piston engine. restricting the flight speed to about 500 miles per hour.

The largest number of fighter aircraft flown at that time was Spitfire aircraft. It had earned fame during WWII's 'Battle of Britain' There were several versions. The most favoured one was Spit 18, with elliptic wing, powered by supercharged Merline 66. There was a clipped wing version, as ground attacker. A version, Spit 19 known as flying tank, for long range operation, when wings stored fuel in addition. Then again a trainer version with tandem sitting arrangement, Spit 9 a late introduction.

Spitfire 18 - the early graceful lady but full of venom if you try to be funny. Germans kept a safe distance during WWII

Air Commodore Frank Whittle brought about a revolution in aeronautical Science & Technology in 1937 when he patented jet propulsion. His persevering effort is an example to all innovative minded S &T personnel that it was not a cake walk for Gp. Capt Whittle before he could get even a hearing from authorities in Command. It was his personal conviction which kept him going, to get aircraft flying at speed greater than sound.

The first aircraft, powered by his designed engine, flew in 1941. The speed restriction induced by the propeller was now removed. The continuous combustion cycle of operation made the engine much lighter and opened up prospects for much greater power for smaller frontal area. His invention opened up the prospect of supersonic flights. No jet aircraft, except one from Germany took part in WWII, because it was too late to get Whittle engine into production.

Germans developed jet engine but with an *axial flow compressor, instead of centrifugal compressor of Whittle engine (Luftwaffe had kept this as secret while developing the engine, and hence it was difficult to verify which one should get the laurel of being the FIRST.). While in the UK, the author had used one W1 engine for some experimental work of his at CIT. It was bought from NGTE (National Gas Turbine Establishment), UK at a throw away price.

* There is a controversy on the type of compressor.

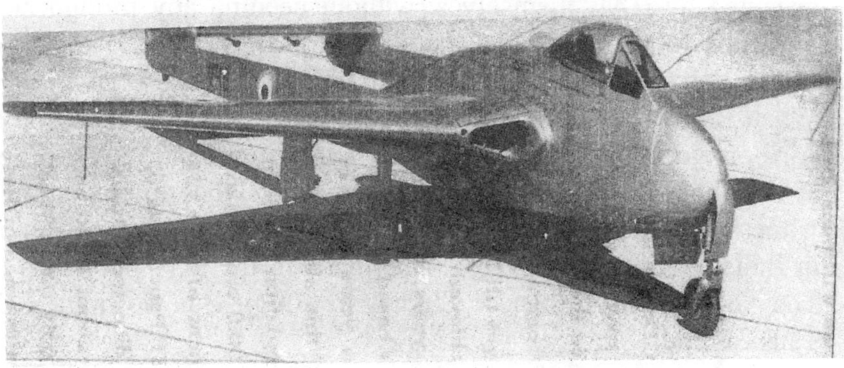

De Havilland358 Vampire

Our Air Force realized the future dimension of Air Power. Four de Haviliand Vampire aircraft were bought in 1948, and a Squadron was formed in Kanpur. Squadron Leader Subbya (Subbie as he was fondly addressed) was the commanding officer. Three other members were (no non-sense illusively mild) Stan White, Nobie Clerk, and bent neck (because of usual posture) Kurian. Jovial but efficient Gyan Singh was the Engineering

Officer. He became a good friend. No outsider was allowed inside that hanger, close to the CO's fortress. These were first subsonic jet aircraft, to fly in Asia. At that time, performance wise they were not much superior to well known fighter aircraft with piston engine, for example, Spitfire. A most thrilling Arial mock fight was done at Ambala; Vampire from Kanpur ***VS*** Spit 18 from advanced training school of Ambala. Ganja (bald) Bose won getting at the tail of the Vampire.

The author (27 years old) was then undergoing flying training at Ambala. Because of earlier extended experience on Spitfire assembly at Kanpur, he tried to help the competitive show, by locking the 'RAD' (Radiator) flap in the open position. This helped to get enhanced turn rate. But the visible evidence for the win was the wrinkled wing's top surface of the Spitfire. subjected to much greater 'g' turn. Yet this was a pre-cursor of much to happen in the future. Later we bought a few other jet aircraft; Hunters and Canberras from UK; Ouragan and Mystere IV from France: - all sub-sonic. The crowning glory was of course the Gnat, and the improved Ajeet, with more than 50 modifications executed by HAL themselves, without needing any foreign help. The fully modified Ajeet version flew on 6th March, 1975. Gnat was a derivative of Midge, flown initially in 11 August, 1954. When RAF (Royal Air Force) was reluctant to have Gnat, Indian Air Force decided to have it. Dasu (Wing Commande S. Das) flew at Farnborough air show in 1956, when the author proudly witnessed. Dr. WEW Petter was willing to set up a design Bureau in India, (Refer page 47 of 'Diamonds in the sky' published by The Society for Aerospace Studies in 2001.) But we invited Dr. Tank instead.

A new Chapter on aviation industry began with the arrival of Dr. Kurt Tank and his team members in 1956. GTRE got involved with his activities, on all occasions at HAL's invitations.. Brief narrations are reproduced below about GTRE's activities, after the initially selected Bristol Siddley's B.Or 12 could not be made available.

.1. Director GTRE was invited to accompany MD., HAL

to assess a substitute Russian engine. The Director pointed out that the engine would not fit .for two reasons. One about interference with the engine accessories, and the other about having a bigger reheat pipe diameter.

2. Dr. Tank felt otherwise. Six engines were bought. On arrival, GTRE 's Director proved to be right. Russian engineers were invited. They endorsed GTRE's view. Left stating nothing could be done to suit the engine to fit the aircraft.

3. GTRE was invited to try and rectify. Working very hard, it got the engine reshaped, but with the original reheat pipe.

It is worth reiterating that the involvement with HAL's aircraft design activities was at the initiative of HAL management. GTRE never offered any help. HAL called for this and with permission from DRDO Headquarter (Scientific Officer's permission) the help was given. The mystery lies in the fact, why invite GTRE when it had it's engine design team.

On all occasions, the work was taken in hand with DRDO's permission. The funding was by DRDO, not HAL. There was NAL (National Aerospace Laboratory). Why this establishment was not invited? It did, but only as analyst.

In our Science culture, a verbose analyst is rated a superior authority, when not offering to soil the hands. That was what GTRE was meant for. There were two kinds of Science oriented personnel. One implementation oriented, the other to write and speak / analyse; the latter was had the upper hand, with no commitment.

The advantage of being one in the latter group, was there was no chance to fail. The implementing party did not have that privilege, once committed to act. The victim is one who wishes to implement / experiment his innovative mind.

Dr. Kurt Tank

INVITATION TO Dr. Kurt Tank

Dr. Kurt Tank's designs in World War II included the Luftwaffe's key piston-engined famed fighter, FW-190 and the multi-engined Condor transport aircraft. After war, he skipped to Cordoba and met M. Dewoirine, the celebrated French aircraft designer. He had converted one room of his large villa at the outskirts of Corodoba as his drawing office, trying to design a jet aircraft with whatever information he had about Rolls Royce Derwent engine. At that time Dr. Hooker was there on a sales mission and joined Dewoitine, named the aircraft as Pulqui (Arrow). When professor Tank surfaced, Dr. Hooker left, and soon Dewoline too, leaving Dr. Tank alone. What happened thereafter is not known. But Dr. Tank's experience on jet aircraft design did not go much beyond. For reason best known to some admirers of German aerospace technology, a decision was preempted to invite Dr. Tank. He arrived in 1956, with his team of 18 design engineers, and soon began his work to design a Mach 2+ supersonic single seated fighter aircraft, to be powered by two B.Or 12 SR engines. These engines were designed by BSEL, UK. The targeted design objective was to meet our Air Force's ASR (Air Staff Requirement). The designed aircraft was designated as HF 24 (Hindustan Fighter)

COMPARISON OF HF 24 Mk I & MARSAL DASSAULT F1

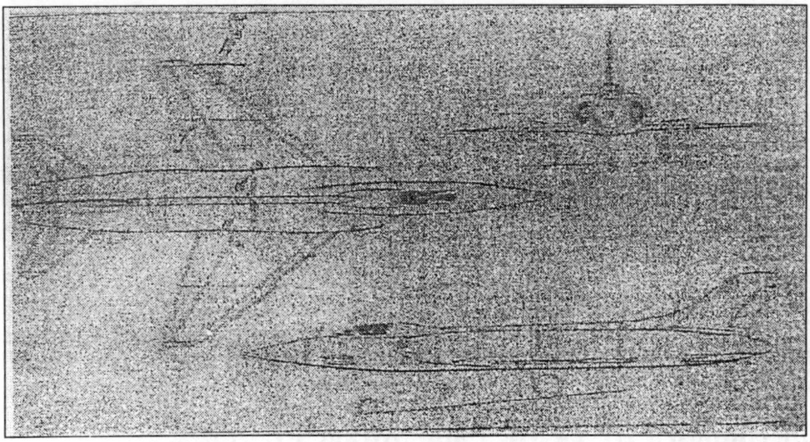

HF24 Mk 1

Note: The tail plane is positioned at the *bottom* of the tail end, at the same level of the wing.

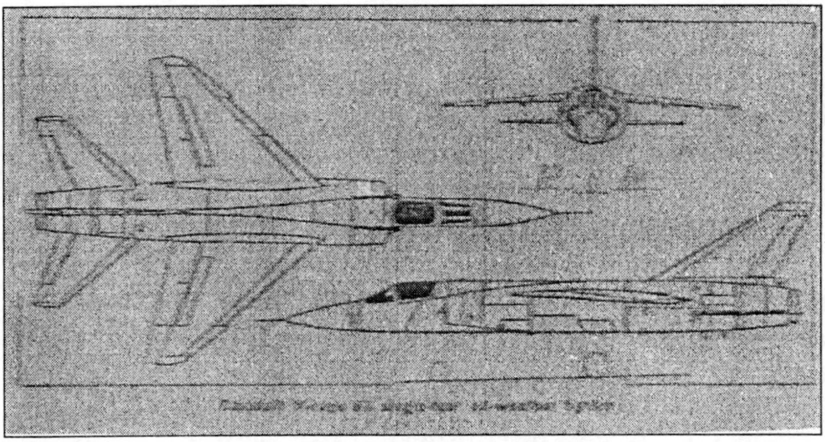

Marcel Dassault Mirage F1

Note: Tail plane at the centre of the of the tail end, when the wing was at the top.

There were views that both originated from the same German stable. This becomes more apparent when their profiles are superimposed.

The rear end configuration differs essentially because F1 is powered by a single Attar 9K engine with a much bigger exit

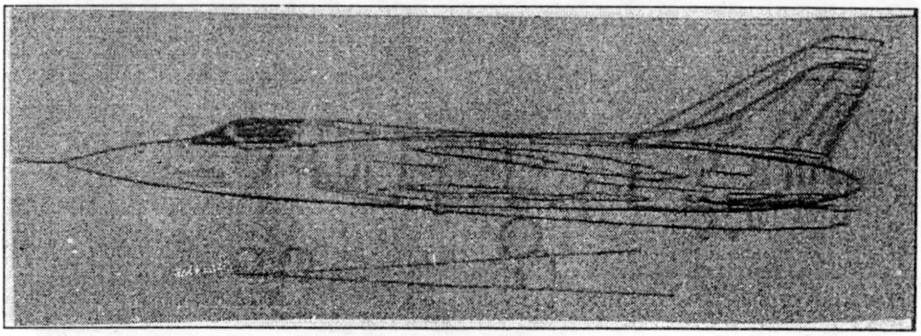

Superimposed HF 24 Mk 1 and Mirage F1

diameter compared to that designed for two B.Or. 12.SR. HF 24 MK 1 was a twin engine version, and hence had a slimmer (darker lined) side view appearance at the rear end. Same wings and tail planes were used in both, but differently positioned.

Who designed these similar aircraft? The selectors, the admirers of this legendry person, - not Dr. Tank alone should share the resultant damage done to the nation's aeronautical S & T. What follows may substantiate this view.

Dr. Petter had designed Hunter, Canberra, and Supersonic P1 before designing the Gnat. Dr. Tank had *no* experience on jet aircraft design, let alone about a Supersonic aircraft. No doubt, he had a very successful run, and was famous for the well known designs of Focke - Wulf 190 subsonic aircrafts powered by piston engines. But he did not fit to meet the country's desire to have a fighter meeting the specifications of ASR.

Dr. Petter had designed English electric jet engine powered P1 (Lightening) aircraft. It attained supersonic speed in it's first flight, without operating reheat. This world's first supersonic aircraft flying at Mach 2+.did not require 78 gliding trials in a wooden mock up to assess the low speed handling characteristic of the designed HF 24 aircraft. This itself is a record. It would appear that such gliding trials were the standard practice in German aeronautical development effort before powered flights. Surprisingly the near replica in France did not require this.

THE MYSTERY DEEPENS

Germany and Japan, members of axis power, were prevented from designing aircraft after the war. So where was the near identical HF 24 and Dassault Mirage F1, as shown above, designed? Was it at HAL design office at such great speed, when the wooden mock up was ready for discussion in a year? If so, how this designed aircraft for supersonic speed was transferred to Marcel Dassault? . Or, reverse was the process?

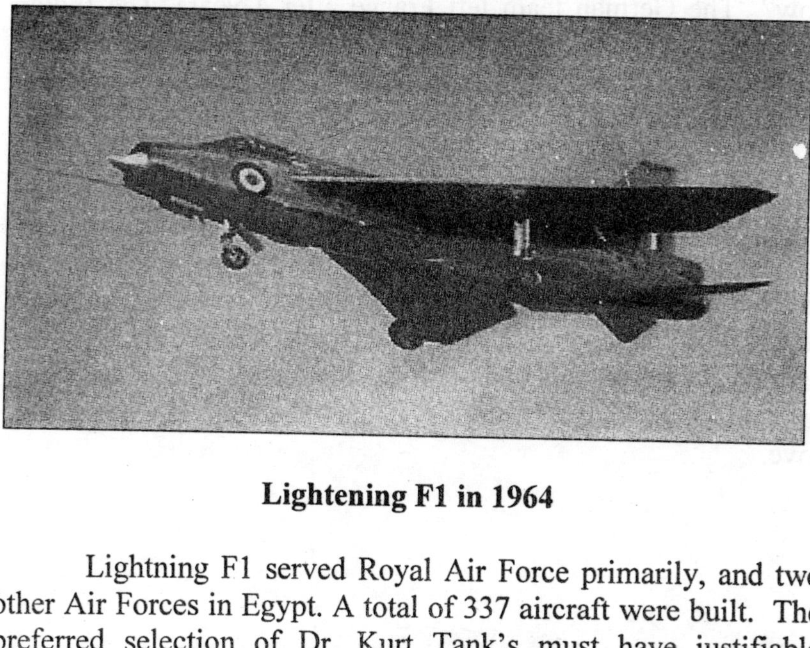

Lightening F1 in 1964

Lightning F1 served Royal Air Force primarily, and two other Air Forces in Egypt. A total of 337 aircraft were built. The preferred selection of Dr. Kurt Tank's must have justifiable support by a responsible and knowledgeable Committee and it's deliberation for invitation of Dr. Tank instead of Dr. Petter must be available in HAL's record. When the Indian sky is currently barren of any *indigenous* fighter and transport aircraft, and the country has recently been forced to consider foreign purchase deal for about 2 bn dollars, (media information), the author believes that the record of the committee needs looking into, when the CV (Curriculum Vitae) of these two would suggest that Dr. Petter would have been a far better choice keeping the ASR in view. Nation must know what was the compelling justification to select Dr. Tank instead, when his past experiences did not indicate anything about his ability to design a supersonic fighter aircraft to meet the ASR.

The above remark would be irrelevant and grossly improper had it not been what presented in later Paras comparing with Marcel Dassault F1, and his actions after the non-availability of B.Or 12 SR. The line diagram comparison of the two, made earlier adds to the mystery. That they were bred from the same stable, secretly in Germany, is a reasonable doubt. A German team had worked at that time in France as well. The question is who owned the stable? Did not the Indian selectors know? The German team left France after 4 years. The Indian team stayed back for twice that period not producing the aircraft they were invited for. Was there any contract? Were they reporting to any?

Supersonic flying caught the imagination of aircraft designers. The period between 1954 to 1958 saw competitive designs in all developed countries, viz., UK, France, USSR, USA, and Sweden, when China, assisted by USSR also phased in a little later. With ban imposed on the then vanquished Germany and Japan with despicable humanism in record, the design of aeronautical store got restricted to the five nations mentioned above.

INITIATION OF GAS TURBINE TECHNOLOGY IN INDIA

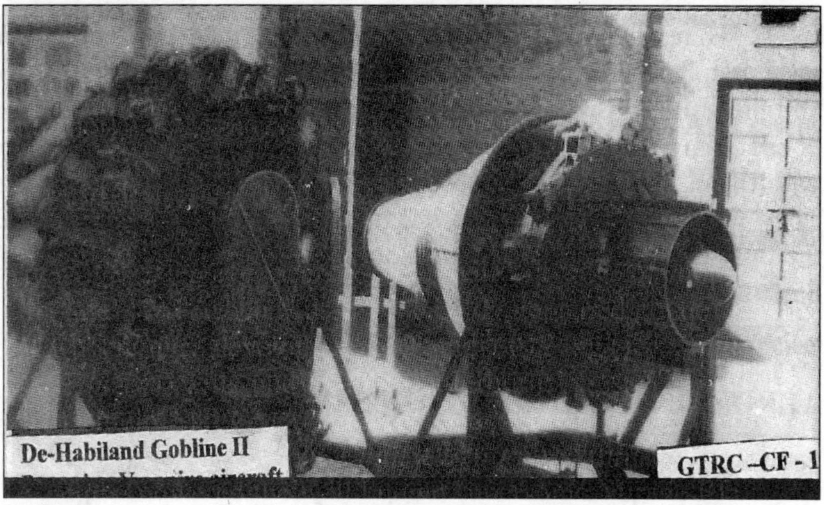

Comparison with Gobline engine with two side intakes and "its copy",
GTRC- CF – 1, with one central intake with a can annular system.

Ratings at SLS (Sea Level Static) : Ambient 14.7 psig, 15^0 C
GOBLINE : 3500 lb Static thrust
GTRC-CF 1 : 2500 lb Static thrust (Design target)

MOVE TO BANGALORE

After making an experimental engine, GTRC-CF-1 at Kanpur, the nebulous unit, GTRC moved to Bangalore, and became a regular DRDO (Defence Research and Development Organization) unit as GTRE.

GTRE arrived from Kanpur, with 14 people with hand tools at cantonment railway station, in November, 1961, to build an establishment of technological excellence working against all odds, and in 20 years, it grew to be a premier institution. Foreign gas turbine manufacturing enterprises exhibited keen interest to collaborate with GTRE's projects. Gas turbine was not even taught in the country, in 1961. The people recruited were those who came from 'employment exchange', mostly with a matriculation certificate and not much in their CV. They had not even heard of gas turbines.

Here the experience at Kanpur described earlier was a great help. The only criteria for selection was basic intelligence and the ability to work with hand tools. They were all trained 'in house', as was done in Kanpur, when the qualified few worked with them. The speed with which they could learn was amazing. They were eager to learn. To reach higher level *competence* was the only qualification to be promoted .with no religion, caste, or hereditary bias. GTRE grew as a compact disciplined body. Everyone worked. What follows prove the above.

AERONAUTICS AND NATION'S DEVELOPMENT

Successfully developed aircraft can create large foreign trade and employment opportunities. An example may illustrate this. During production of Mirage F1, the well known Mach 2 + supersonic fighter aircraft, the total of employment of Marcel Dassault factory, in France, was about 8,550. The ancillary industries employed about ***30,000*** people in 1,500 small units with specialized competence. Generally our labour efficiency co-efficient is about 1.8* poorer compared to a foreign labour (taking into account the reduced yearly working hours because of innumerable religious occasions. and not proficiency alone. These religious occasions are usually performed in cinema halls, restaurants, and other forms of merry makings).

Thus, if we could come up to Dassault production rate, about *54,000* employment opportunities could have been created, in *developed* rural areas, if the first attempt to develop jet fighter HF 24 was a success. They could have multiplied at geometric progression rate, with better technological knowledge, in other diversified industries. The failure to develop this aircraft has set back the nation by 40 years, on indigenous fighter aircraft's design and production efforts.

This is an estimate. Some believe that 1.6 is more realistic.

In our current situation when (a) our industries, trade and commerce are slowly getting out of our grips into foreign hands, except in a few situations, e.g. IT and BT mainly, and (b) when our genetically intelligent mind even though strong but not used, the nation is sliding down with increased disparity ratio between the urban and rural societies.

The country is not competent to make an improved commercially competitive product in a short time though we recognize the spin offs of high science and technology knowledge. To repeat again, this Chapter suggests that after the basic rectification on urban-rural divide,* creating *developed* rural societies, through means described earlier, the need is to adopt an approach which will help rapid GDP growth through non-monsoon dependent industrial activity in rural areas. A survey suggests that aeronautics, coupled with national security, can provide this opportunity, with much less academic exposure.

(Here a major assumption made is on availability of appropriate energy in rural areas. This aspect has been dealt with in earlier paras.)*

Technology oriented *certified* skill is the need, and not academic attainments for most. Success on aeronautical activities, needing multidirectional S & T activities, may also encourage staying abreast with developed societies' attainments. This chapter should be read keeping this in view. What narrated here after is to illustrate how and why we have failed to achieve what Chinese could, when they were way behind us in aviation industry in 1944- 46.

GTRE'S INVOLVEMENT WITH HF 24

Dr. S. Bhagavantam

He was a unique scientist, an associate of Dr. C.V. Raman. He had been the only person allowed to appear for his Master's degree of Science from Calcutta university without going to a college. It is through his book on Raman's work, the world came to know about the Raman effect. His precision mind can be judged when he spoke. Without looking at his watch, he could conclude his talk at the specified time allotted. He was our second Scientific Adviser after Dr. Kothari, when GTRC, now renamed as GTRE as a DRDO establishment moved to Bangalore. The move was not linked with HF 24's development. The main motivation was to become an adjunct unit of the Engine factory .which was established for license manufacture of Orpheus engine to power Gnat/Ajeet aircraft. The primary desire was to make use of specialized facilities of the engine factory for any project which GTRE could design and make prototype.

Involving with HF 24 was not even remotely thought of. But we got involved initially in an advisory capacity when HAL got into a muddle because of non availability of B.Or 12 SR (Simplified Reheat) around which HF 24 was designed. It was a HAL aircraft division's project. The engine factory was not involved. The aircraft division had it's engine design team.

GTRE'S good relationship with the engine factory was established and maintained. It was perhaps more due to their generosity than GTRE personnel's well behaved nature. The operation on expensive machines was offered, when available and needed, as was done in Kanpur, by BRD and AMD. HAL's inspection team provided the help and guidance. They kept a neutral face, not ever asking what was cooking and where.

SEARCH FOR ENGINE FOR HF-24 AIRCRAFT

After an extensive search, eventually a ray of hope surfaced in late 1961 when Russian RD-9F appeared to be a solution. Two engines developed 7542 and 6012 kg.(*73.9 and 59.0 kN st. thrust*) with and without afterburner respectively compared to single SNECMA Attar 9 K, developing 7214 Kg with reheat and 5025kg dry (***70.2 and 49.26 kN***) st.thrust. The SNECMA engine powered the well known supersonic Mirage F1. Thus solution through two RD-9F could have made HF 24 comparable to Mirage F1, provided the aerodynamics was similar.

The same team who made the first visit to USSR to make a preview of MiG 21, was again sent to assess the engine. Taking help of an interpreter, the discussion was interesting, mostly writing equations. The amusing part was the presence of a militia man who did not like writing equations. He grabbed each written page whenever a new page was taken to continue discussion.

Two doubts surfaced before the selection. One was related to the fitment possibility of RD 9F in HF 24 aircraft. This engine. had all the accessories of the engine located at top of the engine. B.Or 12 SR had these at the bottom areas. Secondly, it was observed that the diameter of the reheat system around the final nozzle area was bigger than the aircraft's tail end area. A good deal of discussion ensued when the author, engine assessor of the team expressed his doubt about the feasibility of fitment in the aircraft on both counts. He told the leader that he would disagree the selection, unless the feasibility of fitment is vetted by Dr. Tank. The senior HAL representative also started feeling a little uncertain.

B.Or 12 SR (SR stands for Simplified Reheat)

The leader did not want to take a chance. He wanted these two aspects verified. The senior HAL representative was sent back to India, and had returned promptly after consulting Dr. Tank. Confirming the compatibility for the fitment, he conveyed that the little modification needed at the back end would not be a problem. MOU for the purchase of six engines were signed, amidst much joyous compliments, and greetings on Indo-Ruski 'drusba' (friendship). During the early phase of purchase negotiation the presence of the GTRE representative was not required. The cost of these engines are not known.

Unfortunately major problems surfaced *after* the arrival of these engines. It was soon discovered that these engines *cannot* be fitted in the aircraft! The engine accessories fitted on the *top* of the engine was not properly assessed when the senior HAL member made the short trip back to India, specifically to cross check with Dr. Tank. The bigger diameter of the reheat pipe could be accommodated with in the existing fuselage, but the problem about the rear end was ignored altogether as a minor issue, by HAL. In fact, the author was advised during a senior level meeting not to harp on this *non-issue*.

Unfortunately it was a vitally important issue. This is seen from what presented here after.

Russian help was now called for. A team of three Russian

technologists, headed by comrade Petrov arrived. Actually only two were civilian technologists, and the third person, major Mirashnishankov was the security officer, and the interpreter. He could speak English. (He was posted to Russian embassy, New Delhi, after a few years).

They were lodged within the limited space of GTRE. Their conclusion was that nothing could be done on the engine. The airframe had to be modified, and if necessary, Russians could do that. Dr. Tank was totally opposed to this suggestion. A tussle between Russian and German, surfaced when each was asking the other party to rectify the shortcomings. The Russian team left suddenly. The MD, HAL was obviously in a dilemma now.

This was the *second occasion* when HF 24 missed the opportunity of having the engines it needed. On the first occasion, there was no formal agreement with Bristol Siddley towards the development of B.Or 12 SR. Nothing could be done when it's availability became difficult. It's development was, however, not discontinued in the UK. It was developed up to its full potential beyond 1400^0K reheat, although NATO withdrew its support and UK's aeronautical industry did not require such an engine then.

Air commodore Banks, a well known gas turbine technologist, came to negotiate. But the conditions put forward by him was unacceptable to HAL. It was indeed difficult to accept. HAL was to agree purchase of 50 BSEL fabricated engine for transfer of technology and licensed manufacture. Unhappily lodged at Hotel Imperial on Janpath Road, near Connought circle, he desired the author to meet him. This could be because of his earlier association with BSEL.

In those days it was the best hotel. Hotel Ashok came up a little later. (Air Commdore Banks became the president of Royal Aeonautical Society). During the meeting the author told him that he was no body to talk on the subject. GTRE was not a part of HAL and not associated with HF 24 project. He desired that we could discuss the improved technology, beyond Orpheus engine. The author refused. Cautioning not to be quoted, as an individual his view was that the new license should limit to purchase of 10 BSEL manufactured engines, when HAL engine factory technicians would participate. They were already competent enough executing the on going license production of B.Or 701/703 engine. It should be an extension of the existing license agreement. Air Commodre Banks he was visibly unhappy. So begging leave the author left without waiting for the tea already ordered. So the episode with B. Or. 12 SR ended and also that of Russian RD – 9F.

FORMATION OF GTRE

GTRE felt relieved when the Russian team left. It was occupying office space GTRE needed. We could now get down to building up the Establishment, just outside the rear gate of the engine factory. The entry point to GTRE was opposite to the rear 'workers gate' of the HAL Engine factory. A small shed, about 50X80 ft, was built. It was christened as No.1 workshop. This new born baby became a 'structure' of immense pride, because this was GTRE's first building since inception .

A few common purpose HMT made machines were installed. Now the machine operators could work at any time not needing any body's permission. Next came up it's first office block with two floors. It consisted of just two big halls, one on each floor, and a room at the front end of the first floor. Not to be left out, the sheet metal, and foundry and forge workers erected another shed on the opposite rear side of the office block leaving in-between a 100 ft wide metalled space. We felt immensely proud when everyone was moving about with chest out, including the Director now having a p.a! We decided to have a celebration.

The food was cooked by the GTRE's members. The main best item (assessed till to-date) of the menu was 'BISI BELE BHAT'. This was cooked at the foundry kiln, by the most talented, uncompromising and ever smiling young lady. On an occasion of a turbine disc design, she detected, through application of 'finite element' method, a stress concentration point. Any amount of persuasion could not change her view. We had to change the design of the disc, which meant change of the rear portion of the designed engine.

The scientific culture of GTRE needs a mention here. Decisions on differing scientific views were never decided on the basis of seniority, and when necessary, the issue was resolved through experiments only. The Director took his decisions, mostly through consultations, when a *whole* project was to be submitted to Headquarters. He was the deciding authority on suspected deviation after manufacture on designed parts. Here the quality control (QC) officer was the final consultant. This approach had worked well.

The establishment grew up rapidly thereafter when the power to recruit S & T personnel at lower grades, just below the Grade 1 gazette officer, was left with the director, but only after proficiency tests.

SERVICE BEFORE SELF

The Kanpur culture of hard work and dedication apparently got infused, on all aspects. among the GTRE's newly recruited scientific staff. This helped the formation of GTRE. The above narration has found a place ahead of what happened later is to plant in the minds of the readers why GTRE is still a valued institution. It is culturally different then, and perhaps even now.

Additionally, the purpose is to convey that it was formed by 'migrated' rural youths, now urbanized because of employment. They remained basically rural folks, as can be seen from the fact that most rush back to their rural homes whenever an opportunity for a long period of holidays surfaced.

The most important fact to highlight is that this expansion was possible essentially through an assessment of intelligent mind, general knowledge, and common technical skill. No one was assessed on the basis of having any knowledge of aeronautics, or gas turbine engines. They were common intelligent young people with technology oriented mind. Such young people were not urbanites. Their origins were mostly from poor rural environment.

The focal issue is that if required a Gas Tuebine establishment like GTRE could be created even in rural areas too, if the rural youths are elevated, retaining the root, on agronomy through Fig.3 approach.

The concept of 'out sourcing' from urban industrial activities to rural areas is not an outrageous one. The only requirement is to begin with *developed* rural areas. This is possible, as indicated earlier, through creation of appropriate (not electricity alone) energy source for our vast populous agricultural societies.

The current concept for rural development, through agronomy and cottage industries, *needing no organized energy*, is fundamentally wrong. There is still time to wake up.

GETTING INVOLVED WITH HF 24 DEVELOPMENT

THE FIRST CALL FOR HELP BY HAL

When planning to establish it's own facilities, and trying to find a permanent location, GTRE's help was sought for by HAL. After the breakdown of negotiation with the USSR on RD-9F and the Russian team left, it was felt by MD, HAL as it would appear, that the solution was to convert the RD 9F engine's external feature to be the same as B.Or 12 SR. The design change required was to shift all the accessories from top to bottom. HAL's aircraft design team was aloof and kept it's distance from such a proposal. This might have been because HAL's own engine design team was busy to develop HJE 2500 engine for HJT 16.(Kiron) aircraft.

A view informally expressed view was, who were these novices to meddle with a task which the Russians themselves were not prepared to undertake. The proposed assignment was conveyed to Dr S Baghavantam, then SA. His reaction was typical of what to be expected from a self made man. He reacted expressing that the problem was their own creation, inspite of caution conveyed initially but ignored. There was no harm trying to help. It could be a good learning process. He left GTRE to decide.

It was a time when Chinese attacked us, or did we? Air Marshal A.M. Engineer was then CAS.(1960 – 64) The author's offer to go to Front was gladly accepted by the Director of Technical Services (DTS), the author had initially served under, but rejected by CAS. He wanted HF 24 set right. He was earlier Chairman of HAL.

GTRE'S INVOLVEMENT WITH HF 24

Under such a situation, GTRE was asked to take up the task at a small shed situated at Training Command, Hebbal, some 12 km away from HAL engine factory where GTRE was temporarily lodged. It had just one jeep. Private cars had to be used. We were told that the activity was to be done maintaining complete secrecy. This was followed.

The work was taken in hand with the permission of Scientific Officer. He expressed that the problem was created by HAL, not listening the initial advise given, but there is no harm to try and help.

No special sanction was given. HAL did not provide any support. GTRE officers used their transports to travel this long distance. The task was not simple. Each components were studied and reinstalled at the bottom, The task was completed working round the clock. The old Kanpur culture continued. The same dedicated team worked with the same work culture.

Top engine – Original RD 9F with accessories at top
Bottom engine – Modified by GTRE accessories sifted at bottom, shaped oil tank shifted at top. (Photographed and composed by Author)

Not knowing what was involved, GTRE agreed to take up the task for two reasons. First, it gave GTRE an opportunity to pay back to some extent our gratitude for the support it received from the HAL engine factory; and secondly, it was a moment of great pride to be invited to help the first indigenous supersonic fighter aircraft for the benefit of the Air Force. Besides, the situation involved a very senior Air Force officer. It was our duty to try and do our best of our ability to get this highly respected senior officer out of a likely embarrassing situation. He had acted in the national interest, with consent of .German designers of HF 24. After all it was not his fault which landed him in the unenviable situation. He had signed MOU without consulting Delhi. But his amazing quality of leadership was seen when not once he pointed his finger to anyone for this fiasco. GTRE took up the challenge.

The task was taken in hand on a condition that reheat pipe

would not be modified by GTRE to suit the back end of the aircraft. Our reservation on the rear end dimension was made known even before the initial selection was made. This has been mentioned earlier. Installation with no change in Reheat pipe diameter and the rear end configuration was accepted by HAL as a solvable problem.

We got the modified engine back to HAL to confirm that the fitment (without reheat pipe) was now feasible, and then installed this with the RD 9 F reheat pipe, at the HAL Engine factory test bed which was modified to adopt the new mounting points. It ran up to design potential with no problem. MD, HAL himself came to witness the trial, but no one from the HF 24 aircraft design team came. Even the Chief of the Air Staff (CAS) came from Delhi to witness the trial.

The Air force officers' mess at that time was a small residential house, in fact; - known as Kashmir House situated on Cunningham road. At an informal lunch arranged there, the CAS expressed his satisfaction on the work done. It was felt that our work should be presented to the Russians, who had earlier felt that the engine could not be modified to fit the aircraft. This was done in Moscow, explaining particularly the manner how we retained all the components functioning the same when placed at top. They expressed their approval; and in the evening party, informally wanted to know how the rear end problem of the aircraft was to be solved. The answer was simple. HAL had taken that part as their responsibility.

On return, GTRE was told that the Russian design Bureau had conveyed it's willingness to take up the modification work and negotiation for license manufacture was going on. Our task as a research establishment was over. It was not a simple task, although some felt that it was essentially just rotating the engine round by 180^0 to get the accessories at the bottom, and repositioning the oil tank at the top. (This view implied that the engine could fly in an inverted condition for any length of time!). Another view was that the Russian refusal to do what GTRE did was more due to the WWII legacy and not due to any serious technical problem. However, this kind of remark did not evoke any excitement at GTRE.

When some one remarked as above, our simple answer was: 'please go ahead and try and confirm your wisdom. There were five more Russian engines. We shall supply the fuel tanks.' Surprisingly, the same kind of view was expressed when we built our first demonstrator engine in Kanpur, comparing with De Haviland Goblin II engine. Photographs of these are placed in the earlier part of the book. On both occasions, these views had reached the ears of very senior people, obviously through some senior non-performing 'experts'. There were many. However, we got back to where we left from before taking up this challenging task on RD 9F.

GTRE had done it's job, and no further association was necessary. It was now between HAL and USSR.

An agreement for further development and license manufacture was apparently signed, when GTRE's presence was not considered a necessity, even though the agreement phase had reached because of it's hard work. The agreement did not last. Dr. Tank found a new deficiency. The engine was certified only up to Mach 1.4. He wanted a Mach 2+ engine. This aspect was discussed initially in Moscow. It was a low pressure ratio engine, and had steel compressor blades. The possible need to use Titanium blade was discussed, but no decision was taken then, suggesting that if such a need gives rise to, Titanium blades could be introduced. It was far too early to claim for an aircraft flying at Mach 2+.which was yet to taxi out to runway for take off with any powered engine. It was still a wooden replica glider.

A record number of 78 gliding trials was done to cheek the low speed handling characteristics. While designing HF 24, was B.Or 12 SR certified for Mach 2+ performance, meeting the ASR? Why this sudden demand? At that stage, USSR was making use of titanium material for various applications. When finally agreeing to sign the agreement, the Dr. Tank could have stipulated this requirement, or could have made this as a requirement for development during the license agreement. Why cancel this, making such an issue after signing? Why this after thought? USSR was flying Mig 21 at Mach 2+ since 1956, when HF 24 was not even conceived. Was it because the basic solution came through GTRE – the novices ? What came in the way to consult GTRE before cancellation? GTRE could have made the compressor with titanium material.

HP Compressor made of Titanium material

GTRE built HP Compressor, made of Titanium material for GTX engine needing no foreign help. A collaborative programme for the development of the engine might have been considered. Perhaps the 'non issue' back end problem would have surfaced as well, in addition to needing titanium material blades.

With that kind of back end, as shown earlier, to expect Mach 2+ performance would be far fetched, to say the least, and highly irresponsible. It is for the reader of this book to contemplate the real reason of this cancellation in the manner it was done. What was the cause? The absurd back end, or the steel compressor blade?.

A decision was then taken to use two B.Or. 703 engines, and the aircraft was designated as HF 24 MK 1. A reheated version of this engine was considered for improved performance of the aircraft. The same MD, who purchased the RD 9F, had suggested this development strategy. He was still searching for alternate solution.

HF 24 MK1R

GTRE's help was again called for by HAL. At no stage, GTRE suggested a solution. As before with a precondition that the fitment of the larger diameter reheat nozzle would not be it's responsibility, the reheat project was taken in hand.

B.Or 703 with 1700^0 K Reheat

Again, very hard work was involved. The support from the engine factory was total, although none asked what was cooking. There were several aspects which needed ingenuity, but not once any component was imported. The work done on leak proof nozzle operating jacks, the long ceramic rod with a central hole required to convey high intensity spark to the core of flame holder and automatic shut down with inadvertent reheat operation with nozzle still for dry operation, etc were appreciated by several, except the HF 24 design office.

Dr. Tank could not care less, even when he was no where near meeting the initial ASR he was invited for. He had the support of a few qualified aeronautical engineers of Indian origin. For them Dr. Tank was an infallible hero, even when GTRE had the full support of all Scientific Adviser of DRDO all through except for the last one with his indecisive mind to continue support or not. He did not even express, orally or in writing, the customary words at the retirement time. The CCR&D spoke a few words on his behalf during a meeting at Agra, meant for discussion some other issue. The author made his farewell speech short, politely expressing 'Thank You'.

The establishment grew up rapidly thereafter when the power to recruit S & T personnel at lower grades, just below the Grade 1 gazetted officer, was left with the director, but only after proficiency tests.

Test Bed operation of B.Or. 703 reheated engine

Seen below is the modified rear end of the aircraft with Reheated 703 engine installed. It was an aeronautical engineering marvel (or, nightmare?), worth viewing by all aircraft design engineers, to learn about the status then, on aeronautical sciences, particularly that of the German Design team.

Mentioned earlier, the author was warned at a high level meeting that he should not harp on this *non-issue*. The degradation of aircraft speed, the author was told, was due to reheat installation, and not due to the mutilation of the rear end. This view was supported by some aeronautical engineers with masters degree's. Most pathetic incident was some supported this mutilation, comparing with HF 24 Mk1's good aerodynamics.

Photographed by author: Shows Dr. Tank's brilliance on fitment of a reheated engine, claiming no drag increase supported by engine technologists. (Can be seen at Visveshswariah Industrial museum, Kasturba Road, Bangalore).

This can be compared with the rear end of MK1. This rear end mutilated version of MK 1R had flown for four years, with no attempt to rectify this. The picture below is the one to suit B.Or12SR. In a publication, titled "Diamonds in the sky", first published in 2001 by The Society for Aerospace studies, page 57 states *'The HF 24 was planned so as to offer scope for the introduction of some five successive generations of power plants'.* The author believes that it could not adopt even one of the then generation of engines, (1955-60) till such time the tail plane was positioned at the top, or on the side. Till that was done it would be, at best, no more than a low supersonic aircraft.

Is there any current supersonic fighter aircraft when the tail plane was fitted at the bottom of the rear fuselage?

Tail end of HF 24 mk1 designed to adopt B.Or 12 SR (reheat temperature – 1400^0 k)

UPSIDE DOWN to indicate the exact location and fitment of the tail plane. It was designed to be place *below* the reheat pipe of B.Or. 12 SR

The development of B.Or 12 SR was, however, not abandoned by Bristol Siddley. In house development continued. Earlier, during 1957, the author was deputed to Bristol Siddley when the Reheat was being developed by Mike Williams. (1956 – 1957). He was a friend and a colleague at the Canfield Institute of Technology when our experimental work at the Institute was similar. This deputation had nothing to do with the HF 24's predicament. This was not even known.

The author came to know Dr. Stanley Hooker at that time. At a much later date, when he came to know about our effort on developing reheat system on B.Or 703 engine, advised by Dr. Hooker, Mike visited GTRE, He came ostensibly to check on license production of Orpheus 701/703 engine at HAL engine factory. He was instrumental to advise GTRE to take the first and important step on flight testing of 1400^{0}K reheat system, to begin with. Mike William became Director of Engineering, of Rolls Royce, awarded OBE'.(Order of British Empire).

A close tie with several BSEL's senior engineers developed at that stage. This engine company was still not a part of Rolls Royce. The merger took place later. A decision to merger all engine companies to be one Engine Company under the leadership of Rolls Royce was taken much later. The first flight test with 1400^0 K reheat was done by Flight Lieutenant I. M. Chopra, a competent test pilot, who became the Chairman of HAL (1988-91).

Flight Lieutenant I. M. Chopra

EGYPTIAN COLLABORATION

He also flew at a later date A300, the Egyptian version of HF 24 aircraft for about 145 hrs. with the German designed engine, E300, .fitted on one side in a modified HF 24 aircraft, when the other side had basic B.Or 703 engine. The author was not shown anything when sent by government on two different occasions to check the progress, informed that the engine not ready, although told in Delhi that E300 was flying. Was taken round a machine shop. The author's interest was to see the rear end of the fuselage. This they were not willing to show. However, a picture of the aircraft is available in a book. This shown below;

Egyptian aircraft with E300 engine on the left side and B.Or 703 on the right side. As seen, the aircraft was not what one had expected to see. It was not similar to HF 24, in any way. It was a new aircraft, with delta wing, and no controversial tail plane at the bottom. Only one final nozzle for a twin engine aircraft was a novelty.

The author lost interest. A small car, with an engine at the back, with a designated name, 'Ramsesse', was allotted to the author. The driver sat mostly by the side of the author who loved driving the car. The driver took me to a 'dhaba' looking restaurant, informing me that roasted pigeon, stuffed with buttered perfumed rice was supplied to President Nassar from there. In the evening, before going to formal dinner at the roof of a famed hotel located on the bank of river Nile, I left two well packed, roasted pigeon and a bottle of very good 'red wine', - Omar Kyam - every night, At the formal dinner. the served 'white wine' from Mossel (Ron) valley of Germany, dry and chilled, was no doubt super, but NASSAR's food attracted the author more. The 'white, dry' followed by medium 'red' at room temperature jelled perfectly in my room on return and made me forget about the not so polite Germans, residing in a luxury flat complex owned by the king Farook's sister. The only jarring feature was cracklings, (not very frequently though), on 'Mozart' symphony played through Radio. With free time in hand, gone around Cairo city, the famed Museum where one could see the solid gold mask of Tutankhamen, mummies particularly very well kept of Ramesses II. and the necklace of stone beads. All three are symbols of Egyptian heritage. It is a 'must see' place. On expiry of specified period, returned with no information on Egyptian HF 24 joint venture, but much richer with knowledge on Egyptian civilization.

AN ASSESSMENT OF DRAG

Even when the grossly mutilated tail end of MK 1R, shown earlier, did not convince Dr. Tank and his supportive Indian contingent, a quantified assessment was attempted. The desire was to establish that the problem on increased drag was essentially due to aerodynamic mutilation having the tail plane at the bottom. Static pressure survey at the tail end was decided on, fixing longitudinally a special tape of about two meters length. During the flight, so strong was the suction, (suggesting pulling behind) that the tape got ripped off. The competent technologist who was conducting the test came, saw, and left with no comment. A suggestion for a second confirmatory trial received no response. It was felt that some action would now be taken. The author had been suggesting that in a reheated aircraft the tail plane should preferably be at the top, or may even be on the side, but not at the bottom. Whenever this issue was brought afore, it was confronted with the good aerodynamics of MK 1. A big wall was built to justify the mutilation..

While it was not known what action was being taken, after the conclusive evidence on the cause for the increased drag, a visit was made to Dr. Tank's office to discuss. To present GTRE's view, enlarged pictures of Jaguar and MiG 21 aircraft, as under, were taken to illustrate what perhaps need be done on tail plane positioning. The sole desire was to establish a rapport with the aircraft team. Survival of HF 24 was in the nation's interest, more so when it was the first fighter being developed in the country. A view was conveyed that to achieve what suggested (to shift the tail plane on top), the aircraft itself would need to be redesigned!

The Egypt aircraft could attain a height of about 26,000 ft, and no more. A competent Indian Technical team were assigned to this project. The author did not meet any. Their opinion remained 'secret'. The reason offered was that the aircraft could carry limited amount of fuel. Jaguar had also problem on operating at greater height. The reason offered was that Jaguar, a DPSA (Deep Penetration Strike Aircraft) was not meant to fly at height. It did not participate in any conflict with Pakistan. Whose cause was being served at our cost? Dr. Tank now wanted a smaller engine from his friend!.

HF24 MK!R had routinely flown for four years climbing at 0.9 Mach to 30,000 -36,000 ft., reaching this height in about 4 mts +, slightly greater than Gnat's. If the speed was reduced, reheat flame could not be sustained. Several requests to keep climbing at 0.9 Mach was not accepted by the testing unit at Kanpur. Reason not conveyed. This deficiency on not sustaining the reheat at 0.8 Mach at that altitude was being looked into. The design goal was to attain a service ceiling of 50,000 ft.

EXTRA DRY NOZZLE POSITION

When the drag rise due to aerodynamic mutilation could not move the Himalayan ego of Dr. Tank, claiming that it did not create any increase of drag, GTRE took a corrective step. It developed an 'extra dry' nozzle position to increase the dry thrust. It was observed that at low altitude the Jet Pipe temperature was decreasing. The mathematical justification was seen An 'extra dry' nozzle position (slightly reducing the exit diameter of the nozzle), restored the Jet pipe temperature to the design value, at high higher end of subsonic speed and compensated the increased drag. HAL now blamed GTRE for it's initial wrong assessment on increased drag due to rear end mutilation.

In the meantime, Dr. Tank wrote to our Defence Minister requesting him to withdraw the reheat project. Dr. Bhagavantam was then our SA (Scientific Advisor). He came, heard our verdict and returned. We were told to carry on.

Jaguar Aircraft: Tail Plane on top

A fact needs highlighting at this stage. The desire to have an indigenous fighter aircraft was very strong within the senior orbit of our Air Force, except a small group deputed to HAL. None ever came to GTRE .to discuss. At a much later date, one indicated the reason. It was not pleasant.

MiG 21 with tail plane on the sise at tail end

Earlier in a diagrammatic illustration, the tail plane position, similar to MiG 21, was indicated for Mirage F1. It would be of great scientific interest if any could locate a supersonic fighter with tail plane fixed at the bottom, Also, if any Mach 2+ fighter plane had/ has flown with 1400^0 K reheat system, needing such small reheat pipe. As stated before, HF 24 was apparently designed for the *"introduction of some *five successive generations of power plants."* In fact, it was designed for B.Or 12 SR only, and no other fighter aircraft which flew at Mach 2 + had such a low reheat temperature. The selectors and admirers of Dr. Tank may find one. If possible, why not adopted in any operational Supersonic Mach 2+ fighter aircraft? The doubt is even if B.Or 12 SR was available, would it have achieved our ASR target? The performance Brochures of B.Or 12 was not available to make an assessment.

*Refer Diamonds in the Sky published by HAL, page 57

Dr. HOOKER'S VECTOR THRUST ENGINE

Dr. Hooker and Frank Whittle

During the period when the author was on deputation to Bristol Siddley (1957), Dr. Hooker was working on vectored thrust engine. His door was always open. His innovative thoughts were experimented with simple commonly available objects. For example, he used a bicycle chain to operate the rotating vanes to change the direction of thrust. (Vectoring the thrust). As a Mathematician, he coined the appropriate title. One of his colleague, once remarkéd that the first aircraft to crash with landing wheels pointing upwards, will be with the anti 'g' vectored thrust engine. When this remark was brought to his notice, not only he laughed, he wanted to meet the person with good sense of humour. Our situation is different. Any innovative thought is frowned at, unless the origin is from a developed country. The knowledgeable 'crabs' at the bottom will tear apart, with media help, any with innovative mind. Gossips are the truths; media knows that we love gossips, and they sell better.

One may summarize that modern aviation owe to marriage of innovative minds of the two geniuses shown above.

Both believed in experimental science, making a beginning with inexpensive approaches. When Whittle could not find any to make free vortex 'twisted blade' with metal, he did his experiment with wooden blades, chiseled to his requirement.

Dr. Hooker was a brilliant Mathematician, not an engineer. Both proved that thinking *mathematically*, and proving the concept *experimentally* were the only ways to succeed. Metaphysics is a mental hobby, fit for apparently intellectual discourse of little social value. Our S & T community's bins had been and are over filled with ego-centric Metaphysical minds of senior scientists, (not all) who control S & T .activities of the country, with superfluous knowledge.

HIGH PRIESTS ON AERONAUTICS

Vedic religion was ruined because of germination of Brahmanic religion. A similar clan had germinated, in between, in the society of aeronautics. They held high official positions, had a leader, and suppressed the working Aeronautical engineers. They functioned almost identically as Brahmanas with a noble face and little basic knowledge, harming the nation technologically and financially for many years to come.

Some speculate that Dr. Tank having succeeded to develop a good subsonic aircraft, wanted to retain the same airframe to get a Mach 2 performance by merely changing the engines. After all, Mirage F1 and HF 24 were perhaps from the same still unknown stable and if French F1 could attain Mach 2 performance, why HF 24 should not, with better aerodynamics as was apparent from MK 1's performance. This logic killed HF 24 project.

Three actions were needed to make HF24 a world class aircraft. First, accept and develop RD 9F; secondly, shift the tail plane to top in a manner done for Jaguar; and finally install canards on the contour of air intakes, as done in Mirage F1. Dr. Tank had opposed to first two. The fitment of Canard was opposed by one of the four high priests. He had felt that the

Canard should be placed ahead, and if so done, it would obstruct the look down vision of the pilot. He might have been influenced by the Swedish, JAS 39A. Apparently the pilots of Swedish, JAS 39A did not require to look down!.

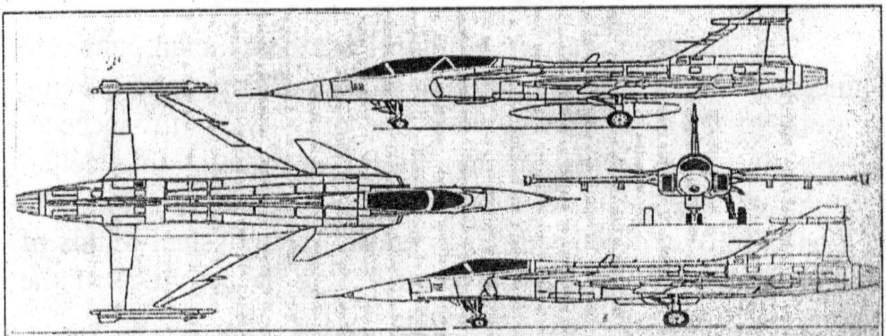

JAS 39A Gripen multirole combat aircraft for the Swedish Air Force, with additional side view (top) of two-seat JAS 39B *(Jane's/Dennis Punnett)*

Sweden Jas 33a Gripen

The concept of Canard had originated in Sweden, but it was not necessary that the original concept should be the only and final answer. Mirage F1 proved that as seen below:

Mirage F1 w ith canard

No engine was acceptable for HF 24.aircraft, unless one could produce an engine similar to B.Or. 12 with a low reheat temperature, needing a small diameter pipe. It was designed exclusively for B.Or 12 SR. The initial reported claim was that the airframe design was such that it could accept several other engines. (Reported early *Diamonds in the sky* published in collaboration with HAL in 2001)

This claim could not be justified with determined reluctance to modify the back end. But such reluctance did not surface for E300 engine, designed in Egypt by Dr, Ferdinand Brandner, a friend of Dr. Tank. Did E300 engine not require a redesigned rear fuselage? Was this not made? But did it work? If the earlier mentioned three steps were accepted, HF 24 would have been a world class aircraft. These three activities were well within the realm of possibility, but not accepted. As regards the solution for propulsion, it is amply clear that he would not have a Russian engine, modified by GTRE, if required.

The reason offered was Air Force now needed a DPSA (Deep Penetration Strike Aircraft). The decision was not related to the most unfortunate fetal accident of the famed test pilot in the first pre-production HF 24 MK1R. This aspect has been dealt with at the later part.

DEVELOPMENT OF GTRE

GTRE was not involved when the negotiations going on around RD 9F. We could now get down to building up the Establishment, just outside the rear gate of the engine factory. The entry point to GTRE, at that time, was opposite to the rear 'workers gate' of the HAL Engine factory. A small shed, about 50X80 ft, was built. It was christened as No.1 workshop. This new born baby became a 'structure' of immense pride, because this was GTRE's first building. A few common purpose HMT make machine tools were installed.

Now the machine operators could work at any time not needing any body's permission. Next came up it's first office block with two floors. It consisted of just two big halls, one on each floor, and a room at the front end of the first floor. Not to be left out, for the sheet metal, foundry and forge workers erected another shed on the opposite side of the office block leaving in-between a 100 ft wide metalled space. The GTRE team felt immensely proud when everyone was moving about with chest out, including the director now having a p.a! We decided to have a contributory celebration. The food was cooked by the GTRE's members, supervised by one of our most talented lady Scientist. The author is yet to test so well cooked "Bisi Bele Bhat".

The scientific culture of GTRE needs a mention here. Decisions on differing scientific views were never decided on the basis of seniority, and when necessary, the issue was resolved through experiments only. The director took his decisions, mostly through consultations, when a *whole* project was to be submitted to head quarters. He was the deciding authority on suspected deviation after manufacture of any designed part. Here the Quality Control (QC) officer was his final consultant (or, dictator!). This approach had worked well.

The most gratifying observation was, how quickly these young matriculates, with some vocational training, sent from 'employment exchange' acquired the competence to become so very useful technicians. The credit goes to floor shop experienced personnel, mostly those from Kanpur, training patiently these new entrants. The dream of converting the rural society with two faces - agronomy as one, and value added agro products and small industrial units the other, became increasingly real possibility in the future.

A training system was evolved. After induction, the new entrants were allowed to work as trainees with experienced ones who were often both craftsmen and academically proficient enough on the work in hand. New entrants were not set aside. They were made to work and learn too to move ahead, and at times given opportunities to work on their own. The work culture was strict, when mistakes were eliminated through repeated trials. Things have improved but the culture of working and learning has been retained. A picture below depicts this. A librarian is not only to issue books but also to teach.

The librarian teaching the fresh entrant on aeronautics

1962-1966 : The growth in five years

(Note: You cannot beat a Sardar! When he could not find a place, he rushed to the near by workshop, got a stool and stood on that at right hand extreme, 2nd row. After all, he had come properly dressed, how could you leave him out!)

The most notable fact was none other than those sitting in the second row and some airmen had any exposure to gas turbines, or aeronautics. Rest were basically rustic people, and proved that given opportunity they could 'concur the world'.

They were a dedicated lot.

The establishment grew up rapidly thereafter when the power to recruit S & T personnel at lower grades, just below the Grade 1 gazette officer, was left with the director, but only after proficiency tests. This rapid growth is shown in photograph above.

TEST FACILITIES

One among our impatient scientists, had specialized on sciences on combustion. He created the first test facility with a diesel engine operating a small compressor to try out some experiments on combustion processes. This was located by the side of the new first building, seen in the back ground.

Stage 1 First test facility (Photograph by the author)

The end room on the first floor, with specially shaped two windows was the director's office. That humble office received many dignitaries, from civil and defence establishments. Some just came without any prior appointment, and held discussions about gas turbine engine's usage in fields other than aviation. Electric Power generation was the most favourite subject. The government had set up a study team and meetings were held. Several ministries were represented. On one occasion, JRD Tata had breakfast with us, before proceeding to the HAL Board meeting.

Earlier, pre-GTRC days, the author, then flight lieutenant, had served as his SO (Staff Officer) at Kanpur, when he came and participated as (Honorary) air commodore, at a special 'Dining-in-night' wearing the formal dress for the occasion. Our commanding officer was also holding the same rank and wearing the same formal dress. Standing side by side, it was difficult to judge who looked more impressive. Both tall, erect, fit with no undue bulges, and in the formal dress, with wing pinned on the dress both looked majestic air officers. It is an occasion to remember. He flew Spit 9, solo. His humility was so impressive that he touched every one's heart.

STAGE 2 TEST FACILITIES

The Kanpur experience of building workable systems from 'scrap' helped. The Allied forces left behind a salvage yard with no inventory, and it was the BRD's equipment depot. Our organised test facility was built coupling a RR Nene engine with a time expired but cocooned Avon Mk1 gas turbine engine, retrieved from the scrap yard. The combustion chambers of the Nene engine were removed and replaced by a suitably made plenum chamber which received partially the exhaust of the Avon MK1 engine. The turbine of the Nene engine already coupled with this engine's compressor, provided for large (nearly 20 lb/sec) air supply, but at low (2 atmospheric) pressure. The excess exhaust hot air of the Avon engine was taken out through another pipe.

LOW PRESSURE AIR SUPPLY FACILITY

The Nene engine compressor's exit pressure was limited because of the now reduced swallowing capacity of the. turbine, receiving low pressure exhaust of the Avon engine. With this unavoidable limitation, the system served several activities.

The RR A1MAK1 coupled with nene engine for low pressure air supply (Photographed by author)

Next to this facility, a large shed was erected. Compressed air from the Nene engine compressor was taken to this shade and connected to a 18 inch (46.0 mm) gallery pipe. Six tapings could provide air supply to conduct several R & D activities /experiments. The turbo-charger for the Arjun Tank project, at CVRDE, DRDO, Avadi, was developed at one point. This project received recognition when the leader of this project received 'Rajiv Gandhi best scientist's' award. The recommendation was made by the user. He could satisfy the user's need.

It is worth recalling that this Scientist was selected during his very first meeting, when he came to meet the author after completing his studies in Bristol, UK. He was requested to join the next day. In those days, a Director of a DRDO establishment could employ temporarily any qualified scientist for a year, and to continue, he had to be selected by the UPSC, against an advertised post, as an individual. He, with his PhD from the University of Bath, UK, proved his worth, and made this valuable contribution, working with a small team he had built up.

Other research activities, e.g., optimization of the flame holder of an afterburner; combustion experiments to determine the required temperature profile to have cooler temperature at the turbine blade root end, and it's efficiency; trials with different kinds fuel other than the aviation fuel; the air and oil seals development; and several others were carried out. These activities lead to the creation of groups for various elements of a gas turbine engine and experimental facilities representing real time situations. Again, the combined exhaust of two time expired Avon engines, driving the turbine to power the full scale test compressors were used in the upgraded test facilities. A different test cell was created for study of reheat combustion.

Two other important labs came up. One to test the fatigue properties of blades. and the other for stress analysis of discs. All combined, the establishment with design and performance evolution (Aircraft and Engine) sections, etc., generated a comprehensive S & T environment, supported by workshops for all kinds of activities.

These saved a large amount of money. The rapid progressed made to set up the test facilities created some flatter in certain minds. The earlier facility was enhanced now adding one more turbine to generate much greater power needed to test 'real time' compressor.

A parallel proposal under consideration by HAL. Learnt that the scheme was to use a large sized electric motor (800 hp) with clutch systems at either ends, to provide alternatively power to air compressors, or test compressors. The use of 'time expired' gas turbines was viewed with disdain. Criticizing GTRE became a hobby house, to a certain section of non performing aeronautical engineers. The director of GTRE became unpopular to the foreign trade agents, but equally liked by several Scientific personnel, except one of the 'high priests' who felt that these are mere acts of iron 'mongers'! And not of any scientific value.

While feeling concerned about the approach made through such 'time expired' gas turbines, three important aspects were not appreciated by the critics. First, there was an urgent need of air supply and power for research activities. Secondly, 'time expired' aero gas turbines are not scraps for ground use. In an aircraft, the engines are subjected to severe tortures. The rapid (slam) accelerations and decelerations as needed in a fighter aircraft create thermal as well as mechanical fatigues. Enough margins had to be left in the engine components for safe use as aero engines. When used for ground installations, these engines would be running at steady rpm's, and could be used for a long period. Lastly but not the least, the facility would be available at any time of day and night without depending on electricity supply.

But the doubts persisted in several minds, and reached the ears of senior officials. The problem appeared when we were not spending much money yet claiming much progress. The fear was, were we doing anything useful? These engines were acquired free of cost. Our friend Gyan Singh of Kanpur (Vampire) days, was now at headquarters. He was a great help to get these engines. Any alternate approaches would have been very expensive. To get the financial sanction, it would have been difficult and a time consuming process. Besides, there was a parallel proposal from HAL as well.

The issue came to such a pass that the scientific advisor to the defence minister, then Dr. Bhagavantam, got such a low cost approach assessed by a well known scientist, Dr. GBR Fielden,- a Fellow of the Royal society (FRS). He was deputed by the scientific advisor to the British government, Dr. PMS Blackett, (Nobel prize winner in 1948). Dr. Fielden was a team member of Frank Whittle, and designed Industrial gas turbines. Three of his designed engines are still used in Assam, using Natural Gas. In 1999, he delivered Frank Whittle memorial lecture, at the Royal Aeronautical Society, London, and spoke at our Aeronautical society as well. Unfortunately, he has expired recently, in 2007. He became the President of British Standards Institution, which functions directly under the Crown, and not the government, as is the case in our country. He decided in favour of our approach to test facilities, with no reservation. He expressed his appreciation, in fact. When enquired to learn about Dr Fielden's assessment, all that Dr Bagavantham, in his characteristic manner, conveyed was that it was alright. We could continue with our approach. GTRE became HAL's biggest enemy when their expensive foreign purchase proposal for 800 HP (not certain) electric motor with clutches at either end did not gain favour..

Dr. GBR Fielden, FRS delivering Whittle memory lecture at Aeronautical society of India

There after he took great interest in GTRE's activities. He desired to be formally recognized as 'consultant' to GTRE. However, his preoccupations did not move to the office of the Crown. He was to make efforts make efforts to change the British system to adopt metric against much opposition. It was a monumental task.

Dr. Bhagavantham was a self made Scientist, an associate of Nobel Prize winner(1930) Sir C.V. Raman, FRS. Dr. Bhagavantam was perhaps the only scientist allowed to appear for his Masters degree examination in Calcutta University, while working as Assistant to C. V. Raman at Science college, Calcutta. A view exists that the world came to know on 'Raman effect' through his book on the subject. His brilliance was felt when he spoke, concluding precisely at the last minute of the allotted time, rarely looking at his watch. The author had the opportunity to work under three other super minds, who believed in science more than bureaucratic ladder. Some climbed down the ladder to serve science. Other than Professor Kothery, the eminent physicist, the other three were Dr. Bhagavantam, Dr. B.D. Nag Chaudhuri, and Professor MGK Menon, FRS. 1956 to 1980 were the golden formative period of DRDO.

At this stage we were disappointed to learn that the negotiation with USSR for RD-9F engine development was called off in 1964. No formal reason was conveyed to GTRE. Based on past experience, one may guess that the need for tail end rectification could have been an issue. Whatever might have been the reason, this was the first *mistake* in our venture to be at per with the world community having a Supersonic fighter aircraft. Two engines combined provided more propulsive force than SNECMA Attar 9 engine used in Mirage F1.

This engine could have been developed with Russian help, if needed. During the very first negotiation stage, the use of steel blades (suited for flight up to Mach 1.4) for a Mach 2 aircraft was viewed as an issue to consider; and this was highlighted on the second occasion too. The compressor needed blades made with Titanium material to withstand higher temperature. The country was still in a 'talking' stage on this material, and yet to grasp the forming technologies of this material of special characteristic.

Our German designers wanted a fully cooked food from USSR. They had no faith on Indian technologists for the up gradation, with Russian help if needed, even though USSR was perhaps leading on Titanium use at that time. GTRE was gearing up to handle Titanium, and mastered this soon. Rolls Royce wanted Rs.2.0 crores to transfer the technology. GTRE developed this needing no collaboration. It bought an EBM (Electronic Beam welding) machine,, the first in the country. It served ISRO's need towards fabrication of pressure transducers.

When approached RR for confirmation the typical British generous characteristics surfaced. They did not hold back the last bit of information. This they gave us free. Titanium was highly fatigue prone. Even a scratch would develop a crack, and eventual failure. The blades needed lapping with a special compound. The two spool compressor of GTX- 37 -14U engine was made of titanium materials of different specifications., IMI 315, 500, 685, to withstand temperatures varying from 450 to 680^{0}C, the outlet temperatures of LP and HP compressors at maximum ratings. Steel blades could operate up to a maximum of 450^{0}C.

THIRD INVITATION BY HAL

After the failure of negotiation on RD-9F, GTRE was again invited by the same MD, HAL to develop a reheat system for the 703 engine. GTRE agreed, but the reheat pipe installation responsibility rested with HAL, as before, when RD-9F was being considered. GTRE optimized that the reheat temperature for that size of the reheat pipe as 1700^{0}K. It was lucky to have some superb technicians.

The reheat system needed not only scientists with good knowledge on fluid flow, but also very competent sheet metal workers, and innovative designers. For example, the leak proof hydraulic jacks, controlling the exit (jet) nozzle system were so designed that even if the rubber seals failed it would not leak and cause fire. This was used in some prototypes of Kavery engine. Imported jacks are used in later versions, when the reheat system is fully variable, unlike 703 reheat which was an 'ON' or 'OFF' system. The ingenuity of design was appreciated by many.

Similarly, a long ceramic rod with a central hole was needed to covey electrical energy to the spark plug at the center of the reheat flame holder. Approaches were made, to manufacturers of ceramic parts, with little success. Innovative minds of some in GTRE provided the solution. Small ceramic rods with a central hole as used in spark plugs of automobile engines, were dressed, joined, to make the long rod.

The flight trial of HF 24 commenced with 1400^{0}K reheat system. Thereafter, almost all flight trials for *four* years, (1966 –

1970) with 1700^0K reheat system was carried out on one prototype aircraft,(No.BD-884,/ 005) by GP. Capt. SURANJAN DAS, the most famed chief test pilot. The author used to be present at the flying control for every test flight of the Reheated aircraft.

It was after that phase, a decision was taken to make two pre-production reheated aircrafts. Only one was made and this was the one in which Gp. Capt. Das met the fetal accident on 10. 01. 1970 on its 10th flight of the first pre-production model.

During this phase of four years of trial using only one aircraft, (BD886/005), before the fatal accident, the establishment got involved with:

1. Type certification tests of B. Or.703 with reheat;
2. Research activities on various elements:
3. Design and development of 2000^0K reheat system developing 3000 kg (29.33 kN) and 2100 kg(20.62 kN) reheat and dry thrust respectfully, replacing the first stage of the compressor with a transonic stage. The desire was to make HF 24 Supersonic with 46 % increased thrust compared to the basic 703 The project was designated as TS 16 R. This should have been possible when the transonic 1st stage and 200K reheat were separately showing promise.

REACTION OF GERMAN DESIGNER ON REHEAT DEVELOPMENT.

At no stage GTRE had expressed any descending opinion on any effort to find an alternate solution to HF 24 development. On the contrary, it made every effort to find a solution at the invitation of HAL management. The importance of this nationally prestigious project was never under estimated. GTRE never volunteered; it acted only when invited. But more it succeeded more unhappiness was generated at HAL. Reason not known.

The German design team took little interest, except during the initial trial phase with 1400^0K Reheat system. On one occasion, the pilot relayed about reheat flame out, and he had reverted back to 'dry' mode. The German team member felt that the flame holder for the reheat system must have got detached, to cause this. . He rushed to the aircraft after it landed and parked. Peering at the back end, he started to retreat with an unhappy face. The flame holder was still attached much to his disappointment.

HAL'S ASSESSMENT ON INCREASED DRAG

After every flight, the (dry) performance was compared with Mk 1. There was about 5-6% deterioration in the level speed with maximum dry power at low altitude. HAL attributed this due to fitment of flame holder of the reheat system, and the resultant pressure loss. GTRE accepted that 2-3 % loss would occur but not 5-6% as observed. This became a major issue when GTRE felt, as was done earlier, that the main culprit was the unusual location of the tail plane at the bottom of rear fuselage.

Unhappiness generated naturally, between HAL and GTRE. The unhappiness was expressed in the most unusual subjective manners. They were so appalling and unethical, that it would be best not to highlight them. All that can be expressed that the author did not deserve these, while working hard, invited to solve *their* own created problems. First, they made a wrong assessment on the fitment of USSR made RD 9F engine at the highest quarter; then after rectification by GTRE; entered into an agreement to accept the engine, from USSR; and quickly cancelled it on a plea of inadequacy of Mach no. clearance: desired GTRE to develop the Reheat system: and finally made a mess on aerodynamic needs for fitment, and then blaming GTRE for all their mistakes! GTRE would be prepared to stand by these remarks, in a *Judicial* enquiry with a penalty clause for the technological and financial harm done to the nation.

Comparing with the tail end of Mk 1, presented below, it would be interesting to learn why no view was taken by our learned high priests. If not a decision, a recommendation could have been made to resolve the mutilated tail end. Or, did they also agree with HAL on no drag rise. However, to save the project, an 'extra dry' nozzle position was introduced by GTRE to enhance the dry thrust, to match with the flight speed of Mk 1. HAL was happy with the flight speed enhancement to the same level of HF24 Mk 1, but not forgetting to mention that "we had always been saying that there was nothing wrong in the aircraft design to cause additional drag." This conclusion defies the basic aerodynamic area rule. The analysis was known to HAL, but no action was taken. Then the abortive effort on experiment to measure static pressure at the tail end, and refusal to discuss the universal practice on Reheated engine installation and several subjective approaches can be a story of our present degraded aeronautical S & T society.

Persuasive effort with HAL to modify the tail end of Mk1R. to reduce the drag was a far cry in wilderness. HAL and all admirers of Dr. Tank, continued believing that the loss of flight speed compared to Mk 1 in *dry* mode was happening because of the thrust loss due to the installation of the reheat system. There was nothing wrong with the aircraft. Dr. Tank had addressed a letter to DM requesting withdrawal of the Reheat project, quoting the German experience on thrust loss of a ram jet at high ambient. The two Photographs presented above prove what had gone wrong. These differences between Mk 1 and Mk 1R can be seen at HAL museum for Mk 1 and, as stated earlier, at Vishveshwaraya Industrial museum, St. Mark's Road, (now Kasturba Road), Bangalore, for Mk 1R.

A pertinent remark may not be out of place. If only these non-performing high priests remained within the true orbit of aeronautical science, the country would be different to-day. It was a project of national importance. When they were ever so eager to express their wise opinions on engine projects, what prevented them to express their opinion on this occasion when the very basics of the aerodynamic (area rule) were trifled with.

Dr. Tank and HAL were treated as infallible. They had

support of a large contingent of senior and well versed Air Fore Officers at HAL. But they did not wish to get involved. Their indifference conveyed much about their views. None ever visited GTRE for discussion on the conflicting issue.

IMPROVED HF 24

While the controversy on the aerodynamics was going on, thoughts on improving the aerodynamics of the aircraft was also considered. New concepts were emerging. Canard, wing body interference, sawed and double delta wings etc. were being actively worked on. world over. Pakistan's MiG 21 had a double delta wing. The author proposed fitment of 'Canard' (small wings), after a visit to Sweden* to learn about this aerodynamic innovation. But the proposal of having this incorporated was rejected by one of the four high priests on a plea that such a fitment would obstruct 'look down' vision. HF 24 was *ideally* suited for incorporating the Canard, having the main fuselage sitting on the wing, and it could have been fitted at the mid section slightly behind the intake, as was done in Mirage F1.

PROPOSAL FOR FITMENT OF CANARD, *REJECTED*

One of the four high priests was an eminent scientist. He showed little interest. First, no interest on tail end modification, and now no interest on canard fitment, the development of the 2000^0K reheat with a transonic first stage became the end of HF 24 saga. The problem on 'look down vision' seems to be a non-issue in several contemporary aircraft, having canard wings Examples of aircraft with Canard are presented below.

**Sweden was the pioneer on Canard wing concept, and hence the visit.

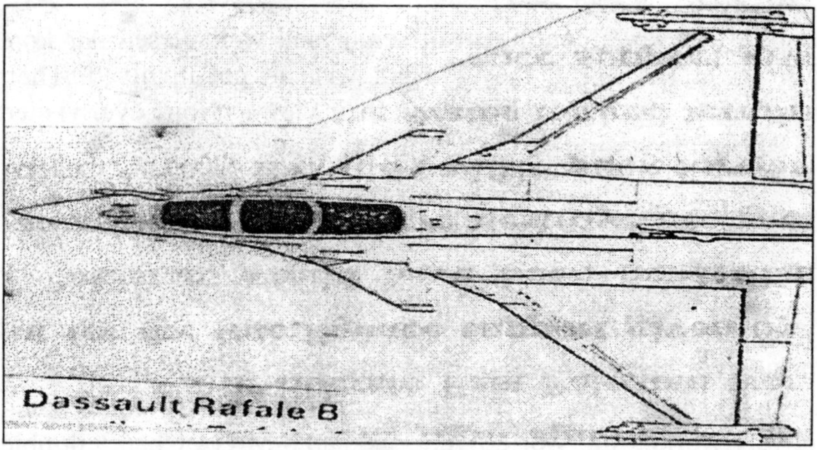

Marsault Dasault Rafale B

J-10 Fighter aircraft

The above named contractors belong to China The project began as a joint venture with Israel. But when Israel terminated this JV, Chinese continued. There were proposals of collaboration with Pakistan.

GTRE's CONTINUED EFFORT

DEVELOPMENT OF MIG 21

Prof. M.G.K Menon, FRS

Pakistan desired to have a better version of MiG 21. The desire to develop our MiG 21 originated because of this. There was no formal directive. A more powerful engine was thought of. A project design and development programme were prepared. Obviously this needed the blessing of our Scientific Officer first. After Dr. Nag Chaudhary, our third Scientific Adviser Professor MGK Menon, FRS was inducted in our DRDO scene. He was our 4th Scientific Adviser (SA). He was the youngest FRS (Fellow of Royal Society). When so honoured, with our characteristic 'crab' mind set, some of his contemporaries, instead of feeling proud, was upset Some did not attend a simple felicitation organised to honour him. Much before he took up the new assignment, the author had met Professor Menon very briefly, during a meeting held by, now defunct COST (Committee Of Science and Technology). It was part of Planning Commission. He was an impressive looking young person who spoke with a clarity which the meeting was sadly lacking The author did not know him. He was a Group Captain, the only service officer present. What he spoke on nation's development made no impact to the hall full of civilian scientists, old and young. The Chairman himself made light of his views. Surprisingly this young scientist was the only person who upheld what the author had said. Later, learning about his credential, the author felt that the participation was worthwhile.

GTX 37-14U

Designed a two spool engine, designated as GTX37-14 U with a Pressure Ratio of 13.15 developing 10,142 lb (43.7kN) and 14,647 lb.(65.3 kN) dry and reheat thrust respectively, and optimized to perform following a new operating cycle, when the initial specified ambient was ISA 30^{0}C, at take off point; reduced to 20^{0}C. (Now IRA +15^{0}C). The assessment temperature was reducing from 45^0 C to 30^{0}C with time, when the ambient temperature is actually increasing!

INITIATION OF GTX 37 14U

Late in the evening, SA returned to his office. Without wasting any time he wanted to know about the designed engine. A few senior officers were present. Those days slide, or pp (power point) projections were not in vogue. One had to use Black Boards and chalks. His power of concentration while listening was apparent, when the author concluded and expressed that he would like to answer any question. Professor Menon pointed out that a part drawn on Black Board was still not covered. The author regretted, explained, but at the same time his respect for the new SA soared. The project was given 'go ahead' as an experimental S & T exercise, with no aircraft in view.

AIR STRIKE AIRCRAFT (ASA)

At that stage, Air force desired to have an ASA (Air Strike aircraft), not a developed MiG 21. Because of past most unfortunate experience, HAL desired that this aircraft should be designed adopting RB 199 engine. It was a well proven classical high by-pass ratio (around I.2) engine developed by Rolls Royce. The past experience on HF 24 fully justifies their selections. However, GTX was running on test bed.

It was designed for operation at the initially designated high ambient. The cycle was evolved to combat the thrust drop with high intake temperature, and to provide better combat high capability..

READER'S NOTE SHEET – beginning of a new phase of GTRE on design and development of two spool high performance Engine adopting Flat rated cycle of operation.

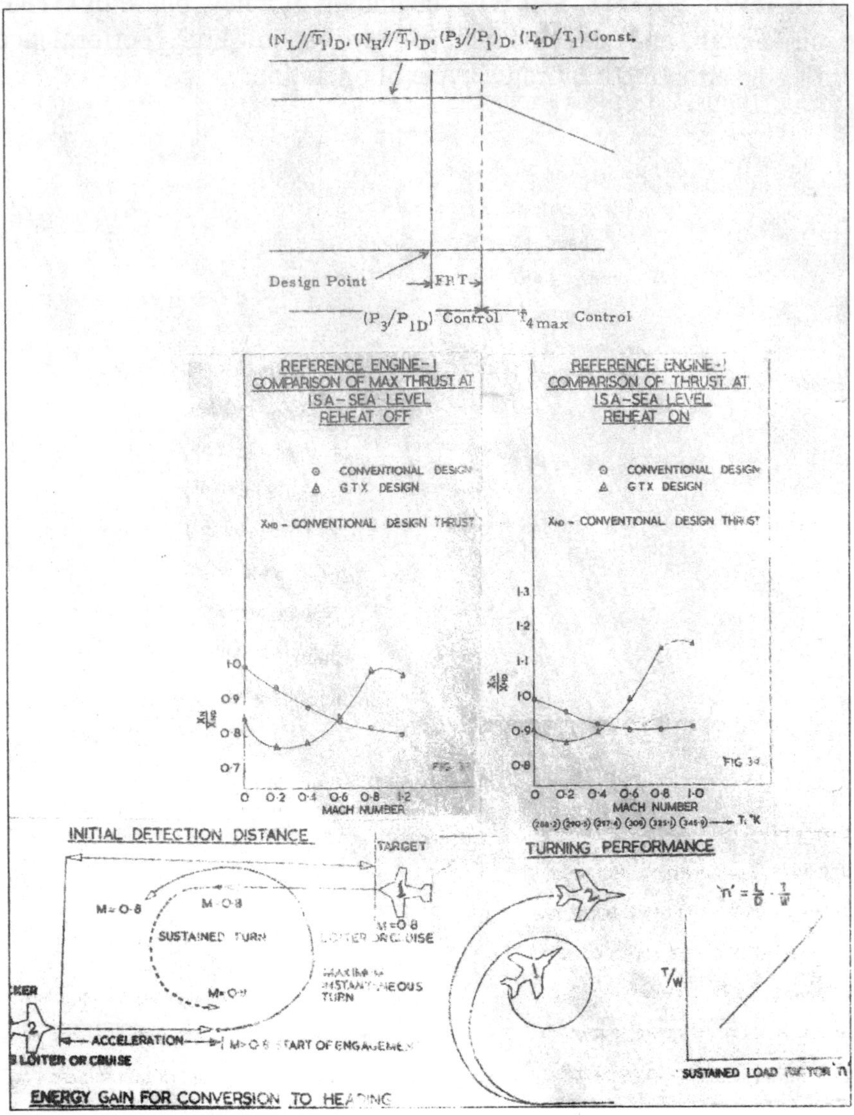

Flat rated temperature cycle (frt) high thrust at high Mach No. Characteristics of high turn rates at high intake temperature

Designation–1 **Designation–2**

Loilering **Enemy attacking. aircraft**

GTX ENGINE &GTX on test bed trial runningwith varying 'surge margin'

GTX Engine

GTX on test bed trial running with varying 'surge margin'

It is seen that the engine did not function stably at around 95 – 97% rpm. (right at the top end). The cause for this could not be established. It could be due to compressor's instable behavior at that rpm, or that of the shaft operating with a squeeze film bearing. Process of elimination was therefore adopted; first to revert back to roller bearing, replacing the inter shaft squeeze film bearing, Fitment of an additional (5th) bearing was also debated about. It was observed that the oil of the squeeze film bearing was leaking; i.e. the film of oil between the shafts for the squeeze film bearing was not retained uniformly. Improvement of the Labyrinth seal was done. The vibration level improved, but not fully. One could operate up to 97%, but a major impediment restricted operation at higher r.p.m. because turbine rub experienced. Cooled turbine blades was not common at that time Single crystal blades were also considered. Equipment to try this was bought and some trials were made Blades with 8 (eight) radial holes were needed to operate at 1400^0 K, the maximum designed TET (Turbine Entry Temperature), A company from France, working for SNECMA, agreed to make these cooled blades. But they could not go beyond 6(six) holed blades. Based on satisfactory operation up to 97% and also restriction imposed due to insufficiently cooled blades, the steering committee accepted the feasibility of the design of GTX engine.

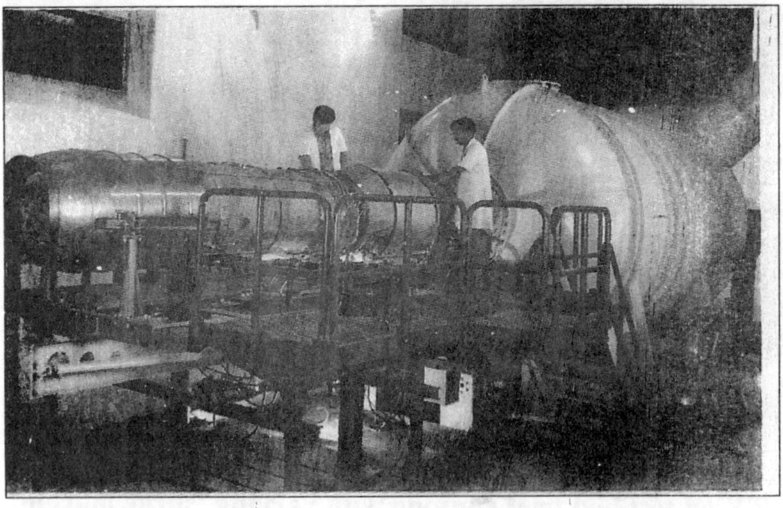

Test facility for hot intake trial using Orpheus engine establishing nil thrust drop with increased inlet temperature

AERODYNAMICS

Improvement of aerodynamics of the aircraft was actively worked upon at Nasik, where this aircraft was being manufactured. This was done by one of our well recognized Aero-dynamist. (He became the first director general of Aeronautical Development Agency ADA). Good results were reported. Pakistan, in collaboration of China had developed their Chinese built MiG 21 with a double delta wing, retaining the original engine, R 13/R-25.

LIGHT WEIGHT AVIONICS

Updating the Avionics, with reduced weight was also under consideration in the development programme.

While GTX was going through the development phase at test bed, a low by-pass (ratio 0.2) variant was designed and getting fabricated. This variant was designated as GTX(B).

*GTX-ADOUR DEVELOPMENT

MiG 21, aircraft, powered by RD–11F, with Mach 2+ performance capability, was acquired by us in 1961. Till then no Russian equipment was used by our defence forces. In 1960, the author accompanied two HAL senior authorities and visited the USSR to make an assessments of then famous MiG 21 supersonic aircraft. In bitter cold, limited assessment was made. The most striking feature was the OSWATITCH air intake. Read about this, at Cranfield Institute, but this was the first encounter with the real use, when such an intake was the first used in a supersonic operational aircraft.

The delta wing, the rear end variable nozzle of the reheat system, and a quick look followed by presentation and discussion left little doubt about this aircraft's claimed performance, This excellence, and the 'beep' from Sputnik, could not but made think about our aviation situation and feel depressed. Yet getting into Moscow city, *his unhappiness disappeared.*

A much bigger team visited USSR to finalize the deal.

The Chinese had also acquired this aircraft around the same time. An attempt was made in 1970 to develop the aircraft with improved aerodynamics, (Nasik, HAL), engine (GTRE, Bangalore), and avionics (ADE, Bangalore) - all initiated as indigenous efforts.

An experimental set up was created to prove the above. This is shown below:

MAINTAINING THRUST AT HIGH INTAKE TEMPERATURE

The improved flat rated engine, GTX-14U was running on test bed of Gas Turbine Research Establishment(GTRE). An evidence to this is presented below. The Steering Committee had certified the feasibility of its development on the basis of performance achieved. The operation was not completely trouble free. This fact was bought to the notice of the Committee and discussed. The engine was designed to have only 4 (four) bearings, with a squeeze film bearing in the front. (RD 11F engine of MiG 21 had 6 (six) bearings, but no squeeze film bearing.)

It was a new approach, being tried out in two shaft engines. Such innovative approaches in the operation cycle (retaining thrust at high ambient temperature at the intake, simultaneously reducing the specific fuel consumption during reheat operation, and some mechanical approaches stated earlier, had attracted attention of leading engine manufactures of the UK (Rolls Royce), France (SNECMA), and the USSR. All exhibited genuine interest on the technology approaches made and offered to collaborate.

GTRE will recall this fraternity for all time to come. Barring a few, the interest shown by the Indian fraternity was no less. Biennial seminars were held in a humble but large asbestos roofed shed, with no frills; for examples, there was no nomination on sitting arrangements. The spirit was one of exchange of knowledge, in a programmed manner. There were several well known participants from foreign countries. During the fourth biennial seminar, held in Nov 27-29, 1979, Mr. R.Ravaud, president director general SNECMA, France was the Chief guest.

Air Marshal S. J. Dastur, PVSM

The ultimate goal in view was most appropriately stated in the concluding remark of the address made by the Chairman of HAL, Air Marshal S. J. Dastur, PVSM "The achievement, its fall out, will give an impetus to our essential industries, transportation, electric power generation, communication etc. "***Bringing in further prosperity to the economically weaker sections of our society***". His was an extempore address, when he was requested to speak that morning after the formally nominated person declined, for reason not known. His decision was not conveyed earlier.

This was conveyed when enquired about his conveyance needs in the morning of the inaugural day. Air Marshal readily agreed to extend his helping hand. This was a mysterious happening. Obviously not bothered to enquired into.

The technology of engine development has to be viewed in the wider perspective, when it can stand alone to serve the society. An aircraft cannot fly without an engine. Rolls Royce, at one stage was earning more selling industrial version of their famous aircraft Avon engine, and had a separate manufacturing division. GTRE also made use of the time expired aircraft engine for its test facilities.

A general feature on aircraft and engine development needs high lighting at this stage. An aircraft receives prominence on its maiden flight. An engine has to wait till it receives the 'type certification' after many thousands of hours ground running and various tests under simulated conditions. Although this is a fully justifiable practice to ensure safety, the time difference between the maiden flight with a different engine, and the 'type certified' new engine can be extremely taxing for the engine developing agency. Often an opinion is expressed that an aircraft should be designed around a proven engine.

Generally speaking, this is a very correct approach, but often difficult to practice. Has not HF 24 aircraft proved this? Was it designed around a proven engine? B.OR12 SR was not a certified engine. Yet the failure of this all important project is attributed to non availability of 'suitable' engine essentially because of the aircraft's unique design. It will be a most revealing discovery, if one can identify a mach 2+ fighter aircraft with a tail end as designed, in HF 24 aircraft, having a tail plane fitted at the bottom of the aircraft. The design was for a subsonic aircraft, but not for a supersonic aircraft reheated gas turbine engine..

If only an engine designer knew what the future aircraft design will be like after 10 years, a well planned approach can be made. But this is often difficult to predict. The answer lies with the aircraft designer to provide flexibility on the kind of power plant to be adopted. Going by what stated in the book titled as "Diamonds in the sky", apparently this provision was made when HF 24 "was planned so as to offer scope for introduction of some successive generations of power plant". Unfortunately, the reality could not justify this lofty prediction.

The design of the straight flow GTX engine, and it's performance with an innovative cycle of operation to provide superior performance at high intake ambient, and with reheat operation, was subjected to detailed comparison with Rolls Royce design RB 199 over a protracted period. It was a by-pass engine of complicated design. For a mission profile needing reheat operation, GTX engine performed just as well.

The GTX engine was then discussed in USSR, when a team consisting of members from HAL, defence Ministry, and GTRE had visited that country to confirm the feasibility of development and installation of the engine in MiG 21 aircraft. After detailed discussion on GTX design, USSR most enthusiastically expressed their willingness to participate the development of the engine and the aircraft as well, if required. Our visit was mainly to assess the design of the GTX engine. To carry forward to this extent needed approval of our government when in addition, the desire was to improve upon the aerodynamics as well as the avionics.

Our desire was to develop further our indigenous S & T. What transpired thereafter in the parlor of Delhi was not known, but our effort on GTX continued. On one occasion, during a lunch break, in the recent days, the then chief designer from Nasik, HAL, (who had experimented and improved upon the aerodynamic performance of MiG 21) stated that the decision of not going ahead with MiG 21's improvement was a mistake. He expressed his view when the then Scientific Officer to the PM, and all senior scientists of NAL were present. This was the second step taken to dismantle Indian aeronautical progress.

Chinese also made a similar attempt to improve upon the MiG 21ML aircraft, and succeeded. The aircraft developed with modified double delta wing, designated as CAC J7 was powered by LM WP7 (The Chinese version of Russian RD-11F-300). It was a very successful venture, with large export order.

CHINESE DEVELOPED VERSION OF MiG 21

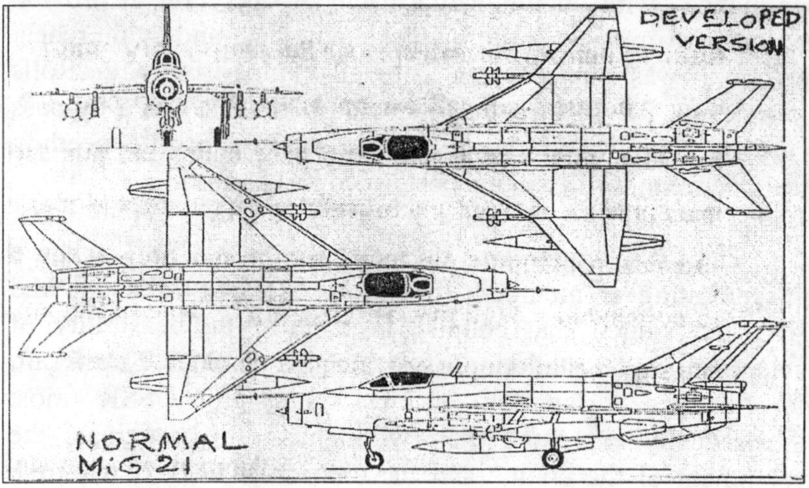

Chinese version of MiG 21 for Pakistan Air force

The justification for not permitting to go ahead with the development of MiG 21M, some 35 (thirty five) years ago is still not clear. The patriotic consortium of four high priests on aeronautics had felt that we should concentrate on developing HF 24 instead. (The fatal accident of HF 24 had not occurred at that stage, and GTRE was looking for new project activity, having completed the HE 24 MK 1R project.). So it took up a project on GTX engine.

ORPHEOUS 703 WITH TRANSONIC BLADE & 2000^0 K REHEAT

Orpheous 703 with transonic blade & 2000^{0}k reheat

Test for 2000 ^{0} K reheat (Photographed by author)

Note: The bigger Diameter, but still can be accepted in existing fuselage. But this was kept in the 'cooler' when the rear end modification of the aircraft was debated about.

DRDO Head Office took no side. It remained, as appropriate, appreciative of the establishment's work, and allowed it to grow.

Continued up gradation of test facilities.

ASSISTANCE TO MISSILE PROJECT.

This was initiated earlier by Dr. B.D. Nag Chaudhury. He was our third SA. who believed in hardware experimental activity; responsible for installation of the first Cyclotron and conducting experiments

TURBO-PUMP: ASSISTANCE TO LIQUID FUEL ROCKET MOTOR FOR MISSILE PROGRAMME

While so occupied with our programmes, the then Scientific Advisor, Dr. B. D. Nag Chaudhury, approached GTRE to make a turbo pump for a Rocket Motor for a missile programme which a Hyderabad based (DRDO) Organization was working on. Apparently and obviously, the programme was 'stuck' up without this component. The turbo pump was made and delivered in the evening at Hyderabad, working nonstop, within a short period of about two weeks. What presented was a pleasant surprise to SA and to the DRDO staff. What we did more than what they had expected, and surprised them.

Turbo pump on top and components of tubular rocket motor

42(Photograph by the author)

TURBINE OF TURBO-PUMP

The most critical part of the turbo pump was the turbine type rotor. A technology to make this with blades integrally machined with the disc was developed. Attempts were also made with powdered metallurgy by another DRDO establishment. Apparently this did not perform well. The details are not known. The developed technology was adopted by VSSC (Vikram Sarabai Space Center), as well. A seminar was held there on this subject, when the Hyderabad Establishment had also presented their effort. However, the GTRE approach prevailed and still continues. Wg. Commander Rao at Delhi office, looking after DRDO, Hyderabad, paid complement stating that the Hyderabad unit got going only after GTRE's effort. In the recent days, an officer then working at DRDO was unhappy about Rao's remark, and advised not to mention this because this may 'raffle' many very senior officers' hair! This example is cited mainly to highlight that innovating actions in our country make enemies, and not friends. Sycophancy makes friends.

ROCKET MOTOR

A thought surfaced to make a tubular structured rocket motor. Without going into technological details of construction,, the main theme was to make inexpensive short range missiles of flexible ratings to halt supply lines to enemy's offensive front line. The current approach would require expensive dies to form the rocket bodies. An example of tubular rocket body and associated components are shown below;

Tubular liquid fuel rocket motor

From: S.V. NARASIMHAN
RETD. SCIENTIST G
GTRE. BANGALORE

DATED: 27-6-
FAX NO: 080-255

To: AVM ROY CHAUDHURY
FORMER & FOUNDER DIRECTOR - GTRE

RE: TUBULAR THRUST CHAMBER

GTRE DESIGNED TUBULAR THRUST CHAMBER WITH INTEGRAL ATOMISER WAS TESTED AT DRDL, HYDERABAD DURING 1974-75(.) THIS THURST CHAMBER LASTED FOR 42 SECDS WITH 4 to 5 FIRING AND DEVELOPED CHAMBER PRESSUR OF 45-48 KSC(.) THE THRUST COULD NOT BE MESUARED BUT THE CALCULATED THRUST CORRESPONDS TO 2.5 to 2.6 TONNES(.) HOWEVER ABELATIVE DESIGN WAS NOT TESTED TO FULL POTENTIAL(.) THIS MESSAGE WAS OBTAINED FROM DRDL OFFICIAL(.)

REGARDS.

(S.V. NARASIMHAN)

The test result of tubular rocket motor

SEMINARS

The need for cross fertilization of research done by various groups of GTRE and elsewhere was felt, when the goal in view was to design and develop a gas turbine engine. A large shed was erected. Initially, it was an in house affair. After the constitution of Aeronautics R & D Board, with financial help, the seminars were organised on a bigger scale. Two events stirred up the aeronautics community. The first was introduction of a transonic first stage in B.Or. 703 engine. This development was demonstrated to the then Chief of Air Staff, O. P. Mehra in 1976, without any prior trial. Rolls Royce had tried this approach earlier, but was not very successful. The other was the design, manufacture, and trial of GTX-37-14U. By this time, very cordial relationship were established with Rolls Royce, UK, and SNECMA, France. GTRE seminar became an International event for exchange of scientific knowledge. The most significant feature was, there was no bureaucratic 'reserved' sitting arrangement. It was truly 'free for all' same type of unoccupied sitting chair for all, anywhere. No special lunch or dinner, or VIP tag. The free for all atmosphere is seen from the picture below

An assembly during seminar

One can see Air Marshal Ranjan Dutt, MD, HAL; SC DAS, his Chief Designer: Dr.Jain, Head aerospace, Indian Institute of Science sitting behind; Mrs. Das, OBE, CEO Cheshire Home; Mrs. Roy Chaudhury, Head Mistress Kindergarden School, ASC center; Dr. Velluri, Director, NAL in front: to name a few, - all listening with great attention to a presentation sitting at random. GTRE truly believed that S & T have no rank barriers other than ability to express these, discuss, listen and learn. In Annexure 3, the names and the subject matters presented in 27 – 29, 1979 seminar should provide an indication that the technology development of GTRE was rapid.

An interesting feature to be noticed that the platform where the foreign dignitaries, mentioned in Annexure 3 and the speakers presenting their views were not in focus. The reason why this omission had happened is known but too subjective to narrate. The author's expensive ZEISS camera was used, by a photographer of GTRE. He received instruction to avoid because defence related subjects were being discussed. Evidence of foreigners participation could cause problem, the photographer was told. There was no doubt on that it was an intentional move to undermine the level of the seminar. It was a move from a sick minded senior Scientist, but did not harm the proceedings of the Seminar. It was a happy occasion when all subjects were discussed with enthusiasm and knowledge.

CONTINUED EFFORT

Simultaneous to test facilities upgradation, during the 4 years trial on Mk1R, GTRE developed the engine further, when the first stage out of seven stages of the compressor of the B. Or 703 was replaced with a transonic stage, and the reheat was developed to 2000^0 K. (The operation with transonic stage was tried out, without any earlier trial, in presence of Air Chief Marshal O. P. Mehra. (He was earlier the Chairman of HAL).

Two such engines would have provided reheat thrust to make HF 24 a supersonic Aircraft, *but only if* the tail end was suitably modified. The similarity of HF 24 and French(Mirage)

F1 has been brought out earlier. Would it be proper to suggest that such dimensional similarities are not accidental. The design similarities are intentional?

To state that Jaguar was bought because of the fa tal accident, which on an earlier occasion was mentioned due to engine failure, can only be justified as a willful attempt to block indigenous development. as to be expected from agents of foreign equipment. At no stage the *reason* for the failure of canopy ejection, - the real cause of the accident, - had remotely been mentioned, although the foreign press did. When the automatic canopy ejection system failed, why did the manual canopy ejection system also failed? Why were the ejection Cartridges fitted wrongly? All these issues were brushed under the carpet. Why? Were they not valid issues?

Gp. Capt Das's humility and unassuming dedication for the country's progress touched many hearts, and these were expressed through his professional competence. But all good things depart after leaving behind their hall mark. Dasu, as he was commonly and affectionately known, was one such person. During the tenth flight of the new prototype, HF 24 Mk 1R No. BD 886 (032), on the 10th January, 1970, he met the fetal accident, soon after the take off. A Board of investigation was instituted to looked into the accident. (Refer. Ministry of defence U.O. NO.286/JS/(ALF)70 date 12th January, 1970)

AN ILLUSTRATION

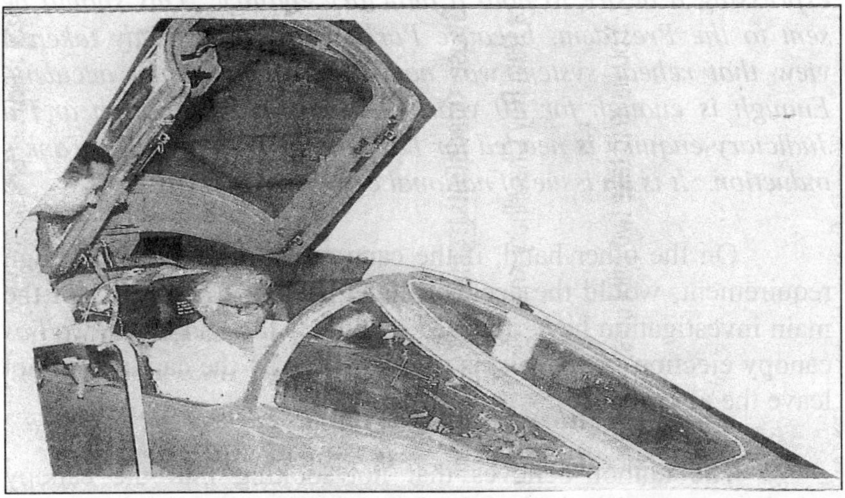

An open canopy representation of what HF 24 Mk 1R's condition was like at take off point when flight speed was about 165 -170 knots, and canopy remaining attached. The general view conveyed is that with one reheat failure, i.e 10 % reduction of total thrust, the aircraft met the fatal accident, the reason for canopy opening and remaining attached were not the primary cause.

A real picture of HF 241R is not available. But it would have been similar.

FOREIGN PRESS

The foreign press reported on this accident. It stated

"On January 10th, 1970, the brilliant career of Gp Capt Suranjan Das came to an untimely and tragic end in the fatal crash of the HF- 24 MK 1R prototype. On takeoff, the canopy opened and *probably* the right engine lost power. *Unfortunately, he could not have ejected out of the aircraft unless the canopy flew off, which it didn't." (Italics by the author)*

Is there any who would like to challenge the press report, not through press, or vocally but it must be formally signed expressing a desire to hold a judiciary enquiry.. This should be sent to the President, because Parliament had already taken a view that reheat system was not responsible for the accident. Enough is enough for 40 years' baseless condemnation and a Judiciary enquiry is needed for happenings including Dr. Tank's induction. It is an issue of national economical health.

On the other hand, if the canopy had ejected as a design requirement, would the accident have happened? Should not the main investigation have focused on both; - the locking *as well as* canopy ejection mechanisms to establish why the canopy did not leave the aircraft?

The author believes that not looking into the canopy ejection mechanism is an intended act. Simultaneous to making wind tunnel trial to confirm that the pilot had failed to lock the canopy, investigation should have been made why canopy release mechanism did not work. During the wind tunnel it must have been so arranged that the release mechanism would not function. During a discussion with a senior HAL pilot, his view was it might have been an inadvertent mistake! similar to wrongly fitting the ejection cartridge. He even felt that this was a sliding type.

Was it of any importance to determine whether the pilot had forgotten to lock the canopy or not. The aircraft was prone to failures on canopy locking. On two earlier occasions the canopy locking mechanism failed but the canopies left as they should have, and the pilots came back with no noise in the media. In this case when the canopy did not leave, he was in a death trap. In the whole history of military aviation has any flown with canopy open?. He knew about the serious danger he was in. He did not relay a word.

On reheat failure, unless no real evidence is produced, the author has nothing to comment on. Was it only the reheat or the whole engine? But when the drag had doubled with open canopy, at such low speed, what could the test pilot do? Many people have earned money for nearly 40 years debating and publishing about the possibilities of reheat failures. The process continues. Why not write about other fatal accidents during the development of HF 24 Mk1? What about SU7's fatal accidents when reheat failed during takeoff ? How many reheat failures on MiG 21? With only one Mk1R, flying for 4 years, and still in one piece, it became a symbol of for all Mk1's fetal accidents, how many no one knows or tell.

English electric P1 lost its canopy on three occasion, once at supersonic speed. But no fetal accident because canopy ejected on all cases. The repeated occurrences of the canopy ejection in English Electric P1 evoked some humorous remark in the internationally famed 'Punch' magazine and printed a cartoon as below, when a rope was wrapped around the fuselage and the canopy with a caption of '*had a little trouble losing cockpit canopies, but I think we have mastered it*'. The pictorial sketch is not in the one in 'Punch'. It is author's reproduction.

Solving canopy ejection problem

Side hinged canopy remaining attached after inadvertent opening during take off

Would it be wrong to suggest that there was deficient technology in HAL about canopy release mechanism.

GTRE and the author were gearing up for the following projects:

1. Powering HF 24 to be a Supersonic aircraft with TS R 2000^{0}K reheat, with 46% improvement compared to basic 703 engine;. flat rating with improved material and cooled turbine blades. Thus having T/W ratios 0.54(dry) and 0.73 (reheat), and tail plane shifted on top.

2. Developed Jaguar with improved Adour engine (collaboration with Rolls Royce;)

3. Developed MiG 21with GTX / GTX(B) engine in collaboration with USSR / SNECMA;

These targets could have been achieved as seen from what stated here after;;

Development of Adour Engine for JAGAUR AIRCRAFT

ISSUED BY : GTRE & RR 3.4.

GTRE/ROLLS-ROYCE JOINT STUDIES

THE GTX-ADOUR FAMILY OF ENGINES

For the last six months, the Gas Turbine Research Establishment, Bangalore, and Rolls Royce have been engaged in joint project studies.

The studies have now established that the operating concepts and the low-pressure compressor, already developed by GTRE for their own GTX engine, can with advantage be combined with the high-pressure components of the Rolls Royce/Turbomeca Adour engine, a licence for the manufacture of which has recently been acquired by the Government of India.

The resulting possible growth versions of the Adour are being designated "GTX-Adour".

The GTX-Adour has already stimulated the creation of a novel after burner concept which is currently being tested at GTRE.

During the next few months GTRE and Rolls Royce will issue joint Preliminary Performance statements which, with the help of the interested Aircraft companies, will lead to a first appraisal of the marketing potential of the engine.

At this stage, the joint work is restricted to the project feasibility studies necessary to establish the prospects of the GTX-Adour family.

P. Young.
(P.H. YOUNG)
Director of Advanced Engineering
Rolls Royce, Bristol, UK
2/4/79.

(S.N.Roy Chaudhury) AVM (Rtd)
Director
GTRE, BANGALORE
2.4.79

Letter from Rolls Royce for collaborative effort.

A year later a team of 5/6, headed by one of the high priest, (under protest from the author being the senior most) visited Aero space, in UK. On return, a report was drafted in the office of the author, when the leader was fetched and sent back, in GTRE's staff car. The report was distorted with regard to Jaguar's further development. The author wrote out a dissenting note. The original report reached Delhi, without the dissenting note.

USSR OFFER OF COLLABORATION ON GTX ENGINE

GTRE's effort to reach upto foreign desin standards got assessed in USSR, when a team consisting of a senior member of Defence Ministry (functioning as an interpreter as well), HAL, and GTRE was sent to USSR to get an assessment on GTX engine design.

SNECMA'S OFFER OF COLLABORATION ON GTX (B) ENGINE FOR FURTHER DEVELOPMENT OF MiG 21

While GTX engine was already undergoing trials in the test bed, a low by-pass version of this engine, designated as GTX (B) was getting ready to provide for increased power to develop MiG 21 with a performance similar to contemporary advanced fighter aircraft. A letter was sent to the then scientific adviser, enclosing a copy of the above letter. Receiving no reply, met him at his Delhi office. He expressed that no such letter had been received. His office confirmed receipt of a letter endorsed, 'personal/ confidential', and knew nothing more.

S.N.E.C.M.A.
2, Bd. Victor
75015 - PARIS
Tel : 554.92.00

Paris, 11 MAY 1978
SD n° 78/8950/40

G . T . R . E .
R and D Organisation
Ministry of Defence
P O n° 1.777
BANGALORE 560017
INDIA

To the kind attention of AIR VICE MARSHAL SN ROY CHAUDHARY

Mon Général,

Due to unavoidable circumstances we could not meet on 2 May 78.

Mr. GARNIER and Mr. BOUDIGUES informed me about your projects and of which you have mentioned in your letter dated 3 May 78.

As you know, SNECMA is prepared to co-operate with the Indian aeronautical industries and particularly with the G.T.R.E. For this purpose, SNECMA has obtained the permission from the French official departments in order to negociate with the Indian Authorities khx over the delivery of a licence for the manufacture of the ATAR 9K50 which equips the aircraft MIRAGE F 1, without any technological restriction and to negotiate with you over a contract for an Engineering advisorx in the GTRE.

As you have already stressed in your letter, the joint-development of a new military engine with high performances necessitates an authorisation from the governmentsof both the countries.

Apart from the authorisations that you have already obtained, if you could confirm to me that such a project had received the approval from the top most Government Authorities, I will do the needful to obtain the same from the French Government.

With the assurances of my highest consideration.

Sd. R. RAVAUD

Copy to : Wing Commander SASTRY
Embassy of India
15, rue Alfred Déhodencq
75016 - PARIS

Letter from SNECMA for collaborative effort with GTRE

GTRE in 1981, beginning at cantonment railway station (author retires) at the age of 59 years then as a civilian director (Normally civilian directors retire at the age of 60 years) Photograph by author

A day after retirement of the author, all the three projects in hand were scrapped. A new engine designed with a five stage high-pressure compressor, named 'KAVERI', for a new aircraft design designated as LCA (light combat aircraft) was taken in hand. The author believes it was a wrong decision. The three on-going aircrafts under development with improved engines with three foreign collaborations (USSR for MiG 21 development with

GTX U), Rolls Royce (Adour for Jaguar), SNECMA (GTX UB), mentioned earlier would have not only supersonic, but could have met the Air Force's need for a) Tactical air superiority, b) DPSA (Deep Penetration Strike Aircraft and c) The ASA (Air superiority Aircraft); though not meeting emerging contemporary aircraft design concept on the horizon in developed countries. But they would not have left our Indian sky barren of indigenous efforts for 40 years. It may not be out of context to mention that this decision to have contemporary aircrafts is yet to materialize. It is difficult to predict when the Indian sky will have indigenous aircraft with current technological status. In the meantime, to meet the defence needs Indian Air force has to buy aircraft at high costs from foreign resources. The rural development needs with co-generation of decentralized 1,00,000 MW might have received a greater financial support, if the three earlier mention aircraft were not scrapped.

This happening is rated by many as if GTRE did not succeed to complete any project. The author believes that the more relevant assessment would be to enquire why it did not

The author was happy to retire one year early (for reason not known) when he could devote his desire to work wholly on rural development. An account of his efforts in this direction has been indicated in earlier Para graphs.

CHAPTER -16

ENERGY SOURCES

Our heritage is the period when our true Indian multi directional cultural splendor flourished and we are so proud of. This is during the mixed indo-Aryan dynasty of about 2700 years, Setting aside the earlier Indus valley civilization, do we have much to talk about other than this period (1500 BC – 1200 AD) If history had kept a proper record, this period would have reflected the contributions made by this subcontinent to develop other countries, particularly in the far East as well.

These countries were aided with the superior minds, skilled artisans and peasants of this subcontinent. But they were made use of as slaves instead, after 1190 AD by the foreign rulers who followed, after the Indo-Aryan dynasty. This sub-continent as a whole became a 'slave dynasty' till 1947, when the country became Independent.

The people who helped the foreigners to rule our country were our own urban countrymen, who robbed the rural poor, simultaneously keeping them locked up in dark with agronomy as their only profession. Tables below prove this.

TABLE 21

QUALITY OF NATIONAL ELECTRICITY GENERATION (MW) IN 2006

Hydro	Thermal (coal)	Renewable	Nuclear	Total
32,726	83,272	6,191	3,900	1,26,089
26 (%)	66 (%)	5 (%)	3 (%)	100 (%)

Total generation: 1,26, 089 X 1000 X0.6 X 0.8 X 24 = 1.45 bn kWh/ day (PLF: - 0.6, Transmission loss – 20 %)

PER CAPITA ELECTRICAL ENERGY AVAILABILITY

(Average)

URBAN - 3.8 KwH/ day for 300 million people

RURAL - 0.384 KwH/ day for 800 million people

Including that used to energize the agricultural pump set.

Estimated population in 2006 is 1,100 million.

(2001 census population was 1,028 million. Assuming population growth rate as 1.7 %, the estimated population in 2006 is $(1.017)^5$ X1,028 = 1, 118 million.

Refer also the earlier estimate on energy generation (3.8 X 300 + 0.384 X800) X10^6 =) 1.45 bn kWh / day, or annual - 529 bn KwH.

ELECTRICITY DISTRIBUTION

The distribution of Electricity in urban and rural areas provides an index to our governance attitude towards rural people. Two quantified illustrations, quoting budgetary allocations on (a) agricultural and rural development; and (b) literacy development have been made to justify that we need an altogether new governance system.

The above on energy consumption proves, without any doubt that the large 800 million rural people are living in dark, to feed the urban society, living in luxury. To be at par with urban society, the deficient electrical energy generation needed by the rural society is about (3.8 - 0.384) X800 = 2.73, bn KwH/ day. Then additional generation need will be 1,37,395 MW, when our current generation is only 1,26,089 MW. That is, the total generation need for our country is 2,63,484 MW. Media often suggests that our deficient energy generation is one lakh MW. This is an achievable estimate. On the other hand, if only the energy policy had accepted as an essential need, then the additional generation need will be 1,00,000 MW as estimated earlier. A separate co-generation energy department, CED, similar to CEA (Central Electricity Authority) need be created, but this needs a close look at our energy resources.

Source: compiled by author using data above.

COAL BASED ELECTRICITY GENERATION

India's current capacity to generate electricity is about 1,24,000 MW, when about 66 percent is through coal. We are short of about 100,000 MW. Serious environmental problems will give rise to if coal is used, as of now to meet bulk of this deficiency. There is a worldwide concern mainly because of $C0_2$ (Carbon Dioxide) emission. We rank third for our coal reserve but our coal with high ash content has low heat value. Much research is being done to get around this problem.

Green coal is feasible. 80 % of Australia's electrical energy is coal based. Obviously we need to adopt a new strategy to get back on rails for appropriate progress. Mindlessly we are trying to catch up with developed society through Nuclear energy. If only our coal is researched on, using a fraction of money spent on nuclear energy, we may get out of our present foreign dependence. Currently, negotiations are going on with USA to buy their aged nuclear reactors. There are several imponderables related to shortage of knowledgeable trained manpower, and, therefore, increased gestation time. They are not receiving adequate attentions. Besides, Nuclear energy cannot create the other side of Rural coin if to be achieved through Fig. 12.

With our large coal reserve, should we not also try to take up research activities to achieve *green* coal combustion with virtually nil pollutant emission. Ongoing efforts in developed societies suggest that this is feasible. Alston, UK and American Electric Power (AEP) jointly hope 'to design, construct and commission an up to 200 MW carbon dioxide capture system on a 450 MW coal fired unit in Oklahoma scheduled to start in late 2011. It is expected to capture about1.5 mn tones of CO_2 to be used to enhance oil recovery. The post-combustion process, using chilled ammonia, reduces the energy required to capture CO_2 and isolates it in a highly concentrated, high pressure form'.

Source: International News, energy World.

Briquetted bio-mass may provide considerable relief to 'green house' problem when it is realized that coal when combusted with biomass reduces CO_2 emission to half.

Our coal reserve is 253.30 bn (10^9) tons. Currently we are mining annually about 529 million (10^6) tons Our reserve is third after China and USA. Assuming we gear up the use double of this, pollution free coal can serve us for about 240 more years, supplemented by unexploited natural and coal gas, mini hydro, wind and solar power not depending on aged Nu-reactors from USA.

Not only we are serious about achieving green coal combustion, we are unmindful of about the raging coal fire since long. Coal fire is a near all the world phenomenon. Attempts to douse this has not been successful. However, a novel new approach has appeared on the scene. Simultaneous to flooding to douse, steam powered electricity production is receiving attention. Our coal worth is Rs. 60,000 Crores. Attempts are being made to save this shifting Jharia, Dhanbad district, Jharkand so that this massive national wealth can be saved.

A LEADER IN EARLY DAYS

A. B. Roy Chaudhury

The author retains an unhappy yet proud memory about his father. He was one of the few Indian colliery manager, - if not the very first, and a very courageous man. In those days, mines were privately owned.

The managers were British. He was a totally apolitical person. His religion was welfare of the miners. At that time, Gandhi was propagating his pledge of 'Purna Swaraj'. He allowed Gandhi to hold a massive meeting in the sprawling land between his Bungalow and the coal mine with a pre-condition there would not be any slogan shouting. He did not attend the meeting. The miners heard him and left silently.

During this time his mine caught fire. The whole structure

looked red hot. Actually it was the glow from fire below. He got down the shaft. At that very young age, not knowing what was happening, looked at his mother. A non-emotional face looked as the cabin started going down. She held the author tight with her arm around his body. After a while the cabin came up with a few miners.

The reason to phase in the above episode is to illustrate a leadership of that quality is needed, to jump in fire to rescue HIS people in grave danger, regardless of the danger to self. How few would do that now, except those in military services? If the present system of giving away awards was in vogue then, he would perhaps have offered one. But the author believes that he would have politely declined, stating that he was merely doing duty. Will it be true that our current concept of leadership has lost regrettably, undergone a 180° turn about, allowing the people starve, or die, Our media heralds this every day.

He walked straight to the Bunglow. My mother followed him. Upto that moment, the author remembers vividly the happenings. He was shifted to Calcutta, where he expired at the age of 47, leaving behind four sons, two daughters, and a very determined widow Goddess mother. Learnt much later that he was infected with carbon monoxide poisoning. The author's mother did not speak much. We shifted to our zamender's big house in East Bengal, now Bangladesh. A new phase of life began. This has been narrated earlier.

NON-CONVENTIONAL ENERGY SOURCES

Some efforts had started to improve upon the life style of rural people, making use of non-conventional energy. sources. A Department of Non-conventional Energy Source (DNES), and a Rural Electrification Center (REC) were formed at CGO complex and Nehru place, New Delhi respectively. The first dealt with were Gobar gas plants, Wind and Solar power, PV (photo voltaic) system coupled with UPS, solar water heaters, efficient wood burning *chullas* (stoves), mini-hydro electric, sea wave power, and so on. Most, except the wind power, did not achieve much success. But for the dispersed nature of poor customers, these did not contribute much to supplement the national energy scenario for rural development, even when heavily subsidized.

OUR WASTAGES ON ENERGY FRONT

An account of energy wastages is indicated below. A caution may be appropriate. This is not easily realizable, and therefore, to designate as 'wastages' may be misnomer. They are not 'free' either. At the same time, with proper planning and research they can contribute much to meet the rural needs. At this stage, much of the table below should be treated as 'possible' recoverable energy opportunities.

POSSIBLE RECOVERABLE ENERGY SOURCE

TABLE – 22

Material	Annual Production	Conversion GAS	Total M gas/yr	Heat value per M^3/Kg	Thermal per-cent	Available cooking energy Kcal/Yr
Dung	9000×10^6 tonnes	0.036 M^3/Kg	32.4 $\times 10^9$	4713 Kcal/M^3	50	76.3×10^{12}
Molasses	2.1×10^6 tonnes	From spent-wash 131.5 M^3/T	276 $\times 10^6$	5336 Kcal/M^3	60	0.885×10^{12}
Agrowaste	4X10 tonnes	-	-	2216.6 Kcal/Kg	15	13.3×10^{12}
Flared NG	17 MMCMD	100%	17 $\times 10^6$	8894.2 Kcal/M^3	62	34.2×10^{12}
Community	150×10^6 tonnes	0.036 M3/Kg	5.4 $\times 10^9$	4713 Kcal/M^3	50	12.7×10^{12}
				Total		137.585×10^{12}

DATA PRESENTED BY AUTHOR DURING THE UN WORKSHOP ON BIO-MASS ENERGY, HELD IN LONDON, ON OCT 1990.

The relevance of inclusion of 'flared NG' was questioned and debated about, but accepted on two counts as under;

1. The origin of natural gas is bio mass; the workshop has not placed a time tag on bio-mass. Besides, the ultimate objective was rural development.
2. It is the most wasted energy source when flared away yet when used through decentralized co-generation can serve much more than other items mentioned.

The author chaired an important session. He explained the approach plan to use such waste energy through densification as shown under.

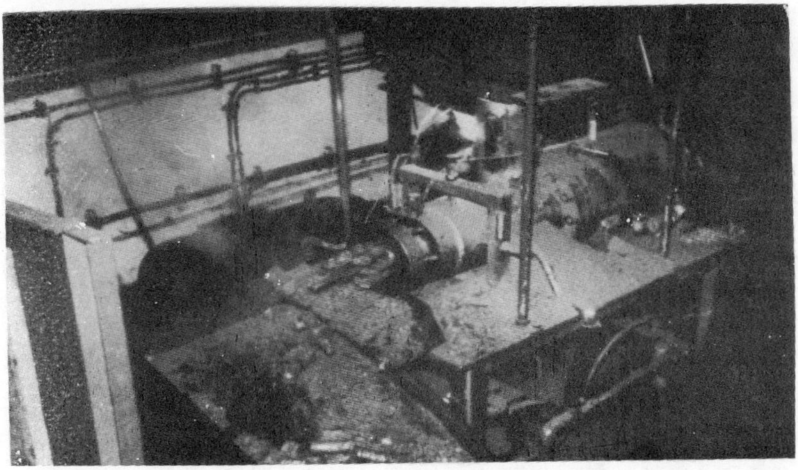

Bio waste densified palatte machine

Palette bundled for collection

Cooking with densified fuel palettes

Group photograph of invited delegates, author front row second from left

Third from right - director renewable source of energy, China. He made valuable contribution explaining the bio-gas strategy through large numbers of community gas digesters placed in a line to collect the gas for distribution.

Annexure „F'

UNIDO

UNITED NATIONS INDUSTRIAL DEVELOPMENT ORGANIZATION

VIENNA INTERNATIONAL CENTRE
P.O. BOX 300, A-1400 VIENNA, AUSTRIA
TELEPHONE. 211 310 TELEGRAPHIC ADDRESS: UNIDO VIENNA TELEX: 135612 uno a FAX: 232156

04 March 1991

Dear Roy

Subject: US/INT/90/201 - Workshop on the Thermal Processing of Biomass. London, October 1990.

I have been advised that the report on the workshop is ready and will be dispatched directly to you by Shell Research. The two volume report contains the workshop proceedings, project formulation frameworks and all technical presentations. UNIDO will be forwarding the report and separate copies of the project prepared by you, to UNDP India. We will also furnish UNDP with information on the background to the workshop and its objectives.

May I suggest you initiate discussions with your authorities with a view to finalizing the proposal and securing its approval by concerned Government Departments. The proposal can then be formally submitted to UNDP for onward transmission to UNIDO. The expert(s) who agreed to link with your particular project during the workshop can be contacted on any technical issues with which you may require assistance. UNIDO will continue to monitor progress of all proposals.

May I take this opportunity to thank you personally and on behalf of UNIDO for your valuable contribution to the workshop. Your hard work in preparing a technical presentation prior to the workshop and in elaborating a project formulation framework assured the success of the project.

I hope to see you again in the not too distant future.

Yours sincerely,

Bob Williams

R.O. Williams
Industrial Development Officer
Chemical Industries Branch
Industrial Operations Technology Division
Department of Industrial Operations

A.V.M. Roy Choudhury
Total Energy Systems
No. 618 80 Ft Road
IVth Block
Koramangala
Bangalore
India

Letter from UNDP

As desired by UNDP organization, the above letter was brought to notice of department of rural development. The net outcome was nil, DG (NIRD) did not respond.

Extracts from file No.A-60011/26/90-CAPART(RD) of discussion on Air Vice Marshall S.N. Roy Choudhury's proposal on Integrted Rural Energy Centres.

Shri E.A.S. Sharma, Adviser(Energy Policy), Planning Commission, Shri L. Mansingh, Joint Secretary, Department of Industrial Development, Shri A. Prasad, DDG(CAPART), Shri Magu from Planning Commission and I discussed the proposal of Air Vice Marshall S.N. Roy Choudhury(Retd.) on his Integrated Rural Energy Centres.

It was concluded that -

(1) The integrated rural energy project as proposed by Shri Roy Choudhury would be feasible only if a tie-up with the Natural Gas is established and the economics worked out.

(2) Secondly, it was necessary to have such a project tied up with an institution dealing with rural development with whom Shri Choudhury could associate in the implementation of the project. Once this feasibility is established, funding from internal and external sources could be considered.

(3) Thirdly, it was felt that Shri T.L. Sankar, DG(NIRD) may be requested to give his comments both on the feasibility of the project as well as associating NIRD with such a project.

Sd/-

(Sarala Gopalan)
J.S.(Admn.)
31/12/1990

Our Government's reaction to UNDP letter

Receiving no response I was advised to approach the Hon'ble Minister of Agriculture.

ef Marshal

O. P. Mehra

PVSM, F.A.e.S.I., M.A. (Retd.)

A-9/34, VASANT VIHAR
NEW DELHI-110 057
PH.: 6873257, 679052

28th April 1994

It was a pleasure meeting you in connection with a project which I feel has promise and needs your active help and guidance.

2. As a follow-up, I enclose a copy of AVM Roy Chaudhury letter dated 28-4-1994 along with enclosures for your sympathetic consideration and guidance to me and my colleague.

3. In view of your pressing engagements please be kind enough to intimate the name and designation of the official in your Ministry with whom, AVM Roy Chaudhury and I can interact. I shall take the liberty of disturbing you only when so advised by the designated officer and also to keep you posted with developments relating to the project.

Shri Balram Jhakhar,
Minister of Agriculture,
Government of India,
Krishi Bhavan,
NEW DELHI - 110001

Copy to AVM Roy Chaudhry.
Room No 24 India International Centre
Lodhi Estate
New Delhi

Letter from Air Chief Marshal O. P. Mehra to agriculture minister

After retirement as CAS (1973 - 1976), Air Chief Marshal O. P. Mehra became Governor of two States. The author was told that the rural development was a political issue, and assistance from a politician would help. The author approached him, because having been governor he would know the condition of rural people more than any politician. Besides, he was a very knowledgeable and approachable helpful person. After learning about the author's need for help, immediately fixed up an appointment with the minister of agriculture. The letter above tells what happened. No reply was received from him or his staff.

DOMESTIC COOKING

To provide organised domestic cooking energy for 800 million poor rural people is perhaps as difficult and a major problem as electrification of their homes.

DUNG, BIO-GAS & ORGANIC MANURE FERTILIZER

India has the largest per capita cattle population, producing about 9000* million tons of wet dung/year. There are two ways this can provide cooking energy to rural community. Let us assume one half will be treated in digesters, i.e., 4500 million tons of dung/year will be treated in digesters, providing 16.2 billion m^3 non pollutant bio-gas/year for cooking purposes, and simultaneously producing enough organic manure to meet the country's need. Assuming that 7.0 cu ft of bio-gas with a heat value of 460 Btu/cu.ft is needed per day/per person, it is seen that 50% of rural population can be served with this gas piped to their homes. Such an estimate has at least two fallacies, and one major technology problem.

* The data mentioned in earlier table was for those partially dried.

First, some farmers believe that once de gassed, the dung loses its fertilizing quality. Secondly, many are not in a position to buy the gas. Therefore, dung is used directly for manure. However, experiment with a 50:50 mix with organic fertilizer has provided better result than exclusive use of organize fertilizer.

The other half is an extension of what is currently practiced. Wet dung cakes are at times mixed with charcoal and dried before use. One may mix with large quantity of powdered coal instead, and make briquettes. An imported briquette making machine was installed in Gujrat, to make briquettes out of saw dust, and used in a hotel. The author had successfully used this machine to make briquettes out of coconut pith, mixing with saw dust, when the mixing became necessary because the coconut pith alone did not have enough natural *lignin* binding material. With some modification, produced in properly designed machines for mixing and briquetting machines, it should be possible to install such systems with commercial viability in rural areas.

Further, we have an estimated 275 million tons/year agricultural residue. In several cases this can be used as good feed stock for the production of bio-fuel. This is presently only a conceptual alternative, although the feasibility cannot be ruled out.

NATURAL GAS USE

Currently we are wedded to the use of chemical fertilizer. We produce about 17 million tons of chemical fertilizer, needing about 25 million m^3 per day natural gas as the feed stock. We are planning to produce 25 million (47 % more) tons of chemical fertilizer by 2010; i.e., one. year hence. Then the natural gas consumption will go up to 36.8 million m^3 per day. Our net yearly production of 30 Bn. m^3 when most is flared away. The author had surveyed and worked in Assam, when Mrigen Jalans and Col. Lahakar, MD, Assam Gas Company Ltd., provided enormous help on all aspects. Our total 'on and off' shore reserve is about 765 Bn m^3 with a life expectancy of about 20 years, or more if the suggested use of Natural gas is implemented initially, before Bio-Diesel from Micro-algae from saline pond is developed.

The Natural gas required to establish 1,50,000 MW co-generation for rural development is about 0.30 Bn m^3/ day. The flared away gas is more than twice this amount. It would be of national interest to make a logistic and cost comparison between the use of Nu-energy, capping and using the required amount of flared away Natural gas, import of this from foreign land; e.g., Iran through Pakistan. and micro algae based Bio-diesel The author desired to present this proposal in a seminar held in Kolkata (Oberoy Hotel) on 19 – 20 November, 2004,and requested DG., CSIR, for financial help to attend this International seminar. The 'all knowing non-performing adviser' most *impolitely* refused. The author spent his own money and as usual, a resolution was accepted but making no mention about the source of funding and selection of a suitable implementing agency.

Bio-gas production and distribution can be a profitable business. The technology is known. Yet to make this a success, the gas has to be de-odorized and substituted by an acceptable strong odor to detect leakage, similar to LPG gas. Since the quantity of the feed stock would be large, the system for collection, delivery, and handling the entire input and output mechanism has to be suitably devised. Bio-gas contains a large amount of moisture, and a system has to be devised to eliminate this. Meters will be required to measure the gas consumed. None of these are beyond the reach of known technology. But affordability and profitable cost are to be assessed. However, since the advantages are related to rural development, dung management needs serious attention. We have already committed a large sum, about Rs.300.00 billion ($6.0 billion) towards infrastructure build up for the production of chemical fertilizer.

If the dung mixed fertilizer is nationally acceptable, then with the saved amount suitable arrangement could be arranged through Panchayats, when the digesters will need to be widely decentralized but connected to bio-gas grid. Even then, it will be necessary not to forget the fact that all these will need substantial R&D effort, experimentation to synthesize proper fertilizer application as stated. At the domestic front the dung gas is to be fashioned to be acceptable with leak detecting strong acceptable odor.

In summary, this book is trying to simultaneously target two vitally important issues. These are rural development, and prevention of global warming, linking them through green energy development. Several possibilities have been discussed. We have just discussed about rain water harvesting. We are considering another green revolution through induction of genetically engineered seeds, and so on. But a breakthrough on soil based food products is not on the horizon as yet.

The belief summary is that if we can shed our foreign dependent culture, through appropriate research, agricultural society can pave the way leading to a reversal of the current situation not only in the agricultural society, but the entire global community.

Science is not a preserve of a community or an individual. If the high science and technology community believes that lunar sourced energy may be the savior of our planet, we must not question that. At the same time, if the enormous solar energy getting trapped relentlessly by the planet, through basic photosynthesis process needs appropriate research, through experimentation on an appropriate scale.

Recently CSIR (Council of Scientific and Industrial Research) has advertised to draw attention of those with innovative minds to provide assistance on Industry oriented research. May be NABARD will follow suit. There are several who have achieved tremendous success through innovative approaches on agriculture. It is necessary to take stock of such innovative approaches, synthesize, and formulate methods which can be circulated for others to learn and apply. How many of their successes have been *patented*? The agriculture science can find new dimension from such successes.

On 25th January, 2005, the Times of India made two conflicting reports on the same occasion, on food front. The first was the right one, reporting the President stating "The first is lifting 290 million people in the rural areas, above the poverty line by setting up 7000 PURAs and encouraging second green revolution to double farm output". The second statement, it reports, "Well, to-day we have a hugely successful space research programmes and *overflowing* granaries". (see Annexure 4) The overflow can be because of shortage of silos, or excess food grain production.

The steaming million below poverty line, the overflowing granaries, and 'food for oil' – all combined can confuse any thinking mind, searching for the truth. Are we becoming a victim of Malthusian prophecy on population growth and reduced means of subsistence? This does not appear to be true. In 1900, Calcutta had a population of only one million. Today it is 22 million, and still surviving. It does not appear that the inadequate means of subsistence is the only real cause of poverty. Scientific developments have kept pace with population growth and means of subsistence in most part of the world.

In our country, the reality is a combined effect of low purchasing power of the rural poor, and also low yield as brought out earlier. The need is to tackle both. Here the efficacy of the governance system, the social system, and the success of our science and technology development for an agricultural society come in focus. Are we on a harmonious and right track?

Our current average annual food grain production is about 200 million tones. This has remained nearly constant for the last decade. The average per capita cereal grain availability is about 0.186 t/year. The actual per capita edible cereal food will be about 0.35kg/day. By 2020, we will have a population of 1400 million; that is, needing 241 millior tons of food grain. The consumption average remaining the same, the cultivated land area of 208 million ha will be needed. This is equal to our gross sown land area. When our cultivated land mass and per capita food grain availability have remained constant as of now for the last two decades, where do we get the additional 30% cultivable land of 48 million ha from? Are we thinking about increasing the unused sown area? What about the grazing area for our large animal population?

Our current budget (2004-2005) has worked out an estimate to ensure that the situation as existed during the last two decade will not deteriorate. The budget in Para III, sub Para 35 states about *bharat nirman*. The target is to *bring an additional one crore hectares under assured irrigation in 4 years time*. Thus 10 million ha will increase the production to about 237 million tons from 200 million (yield increasing to 3.7 tons/ha; but how not mentioned). So we will stay put where we are, assuming the rain God will continue to be kind. Would it be unfair to attribute this coincidence is an arithmetical gimmick, and not an outcome of study on the feasibility of increasing irrigated land and food production?. If this does not happen, the national disaster is not an unrealistic fear. One would be tempted to suggest that even Ashok Sen is optimistic.

POSSIBLE SOLUTION.

It is seen that although we are endowed with several natural resources, we have not been able to exploit them. The fundamental reason is that we may be intelligent but not creative thinkers. Our aspirations are limited to be recognized as knowledgeable human beings, but we stop there. We do not wish to, or perhaps culturally averse to application oriented knowledge based activities.

Obviously, the three biggest challenges we are facing now are population control, increase in per capita income and food availability in rural area, and pollution control. However gloomy the picture is, there are rays of hope. These may provide ways to overcome the challenges. The short term solution may be through *increased yield from land.* Even then we will be short of food in the long run. The feasibility of solving this has been dealt while considering 'Water Management'. Soil based agriculture is rated as a short term solution. Current world population is about 6.5 billion, a third of this is poor mostly living below poverty line.

BIO-DIESEL

An inexpensive, non-polluting, conveyable, compact (high calorific value), yet flexible form of energy system is needed. To elaborate further, it has to be one which should be able to operate in a decentralized manner co-generating (heat and electricity simultaneously) units of 500 kW, or multiples, operating in parallel for operation of Industrial Units in dispersed rural areas. This is receiving attention. A detailed analysis is presented in a subsequent Para. The objective in view is what stated in the beginning of this book.

From the above table a fact which clearly emerges is that in a free sovereign State, literacy is the prime need for progress. When under foreign domination of an European country, this generalization is not valid. If one looks at South Africa (SA), one realizes the anomalous situation. Statistically SA's literacy is 86.4%, its per capita income is $13,300, yet the unemployment and below poverty line are both around 50%.

We seem to miss the boat on most occasions. Recently, a recent feature article has been published in Penguin yearbook 2008 tiled *Empower rural India through knowledge*. Would it not be more appropriate to state *literacy and knowledge*. Knowledge and literacy are not twins. One can be knowledgeable, even when illiterate. Akbar is perhaps a rare example. But for a common man, to extend knowledge literacy. is an first essential first step. Beyond a point, development is proportional to literacy based knowledge, other things being equal.

This civilizations had existed around 8000 – 6000 B.C. This appears to be the earliest well developed urban cum agriculture based civilization of mankind. There are views that because of Geographic location, this sub-continent was insulated from outside world. This is not true. Highly skilled wood craftsmen (carpenters) knew about seafarer ship building. Evidence of trade with distant lands, from a port near Mohenjo-Daro exists.

INDIA AFTER PARTITION

Napoleon once remarked that *an army marches on its stomach.* The world's second largest agriculture based army, (72% of 1100 million, i.e., 812 million) lives in rural India, and most of its members *march* relentlessly on, with their stomachs half empty, so that urban India can move ahead with full stomach. To what destination and to achieve what goal? Can one of the objectives be to create a cycle of continuously improving equal competence based per capita income blended with patriotic emotion, such that there will be no economic disparity between the urban and rural societies; and no evil designs on our nation. Or, is the aim of urban society's march mainly to acquire, ungratefully and often undeservedly, personal glory unmindful of everything else, including what the future threatens the nation?.

Competence based equal income earning capacity is the biggest equalizer, cutting across all manmade barriers, including those created by religions. Once this is achieved, other factors for the appropriate life style for all will follow. The sooner we appreciate the impact of competence based urban-rural equality on the quality of life, the better will be our prospect of avoiding catastrophic consequences by 2020, the time when we aspire to be a 'super power'; that is, in about a decade's time. There are valid reason to be apprehensive when we are moving in opposite directions. Since Independence we have managed to bring about our urban – rural disparity from 3 to 12 in 6 decades. The only improvement we can claim is the quality of printing of manifestos.

The mirage we are currently chasing will only draw us further into the desert. The results of long outstanding neglect and self-centered unwise management on major issues, among others, are viewed as the primary reasons for this subcontinent's present unacceptable situation. A glimpse of our country's rural people since Independence, 61 years ago, and their living condition are presented in Table 1. This table may be viewed as the end result of our governance for 42 years through gram panchayat, (Art.40 of our constitution was introduced in 1950) and the taking note of deteriorating situation, introducing in 1992, Chapter IX, Art. 243 (G), Out of 42 years, Nehru dynasty ruled for 37 years. (17 years by Jawahar Nehru, 15 years by Indira Gandhi, and 5 years by Rajiv Gandhi)

A quantified statement on improvements made on the above situation, in about two years by UPA government and money spent would have been more reassuring about the achievement, comparing also with that anticipated by the present government in their common minimum program (CMP) while forming the new government. We could assess then whether we are on course or not. Most in literate urban society do not bother to ponder on such issues. That the progress has been much to be desired is evident from the fact that no doctor or teacher want to go to these villages, when posted.

PREDICAMENT OF USA

The predicament of USA is easily seen. China with three times more population, a much greater GDP, equal per capita income, and with a comparable military armour will dislodge USA from its current position of No.1 nation, and occupy that seat. What then is the solution for USA? Does India feature in this? Yes, it does but not in the way it is currently moving. Our attempts for maintaining friendly relationships with the three, that is, China, USA, and Russia is a credible foreign policy, so long the Pakistan's alliance with the first two does not drop us in murky water.

The Telegraph, a daily popular newspaper of India, had published in December 2005, an article titled 'Impolite prediction' authored by our eminent economist, Ashok Mitra. He had commented on the prediction made by the Nobel Prize winner, Amartya Sen during his recent visit (2005) to the country.

Normally polite and humble, Amartya Sen did not stand on ceremony and stated *If the economic trends unfolding in the county continue in the manner they have of late, half of India would resemble California, while the other half would be reduced to sub-Sahara.* Concluding, Ashok Mitra stated that '*one is tempted to have his statements slightly amended, the India to-morrow would be only one tenth California, nine tenths would be sub-Sahara; we might then slip down to the status of being one of the poorest five among member-countries of the UN*'. Table 3 provides some indication on such a possibility.

The economic situation of the country is getting confused. It is swinging between becoming an economic giant and one of the poorest in the near future. The World Development Indicators database. World bank, 15 July, 2005 suggests the situation in 2004.(Table 2).

From the above, two facts emerge. Currently China is far ahead of us. With their current growth rate, the possibility of overtaking USA's GDP as well as equaling purchasing power parity (ppp) per capita income are distinct possibilities in another 45 years, i.e. by the year 2050. This is seen from the fact that if China's growth rate is maintained at 8 %, (India's initial projection was 7.8% in our CMP 'common minimum program') the overall growth will be ($1.08^{45} =$) 31.9 times the current GDP. With a growth rate of 4%, the USA's GDP will be a mere ($1.04^{45}=$) 5.8 times more. The GDP of China will then far exceed the USA's. It will be3.3 times more, with PPP per capita income the same as USA's. India will equal USA's GDP with our 7 % growth rate, but PPP per capita income will still be far below, (about a third) with 1.5 times more population. (But we shall live like Americans, our Finance Minister has assured the nation). To equal per capita income of USA, our growth rate should be around 11 %, that is, more than China's. The important question to ask is, can we achieve this, more so with our grossly unproductive 800 million people? Can *PURA, or PURA cluster achieve this apparently unassailable target? Motivated we can if our policy makers and countrymen adopt the six new approaches, mentioned in Annexure 1.

(*PURA stands for Providing Urban amenities in Rural Area)

The remarkable recent development of China which became a sovereign state only two years after ours creates a serious doubt on the efficacy of our governance process and the resultant future. What has caused this magnitude of difference?

Economic comparison with China, 2001

TABLE - 23

	INDIA	CHINA
Popuation (Mn)	1,055	1,288
Urban population (% of total)	28	38
GDP (US $ bn)	599	1,410
Scientist & engineer In R&D	157	584
SHARE IN GDP		
Agriculture (% GDP)	23	15
Industry (% GDP)	25	53
Manufacturing (%GDP)	16	35
Services (%GDP)	52	32
INDUSTRY		
Industry value added (% of GDP)	27	51
Value added in manufacturing	66	375
AGRICULTURE		
Rice (Mn tonnes)	117	177
Wheat (Mn tones)	72	91
Fertilizer consumption (KG)	107	256
Below poverty line (%)	36	8
Personal computer (Per 1000 people)	7	28
Adult literacy (%)	61	91
FDI inflows ($ Bn)	4	54
EXPORT ($ Bn)*	55	438
IMPORT ($ Bn)	70	413
Debt service ratio (%)	15	8
GDP Growth rate	7	8
FE Reserve ($ Bn)	68	291

*Export reflects on indigenous efforts

* Source: Statistical Outline of India 2004 – 2005

The above is a revealing fact when China has only 8 % of their population below poverty line, ours was 36 % -now about 22%,. China was born as a sovereign nation two years after our country became an Independent nation, and it was poorer. If an analysis is made on whole of the sub-continent one will find that India, Pakistan, Bangladesh, and Myanmar sail economically in the same boat, where divide between the rich and the poor is the highest. The birth rates are highest compared (with a few exception) to other nations when the rates in most are below 1.0.

The loud noises which various International assessing institutions are making about are obviously wrong. They prove what the two eminent economists had expressed. Yet, soon after, The Times of India, published a contradictory news originating from London. The first Para of the News item states, "Indians are currently the most positive people to be found anywhere in the world when it comes to national economic conditions, a new global survey has found." If so why what stated in the Paras above and Tables 1, 2, & 3?

Equally heartening but puzzling is the long term projections of global consulting services. On 15. 03. 2006. PWC (Price Waterhouse Coopers) projects that by 2050, as quoted by Prabhakar Sunhat, TNN, 'India will be the second largest economy *along* with USA.'. No justification has been provided, nor any mention has been made about the first position. By implication one may conclude that the suggestion is that China will be in the leading position.

INDIA, USA Vs CHINA

USA's main anxiety, some believe, is to contain China. (This is a debatable but a commonly believed socio-political view). India features in the game plan of USA. But unfortunately not an India with its own mind, when it must be one when the key for its survival will not be in the hands of USA. Has it ever talked about rural poor and it's development? A developed rural society does not fit in the game plan of either the USA, or our own mindless feudal hypocritical society.

USA controlling a populous society, like ours, can be a counterpoise to China's progress. The confusing eagerness of USA trying to come in the way of gas pipe line between Iran, Pakistan and India, and also Russia supplying us Nuclear material may perhaps be better understood looking at the China-USA canvass. One may understand why USA is suddenly getting over interested in supplying Nuclear reactors, ignoring it's earlier opposition for the country's effort in this direction, in 1974. Clearly USA is in a dilemma. It expresses its unhappiness to the extent of reducing Pakistan to 'stone age', and within three days reversed its support for Pakistan, selling (supplying) F18, improved F16 front line fighter aircraft. The other hands extends friendship towards us selling Nuclear reactors.

We are no less confused, when having established new friendship with China,. our recently failed effort on 'long range' Agni III, much less than China's, is designed to develop capability to destroy all strategically important cities of China! Is this an innovative way to prove our friendly gesture, or our equal technology competence, to establish a new doctrine that 'strength respects strength, when friendship last longer if equally strong'?. China has already developed capability to reduce USA and us to dust.

All are nuclear weapon carriers. A quadrilateral game of diplomacy, including Pakistan is going on. Does rural poverty play any part in this game? Should we get into this political game plan when rural people are committing suicide because of poverty?. Shouldn't our priority concentrate on that issue? Or, develop state of art armory at enormous cost?

EFFORTS TO GET ART 243(G) DISCUSSED IN PARLIAMENT

Having failed to get any response, attempts were made get help from Sreemati Sonia Gandhi on two occasions; first when she was the Leader of Opposition, and there after she became the President of AICC (All India Congress Committee.

1

SONIA GANDHI
LEADER OF OPPOSITION
(LOK SABHA)

14, PARLIAMENT HOUSE
NEW DELHI - 110 001
PHONE : 23018705, 23034285
FAX : 23017470

April 9, 2003

Dear Air Vice Marshal Roy Chaudhury,

I have received your letter of 3rd April and taken note of your suggestions regarding a strategy for rural development. Thank you for sharing your views.

With good wishes.

Yours sincerely,

2

Phones : 37 30

ALL INDIA CONGRESS COMMITTEE
24, AKBAR ROAD, NEW DELHI - 110 011

Sonia Gandhi
President

June 21, 2004

Dear AVM Roy Choudhury,

I have received your letter of 17th June 2004 and noted your suggestions and your request.

With good wishes,

Yours sincerely,

Air Vice-Marshal Roy Choudhury (Retd.)
Total Energy Systems
618, Nav Uday, 80ft Road

Replies from Smt. Sonia Gandhi on author's appeal to her for discussion in Parliament about rural development

The response to 9th April, 2003 was positive and helpful. She handed over responsibility to a responsible MP. Discussed on phone when I gathered that the issue had to be discussed first at the Parliamentary. So he addressed a letter to the Chairman of the Parliamentary Committee on urban and rural development.

SHAMSHER SINGH DULLO
Member of Parliament
(Lok Sabha)
Ropar (Punjab)

24, Dr. Rajender Prasad Road,
New Delhi.
Tel.: (011) 3782935
Samrala Road, Khanna,
Distt. Ludhiana (Punjab)
Tel.: (01628) 28711, 27701

Dear Shri Chanderkant Khaire,

June 3, 2003

I have received the copy of the correspondence between Smt. Sonia Gandhi, LOP(LS) and Air Vice Marshal S.N.Roy Chaudhury regarding suggestions for a strategy on Rural Development.

From the letter of AVM S.N.Roy Chaudhury to Smt. Sonia Gandhi I noted that he has been working on Rural Development - Strategy & Implementation since 1982. Two diagrams attached with his letter provide very vital statistics of total energy systems in respect of urban and rural population and its growth rate etc.

AVM Chaudhury has stated in his letter that he was the only Indian Companion (Honorary, Fellow of Institute of Energy, U.K. He is currently working on 'Green' energy, which is enormously compatible with Rural Development.

AVM Chaudhury is the recipient of OM PARKASH BHASIN award in the very first batch when other recipients were Prof. M.G.K.Menon; Dr. Raja Rammana; Dr. Bhipin Pal and others.

I am forwarding herewith the entire set of correspondence with my recommendation to invite Air Vice Marshal S.N.Roy Chaudhury to make his formal presentation before a Committee on Urban and Rural Development which will enable the Committee to make a note of some useful suggestion for a strtegy on Rural Development.

With kind regards,

Yours sincerely,

(SHAMSHER SINGH DULLO)

Shri Chanderkant B. Khaire,
Chairman,
Parliamentary Committee on Urban and Rural Development,
Parliament House Annexe,
New Delhi.

Copy forwarded for necessary action:-

Encl. as above.

1. Shri Pulok Chatterji, PS/JS to LOP(LS) wrt his letter dt. April 29, 2003.
2. AVM S.N.Roy Chaudhury, Total Energy System, 618, Nav Udaj 80ft Road 4th Block, Koramangala, Bangalore-560034.

Followup action by Shamsher Singh to Chairman, Parliamentary Commission

Shri Chandrakant B. Khaire expressed his appreciation and invited the author to meet him at his residence at 8:30 at night. Reaching his house, five minutes ahead of time for appointment, (a customary unwritten rule followed.), well received by his staff in a visitor's room. Informed that he should be on his way. Gratefully received a cup of undrinkable tea, with milk and sugar. However, Shri Khare had apparently lost his way, because he did not surface till eleven. There was no call either. The staff felt that the author should try next morning at 10:30 a.m. Informing that at that time the author would be in air half way to Bangalore, hence not feasible. Leaving with a request to inform about my arrival and departure, the author left burning nearly Rs. 20,000.

From Bangalore, when asked when next I should come, I was told, it would not be necessary.

Informed Shri Shamsher Dullo, and Sreemati Gandhi. but her staff informed that no letter had been received. The courier service investigated and produced document confirming delivery..So the author decided to address a letter to Hon'ble Ministry of Parliamentary affairs when he through media assured that the Parliament was prepared to discuss any issue. He was kind enough to reply as under;

Govt. of India
Shastri Bhawan, New Delhi-110

Ref. No 134/HM?/2005 19-12-2005

Dear Shri Roy Chaudhury,

I thank you for your letter dated 28.11.2005, regarding discussion on rural development in the Parliament. I shall try to act in this regard, on such a vitally important subject.

With best wishes,

Yours sincerely,

(P.R. DASMUNSI)

Shri S.N. Roy Chaudhury,
Total Energy Systems,
618, Nav Uday,
80 Ft. Road, 4th Block,
Koramangala

Letter from Minister of Parliamentary affairs assuring discussion in Parliament

That nothing would happen was clear to the author, when the reply had introduced the escape phrase *'shall try to act'* which was not the impressi>n one received with his earlier positive statement on TV.

MINISTRY OF PARLIAMENTARY AFFAIRS
(LEG.-I SECTION)

Sub: Discussion on Rural Development in Parliament.

Ministry of Rural Development may please find enclosed a letter dated 15.12.2005 in original on the above subject from Air Vice-Marshal S. N. Roy Chaudhury (Retd.), addressed to Hon'ble Minister of Parliamentary Affairs, for appropriate action, as the subject matter pertains to them.

Sd/-
(K.K. Thakur)
Deputy Secretary(L)
Tele No. 23034844

Ministry of Rural Development, Department of Rural Development (Attn. Smt. Smita Chug, Joint Secretary), 199-H, Krishi Bhawan, N. Delhi.
M.P.A. U.O. No. 63(1)/2006-Leg.I Dated 23.01.2006

Copy for information to:-

Air Vice-Marshal S. N. Roy Chaudhury (Retd.),
618, Nav Uday,
80 Ft. Road, 4th Block,
Koramangala,
Bangalore 560034

(K.K. Thakur)
Deputy Secretary (L)

Followup action from Ministry of Parliamentary Affairs to Department of Rural Development

No action was initiated.

We keep on bureaucratic set ups. We began with a department of agricultural ministry, formed a separate ministry, and now a new ministry of '*Panchayat Raj*', with an inaugural function attended by all chief ministers, making 150 recommendations. They are mostly inoperative because of non availability of appropriate energy. A letter was addressed to the Minister, but no reply was received inspite of three requests. The letter was on his table, his secretary confirmed.

A NEW BEGINING

The Author decided at that point to stop his efforts on Rural Development since 1984. He decided to carry out R & D on some items which could have applications on large scale, and could be taken up in by cottage industries of developed rural societies. Innovative approach was the basic theme.

Focused on Natural gas use, began activities on gas stoves, gas flow meters, and gas burners as used in tea processing industries.. For such work, he got an invitation from Jalans who came to Bangalore to discuss. Invited, the author had visited both Jalans, and Assam Gas Company Ltd, (AGCL) Duliajan, Assam. Received good receptions from both. Jalans desired development of burners for tea drying. AGCL desired development of gas flow meters and gas stoves for domestic use..

All three activities adopted innovative approaches Brief description on these are provided in what follows;

1. The approach was to replace many small holes, with one annular orifice. The burner received ISI certification, in one attempt. Handed over the manufacturing right to a well established manufacturer. of various kinds of gas burners;
2. The burner of tea leaf drier adopted the principle of that adopted gas turbine engine burner . It proved to be more efficient than a can burner used. This work was supported by Jalans. The Tea Board at Calcutta preferred to continue the licensed manufacture of a foreign can type, even though it was proved to the Board in a meeting that developed burner was more efficient.
3. The activity on a small turbine type was finance by Department of Science and Technology Research (DSIR),DST, - a CSIR controlled unit. This was patented.

CHAPTER - 17

AWARD

At that stage, 10 well recognized scientists became *the very first J. Om Prakash Basin, 1985*, awardees shown below. The awards were given away by our the then prime minister, Hon'ble Rajiv Gandhi.

The very first J. Om Prakash Basin, 1985, awardees. Author second from right

The author is seen second from the right. Professors MGK Menon is seen at the extreme left. Dr. Satish Dawan is next to him. The lady in between the tallest prime minister and the author is Mrs. Bhasin, wife of the benevolent industrialist whose desire was to promote S & T. Mrs. Bhasin spoke very clearly about the desire of Mr. Bhasin. He had noble desires for the country's development. The citation for the author was read by Dr. Arunachalam, then the Scientific Adviser to the Defence Minister. It was in two parts. First part mentioned about the efforts on aeronautical activities, when the second part dealt with rural development. Simultaneously the 'crab' society's members became very active. These included two ladies. As an invited guest, the author was asked by one, how did he manipulate this honour? in the midst of other crab guests. On the other hand, received a very complementary letter from retired CAS I. H. Latif, then our Ambassador in France.

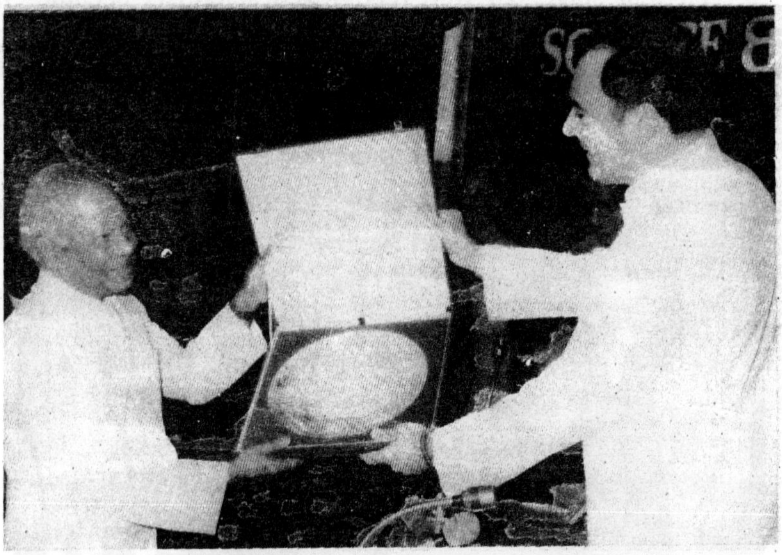

Author receiving award from Honourable Prime Minister in 1994 for Technical Development

CHAPTER 18

FLUID FLOW MEASUREMENT

NEGLECT TO INNOVATIVE REMUNERATIVE ACTIVITY EASIBLE IN ENERGIZED RURAL AREAS.

Turbine type gas flow measuring technology:

A government Order No. III 4(i)/ 97-ET dated 13.1.1998 to provide Financial assistance to develop small turbine type gas flow meter was issued.

Author in his Laboratory, built in his garage, for development of type gas flow meter.

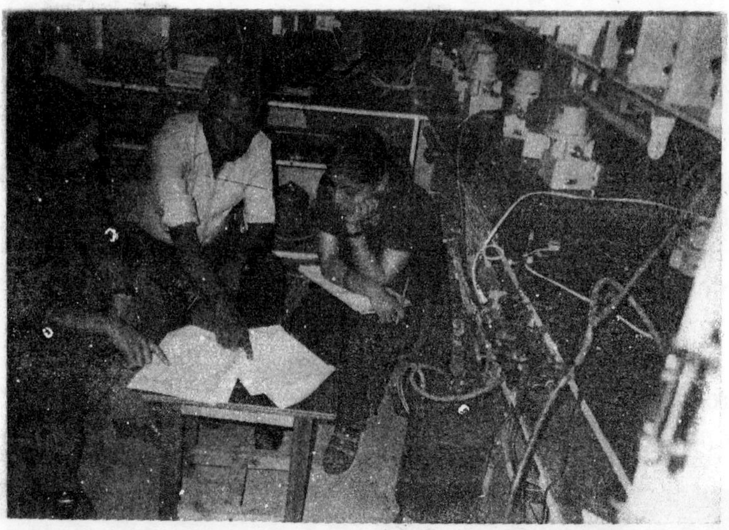

Author analyzing test results

This effort also met unfortunate end, because it was innovative and the accredited testing agency was ignorant about fluid flow behavior of the innovative concept.

CALIBRATION SET UP

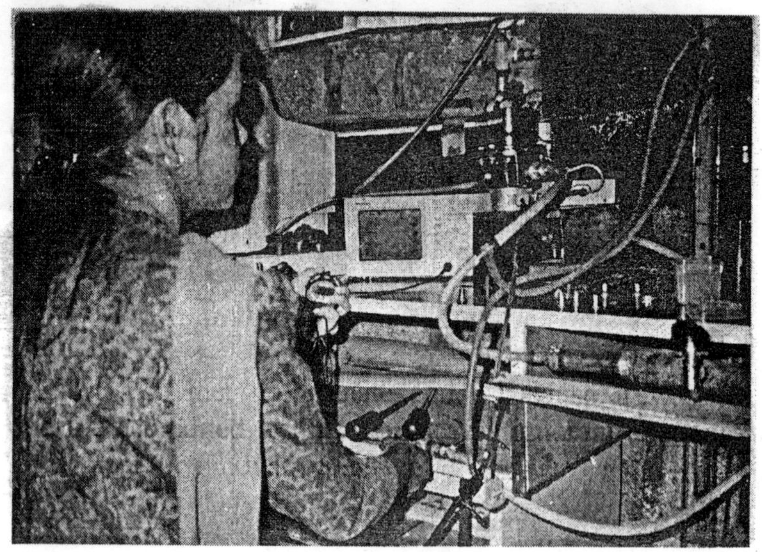

Electronic calibration of the flow meter

50 assembled and tested meters

भारतीय मानक ब्यूरो
BUREAU OF INDIAN STANDARDS

मानक भवन, 9 बहादुरशाह ज़फर मार्ग, नई दिल्ली 110002
Manak Bhavan, 9 Bahadur Shah Zafar Marg, New Delhi

दूरभाष / Phones: 3230131, 3233375, 3239402 | टेलेक्स / Telex: C31-65870 | फैक्स / Fax: +91 11 3234062, +91 11 3239399 | तार / Grams: मानकसंस्था / Manaks

1996-05-14/23.

Our Ref:LM 06/T-36
Subject:Rotary piston and Turbine Gas Meters,
Doc:LM 06(0278)

Dear Shri Roy Choudhary,

We acknowledge the receipt of your letters dated 1996-03-20 and 1996-4-30 and would like to inform you the following in connection with the standardization of Rotary piston and Turbine Gas Meters, Doc:LM 06(0278).

At the last meeting of Commercial Weights and Measures Sectional Committee, LM 06 held on 15 Feb 1996 at New Delhi, the proposal/comments sent by you vide your letter dated 1994-04-04 were placed before the meeting, which was also attended by you in person, for discussion and examination.

The committee examined the proposal/comments and after thorough deliberation decided the following:

a) For Turbine Type Gas Meters, one more set of range having values of Qmax = 1.25 m^3/h and Qmin = 0.125m^3/h in the working range of 1:10 may be included for time being for use in India, even though this range is not covered in OIML recommendation.

b) Data as per the suggestion of M/s Total Energy System, Bangalore, may be included. It was also decided that the inclusion of this range will be suitably taken up at the next OIML meeting so that developments in India also find place in International Recommendations.

c) In view of inclusion of new range as decided above the committee agreed to include the maximum permissible error as given below, applicable only for range Qmax 1.25 m^3/h and Qmin 0.125m^3/h with working range 1:10.

Flow rate	Max. Permissible error on initial verification	In service
Q min ≤ 0.1 Q max ≤ Qt	± 4%	- 6%, +3%
Qt ≤ Q ≤ max	± 2%	± 2%

Where Qt = 0.2 Qmax.

Please note that the Doc:LM 06(0278) will be suitably modified incorporating the above data, for time being, before sending for final printing.

With regards,

Yours sincerely,
(N.K. Sharma)

Shri S.N. Roy Chaudhury
Air Vice-Marshal (Retd)
M/s Total Energy Systems

Certification norm for calibration of flow meter

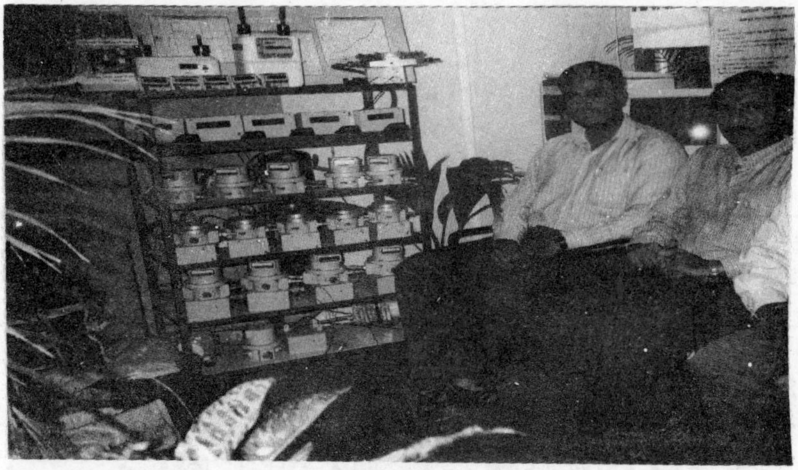

The display at Science Congress of 1954

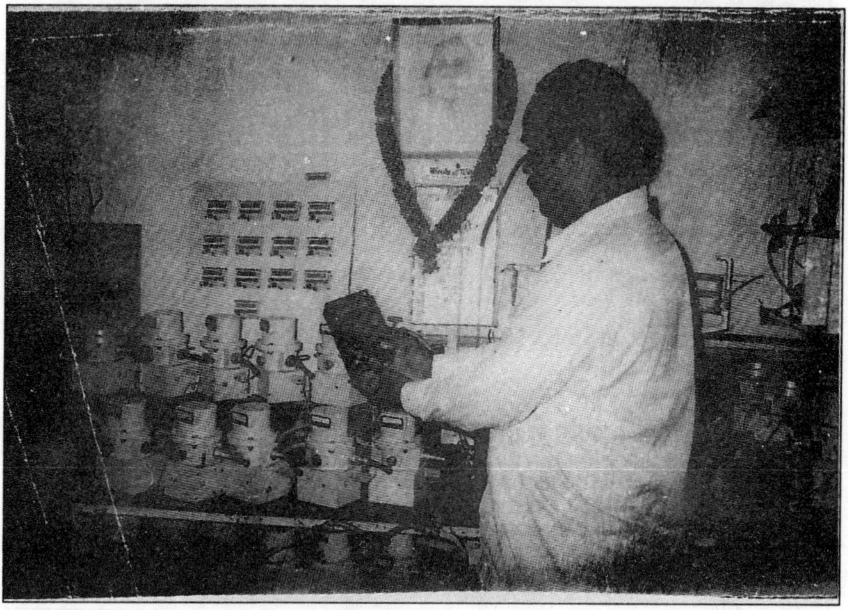

Distance reading

Calibration graph flow vs. √ p

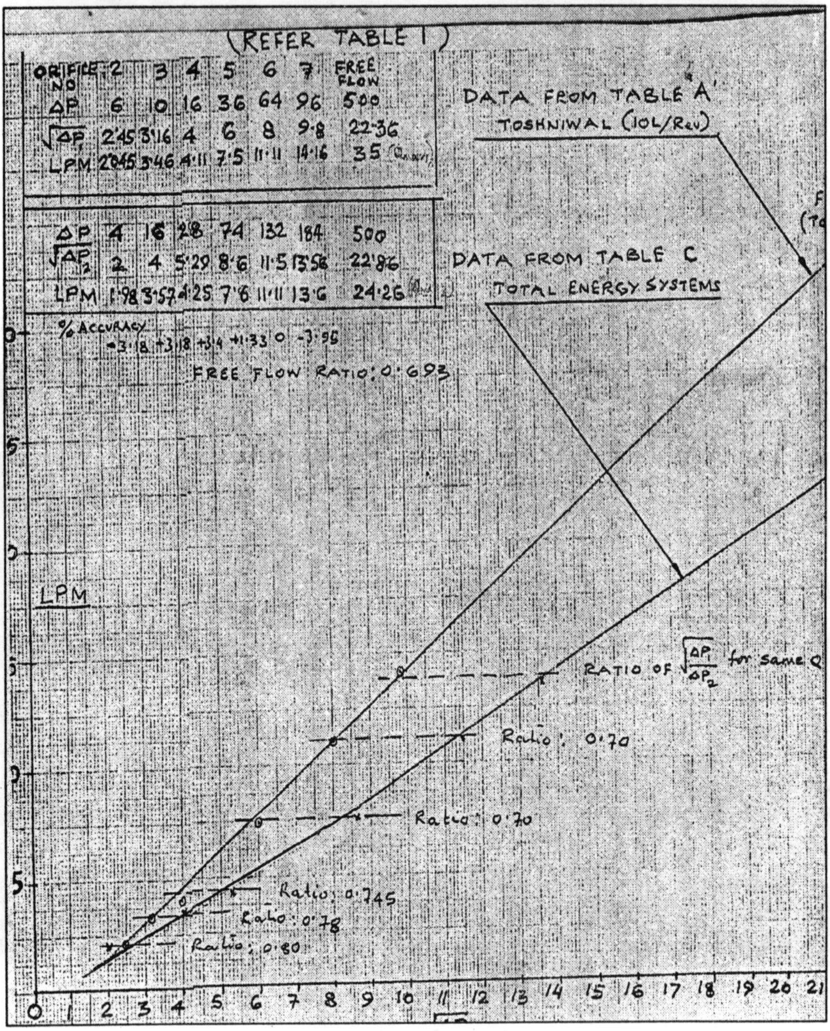

Comparative test result using different capacity reference meters

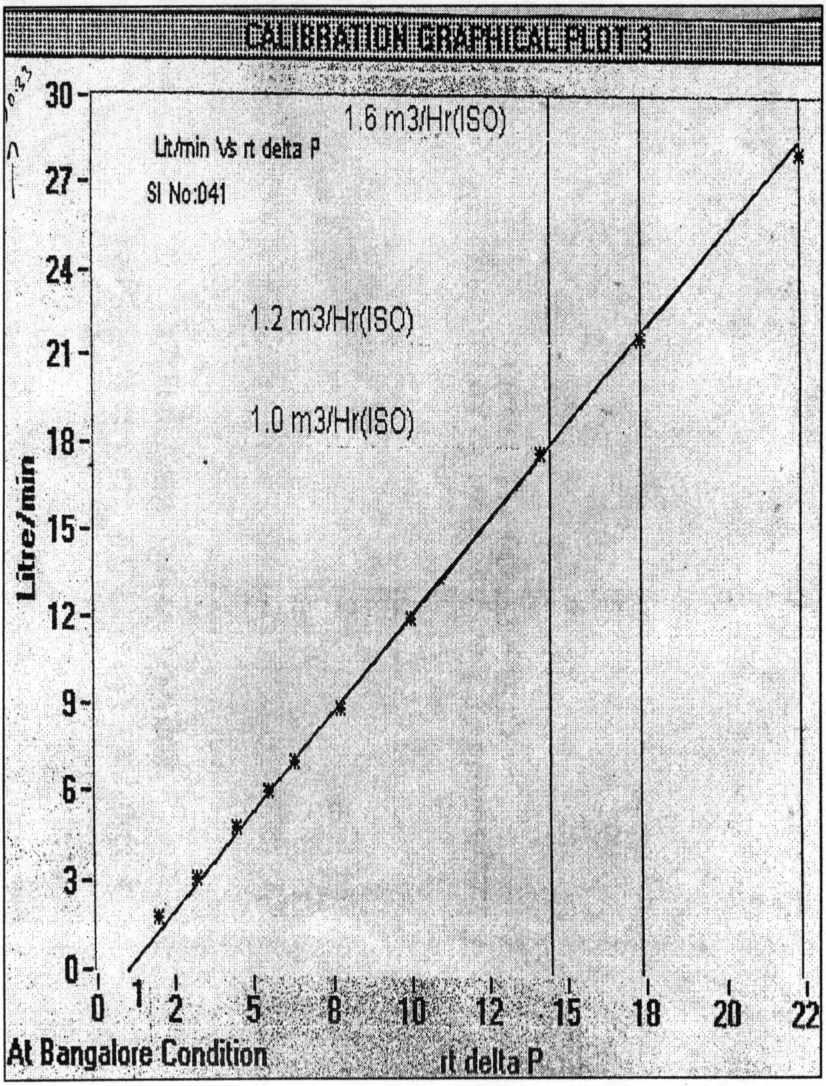

Linearity test

DATE: 19.3.94

CALIBRATION OF TES TURBINE TYPE

DOMESTIC FLOWMETER No. 0005
(BASED ON OBSERVED VALUES ONLY)

1. CALIBRATION OF 1 LIT CAPACITY SMALL TOSHNIWAL FLOWMETER, (TW(s))

1.1. ERROR MEASURED: NEGLIGIBLE

2. FLOW MEASUREMENT USING SEVEN ORIFICE CALIBRATION ROD FOR CALIBRATION OF 10 LIT CAPACITY TOSHNIWAL FLOWMETER, TW(B).

2.1. ENTRY PRESSURE, MAX. PERMISSIBLE FOR 1 LIT CAPACITY: 300 mm of w/c & 3 REV/MIN.

2.2. CALIBRATION ROD STN. NOS.

	1	2	3
TIME/10l, TW(s) Sec	570.85	385.53	224.94
TIME/10l, TW(B) Sec	565.19	383.43	225.19
* ERROR %, TW(B) time basis	(+)0.99	(+)0.54	(+)0.11

ERROR % * = (TW(B) − TW(S)) / TW(S) × 100

3. FLOWMEASUREMENTS WITH TW(B) WITH CALIBRATION ROD & TES(M) FLOWMETER AT 500 mm ENTRY PRESSURE

RANGE: $Q_{min} < 0.1 Q_{max}$, 10:1

STATION NOS.		1	2	3	4	5	6	7	FREE FLOW Q_{max}
AVG ENTRY MANOMETER 498 mm	TIME/10L TW(B) Sec	442.22	297.92	176.84	142.53	80.51	54.03	49.63	
		1.35	2.2	3.77	4.2	7.45	11.1	12.9	
	$Q_{m^3/h}$	0.0814	0.1208	0.2036	0.2526	0.4471	0.6663	0.7254	
500 mm	TIME/10L TES(M) Sec	504.99	288.47	174.74	139.35	79.24	54.21	50.64	26
	$Q_{m^3/h}$	0.0713	0.1248	0.2060	0.2583	0.4543	0.6641	0.711	1.385
		1.18	2.08	3.43	4.13	7.57	11.07	11.8	23
* % ERROR, Q BASIS		−12.41	+7.31	+1.18	+2.56	+1.61	−0.33	−1.99	
		610	1068	1762	2209	3890	5688		

* ERROR = (TES(M) − TW(B)) / TW(B)

TEST JOINTLY CONDUCTED BY
1. FLUID CONTROL RESEARCH INST — SSE (R. MASCOLMANI)
2. TOTAL ENERGY SYSTEMS

WITNESSED BY
1) (K. ANKAIAH) Scientist 'F' GTRE, Bangalore DRDO.
2) VINCENT LOBO

Test conducted by FCRI (Fluid Control Research Institute) and three others Typed version for improved quality is placed below

CALIBRATION OF TES TURBINE TYPEDOMESTIC FLOW METER NO. 0005 BASED ON OBSERVED VALUES FOLLOWED BY *FAULTY* MATHEMATICAL ANALYSIS BY A NOMINATD INSTITUTION FOR CERTIFICATION. .

1. CALIBRATION OF 1 LIT CAPACITY SMALL TOSHNINAL FLOWMETER (TW(S))
   1.1. ERROR MEASURE : NEGLIGIBLE

2. FLOW MEASUREMENT USING SEVEN ORIFICE CALIBRATION ROD FOR CALIBRATION OF 10 LIT CAPACITY TOSHNINAL FLOWMETER, TW(B)

2.1 ENTRY PRESSURE, MAX. PERMISSIBLE FOR 1 LIT CAPACITY & 3 REV/MIN: 300 mm OF W/C

2.2 CALIBRATION ROD STN. NOS

	1	2	3
TIME/10 l , TW (S) sec	570.85	385.53	224.94
TIME/10 l , TW (B) sec	565.19	383.43	225.19
* ERROR % TW (S) ref TIME BASIS	(-)0.99	(-)0.54	(+) 0.11

ERROR %

$$= \frac{TW(B) - TW(S)}{TW(S)} \times 100$$

3. FLOW MEASUREMENTS WITH TW(B) & TES(M) FLOWMETER AT 500 mm ENTRY

PRESSURE

$Q_{MIN} < 0.1\ Q_{MAX}$ ← 10:1 RANGE →

AVG ENTRY MANOMETER	CALIBRATION ROD STATION NOS	1	2	3	4	5	6	7	FREE FLOW Q_{MAX}
498 mm	TIME/10 l , TW (B) sec	442.22	297.92	176.84	142.53	80.51	54.03	49.63	
	Q m^3/n	0.0814	0.1208	0.2036	0.2526	0.4471	0.6663	0.7254	
500 mm	TIME/10 l , TES (M) sec	504.99	288.47	174.74	139.35	79.24	54.21	50.64	26
	Q m^3/n	0.0713	0.1248	0.2060	0.2583	0.4543	0.6641	0.711	1.385
	* % ERROR Q BASIS	-12.41	+3.31	+1.18	+2.26	+1.61	-0.33	-1.99	

TEST JOINTLY CONDUCTED BY:

1. FLUID CONTROL RESEARCH INSTITUTE - R. MASCOMANI
2. TOTAL ENERGY SYSTEMS - Roy Chaudhury

WITNESSED BY:

1. K. ANKAYAN, Scientist 'F', GTRE, DRDO, Bangalore.
2. VINCENT LOBO.- A Watch making Technician

*ERROR %

$$= \frac{TES(M) - TW(B)}{TW(B)} \times 10$$

Dr. G.B.R. Fielen, FRS checking out the meters in a kitchen.

This is another 'Indian crab' culture. Is there one flowmeter developed anywhere similar to one described earlier? Yet recently, invited to New Delhi, interviewed at India International Center (IIC), pictures were taken for viewing by Hindi edition of Doordarshan (DD) for public consumption, as an innovative effort, selected as one among the 10 innovations. But nothing happened thereafter. We continue buying foreign meters.

Dr. G.B.R. Fielen, FRS checking out the meters in a kitchen.

The summary situation is as under:

1 Fielden Associates of UK and British Gas had indicated that such small meters for multi fuel use as was developed for low flow at small pressure might not have been made by any till then in 1989. Current status is not known. A novel approach (E6) working on Doppler effect, needing no moving part, was made in the UK, but it could not operate on LPG gas.
2 It was patented by our Indian patent office.
3 It met our Indian standard specifications.
4 The meter developed was a direct reading mechanical type placed at a height, and extended to electronic LED or LCD reading version placed by the side of electric meter.

5. Further converted into a distant reading type and auto billing facility.

CONCLUSION

The text of this book attempts to draw a canvas of this subcontinent, where perhaps the first civilized human race had originated based on Vedic religion. It is commonly known as Indus Valley civilization. The origin is discovery of 'Flint' from a special rock formation, to light up fire at will, and thus the cavemen came out in the open, free from fear of the wild animals, snakes, scorpions, et al, and observing natural phenomena with inquisitive minds of many sages, derived a non-prophetic religious culture. Simultaneously, a civilized organized way of living developed. (8000 BC till 2000 BC with an un-accounted for period of 4000 years).

The first change came about with nomadic Aryan invasion, but they were not exploitive and got mixed with local inhabitants, to bring about a non-ethnic race. They were appreciative of local civilized way of life, encouraged learned who wrote epics, but did harm creating princely states. The origin of our rich and poor can be attributed to this. So we had three classes, viz, rich princes, poor peasants and a respected learned community.

Two social perversions germinated thereafter namely, the feudal lords oppressing the, poor, and Brahamanic sect, creating a degrading caste system, giving birth to an untouchable poor 'shudra' class.

Invaders came, set up dynastic rules, making the country a slave and weak nation, getting assistance from these two classes of people. The nation was never one, with such a strain, creating rich living in urban societies, and the poor living in rural areas.

The degradation began since 1500 BC and this continues with amalgamation of industrial revolution. It is heading for another phase of slavery, but can be prevented if only the distortions towards rural development are rectified making use of our natural resources in a planned manner.

***FINALLY A REQUEST HAD BEEN MADE TO THE APEX BODY TO ORGANIZE A JOINT PARLIAMENTARY SESSION TO WORK OUT IN QUANTIFIED TERMS A COMMON NATIONAL STRATEGY FOR RURAL AND HENCE COUNTRY'S DEVELOPMENT. THIS REQUEST WAS PASSED ON THE MINISTRY OF RURAL DEVELOPMENT. THIS REQUEST WAS MADE TO GET A LEGAL DIRECTIVE FOR OUR UNDEVELOPED RURAL POOR FROM OUR HIGHEST JUDICIARY FORUM.**

AN ALTERNATE REQUEST HAS BEEN MADE FOR A GRANT OF Rs. 5.0 LAKHS ONLY (BUDGETARY ALLOCATION FOR 10th PLAN PERIOD FOR RURAL AND AGRICULTURAL DEVELOPMENT IS Rs. 76,774 Cr) TO OBTAIN A VIEW FROM 1000 KNOWLEDGEABLE INSTITUTIONS AND PEOPLE, WHEN PARLIAMENTARIANS HAVE NEVER TAKEN ANY INTEREST ON THIS ISSUE, ALTHOUGH ELECTED BY THESE PEOPLE. A POSITIVE DECISION IS AWAITED. IT IS FOR THE PEOPLE OF THE COUNTRY TO DEMAND ONE OF THE TWO ALTERNATIVES.

***Professor U.R. Rao's 'foreword' was written before this development.**

ANNEXURE 1: THE GOAL OF NEW INDIA

SIX NEW DIMENSIONS

1.1. **Unite the nation with universal acceptance of one God and humanism;** religions as personal faith to reach onto Him. One law for all, when religion will have on part to play in the governance.

1.2. ***Bio-energy development to meet our energy deficiency and to suppress green house effect.***

1.3. **Easily accessible Sweet*** (not saline and polluted) potable water, and making it suitable for plant growth; (*Sweet water is the other name of 'fresh water')

1.4. **Irrigated soil and non-soil cultivation** with controlled water borne appropriate Nutrients in inert material;

1.5. **Legally enforced education up to school leaving stage** to be eligible to find a place in the voter's list. Growth of educated population with no gender difference and equal competent based employment opportunities

1.6 **Value addition plans to agro and non-agro products**, and activities with prospects towards increase of GDP. Providing incentive towards innovative minds, and encouragement to creative work are essential functions of Government's Science management Institutions. The emphasis should be to make improved demonstrative models to excel the currently used ones produced by foreign countries. The Government Institutions should also be in search for venues who are likely to be interested to absorb such products for sales. They should be selling/promotional agents rather than science monitoring authorities. Most of the visits from Delhi based institutions serve little purpose in the way they perform now. Like private organizations, the Delhi based organizations should function to justify their credibility through sale, after certification and patenting actions.

ANNEXURE 2 : INNOVATIONS LEADING TO PRESENT WORLD

Discoveries

Discovery	Discoverer	Year	Nationality
Floating Principles	Archimedes	240 B.C	Greece
Printing Press	Johann Gutenberg	1455	Germany
Sun as center of Solar System	Copernicus	1543	Poland
Microscope	Z. Janscen	1590	Netherlands
Law of Falling Bodies	Galileo	1590	Italy
Thermometer	Galileo Galilei	1593	Italy
Laws of Planetary Motion	Johannes Kepler	1609-19	Germany
Air Pressure	E.Torricelli	1643	Italy
Telescrope	Hans Lippershey	1608	Netherlands
Laws of Gravitation & Motion	Issaac Newton	1687	England
Side Rule	William Oughtred	1621	Britain
Nickel	Axel Cronstedt	1751	Sweden
Hydrogen	Henry Cavendish	1766	England
Steam Engine (condenser)	James Watt	1765	Britain
Nitrogen	Daniel Rutherford	1772	England
Ship (Steam)	J.C. Percier	1775	Britain
Oxygen	Joseph Priestly & C.W. Scheele	1772	England, Sweden
Submarine	David Bushnell	1776	U.S.A
Chlorine	C.W.Scheefe	1774	Sweden
Parachute	J.P.F. Blanchard	1785	France
Uranus (Planet)	William Herschet	1781	England
Pencil	Jacques- Nicolas Conte	1792	France
Uranium	Martin Klaproth	1789	Germany
Telegraph	M.Lammond	1787	France
Chromium	Louis Vauquelin	1798	Sweden
Atomic Structure of Matter	John Dalton	1803	England
Typerwriter	Pellegrine Tarrie	1808	Italy
Magnesium	Sir. Humphry Davy	1808	England
Photoelectric Cell	Jalius Elster, Hans. F. Geitel	1893	Germany

Safety Pin	Watter Hunt	1849	U.S.A
Refrigerator	James Harrison & A. Catlin	1850	England
Aluminum	Hand Christain Oerstedt	1827	Denmark
Steel Production	Henry Bessemer	1855	Britain
Electromagnetic Induction	Michael Faraday	1831	England
Transformer	Michael Faraday	1831	Britain
Law of Electric Conduction	Georg Ohm	1827	Germany
Telegraph Code	Samuel F.B.Morse	1837	U.S.A
Silicon	Jons Berzelius	1824	Sweden
Telephone (perfected)	Alexander Graham Bell	1876	U.S.A
Ozone	Christian Schonbein	1839	Germany
Motor Cycle	G. Dairnel	1885	Germany
Ship (turbine)	Hon. Sir C. Parsons	1894	Britain
Wireless (Telegraphy)	G. Marconi	1896	Italy
Radium	Pierre & Marie Curie	1898	France
Speed of Light	Albert Michelson	1887	U.S.A
Rayon	Sir Joseph Swan	1883	Britain
Special Theory of Relativity	Albert Einstein	1905	Switzerland
Steel (Stainless)	Harry Brearley	1913	Britain
Super Conductors	H.Kammerlingh Onnes	1911	Netherland
Optical Fibre	Narinder Kapany	1955	Germany
Photoelectric Effect	A. Einstein	1905	Germany
Nylon	Dr. Wallace H. Carothers	1937	U.S.A
Continental Drift Theory	Alfred Wegener	1912	Germany
Micro- Processor	Robert Noyce & Gordon Moore	1971	U.S.A
Proton	E.Ruhtherford	1919	New Zealand
Radar	A.H. Taylor & Leco C. Young	1922	U.S.A
Television (Electronic)	P.T. Farmsworth	1927	U.S.A
Atomic Nucleus	E. Rutherford	1911	New Zealand
Tank	Sir Emest Swinton	1941	Britain
Transistor	Bardeen, Shockely & Brattain	1948	U.S.A

Atomic Number	Henry Moseley	1913	England
Atomic Structure	Neil Bohr	1913	Denmark
Electromagnetism	Hand Christian Oersted	1920	Denmark
General Theory of Relativity	Albert Einstein	1915	Switzerland
Pluto (Planet)	Clyde Tpmbaugh	1930	U.S.A
Plutonium	G.T. Seaborg	1940	U.S.A
Aero plane	& Wilbur Wright	1903	U.S.A
Electric Washing Machine	Alva J. Fisher	1906	U.S.A
Automatic Rifle	John Borwning	1918	U.S.A
Film (Musical Sound)	Dr. Le de Forest	1923	U.S.A
Helicopter	Etienne Oehmichen	1924	France
Bakelite	Leo H. Baekeland	1907	Beigiums
Ballistic Missie	Wernher Von Braun	1944	Germany
Artificial Heart	Williem Kolff	1957	Netherlands
Compact Disc Player	Sony, Philips Co.	1979	Japan, Netherlands
Hydrogen Bomb	Edward Teller	1952	U.S.A
Atomic Bomb	J.R. Oppenheimer	1945	U.S.A
Jet Engine	Sir Frank Whittle	1937	Britain

ANNEXURE 3: GTRE SEMINAR PROGRAMME (1979)

CONTENTS

INAUGURAL SESSION

GENERAL SESSION

GENERAL SESSION (Contd.)

The seminars held on alternate years provide an indication that the Establishment had acquired a respectable status on Gas Turbine Technology beginning from scratch with a dozen of technicians who had not even heard of a such an engine, in about 20 years. Most were not even Matriculates. The participating members were from most elite Institutions, from our country, as well as from abroad. They were from

Indian Institute of Science (IISc); National Aeronautical Laboratory (NAL); Hindustan Aeronautics Ltd.; Bharat Heavy Electrical Ltd. Indian Institutes of Technology (IIT's), from Madras, Delhi, Kanpur, Karagpur, Renowned Colleges from Roorke, Birla Institute of Technology; Amravati, Maharastra; DRDO Establishments, e.g., DMRL, ADE, GTRE, AND from foreign countries senior representatives of Rolls Royce; SNEMA; Dowty; Lucus and several others. They all presented high quality research papers, when they were discussed and zealously debated about, in a humble large hanger. The attendance for "house full' for two and half days. They all came and made their own arrangements, with no financial support from GTRE.

The subjects discussed in 9 sessions, as under;

1. **Fluid Mechanics in Turbo-machinery;**

2. **Propulsions;**

3. **Combustion;**

4. **Performance and simulation;**

5. **Materials and special fabrication technology;**

6. **Heat transfer;**

7. **Control mechanism**

8. **Small gas turbines and application;**

9. **Measurement technology and data processing**

Compendium of these learned discourse were prepared and widely circulated. They were in demand even from foreign countries. Such seminars are not held in GTRE They were most memorable events, when the preparations for the next started soon after.

ANNEXURE 4: PURA SUCCESS ANNOUNCEMENT

Presidential Presentation:

The Prez then settled down for a chat, "I want to talk about an important subject for 15 minutes. Then we'll have a free-wheeling discussion about anything you like," he promised. And launched into a PowerPoint presentation about how to rid India of poverty by 2020. Broadly, according to the Prez, there are five major interlinked challenges to be tackled. The first is lifting 260 million people in rural areas above the poverty line by setting up 7000 PURAs and encouraging a second green revolution to double farm output. The second is maximizing the potential of India's rich human resource by providing education, health care, social and nutritional security. Third: Boosting information &	Conflicting ⟷ Statement.	You've spoken of completely wiping out poverty by 2020. Isn't that too ambitious? When I was growing up, people scoffed when visionaries like Sarabhai and C. Subramaniam spoke of Indian satellites and fool self suffiency. Well, today we have a hugely successful space research programs and overflowing granaries. You are young, why are you indulging in negative thinking? Remember, dreams lead to thoughts and thoughts to actions. So dream, dream, dream!

communication technology. Fourth: Developing infrastructure.		

He also wanted an article done on three successful PURA (Providing Urban Amenities in Rural Areas) models and had the data all ready. The tasks were quickly assigned. Including electric power and river networking. And finally, developing critical technologies and strategic industries and ensuring economic security so that '*developed countries can't threaten us with sanctions as they did in 1998*'.

By the end of a 90 minute session, he had even hardened cynics amongst us nodding and smiling in appreciation. '*Golden moments*', muttered the same wag as we filed out. Talk about a change of perspective brought on by an ignited mind.

ANNEXURE 5: BRITISH INDIA

Pages from the history of the Indian sub-continent: British Rule in India

Pressures of Loyalism during British Rule

Part One: Loyalist Agents in the Indian Aristocracy and the Early Congress

As has been noted by several historians of British-ruled India, the numerical presence of the British in colonized India was never very significant. Yet, the British were able to maintain a vast and stable empire in the Indian subcontinent for almost two centuries. They were able to recklessly exploit India's natural resources and drain the wealth of its citizenry through the imposition of excessive and unreasonable taxes all without unmanageable challenges to their political authority during much of their debilitating reign.

Although there is no doubt that physical violence (including torture) were important elements of British domination in India, equally important were the successes of political strategies that tool full advantage of rivalries amongst native rules and cynically exploited divisions arising from caste, religion, class and other sectarian loyalist. Not only were the British able to garner the loyalty or acquiescence of the Indian maharajas and other elements of the decadent feudal aristocracy, they were also able to command the support of influential sections of the British educated new urban intelligentsia whose loyalty to the colonial empire remained unquestioned even as nationalist feelings and nationalist currents emerged with greater or lessen intensity after the defeat in 1858. Money –leaders and the landed gentry were particularly reliabilities of the British, and the new industrial class, though critical of British policies, was invariable constrained by its conservations in opposing British rule.

Thus, Loyalist become a powerful political trend in British India that either countered nationalist forces outright, or attempted to diffuse their impact and efficacy through calls for political moderation, non-violence and tactical restraint. Loyalist forces made frequent and fervent appeals to the Indian masses to be patient with the British, to be content with the slow pace of political reforms, and to be grateful for minor concessions concerning self-rule. Those who demanded a more radical and confrontationist approach with the British(Such as Tilak) were branded as "extremists" and dismissed as unrealistic or utopian radicals.

Rooted amongst sections of the Indian elite that feared the power of the restive masses, loyalism was not only a strong political force in Indian territories directly rules by the British, but also had profound impact on Princely India. Recognizing their importance, British administrators feted loyalist elements, rewarding them in accordance with their contribution to the stability of the Raj. In the decades that followed the 1857 uprising, loyalism showed up in a variety of forms (moderate or extreme), and the most anti-national of the loyalist tendencies served as a bulwark against all attempts at overthrowing or ever diluting British authority in India. Not only did such elements collaborate dutifully in facilitating the sustained transfer of wealth from India to England, in their aggressively loyalist propaganda, they matched or even outdid colonial attacks on nationalist currents, spreading disinformation against even those that were politically quite moderate, and essentially reconciled to alien rule.

Acknowledgements

My foremost duty is to express that this book could not have been composed without the help and earlier work done by Gas Turbine Research Establishment (**GTRE**), Bangalore.

I shall be failing in my duty if I do not recall the most useful discussions I had with Professor U. R. Rao, who has written the 'Foreword'.

My mother's concern for the rural poor was planted in my mind,. She did not believe in hereditary caste system. This book could not have been composed without my wife's untiring support, when she took care of all aspects to manage everything, including offering guidance on some aspects related to the text of this book.

This book presents, very positively, that our neglected rural poor can make this country a noble humanitarian society, and a strong sovereign country, self reliant, and secular.

My duty is to express my gratitude to the senior Air Force Officers, senior Scientists, and several who had advised on many issues presented in the book.

I convey my gratitude to Ms. Madhurita Ghosh, for the art work; Shri P.K. Bose, Academician; Gyan Publishing House, Delhi, and Ms.Ujjani Chowdhury for her melodious rendering the 'Bhojan' song.

Finally, I express my gratitude to **Aradhya Enterprises, Koramangala, Bangalore** for their continuous support in the preparation of several draft copies, often working overtimes.

Index

A

J

K

L

M

N